The Psychology of
Ordinary Explanations of
Social Behaviour

This is a volume in
EUROPEAN MONOGRAPHS IN SOCIAL PSYCHOLOGY

Series Editor: Henri Tajfel

A complete list of titles in this series appears at the end of this volume.

EUROPEAN MONOGRAPHS IN SOCIAL PSYCHOLOGY 23
Series Editor: HENRI TAJFEL

The Psychology of Ordinary Explanations of Social Behaviour

Edited by

CHARLES ANTAKI

*Department of Psychology, University
of Lancaster, Bailrigg, Lancaster, England*

1981

Published in cooperation with
EUROPEAN ASSOCIATION OF EXPERIMENTAL
SOCIAL PSYCHOLOGY
by
ACADEMIC PRESS
A Subsidiary of Harcourt Brace Jovanovich, Publishers
London New York Toronto Sydney San Francisco

ACADEMIC PRESS INC.(LONDON) LTD.
24/28 Oval Road
London NW1

United States Edition published by
ACADEMIC PRESS INC.
111 Fifth Avenue
New York, New York 10003

British Library Cataloguing in Publication Data
The psychology of ordinary explanations of social behaviour.
 1. Social psychology — Public opinion
 I. Antaki, C
 301.1   HM251   80-41581

ISBN 0-12-058960-5

Typeset by Colset Ltd.,
Singapore and Printed in Great Britain
by Whitstable Litho Ltd.,
Whitstable, Kent

List of Contributors

CHARLES ANTAKI: *Department of Psychology, University of Lancaster, Lancaster LA1 4YF, England.*

JENNY BROWN: *Department of Psychology, University of Surrey, Guildford GU2 5XH, England.*

DAVID CANTER: *Department of Psychology, University of Surrey, Guildford GU2 5XH, England.*

GUY FIELDING: *Department of Communication Studies, Sheffield City Polytechnic, Totley, Sheffield S17 4AB, England.*

DAN GOWLER: *Oxford Centre for Management Studies, Kennington, Oxford OX1 5NY, England.*

ROM HARRÉ: *Sub-faculty of Philosophy, Merton Street, University of Oxford, Oxford, England.*

BEN HARRIS: *Department of Psychology, Vassar College, Poughkeepsie, New York 12601, U.S.A.*

JOHN HARVEY: *American Psychological Association, 1200 17th Street, North West, Washington D.C. 20036, U.S.A.*

MANSUR LALLJEE: *Department of Extramural Studies, University of Oxford, Rewley House, Wellington Square, Oxford OX1 2JA, England.*

KAREN LEGGE: *Department of Social and Economic Studies, Imperial College, University of London, Princes Gate, London SW7, England.*

PETER MORRIS: *Department of Psychology, University of Lancaster, Lancaster LA1 4YF, England.*

PHILIP PETTIT: *Department of Interdisciplinary Human Studies, University of Bradford, Bradford 1DP, England.*

JOOP VAN DER PLIGT: *Instituut voor Milieuvraagstrukken, Vrije Universiteit, De Boelelaan 1087A, 1007MC Amsterdam, Holland.*

MARC REISS: *Department of Psychology, Middlebury College, Middlebury, Vermont, U.S.A.*

JOHN SHOTTER: *Department of Psychology, University of Nottingham, Nottingham NG7 2RD, England.*

JAMES T. TEDESCHI: *Department of Psychology, State University of New York at Albany, Albany, New York 12222, U.S.A.*

SUE WILKINSON: *Department of Psychology, University of Liverpool, Eleanor Rathbone Building, PO Box 147, Liverpool L69 3BX, England.*

Preface

If we think in the abstract about "ordinary explanations of social behaviour" I imagine most of us would think at first of explanations of the cloudy problems of public life — politics, say, or religion, or economics. We should probably try to give flesh to the abstract phrase "explanations of social behaviour" by recalling some remarkable examples we might recently have come across — the man in the pub's account of why the economy is failing, say, or the television pundit's grand account of some fashionable problem.

If we found ourselves following this train of thought, then the abstract phrase will have led us a fair way from what is really the great bulk and mass of ordinary explanation. Explanations of politics, economics, morality and so on may be standard conversational material, but, compared to explanations of more personal matters, they play a minute part in our ordinary daily lives. Things that need explaining in the ordinary run of events are the small, unspectacular mysteries that would never attract the attention of the man in the pub, let alone the pundit on television: why the milkman did not leave any milk this morning, why the next-door neighbours seem to be so unfriendly recently, what a colleague at work means when he says you look like you need a holiday. These things, and countless others like them, demand explanation and interpretation — not the stand-up explanation of the amateur or professional analyst, but the constant personal effort after meaning that drives our judgment and action in the social world.

What strikes us when we stop to consider these small but vital ordinary explanations of human affairs is that various as they are, they have a common quality; conscious or unconscious, personal or public, conventional or eccentric, all explanations of events have in common the fact that they tell us not just about the event being explained, but also about the person giving us the explanation, and the mental process through which the explanation must have passed. We can look at any explanation clinically and ask : what does this tell us about how this person sees the world? And what does it tell us about how judgments and decisions about his world are arrived at? We can put the question ambitiously and arrive at the purpose and point of this book : what do we know about the social and the cognitive psychology of ordinary explanation?

The psychologist will want to ask three sorts of questions about ordinary explanation : Is it reliable? How is it arrived at? and Why does it happen? These are not easy questions to answer. The first question already has a long history in psychology, stretching back to the first time a curious scientist asked his subjects to tell him how they performed some mental feat such as searching for things in memory or trying to solve an arithmetical problem. What status shall we give to an ordinary person's account of his mental behaviour? The early answers became progressively less optimistic, and today have reached a definite mistrust of introspection into cognitive processes. Introspection into the causes and reasons for actions, rather than thoughts, has suffered the same history — perhaps more because of the family association of the name "introspection" than because of any really insuperable problems with the technique when applied to explanations of action. But voices have recently been raised within social psychology, and outside it, championing people's accounts of their actions as a respectable (and essential) research tool. The questions involved in deciding what to do with people's reports of their reasons for acting as they do are subtle and complex, and must lie at the heart of social psychology. Accordingly, I have asked a number of contributors to devote some time and space to the many issues that weave in and out of the debate.

The second question, the question of how the explanation is arrived at, it is a much more orthodox one. Here we have ground that is farmed by both cognitive and social psychologists: on the one hand we have interests in how the brain manages to process the volume of information that bombards it in any day's social life, and on the other hand we have an interest in how the social individual's thoughts and decisions are mediated and served by his mental machinery. The classic marriage of the two interests is in the collection of theories called person perception, where the social nature of the individual's judgments and the cognitive nature of the processes serving them are seen and treated properly as two sides of the same coin. Currently, the most vital descendant of person perception is Attribution Theory, with its interest in people's accounts of the causes for behaviour. Attribution Theory is proving as popular and as much researched as its parent, and the work done in its name has a special and important relevance to the psychology of the mental processing of explanations. However, again like its parent person perception, Attribution Theory is not a way of thinking that does not have its objectors and detractors; and to give a rounded version of what it

offers a psychology of explanations, I have included contributions for
and against it and discussions on the fundamental assumptions of the
nature of the object it is studying.

The third question we can ask about ordinary explanations is what
function they serve in everyday life. One answer is that they are there to
allow us to manage in the world at all — if we were not capable of
explaining things to ourselves, we should hardly be able to have much of
what we would recognize as a normal human life. Once this has been
said, we can see more refined versions of the questions which really do
need thinking about and which cannot be so easily answered. What
interpersonal needs are served by giving and receiving explanations?
What forms of giving and receiving are allowed? What can we deduce
about people's understanding of the social rules of behaviour from their
explanations of actions which break the rules? Can explanations be used
by psychologists to discover personal and cultural constructions of social
worlds? These questions take us well beyond the strictly cognitive
interests of the considerations we saw above. The contributors who
address this theme are not all psychologists; there are contributions from
sociologists, anthropologists and advocates of a social psychology radically different from the experimental tradition familiar to most research
psychologists.

As the reader goes through the book it will be clear, I think, that the
three questions I talk about here are in practice very difficult, if not
impossible, to isolate and talk about separately. It is the usual fate of
outlines that editors write in prefaces to be swamped by the complexities
and complications of detail in the body of the book. However, I have laid
the sequence of chapters out in a way that corresponds to the sequence of
questions that I put in this preface: this should be of some help.

In the first chapter Philip Pettit sets out the groundwork of explanations and their relation to action. In an interrogative mood he asks
what we, as ordinary explainers, must assume before we can make sense
of behaviour. He proposes five theses about actions and takes us on to
explore the way ordinary explanation develops these to account for
behaviour by investigating the agent's desires and beliefs, and by setting
actions down to matters of policy, profile, personality and position.
Pettit's analysis leads on to the next chapter in which Antaki and
Fielding draw up a provisional map of psychological research on
ordinary explanations, making a distinction between what they call
information-processing and representational psychologies.

The next chapter by Ben Harris and John Harvey fills in an important area on the map with a review and discussion of the contribution of Attribution Theory to the psychology of ordinary explanations, presenting a historical outline of the development of Fritz Heider's "naive psychology". Joop van der Pligt follows this with an examination of the particularly important area of actor-observer differences in explanations. He extends Attribution Theory to account for the tendency for an explanation given for an action by its performer to differ from that given by its audience. An evaluation of Attribution Theory in general is contributed by Mansur Lalljee in his chapter on the relationship between attributions and explanations, and Rom Harré, in Chapter 6, continues the evaluation to ask fundamental questions about the status of Attribution Theory both as a theory in social psychology and as a theory *of* social psychology. In Chapter 7 John Shotter is concerned with drawing a distinction between explanations as retrospections and explanations as avowals of personal states, taking us into the territory of personal and private explanation. Morris in Chapter 8 takes up Shotter's concern with self-knowledge to review the cognitive psychologist's interest in ordinary explanations and self-reports. He examines the most recent versions of the introspectionist and the anti-introspectionist arguments, and proposes a hierarchical model of the mental system that produces actions and can be interrogated for their explanation.

From then on we are concerned with the personal use and functions of explanations, filling out the rest of Antaki and Fielding's map. Sue Wilkinson describes how psychologists can enter into people's private worlds of explanatory concepts by using Kelly's theory of personal constructs. David Canter and Jenny Brown in Chapter 10 are concerned with the effect that role requirements and worldly position have on the giving and getting of explanations, and show how the psychologist has a privileged, and, at the same time, an ambiguous explanatory role. In Chapter 11 Dan Gowler and Karen Legge bring up to date the notion of rhetoric and apply it in an analysis of the context and function of ordinary accounts. Finally in Chapter 12 James Tedeschi and Marc Reiss draw up a comprehensive catalogue of the ways in which explanations can be used to extricate people from difficult interpersonal situations. Tedeschi and Reiss finish by reinterpreting some of the experiments traditionally part of the Attribution Theory literature, bringing us round once again to the theory that has had a galvanizing effect on the experimental investigation of ordinary explanations.

In reading the chapters in this book the reader will discover, as I did, the severity of the conflict in the aims and methods of research into explanations advocated by different writers. Part of the reason for the conflict is the diversity of the disciplines represented. The other part of the reason is the particular controversy over what is and is not proper social psychology. The reader will see that the contributions of Attribution Theory and the radical social psychology advocated by some writers are matters of some contention. This is not an issue about which I can say anything worthwhile here; the reader will see the complexities and the importance of the arguments as he reads the chapters in the middle part of the book in detail. What can be said here is that the controversies, though they are of course arguments over particular claims and particular courses of action advocated by one side or the other, are also representative of the flux and turbulence of modern social psychology itself. Quite radically different matters are recommended to the psychologist's interest by the two sides of the argument (if we can reduce it to two sides for convenience's sake) and quite radically different research procedures are recommended for their investigation. Ordinary explanation happens to be particularly controversial, and the conflict particularly noticeable in these pages, because it is at once a substantive matter of interest — a topic for research in its own right — and, for some, a recommended method of investigation into a great variety of other psychological matters. Probably no other area of contention in the debate over radical social psychology has this special characteristic. An area of substance and also of methodological significance will attract a great deal of attention whatever the climate of opinion in a discipline, settled or unsettled; at the moment, with the debate about the grand issues raging high overhead, and local storms breaking out down below, the attention paid to ordinary explanations is, in some quarters, understandably intense.

It is too early to tell whether the obstacles to eclectic theories of ordinary explanation are resolvable. One obstacle, the language barrier between different disciplines, is all too familiar from other interdisciplinary enterprises, and is a perennial difficulty. Another, the conflict and separation between radical social psychologists and experimentalists, may or may not disappear. Their differences of opinion could polarize into manifestos of opposition — this seems to be what is happening at the moment — or disappear as one side learns and assimilates the other's language. It is too early to tell. But such difficulties hamper a general theory which, if the search for general theories in other areas in psychology is a guide, may be chimerical in any case. The more encouraging thing to say is that if this book is a preliminary map of the territory of ordinary explanation, the survey shows a number of centres of growing activity, and shows some of these centres growing towards each other; we can look forward to a time when they might meet and overlap sympathetically enough for us to be able to call the result a general theory.

In editing this book I have been greatly helped by the constructive help and advice of a number of colleagues. I would especially like to thank Thomas Green, Chris Spencer, Roy Payne and Paul Jackson for early encouragement, and Steve Duck for more specific help in the later stages of the book's organization. I would particularly like to thank Anne Parker, Sylvia Sumner and Hazel Satterthwaite for their patient help in the preparation of the manuscript. I am also grateful to the Medical Research Council for their support during the early part of the book's preparation.

December, 1980   CHARLES ANTAKI

Contents

This book is dedicated to the memory
of my brother Philip Antaki

1

On Actions and Explanations*

P. Pettit

Introduction

This essay is an exercise in the archaeology of action theory. It is an attempt to lay bare the views about action which are assumed in our practice as interactants and interpreters: the practice in which on the one hand we act so as to invite one or another explanation of what we do from our audience and on the other hand play audience ourselves and, whether in fulfilment or neglect of the agent's wishes, decide on how best to explain his overtures to us or some actions of his that we happen to observe. Such a project of excavation may not clearly be something possible and it will be useful to make some further remarks about it.

The possibility of the enterprise is put in doubt by someone who assimilates our interactive and interpretative competence to the ability of a cyclist to maintain balance when riding his machine. We do not think that the cyclist relies on any views about specific gravity and such matters in developing his skill. What he knows in being able to stay upright on his bicycle is something practical, not a piece of theory: in a phrase made fashionable by Gilbert Ryle, it is a form of knowing-how, not of knowing-that. The assimilation of our interactive and inter-pretative competence to such a paradigm of practical knowledge would seem to undermine the idea that there is a theory presupposed to the competence, which awaits our excavation.

It must be conceded straight off that our action accounting compe-tence, to give it a single name, is not learned in the way in which we typically learn bits of theory. The initiate is not given a set of axioms about the antecedents of action, nor is he told any particular story about the workings of the mind. What happens rather is that he is introduced

*Topics covered in this paper were discussed in graduate seminars that I conducted in Spring 1979 at the University of Connecticut and I would like to acknowledge here my indebtedness to the criticism of those who took part in the seminars.

to the use of various concepts by means of which action is explained. He learns when it is appropriate to regard a piece of behaviour as an action proper, what sorts of questions it is then in order to pose, and how one may make a case for one answer rather than another. The concepts which he picks up in learning these things are concepts such as those of intention, desire, decision, perception, judgment, belief and a host of associates. The development of such conceptual skill may indeed seem at first sight to be a practical rather than a theoretical advance, and something therefore not inviting the sort of excavation proposed above.

And yet reflection gives pause. It may be that our accounting competence comes to us in the manner of a practical skill but nonetheless our claim to the possession of it is vindicated only if we display certain theoretical beliefs. We would conclude that someone did not know how to use the concept of intention and its cognates if he did not recognize that to intend something is normally to perform it, that intending is a state of mind for which it is almost always appropriate to seek reasons, that intending is something which supposes the having of certain beliefs about the alternative actions available in a given circumstance, and so on. Knowing these facts is a necessary prerequisite to being able to argue for one or another intentional construal of an action or to being able to anticipate which intentional construal an action will attract in the arguments of others.

But are the facts known not just like certain facts that we may presume to be known by our cyclist, such as that when he puts the right pedal downwards this lifts the left pedal upwards? Not exactly: though even if they were this might be taken to show the theoretical aspect of the cyclist's ability rather than the practical nature of the action accountant's. The difference is that we could ascribe knowledge of the facts about the pedals without taking the cyclist to be disposed to assent to any propositions — the cyclist might after all be a chimpanzee — whereas the knowledge we ascribe in the action accounting case is linked indissolubly to an assent disposition and in that respect distinctively propositional. Pressing the pedals in the appropriate way might be enough to give evidence of the corresponding piece of knowledge about those objects but nothing short of propositional assent would establish knowledge about such conceptually sophisticated matters as intentions and the like.

This must suffice to silence the objection to our archaeological project although it should be mentioned that the objection connects with problems that arise generally for attempts to put a cognitive representation on an agent skill. These problems have been most discussed in linguistics where, on Chomsky's model, for example, one seeks to represent grammatical competence as knowledge of a finitely axiomatized grammar for the language in question. The strongest vindication in the linguistic case takes the correct grammatical theory to describe in detail the implicit propositional knowledge of the native speaker, the weakest takes any theory to be correct which characterizes a form of propositional knowledge that would produce grammatical competence, even though the theory bears no resemblance to whatever it is that underlies the native's competence. The picture suggested by our remarks on the excavation of accounting competence is closer to the first of these vindications. We assume that there are matters propositional known to every competent interactant-cum-interpreter and that the analysis of such competence reconstructs that theoretical knowledge. It may be of course, as we shall see, that one or another analysis will pass as a reconstruction in a given case and that we cannot readily judge on which is correct. Such underdetermination however is commonplace in any intellectual inquiry and does not compromise the representational aspirations of our enterprise.

My paper is in three sections. In the first I isolate five theses about action to which I believe that we are committed as regular action accountants. In the second I look at what it means to explain an event, whether or not that event is itself an action. In the third section I bring together the results of the other two, considering how we put our general theses about action into operation in the devising of explanations for what people say and do. The upshot is a taxonomy of action explanations of a kind which should be of interest, not just to philosophers, but also to psychologists and sociologists who concern themselves with everyday practices: these include attribution theorists, ethnomethodologists, human ethologists, and a variety of other specialists.

Five theses about action

There are a number of theses about action which I wish to put forward in this part of my paper, all of them implicit, as I see things, in our regular practice of accounting. The first is: (1) *Actions, simple or compound, are events*. An event is something spatially restricted like a physical object: there are limits on where one and the same event can be found, limits which vary with different kinds of events. More importantly it is something that takes place at a given instant of time, or, if it lasts over many instants, has temporal parts. What this latter phrase means is that the event, unlike a physical object, is not there to be seen in its entirety at any moment of its existence. We see the whole table or tree if we examine it during any period of its lifespan, but if we see the football match in the last five minutes of the time it lasts then we see only a part of the whole: literally, its last five minutes.

There can be no dispute that as we categorize actions they are events in this sense and not objects or materials, classes or properties, or whatever. The reason for putting in the clause that they are such whether they are simple or compound is to draw attention to the fact that just as objects may be compounds with other objects as parts, so too events, and in particular actions, often display a whole-part structure. A single action like tying one's shoelaces for example is a compound of separable actions of moving one's fingers in such and such ways and it may in turn be a part in relation to the further action of dressing oneself. The question may here be raised as to how far one can go in seeing actions as parts of further wholes, the prospect looming of each of us performing in our lifetime the single action of living or expressing ourselves or doing our thing. It is difficult to set a limit in principle, just as it is difficult to put a theoretical boundary on how far objects can be seen as parts of further wholes, the house being brought under the street, the street under the suburb, the suburb under the city, the city under the conurbation, and so on. In practice we draw the line where the dividends of expressive simplicity begin to be outweighed by the costs of information ellipsis but where that line comes depends on the context of discussion.

The second proposition about actions that I wish to excavate from our accounting practice is: (2) *One action may have many significant properties*. Where the first thesis is scarcely contestable this takes us into an area of active controversy. Those who deny the proposition maintain that an action is an event in virtue of being the instantiation in the agent of a certain sort of property: say, the property expressed in the predicate "is running" or "walks" or "sits down" (see Goldman, 1970). The action qualifies as an event through being an instance of running or walking or sitting down as distinct from being an instance of a non-occurent property such as that of being tall or weighing ten stone. On the approach in question it naturally follows that however they are related the instantiations of different "action properties" cannot be one and the same action. This means that running, running fast, and running fastest in the group, all of which are instantiations of different properties, being expressed in different predicates, cannot be the same action, even when they are things done at a single stroke.

The intent of the second proposition is to deny this result and to say that one and the same action can be a running, a fast running and the fastest running performed within the group (see Davidson, 1967). On this approach the action is not the instantiation of an occurrent property attaching to the agent; it is an entity, on all fours with the agent, which itself has such properties. When we say that John is running we are not ascribing a property to John but rather saying that there is an event which is a running by John and when we add that John is running fast we are not ascribing a further property to John but rather adding that the event mentioned not only has the property of being a running by John but also that of being a fast running.

There have been many arguments put forward on both sides of this debate, none of which has proved knock-down (for a survey see Davis, 1979). Both positions seem tenable and, it must also be admitted, each seems to be capable of being brought into line with our accounting practice. Here it appears that we have an instance of the sort of under-determination that we mentioned as a possibility in the introduction. The evidence available leaves us suspended in respect of which view is implicit in our accounting practice and in respect of which is correct. Nevertheless we must choose one side or the other and in the second proposition I express a decision in favour of the one action/many properties view. This is the more economical theory since it means that when we act, the whole-part aspect aside, there is only one action performed, an action which has many different properties and may correspondingly be described in many different ways.

In connection with the second proposition the so-called "accordion effect" of action may be mentioned (see Feinberg, 1965). This is an effect consequent on the many properties of a single action. What it consists in is the following: that with a given action described as "running" we may generate further descriptions indefinitely by concentrating either on the method of performance, for example, or on its upshot. Taking the upshot side, and pulling our accordion to the right, we may redescribe the event as running faster than competitors, taking the race, beating the existing records, establishing one's name among athletes, or pulling to the left we may redescribe it by reference to method, as making a novel effort, taking huge strides, concentrating everything on one's movement. Each action or action description is an accordion which allows of being extended in this fashion either to left or right.

There are a number of distinguishable ways in which one action description may allow us to generate another which, in the accordion metaphor, is to its right (see Goldman, 1970). A not very interesting means of generation is that in which we augment the given description by the addition of a phrase, as we augmented "running" to "running fast" and to "running fastest in the group": the distinctive feature here is that the augmented description could not be made true without making true the original one. Three other sorts of generation, and the list may not be exhaustive, can be respectively described as causal, conventional and circumstantial. In the causal case the generated description holds true because of a causal effect of the original description being made true: our runner establishes his name among athletes because of the effect of his beating the records. In the conventional case the generated description is made true because of a convention or rule governing the making true of the original: thus running faster than competitors just is taking the race in view of what it means to win in such an event. Finally in the circumstantial case the generated description, and it is taken not to be formed by augmentation, is made true in virtue of some circumstance attending the making true of the original: thus taking the race is beating the records, granted the time clocked and the time on the record books.

So much for the accordion effect and the generation of action descriptions. The third proposition that I excavate from our guiding conception of action is: (3) *Actions are events that are intentionally performed by agents*. There are two claims within this defining proposition. The first is that actions are events performed by agents. This is to say that they are events brought about by agents but brought about immediately and not through the realization of some intervening event. I may bring about a social crisis among my friends but the crisis is not an action of mine since it is occasioned by what I do or say. What I do or say on the other hand does qualify as an action in so far as I bring it about without the intervention of a further event. (Notice here that the formulation of this point is facilitated by the recognition that one and the same action may have many descriptions. We would have to be more circumspect in our expression if we thought that the taking of the race, to return to our earlier example, was a different action from the fast running.)

Although we say that actions are events which agents perform or bring about immediately it should be noticed that this does not force us to recognize a special category of agent causality, contrary to what some philosophers have claimed (e.g. Taylor, 1974). When a person does something like waving a flag it may appear that there is a causal relationship between the agent on the one hand and the waving of the flag, the action, on the other. And this may seem highly distinctive since generally it is events or states of affairs which are thought to enter causal relationships. The mystery however is dissipated when we reflect that just as the agent is said to cause the flag waving, an object such as a kettle may be said to cause a noise, and that where we can say in this latter case that it is strictly the boiling of the water within the kettle that is the cause of the noise, so we can say in the other that it is strictly the onset of a particular state of belief and desire within the agent that is responsible for the action. It may be said that an action caused by an event within me is not an action which *I* perform, being rather something in the nature of the twitch caused by the inner spasm. But this is scarcely compelling. The difference between an action and such an involuntary reflex may not have to do with whether or not they are caused by events but with what sort of an event they are caused by. An action is something that I perform, plausibly, in so far as it issues in the proper way from beliefs and desires by which I more or less rationally hold.

For an event to be an action it is not enough that it be performed, in the sense of being brought about immediately, by an agent. An involuntary cough or shudder or movement of the eyes fits that condition. The further requirement postulated in our third proposition is that the action be intentionally performed (see Davidson, 1971). This condition is reminiscent of the traditional idea that an action issues from the agent's will but two important remarks should be made. One is that whereas the older approach suggested that at the root of each action is an act of will, an action which itself would seem to require a prior act of will and so on *ad infinitum*, no such suggestion is built into the requirement of intentionality. It may be that what makes an action intentional does not have to do with an act of will, although it may have to do with the causal origin of the action, provided this origin is not required to be itself an act, it may for example be a certain sort of state of mind.

A second important remark about the intentionality requirement is that, whereas it used to be said that an action was willed or not willed *simpliciter*, an action can be performed intentionally under one description but not under another. Here the view of action as an event capable of sustaining different properties facilitates the formulation of an important point. An action is performed intentionally, we can say, just so long as it has at least one intentional description: one description such that the agent intentionally made it true. This allows us, whereas the act of will stipulation might not have done, to respect our intuitions and recognize certain accidental doings as actions. Thus if I offend a friend by commenting unfavourably on something he did, my offending him, although I may not have meant to give him offence, is an action for all that. It is an action through being describable as commenting unfavourably on something he did, since that description may be presumed to be one that I intentionally fulfilled.

The third proposition, to which it is hard to deny a guiding role in our practice of accounting, offers a definition of action. One unsatisfactory aspect of the definition however is that it leaves it unclear how we are to judge whether a given description of an action is an intentional one or not. Can we say anything helpful on this? Well it is doubtful whether we can offer a set of conditions necessary and sufficient for describing an action description as intentional and themselves more accessible to judgment than the matter of intentionality. However we can indicate an enlightening connection between judging a description intentional and making judgments of other sorts.

What we can say is this: that a description of an action is intentional if a pro-attitude towards its realization, or towards the realization of a counterpart description transformed in person and tense, played a certain causal role in moving the agent to act. Thus: "John won the race" is an intentional description if John's pro-attitude towards the counterpart "I shall win the race" played a certain causal part in bringing about that event. In this account it is not ruled out that a description may be intentional on the fulfilment of some other conditions: we are told that the description is intentional if the stated condition is realized, but not that it is intentional only in that case. Should we strengthen the account, replacing "if" by "if and only if"? I think that we may reasonably do so, and I propose to follow the line myself, but it should be noticed that there is a small cost to be paid in verbal regimentation. This is that a description which an agent foresaw that he would fulfil in acting cannot be described as an intentional description, if the agent did not desire its fulfilment, whether in its own right or as a means to fulfilling another description, or was not in any way moved by such a desire. It will be a description knowingly, but not intentionally, fulfilled (see Davidson, 1963).

To relate intentionality to the pro-attitudes operative in producing action is illuminating but it does not give us a workable criterion by which to tell when a description is intentional. The reason is that we cannot say exactly what sort of causal role must be played by a pro-attitude in order for the corresponding description to be intentional. Suppose that I get rid of an unwanted visitor by appearing preoccupied, in a case where I have a pro-attitude to getting rid of him, and where this pro-attitude combines with my belief that by appearing preoccupied I will do so, to produce the appearance of preoccupation. Did I intentionally get rid of him? That depends on how the pro-attitude and belief caused the event: if by rationally eliciting it, the answer must be positive; if by momentarily distracting me, the answer must be negative. The reason why our account of intentionality does not offer a criterion is that judging on this matter involves just the same sort of difficulty as judging on whether a description is intentional (see Davidson, 1973).

So far we have seen that as we conceive of them within our regular practice of accounting, actions, simple or compound, are events; that they are events not just in the anaemic sense of being instantiations of certain properties, but in the sense of being full-blooded bearers of properties, on a par with physical objects; and that within the category of events they are distinguished by the fact of being intentionally performed by agents. Along the way we have also discussed, in connection with the second proposition, the accordion effect and the varieties of generation of action descriptions and, in connection with the third, some features of intentional action descriptions. The fourth proposition, to which we can now turn, is: (4) *Actions may be intentional under various aspects*. What this proposition is designed to counter is the idea which one sometimes finds supposed, that there is one privileged aspect under which every action is intended. It may be that for every action performed the agent must have intended it, whether his intending preceded the action or accompanied it. Such intending has been nicely cast as a judgment in favour of the project realized in the action but, unlike the acknowledgment that in such and such a way it is attractive, a judgment of an unconditional kind: a judgment that this project, seen as a concrete entity, actual or anticipated, is what must be done; is, all things considered, the best (see Davidson, 1978). Precisely because intending is an unconditional judgment of value in respect of the action intended, and not a judgment of value relative to such and such a feature, there is no one aspect which it picks out as its special correlate, no one aspect which might then claim to be the primary intentional profile of the action. Any aspect of an action is intentional, roughly speaking, which answers to an operative pro-attitude in the agent.

It may be useful to give a picture of the major varieties of intentional aspects that are to be found in actions. I suggest that an action may be intentionally characterized under at least any of the following ways of being presented to us: as *performed*, being a display of the agent's skill at bringing about things; as *preferred*, being the chosen member of a set of mutually exclusive options; and as *projected* in further aspects that it is likely to have.

There are certainly some performative aspects of any action which are not intentional. When I write I activate my arm muscles after a certain pattern, and doing so is required for the performance of my task, but I do not do this intentionally; indeed I do not even know what pattern it is that is involved. On the other hand some performative aspects are intentional. The so-called "basic" action description is by definition so: it is the intentional description which the agent cannot be said to have made true by making true any other intentional description, and which is not generated by augmentation from any such description. The basic action description of my writing is probably something like "forming letters, words and sentences", this being the bottom description that I intentionally fulfil (see Danto, 1973; Davidson, 1971). Other performative descriptions that are intentional can be isolated by asking: what descriptions beyond this basic one do I fulfil in order to fulfil the description which represents the action as preferred to alternatives?

The description that picks out the action as preferred to alternatives is of peculiar importance. We assume that in any case of action the agent was presented with a set of alternatives, if only "Do this" and "Decide not to do it". Were there no alternatives there would be no need to regard the action as issuing from anything like the will of the agent — the will would not be required to explain its occurrence — and by our definition there would be no reason to see it as an action. The description of an action as preferred depicts it as a member of a set of mutually exclusive options and indicates the primary aspect under which it is presented for the contemplation of the agent. It is only when he comes to think of realizing the action under this description that he will have to think of its performative aspect; and it is only when he has conceived of the action under this description that he can begin to trace out the other aspects that it is likely to have. The description represents the action in that profile in which it is, in the most basic sense, the agent's objective. It may be: going swimming rather than taking the dog for a walk or going to a show; deciding to stay on at university for further study rather than entering employment immediately; or writing a paper on the explanation of action rather than writing one on the connection between the philosophy and the psychology of motivation. In every case it points out to us *what* it is that the agent can be most properly said to have set out to do. (I have misleadingly, if understandably, spoken of it as indicating the agent's intention in Pettit 1976 and 1979.)

Among the effects that an action has, some may not have been foreseen by the agent, as in the case of my offending my friend by something I say, and these will yield non-intentional descriptions of the action. Other effects however will have been foreseen : by effects here I mean effects of making the preferred description true, besides those effects connected with the performative side of the action. These effects will give us intentional descriptions, provided they answer to operative pro-attitudes, so that in going swimming I also intentionally do something pleasurable, get myself some exercise, and surprise the friends whom I told not to expect me at the pool. Here we have descriptions of my action as projected by me and they complement the intentional descriptions of it as performed and preferred. Other intentional descriptions in this category spring from actual effects that were not foreseen by the agent but that were thought possible, and were actively pursued. These give us straightforward intentional descriptions of the form "He brought about so and so" plus intentional accounts such as "He attempted to bring about so and so". Accounts of the latter kind can also be generated from effects which were actively pursued but were not achieved.

Our fifth and final proposition can now be presented. It is: (5) *Any intentional description can be quoted in explanation of an action.* In order to see the point of this proposition it is essential to remember that explanation is relative to background knowledge and that one questioner's answer may be another's assumption. If I ask why the car in which I am a passenger is accelerating unevenly, my question may or may not be answered, and the event may or may not be explained for me, by the information that the mechanism responsible for acceleration is faulty. Whether or not the question is answered depends on what my background assumptions were in raising it: if I assumed that the mechanism was indeed faulty, and sought information on precisely what was wrong, nothing will have been explained for me. The point in the fifth proposition is that, depending on the background assumptions in the interrogative context, any intentional description can reasonably be offered as the explanation of why a given action occurred.

The point will be obvious if we consider a few examples. Take the basic description of an action first. For someone who asks why my hand is going across this page in an uneven pattern an explanation will be provided by the information that I am forming letters, words and sentences. But of course the questioning and the explanation may not stop there. If the person goes on to ask why I am doing that, he will be told that I am writing, the intentional description involved here being still a performative one. And if he presses further resort will probably be had to the description of the action as preferred: he will be informed perhaps that I am writing a paper on the explanation of actions. Still more pressure will elicit explanations that mention descriptions of the action as projected: say, that I am fulfilling a promise, or trying to make a case for a certain approach to the psychology of behaviour. And so on indefinitely.

At this stage we should turn to consider further the nature and the variety of action explanations but before we do so a final remark may be made on the explanatory use of intentional descriptions. This is that, as our examples reveal, there is a certain progression in the descriptions invoked to silence questions, a progression that makes us want to say that some explanations of an action are more basic than others. At the end of the line we can imagine our questioner being finally silenced by the information that in writing my paper I am doing what I consider to be my duty, or what I find most pleasant to do just now, or what I consider to be most in my interests, or a mixture of these. The fact of progression towards this resting point has suggested to some that the agent in action has a chain of goals, each of which is sought for the sake of the next, up to his ultimate goal: his last end. Nothing we have noticed however encourages that calculative picture of agency. The ultimacy of some explanations reflects our assumptions about what it is natural for agents to pursue but it does not mean that we think of agents as actuarial planners of their lives (see Wiggins, 1975).

On explanations

In the last section we charted the conceptualization of action employed by us in our regular accounting practice and in the next our goal is to indicate the nature and variety of action explanations which that conceptualization allows. Before we can hope to fulfil this goal we must consider for a little while what it is in general that makes something an explanation, what it is that gives a statement explanatory force.

There are two grossly distinguishable accounts of explanation to be found in the philosophical literature. The one would identify an explanatory statement or set of statements mainly by its form, and the other by its content and effect: if you like, its force. The standard instance of the first approach is the so-called covering-law theory of explanation which derives from Mill and received its classic formulation in the work of Carl Hempel (see Hempel, 1965). According to this account explanation, whether it be the explanation of an event or the explanation of a standing condition, consists in an argument which guarantees or makes probable the truth of a proposition expressing that event or condition. The premises of the argument are required on the account to contain a law, universal or probabilistic, and they are also supposed to be true or at least well warranted. Further they are each stipulated to be essential in the sense that the argument would not go through without them.

This covering law analysis of explanation has one conspicuous merit, which is that it matches our intuition that an explanation should render what is to be explained relatively unsurprising. We call for explanation of things which, although we know them to be so, we think could have been otherwise so far as our background knowledge goes, and the effect of the explanation is to close or at least constrain this possibility: to show that the possibility of things being otherwise is not as open as it had appeared (see Mellor, 1976). The covering law account captures this feature of explanation, for the possibility that something be otherwise is eliminated or reduced when we realize that it's being as it presently is follows, for certain or probabilistically, from how certain other things are in the context.

The aspiration of the covering law theorist is to provide, mainly in terms of form, a specification of conditions necessary and sufficient for a statement to explain a given event or condition. That goal, I would like to urge, is not capable of being fulfilled and I think that we should therefore go over to an account of explanation from a different angle. The failure of the aim of giving a formal account is seen first of all in the fact that one set of true premises can make a result relatively probable, another lower it. Smith's recovery from his appendicectomy is probable granted that most patients survive that operation, but it is rather less than probable granted that he is ninety years of age and that many patients in that age bracket do not survive appendicectomies. This fact forces a non-formal amendment on the covering law theorist, to some effect such as that in statistical explanation the premises must contain all the information available that affects the probability of the event or condition to be explained (see Hempel, 1965).

Even with this revision made there is trouble in store for the covering law theory. One source of difficulty is that we can construct arguments satisfying the conditions given which we would not consider for a moment as explanations of the events or conditions recorded in their conclusions. Thus we may argue: water boils under normal conditions when heated to 212°; this water is under normal conditions and is not boiling; therefore this water has not been heated to 212°. We have no tendency to regard this as an explanation of the water's not having been heated to the appropriate temperature even though it satisfies the conditions. Again consider: whenever the barometer falls the weather changes; the barometer has fallen; therefore the weather has changed. This would not be taken as an explanation of the weather having changed, for the barometer is only a symptom of the altered atmospheric pressure that gives the true explanation. And a final example: the sun in the sky is at such and such an elevation; the length of the shadow cast by the flagpole is so-and-so; therefore, granted the physics of light, the height of the flagpole is so-and-so. Where we would be happy to quote the height of the pole in explanation of the length of the shadow, we find absurd the reversal of the relationship involved in this example.

It is an irresistible thought that in these examples the premises fail to explain the events recorded because they do not point us towards causes, but rather towards associated or irrelevant factors. This observation may suggest that the covering law theory should be amended nonformally in the way in which it has been amended to cater for the problem with probabilities mentioned above. Such amendments have been proposed, specifications being entered on the explanatory factors, which are designed to restrict them to the appropriate causal ones. Attempts of the kind promise to be no more successful however than have been attempts to analyse what makes something a cause of another (see Brand, 1976; Sosa, 1975). Attempts at the analysis of causality usually specify that the cause cannot be later than the effect, and that in the circumstances the cause is necessary and/or sufficient for the effect, but even when these conditions are elucidated and supplemented they fail to distinguish causal connections from certain other relations. Thus the occurrence of a component will satisfy the conditions for being the partial cause of an event even though we would not regard it for a moment as a cause. Where we find such failure we may expect to find attempts at patching up the covering law account also unsuccessful. Just as we would not regard my lacing up my boots as a cause of my dressing, so we would not find an account which mentioned that factor explanatory of why I dressed.

The source of difficulty in the covering law account, which we have been probing, is its failure to specify that the factors mentioned in an explanation, or at least in the explanation of an event, should be causal. A second source of difficulty is that even where a statement seems not to offend on the first score, it may fail to count as an explanation because of the way in which it engages with the background knowledge of those seeking enlightenment. Suppose one's dog falls ill. It will be explanatory of the event if one discovers that all dogs eating such and such a new brand of petfood fall ill, and the statement can be cast in the format specified by the covering law theory: all dogs which ate Dog-y-dog fell ill; Rover ate Dog-y-dog; therefore Rover fell ill. However if, with the knowledge about the general effect of Dog-y-dog in the background, one seeks an explanation of Rover's illness, the statement which was earlier found explanatory will prove no longer so, despite the fact that it continues to satisfy the covering format.

The difficulty here is that whether a statement constitutes an explanation depends on how it engages with the background knowledge of the person seeking explanation. There are ways in which the covering law theorist may try to counter the problem, just as there were strategies available to him for repairing the other flaw. At this point however there is a temptation, and I have no intention of resisting it, to put aside the attempt to characterize explanations by their form, or by their form plus their fulfilment of certain conditions such as that imported to deal with the problem about probabilities. We may well allow ourselves to investigate the other approach to explanation, which highlights the content and effect — the force — of an explanatory statement, rather than its form.

Let us begin the inquiry with the recognition that there are many uses of the word "explain" and its cognates, and that it would be rash to seek a single analysis of the lot. Since our topic is the explanation of actions, we may restrict our target and concentrate on the explanation of events: the explanation of why one or another event, described as such and such, occurred. When should we say then that a statement will count as explanatory of an event?

One condition that we must acknowledge, consistently with the merit that we admitted in the covering law account, is that the statement must render the event relatively unsurprising. This means that it must make the event seem relatively more probable than it had seemed before but also that it must make it seem sufficiently probable to be less surprising than the alternative would have been: it must give it a probability of greater than 50% (see Mellor, 1976). Some have urged that we sometimes explain an event by revealing it to have had perhaps even lesser probability than had been thought, as when we put the sequence of tails down to chance (see Salmon, 1971). I would prefer to say that in such cases we deny that there is any explanation available for the event, properly speaking; it just is a matter of chance (see Mellor, 1976). More on this later.

To say that an explanatory statement must render an event relatively unsurprising is not necessarily to go the way of the covering law theory and represent an explanation as an argument or inference. That representation is a distortion, although the popularity of the covering law approach may have obscured the fact. For in explaining an event there is no question of wanting to infer the truth of the proposition giving it expression. Normally the truth of that proposition is taken for granted and the last thing required is to put it on a firm inferential footing. The explanation of an event then may be taken to consist in a statement whose effect is to make the event seem relatively unexceptional, and not to involve the construction of an argument with that statement in the premises and the proposition that the event occurred in the conclusion (see Mellor, 1976; Salmon, 1971).

But what more do we say of the explanation of an event than that it is a statement which renders the event relatively unsurprising? The criticisms we made of the covering law theory can help us here. We noted that the factors mentioned in an explanation have a causal bearing on the event explained and that whether a statement is found explanatory of an event depends on the background knowledge of the person seeking explanation. A statement which explains an event then must give us causal understanding; and the understanding it gives us must be an advance on the cognitive *status quo*. In a phrase, the explanation of an event must advance us in the search for the event's causes (see Quine and Ullian, 1978).

As we have already noted, the analysis of the causal relationship between events is notoriously elusive. Some points however must be mentioned if we are to have a grasp of the ways in which our causal understanding of an event may be advanced. The causal connection between two events c and e, where c is a total cause of e, and not just part of a total cause, is usually thought to involve the following: first, that c is not a later occurrence than e, secondly, that c is spatio-temporally contiguous to e, or that it is connected by a chain of spatio-temporally contiguous events to e, and thirdly, that c is necessary and/or sufficient in the circumstances for e. The questions lurking here are legion. The temporal clause allows simultaneous causation but in such a case how do we distinguish cause from effect, since the other clauses treat them symmetrically? One answer may be to say that the events are not so much simultaneous as overlapping and that earlier parts of the cause are always responsible for later parts in the effect. The contiguity clause is obscure for the reason that our notions of what are contiguous and what not, depend to a good extent on prevailing physical theory. Such a dependence makes the concept of causality more fragile than is generally assumed, although if we learn to tolerate it we may eventually come to cherish it.

The very tricky issues however come up with the third clause. A cause need not be necessary in the circumstances because the effect is over-determined. But do we really allow that it may not be sufficient: do we admit non-deterministic causation? That is a first question. A second has to do with the basis for the necessity and/or sufficiency mentioned in the clause. An event c, redescribed as "the event such that it occurs in such and such a position, and at such and such a time, relative to e", will automatically pass as sufficient for c. Clearly the basis sought for sufficiency cannot be the redescriptive one manufactured here and must be something else; the laws of nature. But then we have pressed upon us the unresolved problem of how to distinguish such laws from true accidental generalizations (see Goodman, 1965). And there is a third difficulty which also arises with the clause under discussion. There are cases of event pairs which seem to fit all the clauses but which we would not count as causally related, such as: my saying "Thank" and my saying "Thank you", my sister having a baby and my becoming an uncle, my being born in 1900 and my being seventy-nine in 1979. With these examples one wants to say that the events are not really distinct but the trouble with the remark is that we lack any agreed criterion for deciding whether apparently different events are one or many.

These comments will remind us of what we know and do not know about causality: the cement, as Hume described it, of our universe. What then may it mean for an explanation to advance us in the search for the causes of an event? Suppose we are presented with an event described as an A-event. We may be advanced in our search for its causes by being directed to a B-event which is its total proximate cause or a part of that cause, supposing the total one to be a combination of the B-event with a C-event — a combination which may or may not be describable as a single complex event. We may be advanced instead, or in addition, by being pointed towards a total or partial non-proximate cause: a proximate cause of the proximate cause, or a proximate cause of the proximate cause of the proximate cause, or whatever. Finally, we may be further advanced by having a hitherto ignored feature of the A-event traced to a feature of a given cause of the A-event, the assumption being that causes pass on certain marks to their effects. These three sorts of advancement in causal understanding, and there may well be others, can be neatly characterized as causal embedding, causal excavation and causal enrichment. We embed an event causally when we point to its immediate origin; we excavate it when we turn up its remoter springs; and we enrich it when we see how one or another features is the legacy of its ancestors. These varieties of understanding will be illustrated in the next section by references to our explanation of action.

We had concluded that the explanation of an event is a statement which renders it relatively unsurprising and now we have added that it is a statement which advances us in the causal understanding of the event. It is tempting to speculate at this point that the reason why an event explanation reduces surprise is precisely that it advances causal understanding: in that case it would be sufficient to mention just its aspect as causal advancement in specifying what an event explanation is. Is the speculation plausible then? It is, at least on the condition that causes are assumed to show their effects to have been relatively probable. This condition is fulfilled in the common run of cases and here we can say without hesitation that to explain is simply to advance causal understanding. However there is one special case which requires independent comment, and in conclusion I would like to turn to it.

The case is that of an event e for which the cause c is indeterministic and grossly insufficient: c undoubtedly produced e but indeterminism reigns and we believe that only in a small fraction of exactly similar cases would the counterparts of c give rise to counterparts of e. By tracing e to c we may well be advanced in our search for the causes of e, but we are not led to find e relatively unsurprising; or so it certainly seems. Are we given an explanation of e then by the causal story?

The answer to this question must be that we are not. When e is displayed as the effect c, in a situation where other events than e are actually more probable, what happens is not that e is explained but that it is shown to be an inappropriate subject for explanation: it is depicted as an improbable chance happening. Does this mean then that to explain an event is not simply to advance us in our causal understanding of it? Strictly speaking it does, since in the special case considered we can have causal advancement without explanation. What we can say however is that where evens explanation is available, i.e. where it is possible to render the event relatively unsurprising, it is achieved by a statement that advances us in our search for the event's causes. This formulation highlights the connection between advancing the causal understanding of an event and rendering it relatively unsurprising, while reminding us of the existence of the special case.

The explanation of actions

We concluded the first section with the observation that almost any intentional description of an action, whether as performed, preferred or projected, can be quoted in explanation of an action. With the insight into the nature of explanation that we have developed in the second section we can make sense of this proposition. Whether one intentional description or another is found explanatory of action depends on the background knowledge assumed, as we should expect. That a description does provide an explanation must come of the fact that, granted the cognitive *status.quo*, it advances us in our search for the causes of the action. If someone who asks why my hand is moving unevenly across the page is told that I am forming letters, words and sentences, the implication is that he learns something about the causal origin of the event in question: specifically, that it is produced by my desire to form letters, words and sentences, combined with my belief that I am doing just that in bringing about the event in question. Some philosophers have wanted to construe action explanations as non-causal but this causal reading does seem to be required in order to do justice to the shared assumptions of those trading explanations. No explanation would be given in the example under discussion were it not assumed that the desire and belief mentioned actually produced the action: were no such belief and desire postulated, or were they not thought to have been responsible for the action, then we could hardly expect our questioner to be satisfied by the redescription of my action (see Davidson, 1963).

But, as we have seen before, a questioner may press further on an action such as my forming letters, words, and sentences and may be told in turn that I am writing, that I am writing a paper on the explanation of actions, that I am fulfilling a promise, and so on. How in such cases is he being advanced in his search for the causes of the action? Well, it seems that if the first explanation embeds the action causally, these further explanations progressively excavate it. My desire to form syntactical inscriptions is explained by my desire to write combined with the appropriate belief. Similarly my desire to write is explained by my desire to write a paper, and my desire to write a paper by my desire to fulfil a promise, the desires being combined in each case with appropriate beliefs; and so on. The picture which emerges is that an action issues from a long line of total causes, each consisting of a desire part and a belief part, and that the pursuit of ever more basic intentional explanations presses us on and on in excavation of further ancestors. Notice however that it may be misleading to speak of ancestry here since there is no implication of increasing temporal removal from the action as we move from one desire to another. A cause cannot be later than its effect but it may be simultaneous with it and so the chain of causation back from one desire to another may be pictured not so much on the model of a genealogy as on that of a hierarchy: the causes are not progressively more distant, but rather more elevated and overarching.

We said just now that *if* the first intentional explanation embeds the actions causally, the further explanations causally excavate it. The conditional form of expression is chosen with reason, for it is possible to hold that the proximate cause of an action is the act of intending it, something which we characterized in the first section as an unconditional judgment in favour of the action (see Davidson, 1978). If the intending of the action in this sense is taken as the proximate cause then reference to that intending is what causally embeds the event and reference to the agent's pro-attitude to the basic description is the first step in causal excavation. It does seem that whenever one acts intentionally, one must judge unconditionally in favour of the action and that one must therefore intend it, but consistently with admitting this one might or might not regard the intending as a cause of the action: one might take it as a simultaneous effect, or as something identical with the performance of the action. I do not wish to judge on which of these possibilities is realized, or indeed on whether the same possibility should be assumed to be realized in every case.

We find our first major variety of action explanation in these intentional accounts of action, these ever more satisfying intentional redescriptions of behaviour. It is worth mentioning however, and the point has already been implicit, that among intentional explanations some are of greater utility than others, serving more reliably to silence questions. Of particular importance are, on the one hand, the explanation which gives us the description of the action as preferred to alternatives and, on the other, the explanation which gives us that description, and it may be a description of the action as preferred or projected, which puts the most persuasive face available on the action. The first sort represents the action as one among the mutually exclusive set of options available to the agent and indicates what, properly speaking, the agent set out to do; elsewhere, somewhat misleadingly, I characterized it as the explanation by intention (see Pettit, 1976). The second kind of explanation puts what has been called a desirability characterization on the action (see Anscombe, 1963). It describes the action in terms such that no one who understands the terms can fail to see why the agent should have been moved to try to realize the description: and this, even if the assessor not approve of the agent's choice. Typical desirability characterizations represent actions as dutiful, enjoyable, profitable, friendly or, perhaps most typically, as a mixture of these. We accept that such characterizations can be found persuasive, and we acknowledge that it is wilful to seek an explanation of why an agent should have wanted to realize one, because of a shared model of normal human motivation (see Pettit, 1975, section 3).

With the category of intentional explanations fixed and analysed, we can begin to sketch in the other ways in which we account for action in everyday life, the other ways in which we advance the search for the causes of action. Our strategy will be to ask how, apart from pursuing intentional explanations, we might hope to excavate and enrich an action causally. The picture which we presently have gives us a progression of total causes, each consisting of a desire part and a belief part and each having its desire part explained by the preceding pair, up to the last desire to realize a desirability characterization or set of characterizations. This gives us some loose ends, in particular the belief parts at each level and the desire part at the last; thus we naturally ask how they in turn are explained, yielding a deeper excavation or enrichment of the action.

The explanation of why we hold those beliefs which operate in the genesis of action may take any of a number of forms. It may refer us to the pressure of inductive evidence, deductive reasoning, reliable testimony and tradition or, rather less flatteringly, to the force of conformism, illusion, self-righteousness and the like. When the explanation of an action is sought we often find the focus on the springs of some operative belief and then we are pointed towards such pressures and forces. In asking why someone of a strange religious culture goes through an unfamiliar cleansing ritual for example, we may assume that the operative desire is to do what is holy and our real interest will be in the sources, proximate and otherwise, of the agent's belief that the ritual is a holy deed.

It should be mentioned in passing that explanations by reference to what, in catch-all phrases, we have called desires and beliefs may be more complex than has perhaps been suggested; otherwise the excavation of beliefs, and indeed of desires too, may seem to be a very limited enterprise. We have spoken as if at every level of description an agent's desire to realize that description follows unproblematically from a desire to fulfil a further description which he believes will for sure be fulfilled by the realization of the first. This leaves out of account the complexities of the choice under risk or uncertainty where the agent is faced with the action under its preferred description, but where he is unsure about which of a number of mutually exclusive outcome descriptions will be made true by his fulfilling the preferred one: he is unsure for example whether speaking candidly to a friend will cause offence or clear the air. Here the desire which yields the desire for the preferred description is the desire for the hoped for outcome, the desire to clear the air, but it is geared into the lower desire by complex beliefs about the likelihood of achieving it rather than the unfetching alternative, beliefs such as decision theory tries to analyse.

Apart from beliefs, the other loose end in the causal chain of belief-desire pairs is the last desire mentioned in intentional explanation: the desire for the realization of a simple or complex desirability characterization. In many circumstances the only appropriate explanation of this will point us towards the influence of the perceived external prompt; an anticipated prospect of doing one's duty, enjoying oneself, making a profit or whatever gives one reason just as such to pursue it and no further explanation of the pursuit need be thought to be required. However we often feel that deeper exploration of the last desire is required if the desire prevails over what might have been assumed to be an equally strong or even stronger inclination towards an alternative action. Suppose my writing this paper is given its last intentional explanation by my desire to fulfil a promise: this description is taken as a desirability characterization. The appeal of promise-keeping might normally be thought enough to explain this desire but we would feel that further comment was required were one of the alternatives neglected any of the following: going to visit a seriously ill parent, taking a free holiday on the riviera as a raffle prize or submitting myself to urgently required medical treatment.

In this case what is required is causal enrichment of the desire to fulfil a promise, and ultimately of the action which it produces. The perceived appeal of promise-keeping is the cause of this desire appearing but what we require is a feature of that cause which will explain the feature noticed in the desire: that it prevails over certain other powerful desires that we assume to be present in the agent. Causes pass on certain marks to their effects: if the thunder is near, the noise will be loud; if the fire is widespread, the damage will be costly; if the drinking is riotous, the hangover will be prolonged (see Salmon, 1975). What we seek now is a feature in the perceived appeal of promise-keeping which would let us understand the surprising property in the desire it occasions, that the desire prevails over powerful competing urges. What feature in the cause could have passed on this property to the effect?

There are at least four different ways in which the causal enrichment required in this question is provided (see Pettit, 1976). All of them have in common that they locate the operative feature of the prompting cause in the agent. The first would relate it to a long term policy or commitment on the agent's part, the second to the agent's motivational profile, the third to his character or personality, and the fourth to his social position. The idea is that the perceived appeal of promise-keeping, granted that it has the feature of engaging someone with such and such a policy, profile, personality or position, passes on to the desire occasioned the property of outweighing certain opposed desires. Some remarks will be useful on the invocation of the factors mentioned since the explanations in which they appear constitute the major action accounting varieties over and beyond the explanations of beliefs and the rather mixed bag of intentional explanations, i.e. the explanations of (non-ultimate) desires. The remarks will be brief since the going is relatively easy and it is time to draw this paper to a close.

An agent has a policy, such as the policy of keeping promises come what may, when he makes an unconditional judgment in favour of those actions which he sees in future offing for him, that fulfil promises. It is not just that he finds them qua fulfilments of promises attractive or compelling, a state which would leave him free not to perform them, finding them unattractive under other aspects. He selects in all their particularity those actions that he foresees; he decides resolutely for them. Such a policy resembles a state of intending something in this regard (see Davidson, 1978). What distinguishes it is that whereas the intending is fulfilled by a single action, however complex, the policy remains intact and directive no matter how many actions have satisfied it.

An agent's motivational profile is constituted by the state of his emotions and drives. Emotions are passing states of feeling which are not associated with any very restricted class of action: fear and jealousy, shame and joy, despair and sadness, may sensitize agents to any of a number of promptings and may lead to any of a variety of actions. They are associated with characteristic circumstances of arousal and they usually issue in distinctive involuntary expressions. Drives on the other hand are passing states of feeling which are pointed much more definitively towards particular tracks of behaviour: avarice and envy, revenge and ambition, hunger and lust, are primarily identified by the promptings to which they make us responsive and the actions which they lead us to perform. Like emotions they have characteristic circumstances of arousal but they do not have such distinctive involuntary expressions. As states of feeling, emotions and drives have in common the fact that it does not make sense, as it would with a policy, to think of an agent revoking them: they are conceived of as unwilled, if sometimes welcome, visitations.

An agent's character or personality consists in deeply enduring and only partially controllable habits of mind and heart whereby he may be distinguished from other individuals. It is often described by the use of words associated with certain emotions and drives, the implication being that the agent has a susceptibility to those states. Thus we have fearful and jealous, avaricious and envious, people as well as having the emotions of fear and jealousy and the drives of avarice and envy. Personality is often characterized too, not by habits of the sensibility but by habits of thought. When we speak of someone as obsessional or judgmental, or when we characterize his belief patterns as fascist or xenophobic, we are ascribing personality just as much as when we describe his affective dispositions. In either case we are focussing on something in the agent which, like his policies or his motivational profile, may mean that a given prompting occasions a distinctively powerful desire.

Finally, an agent's social position, in a slightly unusual use of the phrase, is the frame constituted by the relationships with other people which constrain his behaviour at any time. The traffic warden seeing children safely across the road, the bank clerk considering a request for credit, the tourist office attendant giving information to visitors: these are examples of people who so long as they exercise the activities described are in highly visible social positions. Like the other factors mentioned, position is something on the side of the agent which can mean that a given stimulus to desire is exceptionally potent, and that the desire occasioned has the feature of readily prevailing over competitors.

It appears then that as we causally excavate action in progressive intentional explanations, and in the explanations of our beliefs, so we causally enrich it by exploring policy, profile, personality and position. It is fascinating to notice that these four lines of exploration have all been taken up beyond the marketplace of common accounting, within the portals of organized psychological theory. Policy has loomed large, although under various names, in the annals of existential psychiatry, where we are invited to see the ubiquitous influence on an agent of projects and commitments dimly undertaken in childhood. Motivational profile, whether in the form of emotions or drives, has appeared across the spectrum of schools, and under various guises. Personality has been the concern of those who have dealt in character traits but also, less obviously, of psychologists interested in the internal maps or constructions of the world whereby agents orientate themselves. Finally position has been given prominence by theorists from Lewin to Goffman who have sought to represent agents as exhibiting in every circumstance, albeit sometimes imaginatively, the behaviour that is required for the maintenance of their pressing relationships.

In this section we set out to investigate the nature and variety of action explanations and we may be reasonably content with what we have attained. The explanation of an event, we know, is a statement which advances us in our search for causes, whether embedding, excavating, or enriching the event causally. Turning to the explanations sponsored by the action theory described in the first section, it appears that we embed an action causally in a basic state of desire and belief on the part of the agent or in the agent's intending of the action; that we excavate it as we look further into the causes of the belief and the desire or of the intending, this investigation taking us into a hierarchy of belief-desire states; and that we enrich it as we highlight the marking given to what might otherwise have been innocuous initial promptings by such factors as policy, profile, personality and position.

We must be prepared to admit that, even when we have covered the possibility of elliptical formulations of explanations recognized in our taxonomy, we shall come across forms of explanation that we have not identified here. Be that as it may however, we have at least achieved the beginnings of a systematization of our regular accounting practice. We are now at the point where we can raise the question of how far organized inquiry can supercede the assumptions and attainments of regular accounting (see Pettit, 1978, 1979; Macdonald and Pettit, forthcoming). This, fortunately or unfortunately, is the point at which we must stop.

2

Research on Ordinary Explanations*

C. Antaki and G. Fielding

What are ordinary explanations?

In the last chapter Pettit examined ordinary explanations for what they tell us about human conceptions of social action and purposive behaviour. Explanations were taken as causes advanced to account for actions. In this chapter our aim is to outline the variety of research that exists on ordinary explanations, and to suit our purpose we have broadened the conception of explanations to cover rather more ground; in this chapter ordinary explanations are taken as interpretations of behaviour, ranging from unconscious appraisal to considered and polished argument.

There is what one might call a pyramid of consciousness in explanations: at the base of the pyramid there are the unconscious or unrealized accounts we have of actions and scenes presented to us in the ordinary course of events; above this level there are the realized but purely private accounts we articulate only to ourselves; and tapering away towards the top of the pyramid there are those public accounts and explanations whose production and acceptance are governed by social convention. The considered explanations that Pettit examines are based on less articulate thoughts and habits of mind below them; in this chapter, we shall try and describe how psychologists and others have made sense of the various levels of the pyramid. We shall use two sets of distinctions to help us describe its architecture: a distinction between sorts of explanation, analogous perhaps to levels of explanation; and a distinction between types of psychological approach to their research, analogous perhaps to the faces of the pyramid.

TWO PSYCHOLOGIES

We have organized the chapter down two parallel tracks. At every

The authors are grateful to Steve Duck and John H. Harvey for reading and commenting on an earlier version of this chapter.

station of explanation we come to we shall have something to say about work done in the cognitive, or *information-processing*, tradition, and work done within the personal-interpretation, or *representational*, tradition. The information-processing tradition is firmly within the experimental approach to social psychology: it is concerned with *how* ordinary explanations are arrived at. Research in this tradition is aimed at describing powerful models of the way in which people select, combine and integrate social information in arriving at a judgment. What we have called the representational approach, on the other hand, is a heterogenous collection of analysis and research in the disciplines of social anthropology, philosophy, sociology and linguistics, and most especially in the newer forms of radical social psychology. Research and writing in this tradition is less concerned with models of selection and integration of information and more concerned with the *content* of ordinary explanation and its personal, interpersonal and cultural *use*.

THREE TYPES OF EXPLANATION OF SOCIAL ACTIONS

On our parallel tracks through the existing research we have found it useful to reduce the variety of ordinary explanations to three sorts, which we shall come to in the following order: explanations of what an action is (*descriptive* explanation) explanations of why it was performed (*agency* explanations) and explanations of its rightness or wrongness (*morality* explanations). This is based on a reading of Pettit's distinctions of types of explanation (1976; see also Chapter 1, section "On explanations"). The basic idea is this: there are a number of questions that explanations can answer, and each of these questions requires a rather different sort of language for its answer to be cast in. Furthermore, the questions may be organized in a sort of sequence, the question "What's all this about?" and its family needing to be answered before explanations of "Why did this come about" can be advanced. After we have worked through the sequence, we will review the sorts of ordinary explanations it leaves out of the reckoning.

The foundation stone of explanations is the account one gives when one has been asked "What is going on?". One might take a friend from abroad to see a rugby match and he might ask what is going on when there is a line-out, when the players scrum down, when one of them is sent off and so on. Probably he will not need to be told that what is going on is a game, but he will need specific points of information to give him a handle on what is, at the outset, peculiar behaviour even within the context of "games". He needs to be told what this or that activity *is*; other explanations follow later. Everyday explanations of this type — call them descriptive explanations — are of course quite common, since we are forever offering interpretations to people in the way we choose to describe something; but we are only really aware of it when we are deliberately asked for it by a stranger or someone who genuinely does not know what is going on. We seem to need old jokes like "horses sweat; gentlemen perspire; ladies glow" to remind us how ordinary language discriminates between various interpretations of the same fact.

Once the meaning of the event has been sorted out the question of what brought it about can be raised. There are two sorts of follow-up questions that one can ask. One is to do with what happened — a series of questions about the sequence of events, who was there, what happened next and so on. We shall not be much interested in these. The other is to do with the *reasons* for it happening, and it is with these that we shall be concerned. Here, as Pettit (1976) has pointed out, the answer is going to be in terms of motivation, character, intention and policy; as Pettit says, all of these have the property of locating, as reasons do, the operative feature of the prompting cause in the agent. We shall see that attribution theory has taken this as its paradigm of ordinary explanation: its aim is to understand how people set about "perceiving the causes of behaviour" (Jones *et al.*, 1972). However, it has been said that this view of explanations is a limited one, and that it is more profitable to see explanations as more than perceptions of causes. We shall see more of this controversy later in the chapter.

The last question one might be called upon to answer in our scheme is one that assumes that all the others have been answered, since it is about the *morality* of the action. The questioner here knows enough about the action and what brought it about to make him want to ask about its propriety. The answer he will get will use all the explanatory concepts of the answers to the other questions, but in this context they will have a particular force behind them — they will need to persuade his audience not just that things took place for certain reasons, but also that these reasons made what took place all right.

We have been briskly through a categorization of three sorts of explanation ("meaning" explanations, "reason" explanations and "morality" explanations); now, what has psychology to say about them? To begin to answer this, it is worth saying that though there has never been a psychology of ordinary explanation as such, with schools of thought, arguments, crucial experiments and all the other paraphernalia of established research areas, psychology has always had something to say about parts, at least, of the phenomena of ordinary explanations.

We shall now go down the parallel tracks of information processing and representation to discover what parts of the three sorts of explanations have had something said about them. We shall examine in turn analyses of explanations of what, explanations of why and explanations of morality.

Descriptive explanation

The question this sort of explanation is meant to answer is the question in the form "What is . . .?". The general "What's going on?" is the familiar example in adult life. Obviously when one is a stranger or a tourist one will ask a lot of these sort of questions — "Is this a parade, or is it a march?" "What does it mean to be wearing a red carnation?" etc. etc.; but one can also be puzzled by more mundane things. One might ask something like "What was going on between you and him at the party?" or "What did it mean when you started reminding me that I was going to be driving home?" or "What is happening to us?". We are searching for the *significance* of the event: we want to translate what is enigmatic into what is familiar. Privately, the translation may not be any conscious process but, at some point, some translating device will have been used to turn the scene in the external world into a short-hand culturally-given expression like "it's a celebration; or "we are breaking up", and so on.

We have used the term *descriptive* explanation as a shorthand way of saying that this is explanation by *labelling* or *tagging* — explaining something by giving it a name that the audience will understand. This name, as Pettit points out (this volume, p. 11), can be an intentional description of the event, shading descriptive explanation into agency explanation. We shall come to agency explanation later.

THE REPRESENTATIONAL APPROACH TO DESCRIPTIVE EXPLANATION

The labels or tags that people put on events they are asked to explain are evidence of the way those events are represented or filed away in people's minds. Consequently, there is a great deal of research into this type of explanation from those who are interested in mental representations, and the range here is from psycholinguists to radical social psychologists.

The link between what a person says about what he understands a situation to be and what representations of it he carries about with him is not an uncomplicated one, since, of course, many things can interfere with a strictly accurate report, and the very notion of an accurate report of such things may be misguided (Berger and Luckmann, 1971). What is clear, though, is that if one is interested in how people plan their actions then one must work on their fundamental definitions of the actions and of the situation in which they may be performed. For Shotter (Chapter 7) the study of the definition of the situation is the aim and value of a theory of explanations; but more generally it is the concern with the ascription of meaning that is common to the range of research considered here.

Consider the recent developments towards *schemata* in various branches of psychology. A *schema* can be taken to mean here a package of instructions for interpreting something (sometimes also for performing something). There are proposals that schemata can account for as extensive a social phenomenon as attributional performance (Reeder and Brewer, 1979), for example, though the more usual approach is to propose particular schemata as examples of what the concept can do for cognitive psychology. For example Schank (1973) gives a number of packages of mental instructions (scripts) to make sense of how people cope with information in situations where a good deal of what is going on is predictable. In a restaurant, for example, one knows roughly that one will come in and be shown to a table, that one will sit, look at a menu, order, make small talk, eat, have coffee, call for the bill, pay, judge the tip and leave. For Schank, these "predetermined sequences of actions that *define a situation*" (ibid, p. 123) are mental packages which help us make sense of the world by filling in what we cannot see at the time but is likely to be there nonetheless. The psychological use made of this version of a schema is generally a linguistic or cognitive one (e.g. Minsky, 1975; Charniak, 1972), the intention usually being to strengthen theories of comprehension and memory, for example, to account for people's ability to generate consistent, but inaccurate, information when remembering a story whose outline may be familiar but whose details may vary (like the restaurant example above). Scripts have also been proposed as components of social theories: for instance Abelson (1976) uses a script as a conceptual structure which explains for the believer what a specific social action or sequence of actions means. The attraction for the psychologist is that arming the social person with a comparatively smallish number of such conceptual structures allows him to make sense of a great number of events in the *social world* : not at the level of *reasons*, but at the level of how the events are defined in terms of a larger scheme of things. This economy is appealing and large numbers of scripts can be further reduced and integrated by putting them into families or "themes".

What is particularly interesting here is that in applying the notion of schemata to social representations, Abelson is following in the lead of Heider (1958) and his analysis of the elements of stories, fables and so forth. As Harris and Harvey point out in Chapter 3, Heider's contribution to ordinary explanations is wider than what has become known as Attribution Theory. Schemata, in this post-Heiderian context, are means for situating actions.

What is noticeable once one has said this is that the schemata of Schank (1973) and Abelson (1976) are highly *situational*. The notion of personal representation, which might have developed into a more idiographic theory — each individual having his own set of idiosyncratic schemata for his own purposes — is used in the development of a theory about differences between situational schemata rather than differences between people. The converse of this is found in those researchers who are concerned with what differences there are between people in apparently the same situation, and it is worth noting that the search for "situationist" models of anyone's representations is going on in parallel with this search for more personalized models.

One example of this psychology of individuals' representation is the sort of theory that develops from a concern with personal adjustment and mental health. One obvious candidate is Berne's well known Transactional Analysis. Here we are given a reduced and systematized language into which we can translate ordinary thought and feelings, though the rules by which we do the translation of, say, feelings of frustration with one's wife into some question of ego states, games, life scripts, etc. are not absolutely fixed. The status and validity of this kind of theory are controversial but it seems safe to say that, in principle at least, the psychodynamic theory which this exemplifies is a theory of personalized representation.

One important notion of psychodynamic theory we shall not have space to pursue here is the notion that it is not just what people *say* that tells us about what they think, but also *how* they say it, or, in more general terms, in what expressive style (Harré, 1979, p. 5) they perform what they are doing. I may put a £5 note in the collection plate, but whether I do it with a grimace or not will tell you whether or not I have anything smaller to put in. Shotter (Chapter 7) elaborates on this to argue that since something like a piece of style, possibly no more than a nod or a wink, can "explain" something in the descriptive sense (change our notions of what is going on), then something beyond inferential or propositional reasoning must be involved in the ordinary interpretation of actions.

To return to clinical theories of personal representations, modern examples tend to move away from using expressive behaviour in formal diagnosis (though it is unlikely that it plays no part when the clinician is forming some judgment in the unquantified part of the consultation). One example of a modern theory here is the personal construct theory of George Kelly (Kelly, 1955; Bannister and Fransella, 1971). Here the accent is less on applying a clinical language than on discovering the person's own way of seeing the social world. In finding a method of doing so, Kelly laid the grounds for a technique (the Repertory Grid) which is probably now the single most popular research tool used by psychologists interested in personalized representations (though this is not to say that every use made of the Repertory Grid is one Kelly would have endorsed). The central idea is that "A person's processes are psychologically channelised by the ways in which he anticipates events" (Kelly, 1955, p. 46) so that if one can find how he anticipates things one can find out something important about his psychology: and, since "a person anticipates events by construing their replications" (1955, p. 50) this can be done by looking at how he construes, or interprets, things that have happened. His single interpretations, or individual constructs, are couched in bi-polar terms: a thing is either this or that, one thing or another, and a person's construal of an event (or person, or situation and so on) can be fully catalogued by a smallish number of independent bi-polar constructs. Like the cognitive theorists we saw above, Kelly seeks a parsimonious model of representation: the difference is that instead of choosing to model the structure of the situation that is seen, or the story that is processed, Kelly has chosen to model the structure of the interpretative machinery individuals bring with them to the situation, or the story, event, relationship and so on.

The strength of Kelly's model when describing individual representations becomes a weakness when the task we require of it is to an account for how and why *joint action* between people is possible (c.f. Shotter, Chapter 7). It has been shown that the relation between two people's construct systems can be useful in predicting, say, friendship (via what is called the "sociality corollary": Duck, 1979) which is one sort of joint action, but for our kinds of social interaction the question of whether one likes the other people or not or more generally how one's construct system relates with theirs is not an issue. In these areas what is needed is a theory that has a model both of individual action *and* of the representation of the situation. Examples of theories which span social representations (as exemplified by the notion of situational schemata, e.g. Schank and Abelson) and personalistic representation (as exemplified by the work of Kelly) are theories of the generation of social action, since in the nature of things these need to be cast in a form which can mesh individual cognitions with situational constraints. Gowler and Legge (Chapter 11) show us how fundamental is the "giving and grasping of meaning" which such theories take as their target to explain. Perhaps the most widely known, if among the most controversial, theory of this sort in social psychology today is Harré and Secord's theory of ethogenics (Harré and Secord, 1972) — literally, a theory of the birth of ordinary behaviour (Harré, 1974). We shall be seeing rather a lot of this when we look at representation-theory accounts of ordinary explanations of agency, so we shall defer a closer look until then.

THE INFORMATION-PROCESSING APPROACH TO DESCRIPTIVE EXPLANATION

The processing of perceptual information into meaningful categories has been studied extensively by psychologists for the last hundred years, and some of the work in this tradition has had to do with descriptive explanation. The fundamental question is this: you or I might want to explain that is such-and-such a thing, but how have we so identified it in the first place? Let us gear the question down and say that here is a piece of behaviour our foreign visitor finds odd, and we call it something or other for him in explanation. How have we separated that piece of behaviour off from everything else going on around us? How have we processed it into "action" (as opposed to mere movement)? And, most importantly, how have we recognized that it was this type of behaviour rather than that?

There is a good deal of attention by psychologists to the question of their own partitioning up of the social world: this is quite a methodological consideration when one has behavioural data that one wants to chop up into categories (see, for example, Cairns 1979). Since Barker's

1950s work, a lot of effort on this score has brought this corner of psychology quite close to the procedures used by ethologists. Nevertheless this has been strictly what has been called an *etic* question of professionals' own technical considerations in categorizing behaviour and not an *emic* question of how ordinary people do so. The latter has much more usually been left to those concerned with more basic, non-social information (colour, size, shape, etc. etc.). The tide turned when the literal behaviourism of Barker gave way to the more conceptual and analytic disposition of Heider (Heider and Simmel, 1944; Heider, 1958) who bridged the perceptual/social gap by noting that one of people's perceptual jobs was to break down Barker's stream of behaviour into recognizably social units of action. Once made, this bridge invited many perceptual psychologists to cross into social territory. More recently the bridge has been re-invented by social psychologists going the other way — the recent concern with "episodes," for example, is an illustration of this and an interesting echo of the situationism we saw in the cognitive work mentioned earlier.

One sort of crossing over we want to look at closely is Newtson's. (Newtson, 1973, 1976). Newtson and his colleagues, following Barker's and Heider's lead, have conducted a series of experiments which have shown that the behavioural units people use are far from being of a constant length and vary according to who the perceiver is, what the behaviour being looked at is like and the sort of reasons why it is being looked at.

We can take a detailed look at one such experiment to show the sort of experimental method that is necessary to bring out how people process behaviour before they can start to wonder about why it happened. "Chunking" is part of the process of finding out what name to give the behaviour and how confident one can be about the name, as we shall see. Newtson (1973, experiment II) showed experimental subjects a video-tape of someone assembling a large model of a chemical molecule, the kind of thing one would use as a visual aid in a lecture. One group saw the man simply assemble the various stages of the model with nothing untoward happening. Another group saw the man interrupt his model-making to take his right shoe off, remove his sock, and roll up his trouser leg. Each group of subjects had to mark off, as they were watching the tape, the ends of naturally occurring meaningful action in the sequence. In this experiment and in other studies, two things became clear. The first was that the absolute duration of what was seen to be a naturally occurring unit got longer as the sequence progressed, with the behaviour getting more predictable as the subjects stored more and more inform-ation about what the man was doing. The second was that if something unexpected happened (like the man rolling up his trouser leg) then the size of the units became significantly *finer*: people paid more attention to what then happened and chunked it into smaller units.

What Newtson has offered us is a view of the application of temporal rules in the segmenting of behaviour. This is the most basic task of the perceiver of any social action. But as Newtson notes, the perceiver's understanding of the action going on (e.g. its "novelty") is an important determinant of how the temporal rules are applied: in the experiment we discussed, the units of behaviour changed from gross to fine. What such distinctions do not tell us is the difference between the same lengths of quite different information; say a sip of tea and writing a line on a page. Both might take exactly the same time, but the difference in content may be more important than the similarity in unit time. However, the fact that units change when meaning changes suggests that this sort of enterprise, though not informative about sorts of inform-ation in units, is a good measure of the effects on the perceiver when these do change and of how the information is represented in his mind, along parameters of discriminability and absolute and relative size. The promise of this analysis of basic representation is that it can be married to a more conceptual analysis: perhaps one day we shall be able to say that event type A is perceived in units of x size and y discriminability, while type B is perceived in x − 1 units and so on. This is an orthodox vision of reducing social cognitions to algebra, similar to the aim of established social psychological theories (for example cognitive balance, dissonance, cognitive consistency, and psycho-logic) which sought to model social judgments in content-free algebraic terms.

Agency explanations

Agency explanations are usually asked for when there is something ambiguous about the cause of the action, or some reason to suppose that the obvious reason for a plain action is not the right one. By and large they are not asked for when things are proceeding normally, but even here the social individual will necessarily have processed *some* sort of understanding of what is going on around him, so one can also speak of "unconscious" or automatic explanation of this sort.

Psychology has to account for both covert and overt explanations separately, since it seems like that the difference in what is called upon to

be explained in the two ways makes a difference in the sort of explanation given. Run-of-the-mill events, processed as a matter of course,
might be satisfied with a set of explanatory concepts different from those
for events that strike the explainer as needing some public comment
(even, for the moment, barring "moral" events, which we shall come to
later). This harks back to the notion of a "pyramid of consciousness",
and is a theme taken up by Morris (Chapter 8) and by Shotter (Chapter
7). Apart from the content, there is also the matter of the process by
which the explanation is arrived at. Considered explanations may or
may not emerge from the same mental machinery as automatic ones, If
they do, so much the better, since considered explanations are much
easier to research than the other kind; if not, we have to be able to
account for the difference. Whether or not there is any similarity, and
where it may lie, is a question at the heart of the representationist
approach; work done on the information-processing side is much more
concerned with accepting the brief of going after automatic rather than
considered explanations, though, as we shall see, some of its lines do
branch into more public social territory.

THE REPRESENTATIONAL APPROACH TO AGENCY EXPLANATIONS

Bromley (1977) makes the point that when you ask people to describe
the personalities of people they know, the list of terms and phrases they
use is remarkably, and, to a psychologist, alarmingly long. How is the
personality theorist to cope? Exactly the same problem confronts the
psychologist of ordinary explanations when he asks his subjects to
explain the reasons for why people do things. The list of reasons, taken as
a census of each individual's personal favourite reasons for a range of
things people might do, must be endless; add the complication that
favourite reasons — theories about human nature if you like — admit
exceptions for, say, certain well-liked or loved, or even disliked or hated,
agents of action, and you have a well-nigh impossible catalogue the
psychologist must work with. The answer, of course, is that psychologists
simplify and organize; they collect data on what sorts of things seem
representative of the reasons people invoke in explanations of agency,
and find threads of meaning common to large sub-sections of the
collection. This is the orthodox approach to the representation of concepts of agency.
    But this orthodoxy has lately been challenged in two ways. The
method of reducing the variety of causal attribution explanations can

fail for several reasons, as van der Pligt argues in Chapter 4. On the other hand, more radical psychologists claim that the very enterprise of this sort of collection is a misguided one. There is a common link between the two criticisms. Both methodological and radical arguments are contingent on a functional notion of accounts. The idea here is that the account a person produces depends very strongly on the uses to which he wants to put it. In a sense we have already implicitly supported this argument simply by partitioning up explanations, as we have, into three sorts of answers to three sorts of questions.

The strong version of the functional argument says that the use to which an account is put is not discoverable from its superficial content, the words on the surface; on this argument content can be ignored in favour of searching after the underlying motives and intentions of the speaker. The weaker proposition agrees that the deciding factor in the statement of any explanation of agency is the advancement of some hidden purpose of the speaker's, but takes it that there is some important connection between what the words he uses are and what they do. It is this second form, with its greater respect for the content of what people say, which is generally accepted.

The two forms of the proposition have the same implication for the study of explanations, though they differ in degree. If the use to which an explanation is put is more important than the words used in the explanation, then interesting though it may be to catalogue and reduce reasons into a small list of types distinct in their dictionary meaning, for example to divide them up into those that mention the agent's intentions and those that mention his character, this is only a distraction from the real task of finding out the characteristics of the real causal factor, the uses to which such explanations can be put. The representation of reasons is to be found, this argument runs, only, or primarily, in the representation of the part it can play in the speaker's social life.

This way of thinking is manifest in four chapters in this book, those of Harré, Gowler and Legge, Canter and Brown and Tedeschi and Reiss. Now the uses these four sets of authors see their speakers seeking to achieve are rather different, but the central idea that they *do* have uses, and that these uses are the first thing the researcher must inspect, is common to all of them. Perhaps it is clearest in Tedeschi and Reiss's chapter, which follows in the symbolic interactional footsteps of Scott and Lyman's classic functional account of reasons (1968), where the social goal the person is trying to achieve guides the researcher in his cataloguing of the sorts of account he could use to achieve it. Harré is concerned with investigating the special character of psychologists' own explanations, and Gowler and Legge and Canter and Brown show very clearly how in professional life the function of the explanation and the negotiation of its content must be taken into account in its inter- pretation. All these writers' chapters lead one to ask; if the use of the explanation is so important, what is one to do, as a psychologist, when one is out collecting data? The suggestion is that greater respect is paid to the interpersonal and cultural content of data collection, since the problem of the experimenter having an effect on the phenomenon he is studying becomes much more than the mere nuisance it normally is; it can become a chief factor in the nature and content of the elicited account. It seems likely that the psychologist will be on safer ground when he admits that he cannot divorce function from form, and sets out on research procedures which take that into account. The trend has indeed started, and new attribution research shows a real appreciation of these issues (e.g. Orvis *et al.*, 1978).

THE INFORMATION-PROCESSING APPROACH TO AGENCY EXPLAN- ATIONS

Recent approaches to information-processing in experimental social psychology have identified a number of cognitive processes which are important in ordinary explanations of *why* such-and-such happened. We shall discuss the one with most particular relevance (i.e. attribution theory) at some length below, but first some words are appropriate about two theories which alert us to the importance of simply-perceptual influ- ences on otherwise cognitive decisions about the agency of social acts. (1) *Perceptual differences.* According to Bem's self-perception theory (Bem, 1972):

> Individuals come to know their attitudes, emotions, and other internal states partially by inferring them from observations of their own overt behaviour and/or the circumstances in which this behaviour occurs. Thus, to the extent that internal cues are weak ambiguous, or uninter- pretable, the individual is in the same position as an outside observer, an observer who must necessarily rely on these same external cues to infer the individual's inner states. (1972, p. 2)

We should immediately be aware that if the times when our private knowledge about what we are feeling and thinking is weak, ambiguous, etc. are more numerous than we might commonly suppose then this is a very radical proposition indeed. If, on the other hand, this is no more than the statement that when we do not know or cannot tell what we are feeling then we look elsewhere for evidence, and that these times are the relatively rare — feeling bad in the morning (hangover or cold?), feeling excited (the girl next to you or the fear of discovery?) and so on — then this is not so much a radical proposition as one that more straight-forwardly ties down exactly how we go about obtaining and processing evidence to reduce our uncertainty.

According to Bem, when internal private knowledge is weak, our own ordinary explanations of our internal states are no more sure an account of an event or feeling than an untutored observer's account. In other words, ordinary explanation of agency is sometimes no more than logical guesswork in disguise: its data are *strictly* public observations and its judgments *strictly* inference. The disguise fools the explainer into thinking that the explanation is not liable to all the qualifications he would attach to it had he known it had only the status of any other observer's account. To these qualifications the psychologist would add those additional hidden biases that research has revealed (Ross, 1977). What this means is that we are to be alerted, both as ordinary explainers and as psychologists, to new and closer boundaries on the dangers of prejudiced perception: now we have not only to worry about the validity of attributing qualities to other people (cf. Mischel, 1973) but also the validity of attributing them to ourselves.

An equally radical warning about the implications of inarticu-latable influences on social perception is given in Duval and Wicklund's Objective self-awareness theory (1972). Working from the proposition expressed by Mead (1934) that one's self can be either the subject (the doer) or the object (the sufferer) of one's perceptions, Duval and Wicklund propose that simple salience can flip a person from one state to the other, and that this has effect on, apart from other things, the person's ideas about the causes of things happening. "Given that there are two or more objects in the environment which could reasonably cause the event, the theory indicates that the focus of the person's attention will determine the locus of attribution" (Duval and Wicklund, 1973, p. 19).

There can be no doubt that this is as radical a proposition as Bem's. It is not intuitively comfortable to believe that one's judgment of the cause of some event can be affected by the focus of one's attention. We should not easily believe that our judgment of who was responsible for some event reported in the morning's newspaper, say, was affected by where our attention was when we were reading the story, yet in an engagingly simple study of undergraduate girls' explanations, Duval and Wicklund

(1973) found that an equivalent phenomenon could be made to happen. In experiment I, one group of girls was asked to read a series of stories about events which they might hypothetically have taken part in. They were in a room housing a piece of psychological machinery, but they were asked to ignore this and report their judgment of how much they would be to blame for the consequences of the events if they had taken part in them. Girls in another group were given the same stories, but while they were deliberating on the apportionment of blame, they were operating the machinery and their attention, presumably, was directed away from themselves (the task was simply to keep a turntable spinning by the pressure of a finger). Girls in the latter group attributed one-fifth more blame to causes other than themselves for the events in the stories than girls in the former group (a statistically significant difference). In experiment II, girls in one group were seated in front of a mirror, girls in another were not; the judgments (this time of "responsibility to oneself") were a fifth higher for the group who were made self-aware. The conclusions that the authors came to were that the manipulation of attention away or onto the self made the self more or less salient to the person, and this perceptual salience affected the person's judgment of things that should, rationally, be completely unaffected: in this case, judgments of their blame and responsibility for quite independent, hypothetical events.

Once again, the important thing to note is how much this theory contradicts ordinary notions of what is happening when we give reasons for something, and cautions us to beware of unthinking, and inarticulatable, influences on what we say; the strength of objective self-awareness theory and self-perception theory is that by identifying what can happen in the process of collecting information in coming to a judgment, or what can weight the information we receive, they identify strictly non-social (in the sense of more fundamentally information processing) factors which might account for what someone concerned only with the events of the explanation might mistakenly attribute to truly considered substantial differences between accounts.

(2) *Attribution theory*. If information-processing is important in the psychology of perceptions and judgments of a person's agency of action, then it is welcome to find that one of the most popular current research theories in social psychology today is a theory of people's attributions of causality. Harris and Harvey's comprehensive account (Chapter 3) shows the development of psychological principles concerned with the processing of information to one end: to providing the explainer with the

most satisfactory candidate to whom or to which the cause of an event may be attributed. For attribution theorists the content of people's explanations has been sharply delimited to just these causal attributions, and though this may leave it open to some objections, as for example van der Pligt shows, what it does is to reduce explanations to a vocabulary of responses to situations which are much more easily under the psychologists' experimental command than the situations which might prompt other, more wide ranging explanatory responses; and this brings explantions of agency into the legitimate area of experimental social psychology. In discussing Attribution Theory and its findings we should bear in mind that to bring explanations into the laboratory some damage has had be done to them, and we must ask ourselves whether the damage done invalidates Attribution Theorists' claims to be illuminating ordinary explanation as such. This, of course, is an echo of our misgivings about a clinical typology of explanation, expressed above.

Consider the two most influential attribution models, Jones and Davis' correspondent inference theory and Kelley's covariance theory. Both are concerned with the information the individual needs to process, and how that information must be processed, before a judgment about what the event must be set down to can be made. Jones and Davis (1965) propose that in explaining an event, the social individual is seeking to clear away any impediments to making a correspondence between what Mr A did and Mr A's personal dispositions; if obstacles to this inference cannot be cleared away, then the individual can have no great confidence in the exact explanation of Mr A's actions. If they can be cleared away (and the obstacles are such things as likely coercion of the man's actions, the high general desirability of the effects of those actions and likely unintentionality of the man's actions) then the individual can conclude that the person did such-and-such a thing because he had an intention to do it, which sprang from a general disposition. The more the effects of the man's actions are unlikely to be generally desired by anyone else, the more likely it is that he will have specially desired them, so the more they will *correspond* to his private dispositions. While both Kelley's and Jones and Davis's theories divide the world of ordinary reasons into private dispositions and environmental causes, Jones and Davis are concerned with the problem of inference following the observation of a single event; Kelley, on the other hand, is concerned with inferences based on a history of observations. In his model, the explanation for the event is reduced to two causal candidates (the person involved, or the environment in which the event took place) and the information to be processed is reduced to the information necessary to decide the *covariance* of the event with one or other of the two causal candidates. This information is historical information about when the event took place with either or both: for example, in a study by McArthur (1972) the information given to people to help them decide on the explanation of the event was of this sort: "John almost always laughs at this comedian; John laughs at almost any comedian; hardly anyone laughs at this comedian" (after McArthur, 1972, p. 174). According to Kelley's model of information processing — a straightforward application of logical rules of association, or what is sometimes called Mill's method of difference — people reading this should attribute the cause of the event (laughing at the comedian) to John, as of course they do. What Kelley offers us is a systematization of what people can infer from certain patterns of historical fact about the relation between one event and two causal candidates.

Common sense might lead us to think that when it comes to looking at evidence about what caused a particular piece of behaviour, people are reasonably good at deciding what is and what is not pertinent information and making their judgment accordingly. What Kelley's model allows us to do is to test this. In his model the pertinent information can be divided into a small number of types by the experimenter and fed to the subject in various combinations; the subject is then asked to make some judgment about the cause of the event and from this it can be deduced how much he was influenced by each sort of information. When this is done, the results can be counter-intuitive: Nisbett, *et al.* (1976) bring together evidence to show that people are very poor at using what Kelley calls *consensus* information. People take less account than they should of information about how common an event is. One example of this is seen in the work of Miller, *et al.* (1973), who asked college students to read a description of an experiment in which subjects were asked to apply shocks of increasingly painful and dangerous intensity to another subject in an effort to make him perform better at a task of memorizing lists of words. This experiment had actually been performed (Milgram, 1963) and showed that people almost without exception would subject the learner to very substantial and painful intensities of shocks before refusing to go further (though of course, the "learner" was a confederate of Milgram's and the electrical apparatus bogus). This result, that there was nothing *distinctively* evil about those subjects who carried on increasing the level of the shocks, was revealed to one half of the subjects in Miller *et al.*'s study, and not to the others. Both the groups were then asked to rate a person who had ostensibly taken part in Milgram's original study, and who had gone all the way with the shocks. One might have expected that the group who had seen Milgram's data might perceive this man as less distinctively anti-social than those who had not had the benefit of the data on how others behaved; but on eleven ratings of personality characteristics with distinct evaluative undertones (warmth, likeability, aggressiveness, etc.), there was only one difference between the knowledgeable group and the others. On ten ratings there was no discernible difference between the judgments of people who had seen that the man's behaviour was not specially unusual and the judgments of people left to the naive belief in personal traits. This result, whether it is a demonstration of people's poor use of information or of their refusal to allow a certain sort of behaviour to be mitigated by its popularity, is, one way or another, a very clear illustration of the non-effect on explanations of something that we should ordinarily have thought was most important; Kelley deserves our appreciation for putting the apparently obvious in such a way as to allow it to be tested.

Putting the case more broadly, we can look away from Kelley and towards the controversy over whether such rules of inference as he incorporates in his models are available to consciousness. Morris's review of the controversy in Chapter 8 examines the proposition that such rules may be inarticulatable and that this should alert us to certain important deficiencies in ordinary explanations. Morris brings out the special value to the *cognitive* psychologist of a charting of such deficiencies, but is concerned also to warn against overstating the anti-intospectionist case.

The history of attribution theory is bound up in person perception, the study of people's social cognitions of others; like person perception, its aim is to discover an economical way of describing the rules of the organization of social information. By reducing types of explanation to a manageable number of causes of action it succeeds in describing a set of rules which, in given situations, account for a good deal of differences in explanations. The question is whether this reduction is fair or not. Of the main strands of argument, the first is that the reduction of explanations to "causes" is a conceptual mistake, since people use reasons, justifications, etc. in their explanations; in our terms this would be the argument that Attribution Theory has been operating with a language appropriate to explanations of agency but missing the ways people explain the meaning of events (descriptive explanation) and their moral standing (explanations of morality). The second strand of argument is that the main theories of attribution-making have been heavily cognitive in nature and have overshadowed other work done with attributions from a more social-psychological, interactional point of view: for example, the work on "defensive" attribution (e.g. Shaver 1970; and see Bradley 1978 for a review), and self-presentation inter-pretations of attributions (see Tedeschi and Reiss's Chapter 12, pp. 303 ff.). This strand of argument is put in a very strong form by Kidd and Amabile (1980). In a fictitious dialogue they have two speakers, P and G, say:

> P: . . . The rush to a purely cognitive point of view in attribution has taken attribution out of social psychology and social psychology out of attribution. The study of social interaction and attribution has been replaced with an overconcern with the individual, intrapsychic perspective.
> G: . . . There were no dynamics in these models, no room for repetition, negotiation, habit, rote, or short circuits. (Kidd and Amabile, 1981)

Both the strands of argument we have mentioned are taken up at various points in the chapters ahead. From our point of view the two come together if we see Attribution Theory as primarily a theory to do with one sort of ordinary explanation (agency) which could benefit from theories about a prior sort of explanation (descriptive explanation). Clearly a theory about how people explain an event X needs some sort of theory about how people see the event as X and not Y and so on; descrip-tive explanation has been an assumed step in Attribution Theory. The assumption needs bringing out and examining, since the nature of the event being explained will have some important implications for the language the explanation is cast in and the person's reasons for explaining it at all. In other words, the common link between the two strands of argument above is the recommendation that more attention be paid to people's *interpretations* of the events they are explaining; the criticisms about the two kinds of reduction come together in the claim that prior to the attribution of cause is the attribution of meaning.

Explanations of morality

We must leave the controversial shores of Attribution Theory now to consider work on the third and last of our types of explanation. We shall see here that the divide between representational and information-processing approaches is not so wide as it was in researches on expla-nation of agency. The tenor of work is generally theory-driven; that is to say that even the empirical work has been cast in a context of theories about the nature of moral thinking (this is especially so in the literature on children's explanations) and less on its information-processing character *per se*, though this is not unrepresented in the literature.

In explanations of morality the explainer is up against it. His explanation of why he did such-and-such a thing is meant not just to satisfy someone's curiosity, but to get someone (usually himself) out of a bind, or to put someone (usually someone else) more firmly into one. Here it is not a question of neutrally naming the behaviour, displaying its causes or its motivations, etc. in front of a curious audience — what the explainer says is meant to defend the action or to denounce it, so there is some moral force to what is said. Rather than concentrate on actions which are very clearly in the moral domain (broken promises, murder, exploitation, etc.) we shall be talking about whatever elicits in everyday life some question of *propriety*; this is diluting the concept of morality, but in social life the immoral and inappropriate are often reacted to (and explained) in much the same way. What we have in mind ranges from Tedeschi and Reiss's *predicaments* (see Chapter 12) to full-blown moral questions.

THE REPRESENTATIONAL APPROACH TO EXPLANATIONS OF MORALITY

The most significant contributions within psychology to work on the representational aspects of moral judgment have been made by the cognitive-developmental theorists, the most notable of whom are Piaget and Kohlberg. According to their theories, to understand moral behaviour and people's explanations of morality, we have to understand how a person represents his social world, and how variation in the mode of representation determines his thinking and judgments about what he should or should not do. Interestingly, given the comments of van der Pligt and of Shotter referred to earlier (see p. 31) both Piaget and Kohlberg offer structural-functional explanations of moral behaviour. Behaviour is explained by describing the structures underlying and generating it. The *structures* themselves in particular, their developmental sequences are explained as the person's attempts to meaningfully organize the information encountered when dealing with his (social) environment.

Again, returning to a point made earlier, both theorists seek a way of describing the similarities and differences between representations. In this case, however, the source of the difference which concerns them in neither the environment nor the individual, but rather the developmental stage. Differences in the nature of explanations of models seem to depend on the *stage* of moral reasoning a person has reached. Progress through these stages is determined by the *interaction* of the individual with that environment. For instance, according to Piaget the stage reached will be a function of the child's individual's general cognitive development and of the predominant pattern of relationships that constitute their social environment.

Piaget employs two concepts when talking about cognitive structure in general and about the representation of morality in particular. These are schemata and operations. We have met schemata before (p. 31): here a schema is a basic unit of structure, which may take the form of, and which underlies, a simple unitary act. Operations are organizations of schema, having distinctive input-output properties allowing particular logical operations to be performed.

In his extensive work on the general cognitive development of the child Piaget has proposed and elaborated the concept of developmental stages, qualitatively different forms of cognitive organization through which the child's understanding of the world if successively transformed until he attains the final, adult stage.

Over the age range investigated (approximately 4−12 years) Piaget found that the developmental trends in moral reasoning parallcled, in an approximate fashion, those found in the child's general cognitive functioning, with the expressed moralities of the preoperational child contrasting with, and giving way to, those of the concrete operational child. The examination of this developmental sequence points up for us several interesting features of ordinary explanations. For instance, for the preoccupational child the rules of the game of marbles are *not* clearly related to the playing of marbles. The rules can be verbalized, and are regarded as absolute, fixed and externally imposed. However, his playing of the game may not conform to the rules he has himself described, he may well alter his behaviour in ways clearly contary to these rules, and they apparently play little or no part in coordinating his interaction with the other participants in the game. On the other hand, for the concrete operational child the rules *are* the game, clearly organizing his own behaviour and his interaction with the other participants, and great stress is placed on the behaviour of participants demonstrably conforming to these rules.

A second point for us to note is the social character of these rules. The concrete operational child has abandoned the preoperational child's egocentric and asocial view of rules, and recognizes that rules are social, maintained by consent and changeable by consensus. There is an emphasis on rules as devices for establishing cooperation and reciprocity, with an implicit recognition of these processes as the bases of social interaction. However, for the concrete operational child, the social nature of rules extends beyond this. The negotiation of rules, and the creation and modification of rules in order to achieve specific social purposes becomes an important activity in its own right.

It is when Piaget turns to the consideration of more explicitly moral matters, such as stealing, lying, justice, etc. that the significance of representation is most apparent. Here, he was concerned with the exploration of the child's understanding of the concepts themselves: What is stealing? What is a lie? Is this just? He demonstrated that the child's moral knowledge is related to his understanding of the intentions of the participants in an action. The child approaches adult morality to the extent that his ability to analyse the participants' intentions corresponds to those of an adult. It seems reasonable to suggest that this ability depends, not only on the child's developing information-processing abilities, but also on his increasingly adult-like representations of the social world.

A final point of interest to us, although not clearly developed in his writing, is the importance Piaget placed on the social context as a determinant of moral reasoning. He suggested that the development of the child's moral judgment is influenced by the social relationships experienced by the child, this factor being responsible for the rather complicated relationship between stages of moral reasoning and those of general cognition. Particular kinds of social relationships specifically facilitate (e.g. those of equality and mutual respect) or hinder (e.g. those of authoritarianism and unilateral respect) the development of mature moral reasoning. However, Piaget did not explore the immediate effects of such differing relationships upon the form of the moral explanation offered.

In Kohlberg's analysis of moral development we see the extension of Piaget's cognitive-developmental approach. Kohlberg elaborates the notion of stages of moral development, identifying three phases. In Phase One, moral judgments depend upon physical needs and the outcome of events, such as external rewards and punishments. In Phase Two, moral judgments are related to the dictates of others, in the form of adherence to expectations, roles or the social order. In Phase Three moral judgments are with respect to socially negotiated and shared values and understandings. Each phase is sub-divided into two stages, these six stages forming an invariant developmental sequence. (In later versions of his theory some stages are further subdivided and additional stages are added. Kohlberg's system is continually being modified and expanded.) In his investigation of these stages Kohlberg has sought to identify the components of moral judgment, that is, the terms in which morality is represented in each stage, and the way in which these components are used to produce moral arguments or accounts. Each stage is characterized by the particular content and organization of the accounts produced by the underlying representational system.

When we examine the moral behaviour of individuals we find that it is notoriously inconsistent. Repeated investigation has failed to provide evidence of intra-individual consistency across situations, over time, or with respect to developmental influences. To Kohlberg this is unsurprising. For the individual consistency exists with respect to his *representation* of the situation and his behaviour within it, rather than directly in terms of his behaviour. The same cognitive principles are seen as underlying both thought and action, and in order to understand moral behaviour we must discover the terms in which the actor represents the moral significance of the situation. As a developmental theorist Kohlberg is concerned with both how individuals progress from one stage to the next, and with the development of educational programme to facilitate this progression. Moral development is seen as being guided by social experience, the experience of making moral judgments, and by reflection upon those judgments. Although the precise relationships are complex and poorly understood, the implication is that the form of moral representation is a response to the functional demands made upon it.

What we have seen in Piaget is an example of moral representation treated as derivable from general cognitive representations. In Kohlberg's work there is a more specific focus on moral representations in their own right. Moral judgments are perhaps the most complex and sophisticated of ordinary explanations, and they are perhaps the most clearly social. The research of both Piaget and Kohlberg has recognized the social determination of the development of moral reasoning, but it has not dealt directly with the fact that offering an account of the morality of an act *is itself a social act*. This account will be produced in the light of the purposes the account-giver has in offering it, and will be produced knowing it to be subject to processes of negotiation (both overt and covert), revision and interpretation by the particular audience it is addressed to.

Finally, it is perhaps worth noting one of the implications of the developmental emphasis of the research on the representation approach to morality. Such an approach is concerned with the systematic differences between individuals in their understanding of the meaning of a situation, the factors underlying these differences and their behavioural consequences. Whilst its own emphasis is upon understanding the orderly progression from one stage to another, we might instead take note of the importance of individual differences between representations even amongst mature adults, implied by the developmental processes and influences that are seen as responsible for this progressive transformation.

THE INFORMATION-PROCESSING APPROACH TO EXPLANATIONS OF MORALITY

The strictest form of this approach to moral evaluations can be seen in the application of models designed to cope not specially with moral judgments but with judgments in general (e.g. Anderson, 1973; Himmelfarb, 1972). Investigation of morality using models of this kind are concerned with matters of quantity — how much worse is a rape if it is committed on a child? How much less bad if it is committed by a drunkard? Is a promise made by a known liar less binding that one made by an honest person? Putting the issues this way allows one to find empirical answers to the question of how information is combined to yield a moral judgment. What, for example, does the knowledge that the man is a liar add to, or subtract from, the ultimate judgment? Asking question like this allows one to find law-like relations between classes of variable that go into the evaluation of moral judgments: one comes to understand the nature of moral explanation by charting how it changes according to how the information it works on changes.

The general form of experimentation is that subjects are presented with varying collections of information pertinent to a judgment, and their judgment related to particular characteristics of the information. Such pen and paper experiments tell us about moral judgment in the abstract. Though this might not tell us about the ordinary perception and understanding of moral behaviour, where information simply isn't presented in this clear-cut fashion, it does seem likely that if we were called upon to predict how people might perceive *reported* events then such experimentation would form an intelligent basis for what we would want to say.

Within the literature there are two approaches; one in which a psychological mediating variable is postulated to account for the use or misuse of information, and one in which people's performance with information is traced directly back to fundamental capacities of computation, and no mediating variable is assumed.

Let us take the field of attribution of responsibility as an example which shows both psychological approaches at work. Walster (1963) put forward an attractive and far-ranging psychological account of certain sorts of moral explanation. Walster suggested that when looking on a misfortune, people were more inclined to use a moral explanation of someone's being at fault than they were to blame fate or chance, and that this tendency increased the greater the greater the misfortune. This brought into the realm of moral and evaluative judgment considerations which, strictly speaking, were out of bounds for rational ethics. The theory was that people were unwilling to attribute someone's misfortune to chance because doing so would be an open admission that bad luck existed and, of course, such an admission created anxiety as it was then possible for bad luck to strike in their own lives. Walster's often-cited experiment involved presenting subjects with a story of a man who left his car on a hill, parked rather carelessly; in any case, it rolled down causing varying degrees of damage. For instance, in one description it crashed into a shop, in another description it injured some passersby. Subjects tended to explain the latter description of events more dispositionally than the former — that is, by a greater degree of attribution of responsibility to the man who parked the car, and less to simple chance.

Unfortunately, later experiments along the same lines failed to provide consistent support for this notion of "defensive attribution". After a series of contradictory findings, the field was taken to task by Fishbein and Ajzen (1973). They argued that, among other problems, the measure of perceived responsibility used was too gross. After Heider (1958), they recommended that responsibility should be thought of as being five different concepts: responsibility of association (where someone is merely associated with the agent of an action e.g. is his friend, colleague or brother or sister); responsibility of commission, where the person is held "responsible" for the action if he actually commits it in the physical sense of literally causing it to happen; responsibility of foreseeability where the agent could foresee the consequences; responsibility of intention when he not only foresaw but also intended them; and responsibility of justification where "responsible" means that the explainer agrees that the agent was justified in behaving as he did — the result of external factors. These various meanings may not all be obviously of the same status, and one might wish for a more careful analysis of such a difficult concept as responsibility (cf. work in moral and legal philosophy — for example Hart, 1949), but Fishbein's and Ajzen point was well-taken and the original enthusiasm became rather deflated; working with five different "levels" of responsibility complicated the picture and rendered a motivational explanation of the kind that Walster had endorsed more difficult to test.

At the same time, another motivational theory of moral explanations was burgeoning in spite of the drive towards strictly informational accounts. This was Lerner's Just-World theory (Lerner, 1970) which held that learning experiences were responsible for a motivational factor in explanations of moral situations involving victims. This theory has generated an unusual amount of non-pencil and paper experimentation (see Lerner *et al.*, 1976 for a review) and allows more obvious application to real-life explanations.

Returning to the more orthodox information-processing accounts, a good example of the recent trend is Whitehead and Smith's work (1976). Here the accent is on the basic cognitons involved in moral judgments. In particular, the authors proposed that in explanations of responsibility for a morally-questionable action, responsibility is a function of the perception of the likelihood of the action objectively producing the effect X and the perception of the agent's foresight that his actions would bring X about. In other words, the authors proposed that people are influenced by the informativeness of the action rather than, or as much as, its being of one sort or another: this would account for what we might think of two men who have committed the same impropriety, with the same intention, but by actions which differ in the degree to which they were likely by chance to have brought the offence about. If two hosts manage to insult two guests in identical amounts, but one does so in a way very obviously likely to lead to offence as a matter of course (say a public snub over dinner) requiring no great ingenuity on the host's part, and the other achieves the same by something rather subtler and more personal, requiring more homework (say dropping a reference in company to the man's poor marital record), then we might well see the actions as demanding rather different reactions.

The spirit of this approach is to come to understand moral explanations by mapping the way moral and non-moral information is integrated, and unlike the more general interest in the brain's computational abilities, this pays attention to what an *a priori* analysis of what *should* go into moral evaluation has to say about the information whose integration should be studied. Like attribution of responsibility, research was started by an interest in some motivational account, but it is increasingly influenced by the mainstream social psychology tradition of reductive models of cognitive capacities.

Concluding comments: explanations and actions

In this chapter we have tried to describe research on ordinary explanations by using a framework of three types of explanation and by splitting types of research into two camps. In sections devoted to explanations of what, why and explanations of morality, we discussed what we called the representational approach and the information-processing approach, and gave examples of the sort of research programme each would endorse. We saw that a concern for how the explanation was arrived at was the hallmark of information-processing research, while a concern with the interpersonal use and negotiation of explanations was the theme running through the more heterogenous representational approaches. However, we also saw some points of contact belied by our divisive category system; and in this final section we shall draw these out in an attempt to see how a more rounded theory of explanations might develop.

The first point to make is that in a complete theory of ordinary explanations, contact and overlap between the representation and information-processing approaches is necessary rather than merely fortunate. Models of processing will remain cut adrift from real-life explaining, and theorising about the functional aspects of explanations will lack rigour unless one approach borrows from the other. The pragmatic task faced by a complete theory, as we set out saying, is to account for the form, function and process of an explanation, and a complete answer will only be possible when the three things are seen to be not separate but inescapably complementary.

Much of the research we have described within the information-processing approach would normally be labelled as being concerned with "social cognition" or "social perception". But names like these gloss an important point about ordinary explanations. A person's explanation of an event is a matter of "social perception" in that it embodies his perception of that event, but it is more than this: it is the link between the world as perceived and actions performed within it. If we give a theory of explanations the job of specifying an individual's account of what is going on, and how this will affect his behaviour, then what we are doing is asking the theory to make sense of what is invisible to us as psychologists, but is nevertheless crucial in the production of the individual's behaviour.

The information-processing approach has an important role to play within such a theory, for it provides answers to questions concerning, for instance, the mechanisms that translate perception into cognitions, the processes by which discrete items of information are integrated, and information about various cognitive biases and blind spots. However, there are some questions it cannot answer and which it is unfair to ask it. We need a contribution from the representational approach to round the theories out into something approximating a theory of explanations as mediators of action. We need contributions on, for instance, the personal uses to which explanations are put, the rhetorical and social functions of explanations, their negotiation in specific social settings, etc. It is only with the integration of the two approaches that we can ask questions such as: Do specific personal uses involve particular kinds of cognitive biases? Does the negotiation of explanations involve negotiation of the modes of information integration? etc. It is quite clear that if a psychology of ordinary explanations is to be applied to understanding and predicting the patterns of explanation-influenced action, that is, if it is to be more than an elaborate theory of social perception, then the two approaches must come together.

Such an integration is consistent with the recent trend within social psychology to seek explanations of people's behaviour in terms of the meanings they assign to the social situations they find themselves in. As Backman writes, in his epilogue to the recent important volume "Emerging Strategies in Social Psychological Research" (Ginsburg, 1979):

Symbolic interactionism and such newer traditions in social psychology as the ethogenic and ethnomethodology schools of thought have self-consciously made the meanings of situations central to their explanations of social behaviour. However, many investigators whose work derives from the Lewinian or learning traditions seem to have been much less conscious of how their own research demonstrates the significance of the meanings that people ascribe to situations. The work on bystander intervention by Latane and Darley (1970) provides a striking example. Subjects in their experiments failed to respond in ambiguous situations because they defined them as non-emergencies . . . Others coming out of either the learning of Lewinian traditions have made the person's definition of the situation more central to their work. As examples, Berkowitz (1965) and Walster (1971), following Schachter's (1964) emphasis on the role of attributed meaning in defining emotional states, have developed theories of aggression and romantic love that include this element.

Backman goes further, suggesting that these and other developments constitute an emergent paradigm in social psychology.

> The elements in this new paradigm include the view of man as an active agent, an emphasis on the meanings of events and settings in the determination of social behaviour, and a conception of science in which the goal of scientific social psychology is to generate and verify models of the structure of intention. (Backman, 1979, p. 301)

Man's activity as an agent, his ascription of meanings, his intentions and his actions: all these are served by his social explanations. Whether or not it is indeed a new paradigm, or simply a more pronounced interest in the cognitive mediation of social behaviour, the new spirit that Backman identifies guarantees a secure future for the psychology of ordinary explanation. It has a future in both the experimental tradition and in the more radical emerging schools. In fact, its future may lie, as we have suggested in this final section of the chapter, in a joint psychology developed from both.

3

Attribution Theory: From Phenomenal Causality to the Intuitive Social Scientist and Beyond*

B. Harris and J.H. Harvey

Attribution: its nature and how it is studied by social psychologists

In the last decade social psychologists have become increasingly interested in how individuals perceive and explain the actions of their fellow human beings. As a result, much of social psychology has become the study of how social behaviour is affected by individuals' inferences, impressions and attributions concerning social events. More and more, investigators are asking their volunteers, friends, and themselves to give their impressions of (for example) why Ms Acme acted in such a way toward Mr Baker. Was her behaviour caused intentionally, characteristically, by chance, by Baker's bad luck, by Acme's role constraints, and so on? Who is responsible for Baker's fate? Who is to blame?

In the language of social psychologists, the social perceptions of untrained observers (usually thought to be causal in nature) have become known as "attributions". Among social psychologists this focus on causal perceptions is so popular that "attribution" threatens to become a new buzz word, used to describe processes involved in impression formation, labelling, interpersonal perception and personality assessment. It is our opinion that the increasing attention given to attributional phenomena is a healthy development in psychology. Most relevant to this volume, the attributional approach has developed from an emphasis on the everyday, ordinary explanation of interpersonal

*Some of the work reported in this chapter was supported by funds provided by the Vanderbilt Research Council to the second author. The authors are grateful to Charles Antaki and Jerri Town for thoughtful comments on an earlier version of this paper.

events, providing psychologists with new perspectives and a new source of information — the perceptions and cognitions which allow us to navigate our way through a complex social world. We will use the terms "attribution theory" and "attributional approach" interchangeably in parts of this chapter. In doing so, we must repeat Kelley's (1973, p.8) proviso that the term "theory" should be understood in the sense of a group of general principles with a more or less common focus and orientation.

Before reviewing some major developments in attribution research, it is important to mention the diversity of methods and theoretical perspectives that make up the attributional approach to social psychology. Using Antaki and Fielding's (this volume) scheme, for example, there are psychologists who study individuals' attributions with an eye to their biases in perceiving social events (e.g. overestimating the role of a friend's intention in causing event R), while others are more interested in attribution as a guide to the structure of such events and the nature of interpersonal perception. A survey of current attribution theorists and researchers probably would show more that are interested in the *process* of attribution than understanding its content. However, the acknowledged progenitor of the field, Fritz Heider, not only was most interested in the *content* of attributions, but also constructed a general theory of social perception and behaviour, based on ordinary explanations of common social events (Heider, 1958).

This work by Heider was the first systematized study of social attribution, although it took some time for parts of it to be later brought into mainstream social psychology, most notably by Jones and Davis (1965) and Kelley (1967). Much of our account will describe the translation and elaboration of Heider's seminal work at the hands of experimentally-oriented social psychologists. From this description, it will be clear that there has been great heterogeneity in what is called attribution theory. Nevertheless, we feel that there also have been two points of general agreement among those researchers who have adopted the attributional approach. First, there has been a common goal of understanding how individuals make causal explanations for social events — attributing causality to themselves, their fellow humans, or to physical forces in the environment. Secondly, there has been a common emphasis on non-motivational, non-emotional bases for an individual's attributional activity, with several exceptions in recent years (e.g. see Bradley, 1978). Beyond these basic points there frequently are different explanations among theorists for the same behaviour (e.g. theoretical disagreements over how to interpret actor-observer differences). Most often, however, researchers develop attributional-based explanations for a particular phenomenon (aetiology of depression in humans, children's patterns of failure on academic tasks), and do not attempt to integrate their findings into a unified theory of how humans attribute in general. Given the present diversity of the field, it is not clear that such a unified theory of social attribution could be readily defended. Further, it seems clear that attribution approaches of the 1980s increasingly will reflect a concern with the social context in which people make attributions (e.g. Orvis *et al.*, 1976; Stryker, 1977). Such a development indicates the breadth of contemporary attribution work — a breadth that extends from individual-person level to dyad-context level and from emphasis upon rationalistic, naive scientist portrayal to emphasis upon an inter-action of thought, motivation and feeling systems.

PLAN OF THIS CHAPTER

In contrast to the current proliferation of attributional approaches to diverse topics, early contributors to the field attempted to develop broad theoretical statements, most often on the central issue of causal attrib-ution. In this chapter, we will first review such statements by Fritz Heider (e.g. 1958), Jones and Davis (1965) and Kelley (1967, 1972a, 1972b). In so reviewing the early foundation of current attribution theory, we have several reasons in mind. First, the work of theorists such as Heider contains some basic assumptions (e.g. humans act as naive scientists) that still are shared by many researchers in the area, and these assumptions should be made explicit. Second, these early authors' diversity of approaches and subject matter must be recognized both by attribution theory's supporters and by its critics. Third, we feel that many of this volume's readers might be interested in two unique aspects of Fritz Heider's work: his life-long attributional analysis of stories, fables and plays for clues to the ordinary explanation of social events; and his system of symbolizing such explanations using natural-language terms.

After briefly reviewing the basic statements of attribution theory, we will describe the expansion of the area by Bem (1967, 1972) and by Jones and Nisbett (1972) to include primary concern with self-perception and the difference between self perception and the perception of others. In this second generation of attributional approaches, noteworthy features include the interface between behaviourism and Bem's self-perception theory, and the emphasis on attributional errors that marks the literature on what are termed actor-observer differences.

The final sections of our review concern recent proposals either for modification or rejection of attribution theory's assumptions about cognition (Fischhoff, 1976; Langer, 1978). These criticisms are presented both to show the questions being currently discussed by attribution theorists (often with colleagues of other fields), and to allow examination of competing theories within social psychology. Underlying all sections of this chapter is an awareness of challenges to attribution theory from outside of traditional social psychology (e.g. Harré, this volume). With this in mind, we try to stress the basics of the attribution approach — including both enough detail to elicit discussion and enough of our own commentary to suggest our perspective on this complex field of study. In our concluding comments, we outline some general thoughts on the ethogenic alternative to the attributional approach.

Heider's work on attribution

When psychologists review attribution theory they commonly begin with Fritz Heider's book, "The Psychology of Interpersonal Relations," and (sometimes) his earlier theoretical paper on social perception (1944). This is done to introduce the ideas that: (1) it is important whether social events are attributed to the environment or to persons, and (2) making causal attributions can function to help one control one's social environment (e.g. Wegner and Vallacher, 1977, pp. 40 – 42). While these are important concepts, Heider's work has many more insights to offer social psychologists, whether they be interested in the process of causal attribution or in ordinary explanation in general. For example, to understand Heider's influence on attribution theory (our main goal here), one must recognize the view of social events, interpersonal perception, and ordinary explanation that underlies his attribution theory.

HEIDER AND SIMMEL (1944)

One of the best introductions to Fritz Heider's attribution theory is his study of apparent human behaviour using simple geometric shapes to simulate human movement. Previously, Heider had written essays on the perception of inanimate objects (1927/1959; 1930/1959), in which he developed a lens model of perception. However, his earliest interest in psychology was on interpersonal perception as well as the perception of the physical (non-human) environment.

To study social causation, Heider attempted to construct a minimal social situation; a movie of the simplest moving objects that would elicit the perception of human movement in naive observers. His implicit goal was to answer the questions: "What is a social event?"; and "What is social perception?", through the analysis of the minimal stimulus configuration and his observers' reactions to it (see Jordan, 1966).

The actual method they used involved showing all subjects a movie of four stimulus objects in a two-dimensional plane. These stimulus objects were a large triangle, a small triangle, a circle, and the outline of a square with a movable side (which opened and closed). In the experimental movie, these objects move both simultaneously and sequentially in a series of chases, collisions, and other complex interactions designed to suggest a scenario of interpersonal interactions of three human stimulus persons. For example. one scene in the sequence might be described as; "T chases c into the house, while t runs around the house and then closes the door". All but one of the observers of this film, who were asked to "write down what happened in the film", portrayed the movement as if the three stimulus objects possessed human characteristics, with a majority of observers constructing a story with both consistent characteristics (e.g. malevolence) attributed to each of the three stimuli.

Heider and Simmel saw these observers' attributions as reflecting two important types of perceptual organization: (1) movements are organized into figural units of cause and effect, and (2) objects with human traits are seen as "causal centers" or initiators of acts. For example, in one sequence of Heider and Simmel's movie, the large triangle entered and then exited from the large empty square ("the house"). To most naive observers, this did not just seem to be the complex movement of an object through a number of different coordinates. Rather, the triangle was perceived as a person, the motive of "looking for something" was attributed to it and the complex sequence of motion became a simple one. It is easily described and perceived; the attributed motive of the triangle organizes all of the actions (entering, exiting, stopping inside, etc.) into an integrated whole (or *Gestalt*). Thus, observers' reports revealed a causal structure such that "a few events stand out and are seen by all *S*s in the same way; these events are organized into a meaningful whole which contains causal centres (persons)". Events and persons gain their significance by the way they are causally connected".

In other words, when faced with complex physical movement, Heider and Simmel's subjects made not only causal attributions but attributions of personal causality that included attributed intentions, personal characteristics and emotions. As analyzed by the authors, these were highly personalized but fairly accurate descriptions of a stimulus configuration structured by strong *Gestalts* such as the relatively stable nature of human intentional behaviour.

HEIDER'S (1944) THEORY OF PHENOMENAL CAUSALITY

The implications of this demonstration study was described by Heider first in 1944 and then more fully in his 1958 book. Although the latter account is cited more often, the 1944 paper clearly presents two basic (and interrelated) concepts of attribution theory: (1) that personal causality is qualitatively different from impersonal (environmental) action, and (2) that there are potential effects of the perceptual structure on the perceiver's sense of social control.

Heider's first concept, concerning the uniqueness of personal causality, was represented by the phrase "persons as origins", and was an extrapolation of the results of his movie study into the realm of interpersonal behaviour. His second concept was that this type of personified causation adds a simplicity of organization to the social environment. This simplicity is evident on two levels: first is the purely perceptual level outlined in Heider and Simmel's (1944) ideas of figural unit formation; second is the more abstract level of cognitions about social causes. In discussing this second level, Heider saw a major concern of the organism being the establishment of stable cognitions about the origin of environmental change. In understanding an event in the social environment (e.g. a bicycle accident), attributing changes to a person's characteristics (e.g. carelessness) is simpler than looking for a physical cause (e.g. excessive speed) which might interact with a multitude of other physical forces (e.g. wet pavement) or itself be the product of complex forces (e.g. laws of mechanics). In contrast to such a series of infinitely regressing causes, a person can be readily perceived as the origin (i.e. a first and final cause) of the events resulting from his acts (see Jones' comments in Harvey *et al.*, 1978, p. 373).

For an observer concerned with controlling the social environment, Heider hypothesized that locating the final (personal) cause for an event would be preferred to a more complex, environmental explanation.

While this observation of the power of causal attributions to persons may not seem that profound, it seems to take a phenomenological view of social causality, and presents perception as an active process that should not be separated from social cognition. In certain ways, it is consistent with recent progressive developments in perceptual theory (Gibson, 1966), and in non-Humean explanations of psychological causality (e.g. Harré and Secord, 1972; Pettit, this volume).

HEIDER'S NAIVE ANALYSIS OF ACTION

Fourteen years after outlining his views on causal perception, Heider (1958) presented a general theory of interpersonal perception, cognition and behaviour. Most relevant to subsequent attribution research, this theory centred on a more detailed analysis of the person as a causal agent. This analysis was based on Heider's extensive examination of everyday language, and attempted to identify the many interacting factors that enter into the naive explanation of personal causality.

Sketched briefly, Heider asserted that a person's causal force is perceived to be a combination of the factors of ability ("power") and effort ("trying"), such that the presence of a person's ability *and* effort makes him a causal agent in a particular setting (see Fig. 1). Also, a further analysis shows these factors of ability and effort to be made up of component attributes themselves. For example, the concept of "trying" is analysed as being made up of the two factors of "exertion" and "intent". Further, these two factors can combine with other related attributes in the calculus. The many possible combinations and recombinations of attributes allowed by this system show both the flexibility of what Heider called a causal calculus in analysing new phenomena and also show how Heider's theory is a carefully systematized

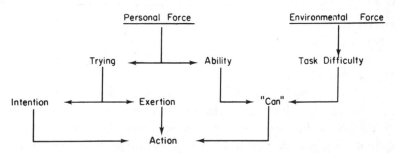

Fig. 1. Factors identified by Heider as constituting personal and environmental causality (after Shaver, 1975).

view of personal motives, worked out to the level of fine details and attributes.

Although we will not attempt a review of all of the many combinations of attributional factors that Heider (1958) discusses, his overall view of causality can be illustrated by application to the attributions of a hypothetical observer O who sees a store window break (event X) as person P is walking by.

According to Heider's view of explanation-by-attribution, O's perceptions of an event can be understood as if he were systematically attempting to solve the attributional equation of an event for its unknown values (attributes). Assuming that the environment was neither a sufficient cause (a gust of wind broke the window) nor totally inhibitory (a shatterproof window), the attributes of interest become those related to P's role as the cause of event X: P's "power" (ability to break window) and his "trying". Assuming that his "power" is sufficient (window breaking is easy stuff) O's attention would turn to the attribute of "try". This attribute is made up of "exertion" plus "intension", and since intention is usually necessary and sufficient for exertion (except in cases of absent-minded effort), the unknown attribute would thus become P's intention. More specifically, evidence of P's intending to break a window (such as his acting nervous before the window broke or his not being surprised and running off after the breaking, etc.) would be sufficient to perceive him as the cause of the entire event, given the previous attribution of ability, environmental possibility, etc.

Although the analysis made possible by Heider's causal calculus has not been widely used, it does prove useful in judgments of responsibility for certain types of events. Weiner and his colleagues (1972), for example, have used the distinction between the personal attributes of ability and effort to help analyse achievement-related attributions. They found that people employ their perception of others' *effort* to a great extent in rewarding or punishing them for achievement-related performance; effort appears to be an even more salient attribute in such situations than is *ability* (see Weiner, 1974, for a comprehensive review of work in this area).

Also, Harris (1977), and Fincham and Jaspars (1979) have found support for Heider's idea that different elements of the causal calculus take on different importance as perceivers mature. For example, when compared with adults, young children assessing responsibility for an event will notice the presence or absence of intention, but may not notice differences in ability (i.e. the forseeability of an accident). Recognizing such developmental differences in the perception of personal causality allows one to understand why children and adults may differ dramatically in their determination of the cause of an action, who is responsible for its result, or the actor's culpability (Heider, 1958, p. 114).

HEIDER'S CONTRIBUTIONS TO MODERN ATTRIBUTION THEORY

It should be noted that Heider's (1958) theory of interpersonal perception consisted of much more than an analysis of the attribution of causality. It also contained chapters on topics such as the relationship between cognition and affect, and the relationship between value judgments and attribution. Most noteworthy, however, was the volume's brief introduction and appendix; it was there that Heider cited as his goal the study of commonsense or naive psychology, and outlined a notational system that would use common English terms in its representation of interpersonal relations.

To Heider, commonsense psychology was "the unformulated or half-formulated knowledge of interpersonal relations as it is expressed in our everyday language and experience" (1958, p. 4). Such knowledge was worthy of study, he argued, for a number of reasons. From an epistemological viewpoint psychology did not need more investigators "seeking further empirical and experimental facts". Rather, it needed "conceptual clarification as a prerequisite for efficient experimentation" (p. 4), and Heider saw the study of ordinary language and ordinary explanation as logical paths to the understanding of concepts such as causality. On the level of tactics, naive psychology was likely to contain at least as many truths about human nature as falsehoods. Moreover, it would allow one to see the implicit theories (however invalid) that help determine the behaviour of one's fellow human beings.

In order to analyse this shared, commonsense system of psychological beliefs, Heider felt the need for a flexible yet exact language of symbolizing interpersonal beliefs, perceptions and attributes. He developed this by first analysing English grammar (contained in fables and novels as well as conversation) for concepts that underlay both common language use and interpersonal relations. He then abstracted basic relational concepts (e.g. causation, sentiment, ability) and expressed them in common language terms (i.e. "cause", "want", "can") — which in turn could be used to represent interpersonal relations. As mentioned above, Heider developed a sort of attributional calculus or "factor analysis" (p. 297) using these terms. This was partially inspired by Cassirer (1944) and was indirectly following the example of Heider's colleague Kurt Lewin (see Harvey *et al.*, 1976, p. 7). Lewin's influence can be most clearly seen in Heider's insistence that the laws and concepts of psychology should be developed autonomously of other disciplines, and in Heider's concept of an interpersonal life-space that would be studied for the relationships that it contains (see Jordan, 1966; Heider, 1960). Based on systematic analyses of hundreds of such interpersonal accounts, Heider came to identify regular relationships between elements of ordinary explanation (e.g. an action = "can" + "want" + "try"), and was able to formulate hypotheses such as those related to interpersonal balance and imbalance (see Harvey *et al.*, 1976, pp. 13–14, for Heider's description of the latent imbalance in Ibsen's "A Doll's House").

In the more recent statements of attribution theory reviewed below, the influence of Heider's (1958) comprehensive work is freely acknowledged by writers in the area. While his idea of common language analysis and his system of language-based symbolic representation have not been generally utilized there are clear reflections of Heider's overall work in modern attributional approaches. On the most general level, Heider's emphasis on cognitive (e.g. attributional) processes as determinants of behaviour is reflected both in modern attribution theory, and also in much of the rest of social psychology.

A second, frequently accepted feature of Heider's work is the role of attributional analyses in promoting personal control over one's social environment. As Heider explained, an understanding of interpersonal causal sequences allows us both to (a) know the abilities, dispositions, and other invariants of our fellow humans; and to (b) predict and control their future actions. In the formulations of Kelley and others, this second function (control and prediction) has been more often cited than the first (understanding).

This analogy between the concerns of psychologists and everyday folk should be recognizable as Heider's concept of naive psychology, and is the third major contribution of Heider's that has become central to the attributional approach (e.g. see Kelley, 1973, p. 109). To some, it is the most questionable of attribution theory's basic assumptions (e.g. Fischhoff, 1976; Harré this volume). In defence of Heider's concept of naive scientist, two brief points need to be made. First, Heider's basic assertion seems to have been not too different from that of many of this volume's contributors: that the ordinary ("naive") explanation of social action is a proper subject of study (see Pettit, this volume, for a defence of this assertion). To this end, Heider seems to have said that the explanations of ordinary folk are no less important and no less lawful that the explanations which scientists employ. A second noteworthy aspect of Heider's "naive scientist" analogy is the extent of its intended applicability. While contemporary attribution theory may be offered by some as relevant to all social behaviour, Heider himself did not consider that we were intuitive scientists in all our social interactions. At the same time, however, he *did* see this model as valid for "that part (of inter-personal relations) which, let us say, inclines toward the side of 'intellectualism' " (1958, p. 298).

To summarize, the features of Heider's theory that have survived in most undiluted form are his general cognitive emphasis, the functionalistic implications of his work, and his model of humans as problem solvers using a naive, scientific methodology. Coupled with his insights into the structure of interpersonal causality and relations (e.g. personal versus environmental forces), these concepts have been applied by experimental social psychologists to better explain the existing literature (e.g. on social influence — see Kelley, 1967, and to the further understanding of attributional phenomena.

Jones and Davis' theory of correspondent inferences

Jones and Davis' (1965) theory was the first systematic attempt in social psychology to generate testable hypotheses based on attributional concepts. It was more limited in scope than later formulations by Kelley (1967, 1972a, 1972b) in that it did not discuss attributions to one's self, but rather discussed factors which affect an observer's willingness to infer another person's intentions or dispositional traits.

In their theory, Jones and Davis attempted to use an attributional approach to resolve possible conflicts between the then-current paradigm in research on person perception, and the concept of self-presentation in social life. Traditionally, person perception researchers had presented subjects with various lists of adjectives or traits describing a (hypothetical) "target person" and then sought to see how the arrangement of such lists (e.g. placing the most negative trait last) affected the subjects' impressions of the target person. However, Jones and Davis recognized that in actual social life target persons often choose to present different trait characteristics, depending on the requirements of different social roles. In fact, being observed by another is itself a social role with its own constraints. Thus, the explicit question posed by these authors was: What are the limiting circumstances that reduce one's willingness (or ability) to attribute motives or traits to a person based on the actor's behaviour?

ATTRIBUTION OF INTENT AND DISPOSITION

To analyse the process of inferring others' intentions and dispositions from their actions, Jones and Davis developed attributional principles based on Heider's (1958) work. In their formulation, a *correspondent inference* was an inference about individuals' intent and disposition that follows directly from their behaviour. If, for example, Bill makes a very hostile remark to Don, leading to distress on the part of Don, we may examine Bill's behaviour and make the *correspondent* inference that Bill dislikes Don and intends to abuse him verbally. We may also make the dispositional inference that Bill is basically a malicious person. Alternatively, there might be circumstances under which we would infer that Bill's hostile remark was not intentional and that he means Don no ill will; while this inference of non-maliciousness might be accurate, it would *not* be correspondent to Bill's actual behaviour. In Jones and Davis' analysis, there are a number of factors that determine whether a particular situation promotes correspondent inferences or not. The most central of these factors is the social desirability of the act.

SOCIAL DESIRABILITY: A CENTRAL DETERMINANT OF CORRESPONDENT INFERENCE

Jones and Davis viewed a behaviour's social desirability (or consistency with social norms) as being inversely related to the correspondence of the inferences (or attributions) that it elicits. In other words, if an actor's behaviour is high in social desirability, it does not allow many strong inferences to be drawn about the actor. (In this conception and related research, "correspondence" in attribution is typically operationalized as how confident the attributor can be in making an inference.)

A classic study by Jones, Davis, and Gergen (1961) provides evidence about the prediction that behaviour which is inconsistent with a particular role (out-of-role behaviour) will be more informative to a perceiver than will behaviour which is consistent (in-role behaviour).

In this experiment, subjects listened to prepared tape recordings in which a stimulus person was interviewing for a job either as an astronaut or a submariner. Before listening to the taped interview, subjects were given instructions in which the ideal astronaut was described as a person who is essentially inner-directed (is autonomous, can get along well without others); the ideal submariner was described as a person who is essentially other-directed (gregarious, likes frequent contact with others). In the actual interview, the stimulus person, who was thought to understand the requirements for the job, made remarks designed either to reveal himself as a person who was fit for the job (in-role condition) or as a person who was not fit for the job (out-of-role condition). Subjects were then asked to give their impressions of the person on several traits and how confident they were in their impressions.

Jones and associates found that subjects made more extreme judgments and were more confident about them in the out-of-role condition than in the in-role condition. For example, they felt strongly and confidently that the astronaut interviewee was an affiliative, conformist type of person when he acted in that manner despite the nonaffiliative, independent nature of the job. Thus, in a sense, the out-of-role person was seen as breaking out of the constraints of the situation to show his true self — or at least his true dispositions.

COMMENTS ON JONES AND DAVIS

With fifteen years' hindsight, we may look at correspondent inferences theory as adopting a rather unsophisticated view of social relations (cf. Harré, this volume). For example, in asking college students "what do you think he is *really* like as a person", the authors seem to imply that a human being *has* a basic character or dispositional structure; theorists such as Erving Goffman might object that there are always roles beneath roles, and scripts to be followed when one is told not to act by a script ("act naturally").

Such a criticism has some merit, and one can indeed detect in Jones *et al.* reflections of "The Organization Man" (Whyte, 1956) and of the idea that one naturally acts differently on the job (ruthless, subservient) than in one's "home life". On the other hand, Jones *et al.*'s study is based on the realities of pressures to conform to job descriptions and work norms, if only during one's job interview or probationary period. Also, in the context of the then-current person perception research, Jones and Davis seem quite progressive in their inclusion of more socially relevant variables (e.g. social norms) in the determination of interpersonal attribution. Although they did accept the reality of personal, "true" dispositions, this seems to have reflected a Heiderian emphasis on accurately predicting behaviour; we would assert that separating out environmental coercion does indeed allow one to better predict another person's future actions.

A final comment on Jones and Davis is to note their recognition that observer bias may be a factor whenever persons perceive others. Such a possibility was included in Jones and Davis' theory through the variable of a behaviour's hedonic relevance. This variable was a final determinant of an act's correspondence, such that the more relevant an act is to an observer (e.g. the more it affects his or her life) the more the observer will see it as correspondent. While Jones and Davis did not cite strong evidence for this factor's operation, its formulation is noteworthy in suggesting that its authors did not see observers of social behaviour as completely impartial, decontextualized arbiters of action, inference and disposition.

Kelley's attributional conception

Appearing shortly after Jones and Davis' theory of correspondent inferences, Harold Kelley's (1967) analysis of interpersonal attribution gave social psychologists a broadly conceived theory that could be integrated with a popular topic in social psychology: interpersonal influence. At the same time, Kelley expanded the scope of attribution theory to include individuals' perceptions about their own emotional states and the determinants of their own behaviour.

As will be discussed more fully below, Kelley's theory was in many ways a departure from Heider's early structuralist epistemology, while at the same time it was also a development of the cognitive functionalism contained in "The Psychology of Interpersonal Relations". Although Heider first had stressed the immediate quality of perceived personal causation, Kelley (1967) focused on perceivers with more information, more analytic propensities, and more concern with the partialing out of environmental determinants of behaviour.

THE ANALYSIS OF VARIANCE (ANOVA) MODEL OF ATTRIBUTION

In his most frequently cited contribution to attribution theory, Kelley updated Heider's (1958) assertion that as social beings, we often use a naive version of J. S. Mill's method of difference. Developing the heuristic value of this observation (see Kelley's discussion in Harvey *et al.*, 1978), Kelley argued (1967) that people often make causal attributions as if they were analysing data patterns by means of an ANOVA, a statistical technique for determining whether differences in variance exceed the differences to be expected by chance. The principle of *covariation* between possible causes and effects is the fundamental notion in Kelley's (1967) attributional approach. Covariation here means linking effects to their proper causes. For example, we as attributors may infer that a student's performance on an exam uniquely covaried with the student's motivation to succeed and not with other factors such as the difficulty of the exam.

How do attributors verify whether they have correctly linked cause and effect? For instance, how does an individual account for the feeling of liking a certain new food? Was the food really that good, or is the person simply a "food freak"? According to Kelley's ANOVA model, an individual can know that attribution to a cause is valid by using these criteria:

(1) It is associated *distinctively* with the cause; for example, the person's particular and positive reaction to the new food would occur in other situations; for example, the person does not necessarily have to be at a banquet in order to enjoy the food.

(2) It is similar to those made by other persons to the same cause (for example, there is *consensus* among others about the high quality of the food).

(3) It is *consistent* over time; on successive exposures to the causal situation, the person related to it by different sensory and perceptual modalities (such as looking at, smelling, and thinking about the food), and it was good each time.

In sum, Kelley proposed that individuals use the criteria of distinctiveness, consensus and consistency over time and modality to validate their attributions. Thus, in this illustration, the individual may infer that the new food was really good if there is no positive response to all new foods (rather, the person responds distinctively, or differentially, and in various situations), if other people liked it too, and if the person had a sense of good taste and smell, as well as good thoughts regarding the food.

Several investigators have reported evidence supporting Kelley's (1967) ideas. In one such study, McArthur (1972) examined the causal attributions made by observers of another person's behaviour. She presented subjects with person-entity statements (e.g. "Tom is enthralled by the painting") and three accompanying statements providing information about high or low consensus (high: "Almost everyone who sees the painting is enthralled by it"), distinctiveness (high: "Tom is not enthralled by almost every other painting"), and consistency (high: "In the past, Tom has almost always been enthralled by the same painting"). For each set of information, the subjects were asked to decide what probably caused the event to occur. They could attribute it to something about the person, something about the entity, something about the particular circumstance, or some combination of two or more of the first three factors. McArthur found that stimulus attribution (i.e. something about the painting) was relatively frequent when a response was characterized by high consensus, high distinctiveness and high consistency. Further, she found that person attribution (i.e. something about Tom) was relatively frequent when a behaviour was characterized by low consensus, low distinctiveness and high consistency. Overall, McArthur's results suggest that people may be quite sophisticated in their analysis of information and related causal inference activity.

CAUSAL SCHEMATA

Kelley (1972a) has suggested that the ANOVA model is appropriate for certain cases when the individual can engage in a relatively complete causal analysis. However, he suggests that this model is descriptive of most attributional work (recall the type of "basic perception" attributional analysis Heider proposed). According to Kelley, the inferential problem for the individual is only infrequently so imposing that it necessitates a full-blown analysis. The exigencies of modern life frequently lead to hasty deliberations in which decisions are made by reference mainly to present feelings, thoughts and perceptions, the advice of others, and our past experience. Kelley contends that past experience may provide individuals with a backlog of understanding relative to causal relations and that they can thus call on this store of knowledge when an inference has to be expeditiously made. This backlog of causal relations represents what Kelley refers to as causal schemata. Although Heider does not label this backlog of past experience, he too seems to be advancing a notion similar to causal schemata in his assertion that people readily make hundreds of attributions every day.

According to Kelley's conception, causal schemata are learned, stored in the person's memory, and then activated by environmental cues; they presumably generalize across a broad range of objects and situations and may be activated by numerous types of cues. For example, a person relying on a schema for understanding why two people would be affectionately and happily embracing at an airport terminal might readily infer that the people have a warm friendship and that they have just been reunited. On the other hand, the sight of tears might suggest that they are about to be separated from one another.

Kelley's causal schemata model has not yet received sufficient empirical attention. One hypothesis derived from the model that has been examined is that the more extreme the effect to be attributed, the more likely the attributor is to assume that it entails multiple necessary causes. A study by Cunningham and Kelley (1975) tested this hypothesis by asking subjects to make attributions about hypothetical social events that varied in terms of extremity of effect. An example of an extreme effect in this study was "Norm always avoids Al". In this example, multiple necessary causes might include the facts that Norm does not like people very much and that Al is not a very pleasant person to be around. Cunningham and Kelley found relatively strong support for the hypothesis across a wide array of hypothetical social situations. An important question that future researches in this area should address concerns how causal schemata develop. At different states of development, do people display different causal schemata?

DISCOUNTING

Let us suppose that an average student consistently flatters an instructor about the quality of the instructor's lectures. Further, consider that no other student in the class flatters the instructor, who also typically does not receive high teacher ratings. While the student who does the praising may claim that the lauding of the teacher was well-deserved, an attributor might readily *discount* this claim and instead infer that the student was trying to ingratiate himself to the instructor so as to achieve a higher grade in the course. The idea of discounting in attribution was articulated by Kelley in another of his important analyses (Kelley, 1972b). This principle relates to the situation involving an attributor who possesses information about a given effect(s) and a number of possible causes except one. Kelley offers this definition for discounting: "The role of a given cause in producing a given effect is discounted if other plausible causes are also present" (p. 8). According to Kelley, discounting is reflected in ways such as a person's feeling of little certainty in the inference that a particular cause led to a particular effect. In the example above, the attributor might feel that not only is ingratiation motivation a plausible cause of the student's praise, but also the attributor might feel quite certain about the matter.

Kelley discusses a well-known pair of investigations by Thibaut and Riecken (1955) as a way of illustrating the discounting principle. In one of two parallel studies, an undergraduate student worked with two other subjects (both were actually the experimenter's accomplices), one of whom was revealed to be of higher status (he had just finished his Ph.D. requirements) than the other subject who presumably had just finished his freshman year of college. As the experimental procedure developed, the true subject found it necessary to attempt to influence the two accomplices to help him. Eventually, and at the same time, both agreed to do so. Thus, compliance constituted the effect for which the subject had various plausible causal explanations. He was asked whether each person complied because he wanted to (an internal cause) or because he had been forced to (an external cause). The results showed that subjects attributed the high-status person's compliance to the internal cause and the low-status person's compliance to the external cause.

This study relates to the discounting principle as follows. The possible causes of compliance by both the high- and low-status persons are the internal one (the person's own preference) and the external one (the subject's persuasive power). In the case of the high-status person, the subject's power is not a plausible cause for compliance; thus, the compliance is attributed to the internal cause. However, the subject's power is a plausible cause for the low-status person's compliance, and, given the two plausible causes (including the low-status person's own preference), the role of the internal cause is discounted; thus, the low-status person's behaviour is attributed to external pressure.

It seems likely that discounting processes will continue to represent a focal topic for future research in attribution theory. Theoretically, there are a number of major questions that remain to be investigated. For example, what decisional rules do people use in deciding which of seemingly equivalent causes to discount?

Summary and comparison of early statements of attribution theory

Both the strengths and weaknesses of the attributional approach are revealed by comparing Heider's (1944, 1958), Jones and Davis' (1965), and Kelley's (1967, 1972a, 1972b) viewpoints. Important strengths are their explanation of a tremendous range of human social behaviour, and their use of empirically testable formulations. A possible weakness, however, is their study of a more narrowly defined, disparate array of social situations, rather than focusing on one type of social behaviour and developing a unified attribution theory.

To begin with Heider, attribution is seen as a rapid, perceptual process that uses the immediate structure of a given event to determine personal or environmental causality. Heider argues that whenever a person cognizes the environment, attribution is occurring (see Weary, *et al.* in press). Often, Gestalt-like forces or the lack of contextual information lead to attributional errors as the perceiver attempts to differentiate degrees of personal causality. While Heider stresses the compelling nature of attributions to persons, Jones and Davis focus on situations in which environmental factors limit such attributions. They see the actor's alternative behaviour and personal preferences as additional data for the attributional process. Compared with Heider, the focus of Kelley's attributional theory is the other end of the personal-environmental continuum (see Shaver, 1975). Kelley's attributor is a relativistic information analyst who considers his role as an observer, as well as contextual data on time, place and actor.

As one may imagine, each of these three different approaches to attribution has a type of social behaviour that it explains best. Interestingly enough, these spheres of best explanation are related to problems to which the theory's author(s) had first applied an attributional perspective (see Harvey *et al.*, 1976, 1978). Heider's theory, for example, does best on attributional biases and on situations requiring a differentiation of degrees of personal causation based on limited information (e.g. attributions of responsibility — see Harris, 1977). This corresponds to Heider's initial interest in (a) interpersonal disagreements over attribution, and (b) describing the fine structure of both natural and social events. Jones and Davis' theory, in turn, is at its best when explaining subjects' unwillingness to make personal attributions when given limited but qualifying information about the environment or alternative behaviours. Such situations can be seen as boundary conditions to the problems in person perception and clinical judgment that were of initial interest to Jones. Finally, Kelley's ANOVA model is designed to work best in situations where the attributor has both the opportunity and incentive to consider a wide range of alternative causes (e.g. see MacArthur, 1972). This type of setting, and the model of the human as an information analyst, correspond well to the demands of highly structured "minimal social situations" that Kelley earlier had investigated in his work on cooperation and conflict (e.g. Kelley *et al.*, 1962).

Most attribution research is based on eclectic mixtures of the above-mentioned ideas, combined with other trends in social psychology and related areas. A good example of such electicism is the attributional facets of the self-perception theory of D. Bem (1972). This theory, similar to the ideas of Jones and Nisbett (1972), and Weiner and colleagues (1972), can be seen as a sort of second generation of attributional approaches addressing more limited questions, and in doing so, generating much research. In recent years a prominent topic of such research has been the general topic of self-attribution, its nature and differences between it and the perception of others.

Self attribution: understanding one's own behaviour

A major focus of attributional theorizing has been on nonmotivational, information-processing aspects of attributional activities. This emphasis upon non-dynamic modes of explanation is best exemplified in attributional approaches to self-perception and self-knowledge, topics traditionally found in trait-oriented personality theory. In contrast to most "self" theories of personality, the attributional approach sees the process of self-attribution (e.g. looking for the causes of one's own behaviour) as obeying the same general laws as attribution to environmental events. This view derives from the assumption that human behaviour is best explained without reference to actors' internal traits or attitudes. Thus, an individual's self-knowledge cannot be based on his or her unique access to, or motivation by, internal dispositions. Instead, the individual must engage in the same process of self-attribution as would an observer who is also looking to understand the actor's social behaviour.

Current research on self-attribution has mostly followed the original statements by D. Bem (1967, 1972) and Jones and Nisbett (1972), along with reliance upon ideas found in Heider's and Kelley's writings. In sketching the basics of these statements, their implications for social psychology is obviously our primary interest. However, it should be noted that some of the most interesting applications of cognitive self-perception theory has occurred in the areas of clinical and personality/motivational psychology (e.g. the work of Schachter, 1964). The implications of these analyses for a general theory of psychology, as well as for the understanding of perception and behaviour in social contexts, appear to be substantial.

BEM'S THEORY OF SELF-PERCEPTION

Approaching social events from the perspective of radical behaviourism, D. Bem's initial impact in social psychology was in a dispute with cognitive dissonance theorists. His novel proposal (Bem, 1967) was that a well-known type of experimental social influence (forced compliance effects) was best explained by treating individuals as ignorant of any internal causes for their behaviour. As initially recognized by Kelley (1967), Bem's (1967, 1972) theory of self-perception is of significance for attribution theory as well as for theories of attitude change. On the theoretical level, Bem's contributions have become known as self-perception theory; on the empirical level, they have led most substantially to the study of overjustification effects.

Most generally, Bem's work has helped promote the idea that self-knowledge can be reduced to self-attribution, all other things being equal (see Jones and Nisbett, 1972, below for an exception). According to Bem's (1972) theory of self-perception, people come to know their own attitudes, emotions, and other internal states partially by inferring them from their overt behaviour and the context in which this behaviour occurs. Rather than knowing what they think, feel, or believe, before they act, people are viewed as strictly information processors, making attributions about themselves based mainly upon observable data. For example, Sue may infer that Ann is in favour of municipally flouridated water from the observation than when this issue was placed on the ballot during a recent election, Ann voted for flouridated water, without being coerced to do so. According to Bem, Ann would use the same information to infer her own attitude as Sue had used, assuming that Ann did not have strong, unambiguous internal cues (e.g. a previously developed strong attitude on the subject).

OVERJUSTIFICATION EFFECTS

Bem traces much of his work to Skinner's (1957) radical behaviourism, noting that self-perception theory eschews any reference to internal physiological or emotional processes. However, in certain situations Bem's quasi-cognitive formulations seem to predict the opposite results as Skinner's operant psychology.

Consider, for example, a situation in which someone is rewarded for performing a behaviour that is already intrinsically interesting or rewarding. Presumably, if external reinforcers (such as money) are contingent on performance of an already pleasurable task and if these reinforcers are highly salient to the person, he or she may infer that this interest in the task is due to the external reinforcers. If however, the external reinforcers are not contingent on performance or are not highly salient to the individual, personal interest may be attributed to internal factors. Thus, interest, enjoyment, and actual performance should be greater than in the former case where external reinforcers prevail. In other words, salient external reinforcers may undercut individuals' interest in a task that they find to be intrinsically rewarding.

As developed by Nisbett and Valins (1972), this view suggests that people acting in social situations often ask "why am I engaging in this activity?", and their answers are said to govern a host of their future behaviours related to the activity. For example, a person may answer the question this way: "If I'm doing it for the money, then I must not like the activity very much". This general line of reasoning is referred to as the over-justification hypothesis, because external reward for an activity is *overly* sufficient justification if the individual already has found the activity to be inherently rewarding.

This hypothesis is illustrated by a study on children's choice behaviour by Lepper *et al.* (1973). In this experiment, a group of 3 to 5-year-old children were first asked to draw pictures — an activity for which they had previously shown a high degree of interest. Subsequently, one-third of the children were first promised and then given an award (a certificate with a gold seal and ribbon) for their drawing, one-third unexpectedly received the same award, and one-third received no award. One to two weeks later, the children's behaviour relative to the same drawing activity was observed. As the investigators had predicted, children who had received no award and those who had received an unexpected award showed more spontaneous interest in the activity than children who had received an expected award. The no-award and unexpected-award groups did not differ in spontaneous interest. Thus, Lepper and associates concluded that the expected award had indeed undercut the intrinsic motivation of the children to engage in the activity.

JONES AND NISBETT'S (1972) DIVERGENT PERSPECTIVES HYPOTHESIS

In discussing Bem's theory of self-perception, Kelley (1967, p. 214)

argues that Bem's position is tenable only so far as self-attributors ("actors") have the same information about themselves as someone who is watching them ("observers"). In other words, an actor's self-perception and observers' perceptions of the actor cannot be equated if there are perceptual differences leading to disagreements over what is taking place. In a widely-read essay, Jones and Nisbett (1972) developed this conception that actors' and observers' may have diverging attributional perspectives. Pursuing the insights of Heider (1958), Jones and Nisbett proposed that actors and observers alike are prone to exhibit bias in their attributions. They hypothesize that actors attribute causality for their behaviour to situational influences, whereas observers attribute causality for the same behaviour to stable dispositions possessed by the actors.

According to Jones and Nisbett, this tendency is due in part to actors and observers possessing different background data for evaluating the significance of an action. Actors generally know more about their behaviour and present experiences than do observers. Jones and Nisbett suggested that this background knowledge may divert actors from making a dispositional attribution (i.e. actors' attributions may be influenced by their memory that their behaviour has shown variance across similar situations in the past). Observers, on the other hand, probably lack information about the distinctiveness and consistency of the actors' behaviour. Because of this deficiency in background data, observers may tend to focus their causal analysis on actors and their presumed stable personality dispositions.

Jones and Nisbett also contended that different aspects of the available information are salient for actors and observers and that this differential salience affects the course and outcome of the attribution process. Because actors' sensory receptors are poorly located for observing themselves in action, they may tend to direct their attention to the situational cues with which their behaviour is coordinated. To actors, these salient aspects of the environment are the determinants of their behaviour; from the observer's perspective, these situational cues may be obscured by the actors' behaviour. The observer, therefore, may tend to assign major responsibility for the actors' behaviour to dispositional qualities possessed by the actors.

SOME EVIDENCE ABOUT THE DIVERGENT PERSPECTIVES HYPOTHESIS

Nisbett *et al.* (1973) and Storms (1973) have provided the most direct evidence in support of Jones and Nisbett's divergent perspectives hypothesis. Nisbett and associates created one experimental situation in which observers watched actors either comply or not comply with an experimenter's request that they volunteer their time in service on a particular project for their university. As the investigators had predicted, observers tended to assume that actors would behave in the future in ways similar to those they had just witnessed, whereas actors made no inferences about their own future behaviour. In other words, observers saw actors as very fixed and static in their behaviour, but actors did not have the same image of themselves; they perhaps thought that their future behaviour would depend on the circumstances then prevailing. In further support of the divergent perspectives hypothesis, Nisbett and associates found that college students described their best friends' choice of girl friends and college majors by reference to dispositional qualities of their best friends, but they described their own similar choice in terms of properties of the girl friends or majors.

The study of Storms (1973) provided additional evidence that an observer attributes an actor's behaviour to his or her disposition, whereas the actor attributed the same behaviour to the situation. More importantly, perhaps, Storms showed that these tendencies can be reversed (the observer now making more situational attributions than the actor) by using videotape to provide the actor with the observer's view of his or her behaviour and the observer with the actor's view. Thus, Storms' study provided evidence in support of Jones and Nisbett's (1972) argument that actor-observer divergencies are due in part to differential foci of attention; his results suggest that when the foci are reversed, the attributional divergences may be reversed too.

In a recent step toward reformulating the divergent perspectives hypothesis, Monson and Snyder (1977) have reviewed data relevant to this hypothesis and develop a number of qualifying propositions. A few of these propositions are: (1) when a behaviour has been performed in a situation *chosen* by the actor, actors will make more dispositional attributions than will observers; whereas for behaviours performed in situations not chosen by the actor, actors will make more situational attributions than will observers. (2) Whether actors or observers, individuals may differ in a *general way* in their inclinations to make situational or dispositional inferences. (3) When an act leads to an outcome that is *not intended*, the attributions of actors ought to be more situational than those of observers. (4) When observers are led to empathize with the actors' position, observers should be no more likely to make dispositional attributions than actors (Regan and Totten, 1975).

Monson and Snyder have made the very reasonable suggestion that researchers turn from attempts to verify the divergent perspectives hypothesis to systematic investigations of when, why, and with what implications for attribution theory do differences between actors and observers occur. Some relatively obvious limiting conditions for this phenomenon, for example, involve the context of the event being observed. Thus, actor-observer differences are affected by participants' expectations of the event (Harvey et al., 1974) and whether actors and observers make different attributions when undesirable outcomes are associated with an actor's behaviour (Harvey et al., 1975).

Critiques of the attributional approach

Social psychological research using an attributional approach continues to flourish, as judged both from its quantity and from the variety of problems addressed (see Harvey et al., 1976, 1978). While this research has not resulted in a codified, unitary theory of social attribution, it has produced a general orientation to social behaviour that is clearly recognizable and easily contrasted with non-attributional approaches.

To cite just one example of the changes brought on by the attributional approach, consider the learned helplessness theory of Seligman (1975). When initially applied to humans, this theory predicted that cognitive and motivational deficits in problem solving would result from the experience of non-contingent success and failure (e.g. failure to solve problems regardless of effort, varied behaviour, etc.). To psychologists well versed in the attribution literature (e.g. the work of Weiner et al., 1972), a shortcoming of learned helplessness theory was its inattention to humans' tendency to make a variety of causal attributions for both failures and successes in problem solving. Fortunately, the need to consider subjects' attributions following helplessness induction was eventually recognized by Seligman and colleagues (Abramson et al., 1978); at approximately the same time, a number of attributional reinterpretations of helplessness phenomena were formulated by others (e.g. Miller and Norman, 1979; Wortman and Brehm, 1975; see also Wortman and Dintzer, 1978). Although the strength of these formulations (and Seligman and colleagues' revised theory) remains to be fully evaluated, they have already clarified a set of seemingly contradictory data in the human helplessness literature.

While attributional formulations have begun to influence fields such as experimental psychopathology, serious critiques of the area have increased. In recent years, challenges to the attributional approach have come from both (a) those who are pessimistic about the ability of humans to process in an elaborate and accurate way social information and, (b) those who question whether humans analyse social cues at all in their day to day interactions (Langer, 1978). While both of these positions are critical of attribution theory, the first promotes an image of the human as a faulty information analyst; the second position would scrap the "person-as-scientist" or "person-as-mathematician" image altogether.

LIMITATIONS OF THE INDIVIDUAL'S COGNITIVE AND ATTRIBUTIONAL ABILITY

For many psychologists who study human decision making, the social attribution approach that we have outlined is based on a number of unexamined assumptions about human cognitive abilities. As noted by Fischhoff (1976), social psychologists have generally studied processes such as causal attribution without recognizing the existence of a large, related literature on the cognitive psychology of processes such as decision making and probability estimation. While there are methodological differences between this cognitive and traditional attribution research (e.g. the former stresses the prediction of events rather than the understanding of social behaviour), these differences are not too great to prevent comparison of general ideas and findings.

According to judgment theorists, the attributionist's model of the human as a systematic, relatively unbiased *intuitive* scientist may be greatly in error. As reviewed by Fischhoff (1976), the work of judgment researchers reveals people to be quite inept at all but the simplest inferential tasks — and sometimes even at them. People are portrayed as "muddling through a world that seems to let them get through life by gratuitously allowing for a lot of error" (1976, p. 421). While attribution researchers make substantial and more explicit assumptions about people's sophistication in making causal inferences (cf. Jones and McGillis, 1976), judgment researchers have often gone in quite the opposite direction, looking for even more biases in people's judgments and for ways in which fallible people can be wholly or partially removed from their own decision-making processes.

In an influential demonstration of the fallibility of human judgment, Kahneman and Tversky (1973) asked experimental subjects to predict the characteristics of an unknown individual, using information about the population from which the individual had been selected. They found that potentially useful base rate information (e.g. on the prevalence of a characteristic in the population) was not used by subjects, while dramatic but logically unimportant details tended to be used and to bias judgments. As seen by Kahneman and Tversky, such bias is one way of coping with too much information. According to this view, human perceivers tend to avoid processing all the potential information related to a population that they are studying. Instead, perceivers use a heuristic, such as *availability*, to select the most available subset of the provided information.

In the case of predicting one of an individual's personal characteristics — such as occupation (the characteristic used in the task for Kahneman and Tversky's subjects) — the heuristic of availability would lead a subject to select the most available information (usually something memorable about the individual person) and ignore any relatively unavailable information (e.g. undramatic data about the person's reference group). Applied to a more naturally-occurring judgmental task, the use of the availability heuristic can account for frequently seen types of attributional bias. To cite just one example, if one had to judge the chances of a discharged mental patient being dangerous, one might only access dramatic memories of particular discharged patients (e.g. memories of their violent behaviour) presumably because such memories are more available. If so, then one would judge a particular patient as having a greatly inflated chance of being dangerous, ignoring data which suggest, in general, that discharged mental patients are most likely to be docile and non-violent.

Evidence that the kind of bias described by Kahneman and Tversky may operate in social situations has been reviewed by Nisbett *et al.* (1976). Translating Kahneman and Tversky's concepts into the language of Kelley's ANOVA model, they asserted that people are relatively insensitive to consensus information in making attributions; instead, they often use small, possibly non-representative cases in their explanations of social events. For example, automobile drivers may be relatively inattentive to statistical reports of the great number of people who, over the past years, have died as a result of driving after drinking. However, an individual driver may give great weight to the possible effects of alcohol on driving after personally witnessing the grisly results of just one alcohol-related fatality on the highway.

To test for such judgmental biases, Nisbett and Borgida (1975) presented college students with the accurate but counter-intuitive information that most subjects in a psychology experiment obeyed an experimenter's instruction to deliver strong shocks to themselves (see Nisbett and Schachter, 1966). After receiving this base rate information, the students were asked to estimate the chance that one particular subject delivered severe shocks to himself; the students's estimation followed their intuition (low probability) rather than the base rate information. By contrast, when an additional group of students was given specific descriptions of only two subjects' shocking themselves, the students were willing to generalize this to all subjects in an experiment. As analysed by Nisbett et al. (1976), this evidence exemplifies humans' willingness to make predictions that (a) ignore base rate (consensus) information, and (b) show reliance on salient but unrepresentative information.

While there are differing views of what types of attributional biases exist and under what circumstances (see Wells and Harvey, 1977), there is agreement that human attributors can often show biases, irrational judgments apparently based on use of simplifying heuristics, or misleading schemata. As a result, the question arises as to the appropriateness of the model: "attributor-as-scientist" or "attributor-as-psychologist," which is implied in much attribution research. Fischhoff (1976), for example, suggests that we adopt a model whereby social beings are seen as "naive historians" rather than naive scientists.

One alternative to abandoning the concept of persons as naive scientists is not to tie the concept to a particular method of data analysis. Certainly, as Fischhoff (1976) notes, there are alternatives to methodologies based exclusively on ANOVA procedures, such as Heider's naive "factor analysis" (1958, p. 297). Thus, it is entirely possible that attribution theorists may eventually want to revise Kelley's (1967) identification of a specific type of social science methodology used by the naive scientist. While the degree to which this revision is necessary is still a matter for debate and empirical test, it is useful to remember that the attributor-as-scientist analogy does not necessarily depend on one type of scientific method.

A second alternative to abandoning the Heiderian concept of persons as naive psychologists is to recognize the frequent biases of professional psychologists who are far from naive, and thus de-mystify the "social scientist" component of this concept. In clinical psychology, for example, the literature on the fallibility of clinical judgments suggests that we would not be over-estimating the cognitive ability of anyone by calling him or her a "naive clinician". In social psychology, similarly, much recent history of the field has been analysed as demonstrating professionals' repeated underestimation of the effects of environmental forces (Ross, 1977). In fact, dispositionalist bias of professional "scientists-as-attributors" is so prevalent among social psychologists that certain experiments gain notice mostly through the exposure of this error (e.g. Milgram, 1965). Thus social psychologists may provide at least as good a fit as historians for the cognitivists' models of judgmental bias.

REJECTING THE VALUE OF SOCIAL ATTRIBUTION

As concluded by Fischhoff (1976), humans are sometimes quite poor as "intuitive information processors", and might best be considered as intuitive social scientists (e.g. historians) rather than intuitive mathematicians or natural scientists. In proposing such an analogy between our cognitive processes and historical or sociological methodology, Fischhoff is proposing a modification of Kelley's intuitive scientist notion; at the same time he was accepting the general idea that humans process information in their everyday decision making and social life. His assumption, that interpersonal perception and cognition play a primary role in social behaviour, has, of course, been a basic tenet of most social psychology in the last twenty years, with an occasional exception (i.e. Bem, 1972). Recently, however, this assumption has come under attack by social psychologists, most notably by Abelson (1976) and Langer (1978) in the United States, and by Harré (this volume) and Shotter (this volume) in Britain.

While Harré and his colleagues have produced possibly the most extensively described alternative to traditional social psychology (e.g. Harré and Secord, 1972; Gauld and Shotter, 1977), they have only recently begun to focus their attention to attribution theory, and have produced little empirical research that can be directly counterposed to the attributional paradigm. Of course, this is not a criticism of Harré and his colleagues' work. In fact, it may be interpreted as evidence of a Kuhnian paradigm clash where competing paradigms utilize radically different methodologies. However, Langer (1978) uses an empirical research programme to show inadequacies in the attribution approach, and her critique is that of someone quite familiar with the attribution literature in all its diverse forms. In this section, we will focus on Langer's work as the best informed rejection of attributional assumptions;

some general comments on Harré's essay will be presented with our concluding remarks.

THE "MINDLESSNESS" ARGUMENT

According to Langer (1978) and Abelson (1976), people engaged in social interactions do not base their behaviour on thoughtful analyses of interpersonal information. Instead, they act in a "mindless" (attributionally unaware) manner. Rather than approaching social interactions as naive scientists who will analyse the social environment, people are seen as routinely following a pre-set scenario or "script", which guides their behaviour more than attributions, social perceptions, etc.

According to Langer, scripts are formed of overlearned sequences of behaviour that become known to an actor or observer, and that are anticipated in certain settings. Each script contains cognitive features abstracted from many single vignettes (e.g. the image of successfully explaining one's ideas on a theoretical point to a colleague) that are grouped together by theme. With experience, these abstracted features come to be processed instead of the social interaction actually taking place; hence the script follower becomes "mindless" of interpersonal attributes once the stored scenario is accessed.

Evidence regarding Mindlessness. As direct evidence of the operation of mindlessness, Langer (1978) cites three field studies, two of which will be described here. In the first study, (Langer *et al.*, 1978), adults about to use a public copying machine in a university library were asked by an experimental accomplice to let the accomplice use the machine first. To assess the extent to which compliance in such a situation is mindless (script-determined), the accomplice used three different types of request:

(1) *Request only*: "Excuse me, I have 5 (or 20) pages. May I use the Xerox machine?"

(2) *Placebic information*: "Excuse me, I have 5 (or 20) pages. May I use the Xerox machine, because I have to make copies?"

(3) *Real information*: "Excuse me, I have 5 (or 20) pages. May I use the Xerox machine, because I'm in a rush?"

As analysed by Langer *et al.*, the first and second type of request are identical in semantic content (requester desires a favour), while the second and third type of request are identical in their structure (request for favour plus reason for request). Thus, if subjects complied equally often to the first and second request (and differentially to the third), they must be processing the messages' actual information content. On the other hand, if compliance were the same for requests number two and number three (and different for number one), then subjects could be following a script (i.e. "comply when a favor is asked with reason attached") and ignoring the messages' actual information content.

As predicted, when only a small favour was asked of Langer et al.'s subjects (a few pages to copy), their compliance followed the pattern analysed as mindless (requests two and three had the same result). By contrast, when a large favour was asked (many pages to copy), subjects seemed mindful of the content of the requester's message (requests one and two had the same effect). Thus, Langer et al. conclude that the apparently mindful interaction of two humans over a copying machine can, in fact, proceed by predetermined script rather than by an on-line analysis of the semantics of verbal communication.

In a second experiment, Langer et al. (1978) again studied whether compliance can be mindless. To do so, they formulated two types of requests for compliance, in the form of two inter-office memoranda. The content of both requests was the same: that the memo's recipient should immediately return it by inter-office mail to a designated (but actually nonexistent) room. Unknown to the secretaries, the experimenters would monitor the mail and intercept any returns. The form of the request was varied to be either consistent with standard memos (an unsigned, polite request) or inconsistent (either signed by the sender or overly demanding, or both). As analysed by Langer et al., compliance with memos is an overlearned, scripted behaviour, but one that can be *mindful* when the requirements or cues for a script are not met. This analysis suggests that the degree to which secretaries comply with the instructions of meaningless memos (meaningless because they require no action other than their own return) should depend on the memos' structure, rather than semantic content — since structural properties determine consistency with script cues. As predicted by this analysis, university secretaries who actually received Langer et al.'s bogus memos were significantly more likely to return them if the memos' format conformed to that of normal university memoranda. When this condition was met, 90% of the sample of secretaries complied with what Langer et al. termed "meaningless communication."

Comments on the Mindlessness Argument. In her exposition of the mindlessness concept. Langer (1978) is careful not to overstate its implications for attribution theory and other cognitive social psychological theories. Rather than categorically denying the validity of attribution theory, she simply questions its applicability to non-laboratory situations in which people follow scripts. (In doing so, she notes that traditional laboratory subjects are too aroused and in too novel a situation to follow any particular script.) While this is not a complete rejection of the attribution approach, it is a denial of its applicability to most of the social events of everyday life, since Langer *et al.* (1978) assert that "mindlessness may indeed be the most common mode of social interaction" (p. 641). In response to this view and to the research described above, we feel that it raises interesting and worthwhile questions about certain everyday, non-laboratory situations. At the same time, it is beset with problems of internal and external validity.

In Langer *et al.*'s (1978) study of copy machine etiquette, the authors' invocation of mindlessness depends on the idea that the "placebic information" request (". . . may I use the Xerox machine, I have to copy something?") is semantically identical to the simple request (". . . may I use the Xerox machine?"), while at the same time its syntax provides a reason for the accomplice's request (although the reason is one that's devoid of content). Thus any additional effectiveness of the placebic request over the simple request may be due to the fact that the syntax of the former cues a script of favour-giving.

Contrary to this argument, it seems to us that in this study of compliance, there is significant attributional content in the message that the authors label as "placebic", and that subjects' compliance can be explained in attributional terms. The attributional content of the placebic request is the implied or inferred message that the requester is indeed in a hurry or otherwise under some environmental pressure to use the copying machine. This is expressed in the phrase "I have to . . .", which is a more important part of the requester's sentence than the admittedly redundant goal of ". . . copy(ing) something". The use of the phrase "I have to" as well as the fact that the requester provided a reason for his request tells us something about *him* (e.g. he is too preoccupied to give a better reason) and about his environment (it may be putting him under pressure), as well as invoking the norm of favour-granting.

While we note the requester's use of the phrase "I have to", we recognize that his (her) real meaning may be "I need to" or "I want to", and that custom dictates the reference to an environmental press (I have to = I am compelled to), thus avoiding personal responsibility. This possibility would still be amenable to attributional analysis, however, since it suggests the differential effectiveness of internal and external attributions. More generally, although such phrases as "I have to" (a weak form of "I must") fail to properly locate the source of the actor's apparent coercion, in social life such phrases are still quite informative. To the extent that they reveal the strength of either an internal or an environmental press, they can be cues for attributional analysis as well as for scripted compliance (see also Harré and Secord, 1972, Chapter 8).

Thus we see Langer *et al.*'s subjects as having a valid, attribution-related reason to grant the placebic requester a small favour (small number of copies), while reserving a larger favour for the requester providing a better differentiated, *internal* reason ("I'm in a rush"). While we do not dispute the operation of social norms and conventions, it is important to point out the presence of real causal information that may be affecting subjects' compliance as much as cues for scripts.

In the case of Langer *et al.*'s memo study, a similar alternative exists to the proposition that secretaries' compliance with meaningless instructions is chiefly determined either by the presence or the absence of cues for a compliance script. While it may seem irrational to ask someone to forward a memo to another room with no other action to be taken, it may also seem to be part of a study of employee efficiency, a check on the reliability of the campus mail service, or someone's failure to enclose the first page of a two page memo (e.g. "please read and initial this; please then send it to office X"). If we assume for a minute that any of these meanings were attributed to Langer's memos by mindful secretaries, why would some of them fail to return the memo as requested? One strong hypothesis is that they returned them as long as the secretaries attributed a normal amount of courtesy and sincerity to the memo's sender. While speculative, this possibility would be consistent with Langer *et al.*'s finding that in general, demanding memos and memos that were overly solicitous (compared with university norms) were returned less often than memos that were polite but impersonal.

In writing on mindlessness, Langer *et al.* (1978) admit that valid alternative explanations can be proposed for their data, and it could be that they would agree with much of the above commentary. What seems to be more at issue is the degree to which these studies can be generalized to natural social situations. In a critique of laboratory-based social psychology, Langer suggests that theorists such as Heider and Kelley have based their work too much on the self-reports of over-aroused laboratory subjects whose behaviour in more natural settings would likely be scripted. Thus, she asserts that "attribution theorists, by and large, may have presumed too much mental activity on the part of individuals engaging in many of their everyday activities" (1978, p. 50). Putting aside the problems of internal validity already raised, the question of external validity can be posed: how applicable to general social interaction are Langer's argument and field studies?

Based on our knowledge of most secretarial work loads, our experience with copying machines, campus mail, and overcrowded, understaffed university libraries, it seems as if most secretaries, university employees and students are either encouraged or forced to act much more "mindless" than they really are. That is not to say that they are forced to act out scripts as a defence against an oppressive environment, but rather that they are in an environment in which attributional agility and mindless script-following may produce the same apparent effect.

As an example, during the time that the first author of this chapter had set aside to re-read Langer *et al.*, he received a routine memorandum from a dean of his college. The memo said (in full):

> It is against the (college) fire regulations to smoke where there are "no smoking" signs in academic buildings. Many students and faculty in past years have voiced displeasure or abhorrence at abuses of the regulations. No rules can meet the desires of everyone. May we try to make civilized adjustments to the differing views and needs of others in respect to smoking? I shall be grateful for your cooperation.

Even after having been read a number of times, this note seemed to be at least as devoid of meaning as Langer *et al.*'s bogus memos, and possibly as redundant as their placebic request for the Xerox machine. However, many of us live in environments in which we are frequently exposed to similar requests — that are either redundant, self-contradictory, or both. That we do not immediately throw all memos into the trash or publicly challenge the intellectual ability of their senders does not mean that no one is paying attention. It suggests that certain overt behaviours (e.g. defiance) are under the control of job requirements, politeness and institutional power hierarchies, and that one can usually find attributes that will justify politeness and small favours to fellow employees in an alienating environment (cf. the Xerox and memo studies). Thus, while Langer *et al.* focus on the over-learned nature of some behaviours (e.g. granting favours), they could have also looked at how other behaviours (challenging superiors) are either unlearned or temporarily suppressed. Either way, one should be just as careful about generalizing from an alienating work environment to general social interaction as one is about generalizing from a socially sterile psychology laboratory to everyday life. To the extent that Langer has exclusively presented a psychology of alienation, it is to be hoped that her insights and methods will also be applied to other types of settings, to strengthen the relevance and applicability of her work.

Concluding comments

As implied by the title of our essay, we feel that attributional conceptions will continue to change as much as they already have changed since Heider and Simmel's experiment on apparent behaviour. While we cannot predict the nature of such future changes, we can offer comments on the current state of the area, which may be the best guide to its future health. On the positive side, there is no lack of research that aspires to develop an attributional approach to laboratory and real life problems (Harvey et al., in prep.). Recent subject indexes of "Psychological Abstracts" show almost as many studies listed under "attribution" as under "attitude" — the latter referring to possibly the most heavily researched sub-area within social psychology in past years. Not only are many new topics being analysed within the attribution perspective (e.g. close relations, see Orvis et al., 1976), but also analyses in other areas (e.g. achievement) have become more sophisticated over time. Of possibly greater importance, this flourishing of research has been accompanied by attempts at theoretical clarification of the explanatory concepts of "causal attribution" (e.g. Kruglanski et al., 1978; Buss, 1978; Harvey and Tucker, 1979) questioning of basic assumptions (e.g. Fischhoff, 1976), and interdisciplinary enrichment (Harvey, in press).

Simultaneous with the permeation of attributional concepts into most areas of social psychology, critics of traditional social psychology have begun to turn their attention to attribution theory as a specific trend within the field. In doing so, they have voiced their disapproval of the methodology and metatheoretical assumptions of attribution theory, and have proposed alternative systems for understanding social behaviour, most notably the ethogenic approach (Harré, this volume; Shotter, this volume). While we have devoted most of our attention to a review of attribution theory's development, a few brief comments are in order on the challenge of the ethogenic perspective (see also Argyle, 1977).

A primary difference between attribution theory and ethogenics seems to be the range of social events that qualify for study. As Heider

(1958) indicated, attribution theory is designed to look at the human perceivers who are analysing and responding to the behaviour of others in a shared physical and social environment. Thus, Heider and subsequent attribution theorists have been interested in how individuals perceive a wide range of events, such as: intentional human actions, accidents without human origin, tasks requiring both skill and luck, uncontrollable success and failure, unintentional accidents involving humans, behaviour in coercive environments, interactions with acknow-ledged accomplices of experimenters, and so forth. In other words, the subject matter of attribution theory has been people's perceptions of events ranging from Heider and Simmel's filmed interaction of geometric shapes to Jones and colleagues' simulated job interviews.

Our understanding of the ethogenic approach is that it sees self-reported intentional behaviour as its chief subject matter, and is most interested in how individuals verbally communicate their intentions and internal states to others. As Harré says about the importance of inten-tionality: "To recognize him as an actor is to see his actions as informed by his intentions and he, as an actor, realizing them in actions" (1977, p. 290). Similarly, on the issue of verbally reporting one's intentions, Shotter (this volume) notes that "In everyday social life, people in general . . . treat one another as having the ability to make avowals . . . and in a large part, people are normally treated as meaning what they say" (p. 173).

Certainly, attribution researchers share the ethogenists' interest in intentional, verbally mediated behaviour (see Jones et al., 1961). At the same time, however, the attributional approach was developed to explain human behaviour in a wider range of what we see as social situations. One reason for this broad perspective is that humans tend to project attributes such as intentionality and forseeability into behav-iours and events that are accidental and unforseeable (e.g. Walster, 1966). If one only studies how humans explain intentional events to themselves and others, one must ignore the topics of, for example, how we are affected by social accidents, how we explain the (possibly unintentional) behaviour of anonymous strangers, and how we interpret our own failures and successes on academic achievement tasks (see Weiner, 1974). One also would neglect analysis of how we process limited or misleading social information.

Because the attributional approach addresses such questions, its theories (e.g. Kelley's ANOVA model) may be criticized as only useful in analysing relatively impersonal interactions — such as minimal social situations in the laboratory. However, much of everyday life involves the attempt to explain relatively impersonal interactions, based on limited information and no reliable statement of intention. Consider the behaviour of an employer who decides to give one worker a large raise, to fire another, and to re-assign a third. Certainly, such an event is probably the product of intentional behaviour and may eventually be studied using the ethogenic approach. However, to understand each of the participants' short-term reactions, or the reactions of an interested observer (e.g. a shop steward) who has limited information, an attributional approach seems to be highly useful.

On a different level, attribution theory seems to make another unique contribution. That is its traditional focus is not just on intentional and unintentional behaviour, but also on the interface between them (Heider, 1944). Because of this broad focus, attribution theory has the ability to help answer the question of *why* the distinction between intentional and unintentional behaviour is of such great importance to those engaging in social explanation, on both a naive and a professional level.

In addition to its carefully defined subject matter, another significant feature of the ethogenic approach seems to be its analysis of the activities of social psychologists themselves; we will conclude this chapter with comments on this aspect of the writing of Harré and colleagues. As stated by Harré (this volume), experimental social psychology can be seen as a particular type of social interaction or ritual, with its own rules and norms; it can also be seen as artificially eliciting attributions to descriptions of contrived social events, rather than to more natural stimuli such as gossip and folk tales. Certainly there are many flaws in artificial laboratory settings, and in the artificially dichotimized choices that are employed in some attribution research (e.g. "it was due to the environment" *vs* "it was due to the person"). However, acceptance of this criticism should not necessitate the rejection of attribution theory, its laboratory basis, or the acceptance of ethogenics.

On the question of the artificiality of attribution research, it should be noted that attribution theorists have themselves become increasingly critical of the exclusive use of simple forced choice formats and overly artificial stimulus events. As a result, field studies and more naturalistic modes of assessing attribution have increased in popularity (e.g. Harvey *et al.*, in press). At the same time, however, field studies are no guarantee of external validity (as our discussion of Langer *et al.* suggested), and we have yet to see convincing evidence for the lack of validity of the basic attributional studies reviewed above (e.g. Jones *et al.*, 1961).

On the question of accepting ethnogenics, a comment is necessary concerning ethogenicists' recognition that attribution theorists, among others, are engaged in social rituals. If one assumes the validity of this reasonable observation, it does not mean that one should accept the implication that ethogenics can do a better job than attribution theory in explaining interpersonal perception. Stated more directly, one should attend to the level of analysis that is appropriate for one's subject matter. If it is the general behaviour of groups of social scientists in various cultures, there is no reason to look to ethogenics, Marxist sociology, or even attribution theory (e.g. Ross, 1977). However, social psychologists most often are concerned with the individual's behaviour, cognition, perceptions and feelings, and with dyadic and small group activities in social situations that are relatively confined both temporally and spatially. At this level, and assuming an empirical approach to social behaviour, the effectiveness of alternatives to attribution theory has yet to be demonstrated.

Before concluding our statement, we will briefly address certain major issues raised by Harré in his analysis of attribution theory in this volume. First, Harré suggests that attribution theorists have been remiss in considering reflexivity. In fact, however, this issue has been of concern to attribution theorists for several years. Kelley (1977), for example, presented several warnings aimed at enhancing recognition of the parallels between scientific and naive attributional process. He suggests that the attributional perspective may invite a level of recognition not often found in social psychological inquiry. As an illustration of his concern, Kelley says

> One central question raised by the attributional perspective is how the instances from which they (the respondents) make their inferences correspond to those from which we (the investigators) make ours. In an observer's rating of a family decision process, he is likely to give approximately equal weight to each part of their discussion. However, participants in the decision may recognize that a particular suggestion or comment played a crucial part in the decision and that others were trivial. (1977, p. 105)

It would appear to us that Kelley and many other contemporary attribution investigators need no more "reforming" (to use Harré's phrase) in this area than do ethogenic scholars or social scientists in general.

A number of Harré's other arguments appear to be as applicable to practically any type of social science work now being conducted as they are to attribution work in particular. We all exhibit ethnocentricity to varying degrees in our theories and methodologies, and most of us have been too prone to aim our investigative focus at middle class, typically white, respondents. It is true that American values and peculiarities of the American social order may pervade the concepts and findings of attribution theory and research. But given the socialization experiences of so many researchers in the area, how else could it be? Is it not similarly likely that British and/or European values and societal features have had some impact on ethogenic work? Perhaps we all should try to recognize these limitations and exercise not only more humility in our claims about knowledge, but also more attention to possible trans-cultural and trans-ethnic differences in the phenomena we study.

Finally, Harré seems not to appreciate the emerging and substantial interest among attribution investigators in the role of self-presentation management and dramaturgical factors in attributional processes. But such interest is clearly evident in recent writings. A careful reading of Bradley (1978) reflects a well-considered emphasis upon the role of self presentation in attributional processes, and more recently, Stryker and Gottlieb (in press) articulate elements of a meaningful convergence between dramaturgical ideas and central attributional concepts. Indeed, we welcome this convergence and its concomitant implications regarding the interdisciplinary broadening of contemporary attributional analysis.

To conclude, we shall repeat the observation of Argyle (1977), that the ethogenic approach most often does not lead to testing of falsifiable hypotheses. Whether this is a weakness in the theory or — as Argyle implies — a sociological characteristic of holding this minority position in social psychology, is an open question. More important to us is the need for proponents of ethogenics to develop and consistently use a method of validating their theoretical statements. This is said with the best intention, because there is certainly room for innovative, carefully constructed and *tested* theories in social psychology. In other words, philosophical elegance is, by itself, not sufficient to ensure a theory's utility or acceptance. That seems clear from looking at the fate of, for example, Heider's linguistic calculus, which has had very little impact compared with the rest of his theory. Unfortunately, the important question of why this is true — why certain aspects of a theory such as Heider's come to be developed while others are ignored — is beyond the scope of this paper.

4

Actors' and Observers' Explanations: Divergent Perspectives or Divergent Evaluations?

J. van der Pligt

Introduction

Understanding how people perceive and explain their own behaviour and the behaviour of others is one of the fundamental problems in social psychology. The *attributional approach* to these and related questions refers to a framework or perspective rather than a theory; the main element of this perspective is the emphasis on everyday, ordinary explanations of events. Harris and Harvey present a clear review of attribution theory in Chapter 3. The major concern of the present chapter is with one of the later developments in attribution theory, i.e. the study of the differences between self perception and the perception of others. In 1972, Jones and Nisbett proposed that actors and observers make divergent attributions when they explain a specific behaviour. Their argument was that "there is a pervasive tendency for actors to attribute their actions to situational requirements, whereas observers tend to attribute the same actions to stable personal dispositions" (Jones and Nisbett, 1972, p. 80).

This hypothesis led to an explosion of research on attribution, and a wide variety of different methodologies have been employed to verify this general attributional hypothesis. The first experiment to test this actor/observer hypothesis directly was conducted by Nisbett *et al.* (1973). Results of this study showed that people assign more personality traits to others than to themselves, a finding that is interpreted as indicating that people see personal dispositions in others but believe that their own behaviour is primarily dependent upon the situation. For recent reviews of the many studies supporting this hypothesis, see Harvey, *et al.* (1978); Jones (1976); Monson and Snyder (1977); and Ross (1977).

Yet, despite the impressive track record of studies confirming this hypothesis, recent proposals suggest possible limitations. For instance, Buss (1978) argued that the conceptual framework of attribution theory is inadequate to explain how people attribute dispositions and other explanatory properties. Buss' critique is explored in more detail by Lalljee in Chapter 5 of this volume. Other proposals challenge attribution theory's assumptions about human cognition (Fischoff, 1976), or question the metatheoretical assumptions and methodology of attribution theory (Harré, Chapter 6, this volume).

The present chapter focusses on methodological problems of studies in attribution theory. Unlike other chapters, this one will be concerned with the *procedures* of experimental research on attribution; the intention is to examine whether the procedures generally used in attribution research provide clear evidence regarding the dispositional versus situational locus of attributions to one's self and others. In doing so, we will follow Ross' (1977) classification of the different tasks used to study the divergent-perspectives hypothesis.

The first task is *causal judgment*: the observer is asked to identify the cause, or set of causes, to which a particular outcome or action may most reasonably be attributed. Measures of causal attribution that have been used include both open-ended and structural response measures; in both cases responses are usually classified on a simple internal-external or dispositional-situational continuum.

The second task is *social inference*: the observer of a particular action is asked to what extent characteristics of the actor caused that specific course of behaviour. These two tasks, causal judgment and social inference, have been widely used in attribution research and, until recently, most of the research on the divergent-perspectives hypothesis used one of these tasks.

Recently, Ross (1977) stressed the importance of a third task, i.e. *the prediction of outcomes and behaviour*. According to Ross, observers not only seek causal explanations and make causal inferences, but also form expectations and make predictions about future actions and behaviour. In his view, the psychology of intuitive prediction is a natural extension of the domain of attribution theory.

Results obtained with these three tasks used to test the divergent-perspectives hypothesis will be reviewed in this chapter. Methodological problems and problems of interpretation plaguing attribution research of this type will be discussed. We will focus especially on the task of *attributional inference*, and argue that most research in this area fails to distinguish between descriptive and evaluative aspects of attribution. Furthermore, it will be shown that the observer's evaluation of the actor and his/her behaviour plays an important role in the attribution process. Evidence will be presented indicating that actor-observer differences could be related to different evaluations of own and other's behaviour. Finally, it will be argued that attribution theory should expand its conceptual framework, to include both descriptive and evaluative aspects of the attributions made by actors and observers.

Actors' and observers' causal judgments

Research exploring the causal judgments made by an observer in order to explain the occurrence of social events, generally relies upon a simple internal/external or dispositional/situational dichotomy. Both open-ended procedures and structured ratings have been used in studies testing the divergent-perspectives hypothesis. An open-ended procedure involves asking a subject to explain in his/her own words why a particular event has occurred. Nisbett *et al.* (1973, study 2) used this procedure and found that observers make more dispositional attributions to both positive and negative behaviours than actors.

The major problem of interpretation of open-ended responses is caused by the fact that usually responses to the question, "Why did John do this?" are coded as "situational" or "dispositional" on the basis of the *form* of the response. Thus the response: "John doesn't want to go to this Saturday's match because of football hooliganism", is coded as an external/situational attribution, while the response, "John will not go because he is afraid of getting mixed up in a fight", is scored as an internal or dispositional attribution. It is clear from these examples that when one attends not to the form of the explanation but to its content, the legitimacy of the situational/dispositional distinction becomes rather dubious. Most situational explanations seem to imply assumptions about relevant dispositions, and similarly, most dispositional attributions assume the influence of relevant situational determinants of behaviour. Lalljee in Chapter 5 goes into the problem in some detail.

A recent attempt to solve the problem is formed by the work of Ross (1977) and Monson and Snyder (1977). Both retain the traditional distinction but suggest that one should categorize as situational attributions only "those explanations that state or imply no disposition on the part of the actor beyond those typical of all or most actors". Similarly it is suggested to consider as a dispositional attribution only "those explanations that state or imply something unique or distinguishing about the actor" (Ross, 1977, p. 5). These definitions do not necessarily represent a dichotomous classification, but may instead reflect the relative impor- tance of dispositional and situational determinants in explanations of a social event.

However, these more stringent definitions of situational and dis- positional attributions do not provide a solution for the problem that situational attributions imply certain dispositions and vice versa. This is illustrated by a recent study (Antaki and McCloskey, 1978), in which persons were asked to explain five aggravating or annoying events. The obtained (open-ended) responses were coded according to the above definitions. Results, however, showed little agreement between the judges. Even after a considerable relaxation of the criterion of inter- judge reliability and the adding of a fourth judge, only 43·5% of the statements could be coded as either a dispositional or situational explan- ation of the event. On the other hand, classifying the statements in evaluative categories proved less problematic and showed a highly significant interjudge reliability. In research on causal attributions for success and failure, several researchers attempted to develop coding procedures for classifying open-ended responses (see e.g. Elig and Frieze, 1975). However, open-ended procedures have never been very popular, which is probably related to the necessity to train coders and the time-consuming nature of assessing causal attributions in this way. Recent results confirm the view that open-ended response measures do not provide an adequate measure of causal attributions. Elig and Frieze (1979) compared five different measuring instruments, and their results showed that open-ended measures of causal attributions have a relatively poor inter-test validity and reliability.

One way of avoiding the disadvantages of the open-ended response technique is to present persons with a list of alternatives of which some are assumed to indicate a dispositional and some a situational attribu- tion. However, some of the problems associated with the open-ended response method do also apply to this measure. For instance, Regan *et al.* (1974) conducted a study to test the relationship between causal attributions of another person's behaviour, and the affection for that person. In their second study, subjects were asked to explain a specific behaviour (helping a confederate) by selecting the "primary motive" out of a set of four explanations. Both the response, "He helped because he was in a good mood", and "he helped because of something about the situation, e.g. because he didn't want to leave a bad impression with the other people in the room, or because he wanted something to do during the wait", were scored as situational attributions. It is clear from this example that using a structured response measure does not guarantee a solution for the confounding of situational and dispositional aspects of an explanation.

Another way of avoiding the above problems is simply to ask people to indicate whether a behaviour was caused by the situation or by dispositional factors. For instance, Storms (1973) asked both actors and observers to describe their own and the actor's behaviour along four standard behavioural dimensions (friendliness, talkativeness, nervousness and dominance). Then for each of these behavioural dimensions, subjects were asked to indicate how much influence they thought the following two factors had in causing that behaviour:

(a) Personal characteristics about yourself (or your matched participant): how important were your (his) personality, traits, character, personal style, attitudes, mood, and so on in causing you (him) to behave the way you (he) did?

(b) Characteristics of the situation: how important were such factors as being in an experiment, the "getting acquainted" situation, the topic of conversation, the way the other participant behaved and so on in causing you (him) to behave the way you (he) did? (Storms, 1973, p. 168).

Subjects were asked to indicate of *each* of these two factors how important they thought them to be in causing the actor to behave in the way he/she did.

Storms' results strongly confirm the actor/observer hypothesis and extend previous results by showing that these differences are highly related to the visual orientation of the rater, i.e. both actors and observers attribute causal attributions to what is most prominent in their visual field. From this point of view, the situation is most salient for the actor while the observer's visual attention is aimed at the actor, hence their divergent attribution. Furthermore, these results provide strong support for the divergent-perspectives hypothesis, because the obtained differences were unrelated to the perceived extremeness of the action on the four behavioural dimensions.

Taylor and Koivumaki (1976) used an even more direct measure of causal judgment by simply asking subjects to rate 6 different behaviours on an 11-point scale, where '1' indicated situational causality and '11' dispositional causality. Subjects were told that a dispositional rating meant that personal qualities of the individual had prompted the action; a situational rating on the other hand meant that factors in the situation incidental to the stimulus person had evoked the behaviour. In a second study Taylor and Koivumaki (1976, study 2) asked subjects to rate dispositional and situational causality on two separate 9-point scales, i.e. the two explanations were treated as independent rather than mutually exclusive. These studies do not show that the behaviour of one-self is generally viewed more situationally than the behaviour of another person. Results showed that positive behaviours are generally explained by reference to dispositional attributes while negative behaviours are easily dismissed as caused by the situation, both for oneself and for others, suggesting that *social desirability* or value of the behaviour is an important factor affecting the kind of attribution one will prefer. Overall support for the actor/observer difference was weak and Taylor and Koivumaki (1976, p. 407) conclude that "motivational processes as well as cognitive ones must be taken into account when one attempts to predict how people perceive the behaviours of themselves and of others".

One obvious drawback of this procedure is that one severely limits the answering possibilities of subjects. The use of *one* 11-point scale (ranging from "situational" to "dispositional") forces subjects to use the explanatory framework that the researcher thinks is most relevant and also forces subjects to see the two factors as mutually exclusive. These two complications may be responsible for the fact that subjects in Taylor and Koivumaki's study found the "situational" category of causality particularly troublesome and vague.

Finally, McArthur (1972) and Eisen (1979) used a structured method that is related to the method used by Storms. Instead of rating a number of response alternatives, subjects were asked to *select* the alternative that in their opinion was the most probable cause of a particular behavioural response. The four alternatives were:

(1) Something about me (actors)/this student (observers) probably caused me (actors)/him or her (observers) to give the Y response.
(2) Something about the specific item probably caused me/him to give the Y response.
(3) Something about the particular circumstance probably caused me/him/her to give the Y response.
(4) Some combination of 1, 2 and 3 above probably caused

me/him/her to give the Y response. Subjects were asked, if they chose this alternative, to specify the particular combination of factors they thought could best explain why they (or their matched actor) gave the Y response (see Eisen, 1979, p. 268).

Eisen attempted to relate actor/observer attribution differences to differences in perceived distinctiveness, consistency and consensus of own and other's behaviour. Results of this study showed no *general* actor/observer differences in perceived distinctiveness or consistency, nor in causal attributions. However, there were a number of significant interaction effects, all suggesting that the *social desirability*, or *valence*, of the behaviour in question plays a crucial role in attribution differences. Actors saw their negative behaviour as more distinctive than their neutral behaviour, while their positive behaviour was estimated lower in distinctiveness than their neutral behaviour. Observers showed no significant difference in their estimates for positive and neutral behaviours, but also estimated negative behaviour to be more distinctive than neutral behaviour. The one clear actor-observer difference concerned the distinctiveness of negative behaviour, which was estimated higher by the actors than by the observers. Consistent with this finding, actors inferred lower consistency than did observers only for undesirable behaviours, although this difference did not reach statistical significance.

Results in dispositional attribution differences between actor and observer were in accordance with the findings on distinctiveness and consistency. Actors tended to attribute positive behaviours more and negative behaviours less to their own personal dispositions than observers. Results on situational attribution differences, however, showed no actor-observer differences.

SUMMARY AND COMMENT ON CAUSAL JUDGMENT RESEARCH

Predictions on actor-observer differences have been supported both by studies using open-ended response methods (e.g. Nisbett *et al.*, 1973, study 2) and structured response measures (e.g. Storms, 1973; Harvey *et al.*, 1975). However, subsequent research on actor-observer differences does not provide strong support for the actor-observer hypothesis, and shows that actor-observer differences are strongly related to the social desirability of the behaviour (e.g. Eisen, 1979), i.e. actors attribute their negative behaviour more to the situation than observers, and explain their positive behaviour more in terms of personal characteristics than observers. This is consistent with self-serving biases found in previous research (Arkin *et al.*, 1976; Miller and Ross, 1975; Sicoly and Ross, 1977; Stevens and Jones, 1976). Whether these differences are related to motivational or informational differences is not yet clear (see, e.g. Bradley, 1978; Miller, 1978; Ross and Sicoly, 1979). An increasing number of studies suggest that evaluative aspects play an important role in attribution processes. It has been argued that attributions are not based solely on cognitive processes, and that attribution theory should incorporate the social desirability of the behaviour and the attitude towards the person committing the behaviour (see, e.g. Taylor and Koivumaki, 1976). The influence of these evaluative factors will be discussed in greater detail in the section on attributional inference.

Methodological problems in research methods used to assess causal attributions are most obvious for open-ended response measures, the main problem being that most dispositional attributions imply situational determinants and vice versa. Although there are some problems associated with structured response measures, they generally show acceptable levels of validity and reliability (Elig and Frieze, 1979). However, it should be pointed out that Elig and Frieze limited their analysis to explanations of success and failure on various tasks. It would be premature to extend their findings on the reliability and validity of the attribution categories to explanations of other kinds of behaviour.

Actors' and observers' attributional inferences

The second task, the formation of social inferences, is probably most frequently used in attribution research. The divergent-perspectives hypothesis states that individuals tend to *explain* their own behaviour in more "situational" ways and the behaviour of others in more "dispositional" ways. The use of the attributional inference task extended the hypothesis to also include *descriptions* of one's self and others, i.e. it is suggested that people tend to describe themselves in "situational" terms, and others in "dispositional" terms.

Usually subjects are asked to describe a certain actor or a course of behaviour. Most commonly subjects are presented with brief anecdotes about the responses of one or more actor(s) and are asked to rate the actor on Likert-type scales. Extreme responses are interpreted as dispositional attributions, while the middle categories are interpreted as indicating a situational attribution. A similar task is presenting subjects with lists of trait descriptive terms and asking them to indicate of each presented adjective whether it is:

(a)   a good description of the target person;

(b)   not a good description of the target person; or whether,

(c)   they can't say, "it depends on the situation".

Similarly to the Likert-type measure, the first two alternatives are interpreted as willingness to infer personal dispositions to explain the behaviour, while the third option is assumed to indicate a more situational attribution.

One of the earliest tests of actor-observer differences using a measure of attribution inference was conducted by Nisbett *et al.* (1973, study 3). In this study subjects were asked to indicate whether each of 20 trait terms, their antonyms, or the phrase "depends on the situation" provided the best description of four persons (their father, their best friend, an admired acquaintance, and Walter Cronkite) and of themselves. Results showed a significant tendency for subjects to use the dispositional option more often for others (14 times out of 20, on average), and least often for oneself (12 out of 20).

McGee and Snyder (1975) used the same list of trait adjectives to test whether preference for either dispositional or situational self-attributions is related to actual behaviour. Ross (1977) asked subjects to rate various persons on a number of Likert-type scales, instead of providing them with three alternatives as was the case in the above studies. Increasingly extreme scores were interpreted as reflecting increasing confidence and a dispositional inference. Unfortunately Ross' (1977) main hypothesis concerned differences between attribution inferences about persons who behaved like or unlike the rater. Although subjects were asked to rate themselves, these scores did not receive detailed consideration. The main finding of this study was that observers are more inclined to attribute dispositions to behaviour that differs from their own.

Herzberger and Clore (in press) asked subjects to indicate whether each of 16 trait-terms, their alternatives, or the phrase, "depends on the situation", was the best description of themselves and of their best friends. They found that on some antonym pairs subjects preferred the situational response option more often for descriptions of others.

Finally, Goldberg (1978) conducted a series of experiments using a similar method as Nisbett *et al.* (1973). In these studies subjects were asked to rate the degree to which each presented term described themselves and each of three self-selected peers — one of whom they liked, one to whom they felt indifferent, and one of whom they disliked. Subjects were presented the following rating scale:

0 = the word is *not* a good or accurate description.
1 = the word is *only partly or occasionally* descriptive.
2 = the word *is* a particularly good or accurate description.
    (Goldberg, 1978, p. 1014)

It is assumed that the 1 response is more "situational" than the 0 and 2 responses.

In his main study, a total of 2800 terms was used. Results provide strong support for Nisbett's (1973) proposal; i.e. subjects showed a significant tendency to use the situational response option most often for themselves, and least often for a well-liked and disliked other. Neutral others were also rated more situational than both a well-liked and a disliked other. Furthermore, Goldberg replicated these results in two further studies (Goldberg, 1978, study 2 and 3).

Taylor and Koivumaki (1976) tested actor-observer differences in attribution inference by asking subjects to indicate of each of 30 adjectives whether it was a good description of two others (an acquaintance, one's spouse), and of oneself. Answers were indicated on a rating-scale ranging from $+3$ (definitely describes the person), to -3 (definitely does not describe the person); the middle category was labelled "sometimes describes the person, sometimes not". Results showed that the self was seen less dispositionally than the spouse, but not less dispositionally than the acquaintance, providing no strong evidence for the actor-observer hypothesis.

Overall support for Jones and Nisbett's hypothesis from research using attributional inference measures seems quite strong. Goldberg's (1978) replication using a comprehensive set of 2800 terms seems to provide especially solid support for the findings of Nisbett *et al.* (1973). However, after a detailed psychometric analysis, Goldberg concluded that most studies do not, in and of themselves, provide compelling evidence regarding the situational versus dispositional locus of attributions to oneself and others. The methodological problems mentioned by Goldberg and some related problems of interpretations will be discussed in the remainder of this section.

ATTRIBUTIONAL INFERENCE AND SPECIFICITY

A prime weakness of trait-rating measures is that preference for the option "depends on the situation" or a neutral response on a rating scale could indicate the rejection only of a broad or general dispositional attribute. Several important papers in the attribution area (Jones and Nisbett, 1972; Nisbett *et al.*, 1973) fail to distinguish between the *absence* of a trait inference, and the rejection of broad trait labels in favour of narrow or situation-specific dispositional attributes. The fact that actors do not like to explain their own behaviour as being caused by broad and often clearly evaluative traits does not necessarily mean that people perceive themselves as being led by situations. Presenting people with lists of general trait-terms and asking them to describe others and themselves on the basis of these trait terms seems to be a task that is related to stereotyping. (Actor-observer differences follow a similar pattern as ingroup-outgroup differences, e.g. Stephan, 1977; Triandis, 1977.) If this is the case, it is not surprising to see that people are more prepared to attribute simplified, broad trait-terms to others than to themselves.

ATTRIBUTIONAL INFERENCE AND UNCERTAINTY

Although Goldberg (1978) replicated the earlier findings of Nisbett *et al.* (1973) he also concluded that the procedures employed in his own studies, and those employed previously by Nisbett *et al.* do not provide compelling evidence regarding the hypothesis that actors prefer to describe themselves in situational terms, while as observers they tend to attribute dispositional terms to the other. His main argument is that the meaning of the situational response option is likely to be confounded with response ambiguity and/or uncertainty on the part of the respondent. A psychometric analysis of his data revealed that the use of the situational response is highly related to the degree of consensus on the two dispositional response alternatives, i.e. terms with a high interjudge agreement on whether it *is* or *is not* descriptive of the target, tend to elicit relatively few situational responses. On the other hand, terms which equal numbers of individuals consider to be an accurate description and an inaccurate description tend to elicit a relatively high proportion of situational responses. Since it has been shown that interindividual response variability is related to both response instability over time (e.g. Fiske, 1957) and response uncertainty (Goldberg, 1968), the above findings could suggest that increased preference for the situational option is related to increased uncertainty. Unfortunately, Goldberg did not collect independent measures of response uncertainty.

Recently van der Pligt and Eiser (in prep, a) conducted a study in which subjects were asked to describe two hypothetical others and themselves, using a procedure similar to Goldberg's. One sample received forms in which the situational option was phrased, "Only occasionally an accurate description", for a further group the situational option was phrased, "Sometimes accurate, sometimes not". The remaining subjects rated each of the 22 presented terms on a 5-point scale ranging from "definitely an accurate description" to "definitely not an accurate description", the intermediate categories were labelled as "probably (not) an accurate description" and "don't know".

Results of the self and other-descriptions showed a similar pattern in the three versions. Furthermore, increased perceived difficulty of describing a target led to a higher preference for both the "uncertain" categories and the "situational response option", again suggesting that response uncertainty and preference for the situational option are highly related.

At first sight, the above results seem to provide unambiguous support for the proposed relationship between uncertainty and preference for the situational option. However, some cautionary notes are in order. Firstly, the task used by Goldberg is distinctly different from the one used by Nisbett *et al.* (1973). Nisbett provided the respondents with 20 *pairs* of adjectives, with the "situational option" as a third alternative. Both Goldberg (1978) and van der Pligt and Eiser (in prep, a) provided the respondents with a set of adjectives and of *each* adjective it was asked whether it was or was not an accurate description with the situational option as a third alternative. It is questionable whether the response "the word is not an accurate description" should be interpreted as a dispositional attribution. Secondly, if preference for the situational response is related to uncertainty, one would expect individuals to be less certain in describing themselves than others. This corollary is incongruent with an extensive body of literature on self-other differences in processing personal information. For instance, Kuipers and Rogers (1979) conducted a series of experiments in which subjects were asked to make self-referent (describes you?) and other-referent (describes experimeter?) ratings of trait adjectives. Results showed that self-ratings were consistently judged as easier to make and that subjects always placed more confidence in these judgments. Furthermore, recall for self-descriptions was superior to that for other-referent descriptions, a result that replicated earlier findings of Rogers *et al.* (1977). In other words, self-ratings were made with more confidence and showed less intra-judge instability, findings that contradict the proposal that increased uncertainty could explain the preference for the situational response in describing oneself. This is supported by the results of two studies by van der Pligt and Eiser (in prep a and b), in both studies subjects were asked which of the three targets they found most difficult to describe, percentages of subjects who found it most difficult to describe themselves were 29% (study 1), and 39% (study 2), again suggesting that people do *not* find it more difficult to describe themselves compared to describing others, and are more confident when describing themselves.

Although Goldberg's results seem to suggest a relationship between uncertainty and preference for the situational option, further evidence will be required to establish whether this preference is caused by response uncertainty. Besides some methodological problems, e.g. the interpretation of the response alternative "not a good or accurate description" as a dispositional response, results on information processing clearly contradict the suggestion that people are less certain when they describe themselves.

EXPLANATION AND EVALUATION

Past studies within the attributional framework have generally neglected three factors that could affect the kind of attribution one makes: (a) the evaluation of the target person or behaviour by the observer, (b) the actor's self-evaluation, and (c) the evaluative aspects of the attributions.

(a) *Evaluation of the target person.* In their original paper Jones and Nisbett (1972) emphasize cognitive and perceptual factors in attribution processes, and only briefly discuss the possible effects of motivational variables on the tendency of actors and observers to engage in divergent causal attributions. Furthermore, these authors suggest that the best support for their proposition would be found in cases where the act in question is neutral affectively and morally and the observer holds a neutral opinion towards the actor. In contrast, in situations where the act is negatively or positively evaluated by the observer, or the observer's relation to the actor is not affectively neutral, different attributions regarding the cause of a specific act may result.

Unfortunately, studies in which observers are asked to explain a relatively neutral act or describe a person towards whom they feel relatively neutral are the exception rather than the rule.

Most studies pay little attention to the effects of the evaluation of the target person by the observer on the attribution process. For instance, Regan and Totten (1975) included evaluative measures of target behaviour on four dimensions, but did not take these into account in their analysis, since "the hypothesis was concerned with the relative strength of situational versus dispositional attributions" (p. 853).

One of the few studies that made a direct comparison between attribution of an admired, a disliked, a neutral other and attribution of oneself is that conducted by Goldberg (1978). Results showed that attributions of others become more dispositional to the extent that the actors were more evaluatively polarized, i.e. neutral others were not described in a more dispositional way than the self. (proportion of situational responses for self and neutral other were respectively 0·45 and 0·43). Similarly, van der Pligt and Eiser (in prep, b) found that attributions of dissimilar others were more dispositional than attributions of similar others, neutral others and oneself. Both studies suggest that the evaluation of the target person is an important factor in attribution processes. Furthermore, if the comparison of attributions towards neutral others and to oneself provide the "best test" for the actor-observer hypothesis (as Jones and Nisbett suggested), the above results clearly do not support this hypothesis.

(b) *Self-evaluation*. Since attributions of others appear to become more dispositional to the extent that the targets are more evaluatively polarized, it could be the case that individuals simply see themselves as relatively neutral and hence prefer not to describe themselves with evaluatively polarized attributes. The work of Ross (1977) on the so-called "false consensus bias", suggests that people tend to see their own behaviour as relatively moderate and appropriate to the circumstances and that they tend to overestimate the commonness of their behaviour. Goldberg (1978) correlated the favourability of adjectives with the tendency to endorse them; results showed that this correlation was slightly higher for positive others than for oneself. Furthermore, in a recent study, van der Pligt and Eiser (in prep, c) asked subjects to select two trait-adjectives to describe themselves, a similar other and a dissimilar other. Evaluative sign of all presented adjectives was assessed in a pilot study. Results showed that self-descriptions were less positive than those of similar others and more positive than those of dissimilar others. As a consequence, it seems necessary to incorporate self-evaluations in studies on attribution inference.

(c) *Evaluative aspects of attributes*. Since the evaluation of the target person and his/her behaviour is an important variable that could influence the type of attributions one makes it seems necessary to pay close attention to the evaluative aspects of attributions.

Some years ago, Peabody (1967) was the first one to notice that in most trait-inference research, the role of the evaluative meaning of trait-descriptive terms is overemphasized. Furthermore, he showed that the evaluative response was confounded with the descriptive meaning of the trait. Further research based upon his work resulted in the conclusion that descriptive aspects are at least as important as evaluative aspects in processes of trait-inference and impression formation (see e.g. Felipe, 1970; Peabody, 1970; Selby, 1976). In attribution research, on the other hand, we see the opposite. Perhaps as a result of the prevailing cognitive approach in social perception and attribution, results are interpreted solely as descriptive explanations of the target person's behaviour. Hence, describing a target person as e.g. "overcautious" is interpreted as referring to that personality characteristic as a causal agent of some specific behaviour and *not* as an evaluation of that person or behaviour.

Recently, Fiske (1979) suggested that cognition and affect should be treated as two separate systems and that cognition does not necessarily have to precede affect.

It is important to underline that in the typical attribution-inference study dispositional explanations have a clear evaluative component, while the situational response has no *direct* evaluative implications. Unfortunately, in most studies the descriptive and evaluative aspects of attributions are confounded. Nisbett was aware of the possible confounding of evaluation and description, for instance in Nisbett *et al*. (1973, study 3) the authors tried to unconfound evaluations and attributions by including only terms that were socially desirable. However, the effort to create adjective pairs of equal desirability, so that the evaluation factor would enter as little as possible into subjects choices was largely unsuccessful (p. 161). Another solution is to include evaluatively balanced sets of trait-adjectives or rating-scales, but even then it seems necessary to perform separate analysis for evaluatively positive, negative and relatively neutral attributions. Studies in which separate analysis were performed show clear effects of the favourability of the presented adjectives upon the types of attributions one makes (see Taylor and Koivumaki, 1976).

Unfortunately, most studies pay little attention to the evaluative aspects of the presented trait-attributes. For instance, Ross *et al*. (1977, study 3) compute a dispositional score by simply combining all ratings irrespective of the evaluative sign of the selected adjectives. Other studies (e.g. McGee and Snyder, 1975) used the list of terms first used by Nisbett *et al.* (1973, study 3), although the latter explicitly mentions the fact that the adjective pairs were *not* equal in desirability.

THE IMPORTANCE OF EVALUATIVE FACTORS

Fiske's (1979) suggestion that affect and cognition should be treated as separate systems seems relevant to the area of attribution. There is evidence that evaluation plays an important role in attribution processes as argued in the foregoing section. For instance, Taylor and Koivumaki (1976) found that people are *generally* regarded as causing good behaviour and that situational factors are *generally* regarded as causing bad behaviour. There is some indirect evidence that evaluative factors may even override the descriptive aspects of attributions. Van der Pligt and van Dijk (1979), asked subjects to select adjectives to describe persons with different opinions about the use of drugs. Results showed that extreme agreement or disagreement with the position of the actor leads to an increasing neglect of the descriptive properties of the presented trait-adjectives; i.e. one selects only adjectives that are congruent with one's own evaluation of a particular attitude. This results is in line with Fiske's (1979) proposal that affect can sometimes precede cognition.

Indirect support for the proposed interpretation comes from a recent study (Fiske and Cox, 1979) where people were asked to describe persons using a free response method. Results indicated that people generally do *not* describe unknown others with the help of personality characteristics but pay more attention to things like physical appearance and concrete behaviour, a finding that suggests that the descriptive aspects of the attributions are less important when one describes unknown others (which is frequently the case in attribution research). According to Fiske and Cox (1979), personality characteristics become more important when describing oneself or well-known others, a finding that contradicts most attribution research, which suggests that personality character-istics are most important in describing others. Furthermore, the validity of attributions made to an unknown other is extremely low (Norman and Goldberg, 1966). It would be interesting to see whether the evaluation of the actor is relatively stable over time. Comparing the validity and reli-ability of descriptive and evaluative aspects of the attributions one makes would give more information on the relative importance of these two factors.

SUMMARY AND COMMENTS ON ATTRIBUTION-INFERENCE RESEARCH

The foregoing arguments indicate that the evaluation of the target person by the observer does influence the types of attributions one makes. Furthermore, regarding attributions as causal explanations only is too limited an interpretation. It seems necessary to expand attribution theory to include these evaluative factors. One way could be to include balance theory notions to conceptualize the evaluations of a specific actor and his/her behaviour by the observer.

The most obvious shortcoming of attribution inference studies is that people can *only* respond by either endorsing personality characteristics or denying them, without offering them a separate possibility to *evaluate* the behaviour that they are asked to explain. In other words, subjects' only possibility to *evaluate* the behaviour or person they are asked to explain is by selecting evaluatively positive or negative adjectives to describe the person who displays the behaviour. Since these evaluative aspects are important, further research to unconfound attributions and the evaluative implications is clearly warranted.

In the typical attribution study, the experimenter provides the relevant background information on the basis of which the subjects make their judgments and, in so doing, has manipulated variables like degree of familiarity with the target and the apparent evaluation of the target. This research strategy has the disadvantage that one overlooks potentially crucial phases in the attribution process, preceding data analysis, during which the data are *evaluated*. Aspects that are of special importance are (a) the relationship between self-attribution and self-evaluation and (b) the question whether the curvilinear relationship between evaluation of the actor and preference for dispositional attributions holds for both other-attributions and self-attributions.

At the present time it seems unclear whether preference for the dispositional option reflects a genuine dispositional attribution, increased response certainty or a relatively extreme evaluation. In summary, results of attributional inference studies suggest that evaluative/motivational factors should be taken into account to explain the attributions people make. Furthermore, the paradigm used in most attribution-inference studies has serious methodological shortcomings which makes it impossible to disentangle a number of alternative explanations of the results obtained.

Actors' and observers' predictions of behaviour

The third type of attribution task is prediction of behaviour (e.g. Nisbett and Borgida, 1975). According to Ross (1977), this procedure permits simple straightforward questions and produces responses that can be scored objectively. For instance, someone watching John marching in an anti-nuclear demonstration is asked to predict John's behaviour in a series of related episodes. Similarly, one could ask the observer to estimate the percentage of people that would have behaved in a way similar to John, i.e. decide to join a demonstration to support the anti-nuclear movement.

Most research in this field (Ross, 1977; Ross et al., 1977) — focuses on the second type of prediction. The main hypothesis is that people tend to perceive a "false consensus" — to see their own behavioural choices and judgments as relatively common and appropriate to the particular circumstances while viewing alternative behaviour as uncommon, deviant, or inappropriate. The logical relationship between these two tasks and the tasks of causal judgment and social inference is that:

(a) a dispositional explanation will result in increased willingness to make confident and distinguishing predictions about the actor's subsequent behaviours, and

(b) a dispositional explanation leads the observer to estimate that most other people will behave differently in that particular situation, and conversely, a situational explanation will lead the observer to estimate that most other people will behave in a similar way since the behaviour is under situational control.

It is clear that (a) is related to the "consistency" and "distinctiveness" of the actor's behaviour, while (b) is related to the perceived "consensus" of that particular behaviour.

Strong support for the "consensus" predictions is provided in a series of studies by Ross et al. (1977). In a first study, subjects were presented with short descriptions of hypothetical conflict situations of the sort they might face in real life. Subjects were asked (a) to estimate the commonness of the two response alternatives (to comply or not comply with the request), (b) to indicate the alternative they, personally, would follow, and (c) to assess the traits of the "typical" individual who would follow each of the two specified response alternatives. Results of this study showed that people overestimate the commonness of their own behaviour, and are more prepared to infer dispositions of those who selected a response alternative that was different from their own preferred alternative.

Following these findings, Ross (1977) suggests that actor-observer differences may arise from the attributors' miconceptions about the degree of consensus of their own behaviour and of alternative behavioural strategies. He concludes:

> . . . To the extent that particular responses by one's peers differ from one's own responses in a given situation, such responses are likely to be seen as relatively odd or deviant — the product therefore, not of situational forces (which, presumably, guide one's own contrary responses) but of distinguishing personality dispositions or traits. Moreover, since any peer responds differently from oneself in at least some situations, it is inevitable that one's peers be seen as the possessors of more numerous and more extreme distinguishing personal characteristics than oneself. The false consensus effect thus allows us to account for many of the phenomena and experimental results that have been mustered in support of Jones and Nisbett's thesis . . . (Ross, 1977, p. 191)

Van der Pligt and Eiser (in prep, b) asked subjects to rate 5 others with favourable attitudes towards drugs, 5 others with neutral attitudes and 5 people with unfavourable attitudes. Results confirmed Ross' findings, i.e. dissimilar others were rated more dispositional than others with similar attitudes. Degree of dissimilarity could affect the attributions one makes, since e.g. pro-judges rated only anti-judges in a more dispositional way than similar others, while others with a neutral attitude were not rated more dispositionally.

However, as shown above, it is simply not true that actors and observers always differ in the direction predicted by the "false consensus bias" (see e.g. Monson and Snyder, 1977). Furthermore, it has been shown that observers *also* overestimate the extent to which others would behave similarly to actors whom they have observed (Nisbett and Borgida, 1975).

Eisen's (1979) study is of special relevance to Ross' thesis, since it makes direct comparisons between perceptions of consensus by actors and observers. Results of this study show that the actor/observer differences in perceived consensus are more complicated than Ross suggests. Observers who responded with the same response to a specific item estimated a *higher* consensus than actors did, while observers who differed from the actors, estimated the consensus to be *lower* than actors. Furthermore, her results indicate a clear overall effect of valence upon perceived consensus, i.e. positive behaviour was seen as more common than affectively neutral behaviour which in turn was seen as more common than negative behaviour. However, actors did not see positive behaviours as more common than observers did; nor did they see negative acts as less common. The actor-observer differences obtained in Eisen's (1979) study seem to be unrelated to perceived consensus, and Eisen concludes that attribution biases may be related to biased estimates of the distinctiveness and consistency of behaviour. Furthermore, in accordance with the previous section, she recommends that motivational aspects should be taken into account.

Research on information processing casts serious doubts on the relevance of Ross' claim that the "divergent perspectives" hypothesis can be derived from the false consensus bias. A number of studies provide strong support for the view that people do *not* utilize consensus information in making attributions. McArthur (1972) presented subjects with one-line descriptions of the form "actor responds to stimulus x in fashion y" and were additionally given information on the dimensions of consensus, consistency and distinctiveness. Consensus information accounted for less than 3% of the variance in causal attribution and prediction of future behaviour of the actor. Miller *et al.* (1973) asked subjects to read the procedure section of the Milgram (1963) study on obedience. Half of the subjects were given the actual data of Milgram's study, showing that nearly all the subjects administered a very substantial shock to the confederate and that a majority went all the way to the top of the voltage scale. Other subjects were not given these counter-intuitive results. Subjects were asked to rate two individuals, both of whom had gone all the way, on 11 Likert-type scales. Results showed that for only one of the 11 scales, consensus information had a significant effect, implying that the knowledge that most people administered the maximum shock did not affect the attributions one made. These results are clearly supported by Nisbett and Borgida (1973) and Nisbett *et al.* (1976).

Finally, one of the methodological problems related to attribution inference studies, also applies to research on the "false consensus bias". Since both self-evaluations and the evaluation of others are not assessed independently, Ross' (1977) findings and the findings of van der Pligt and Eiser (in prep, b) could also be interpreted as indicating that similar others and oneself are seen as relatively neutral, while dissimilar others are judged more extreme on the evaluative dimension. Similarly to attribution-inference studies it seems necessary to unconfound attribution and evaluation.

In summary, the procedure to assess dispositional versus situational attribution that is used in this type of research has the same drawbacks as those used in attribution-inference studies. Although Ross's claim that the task "prediction of behaviour" permits unambiguous questions and produces responses that can be scored objectively is unchallenged in the literature, we have seen that there are distinct problems with it. The perception of consensus is affected by the valence of the behaviour, and a number of studies fail to verify the predicted actor-observer differences on perceived consensus. The most obvious drawback of this approach however, is the repeatedly reported finding that observers do *not* use consensus information in the attribution process, implying that Ross' claim that differences between actor's and observer's attributions are caused by different perceptions of consensus is unlikely to be correct.

Concluding comments

In this chapter an attempt has been made to critically examine the research procedures used to test the divergent perspectives hypothesis. Although this hypothesis has been verified with a number of different methodologies, empirical support is not as strong as is often suggested. Each of the experimental tasks used to test actor-observer differences, i.e. causal judgment, social inference, and the prediction of behaviour shows serious shortcomings. Because of a number of interpretational ambiguities, the prevailing procedures do not provide clear evidence regarding the dispositional versus situational locus of attributions to one's self and others.

As a cognitive model of social behaviour, attribution theory stresses the importance of information processing aspects of social cognition. Actor-observer differences have been interpreted as a function of the information available to the actor and the observer. The usual argument is that because one has more information about one's own behaviour and its inconsistencies, one is better placed to see situational influences operating on oneself than one is to see them operating on other people.

My main argument is that this narrow informational approach has led to an underestimation of the influence of evaluative factors upon attributional processes. Past studies within the attributional approach have generally neglected both the attitude towards the target person and the evaluation of the behaviour committed by that person. Furthermore, in most attribution inference studies the evaluative and descriptive aspects of the attributions one makes are confounded. Close inspection of most of the obtained results in this field show that support for a *general* attributional difference between actors and observers is not very strong. Studies in which evaluative factors are taken into account show that the kind of inferences one makes is related to the evaluation of the actor and his or her behaviour. The major influences of evaluative factors can be summarized in the following three points: (a) *positivity bias*, i.e. good behaviour is generally regarded as being caused by the person, while bad behaviour is more likely to be interpreted as being caused by the situation; (b) *evaluative consistency*, i.e. consistency between the evaluation of the target person and the target behaviour generally leads to a dispositional attribution, while evaluative inconsistency is more likely to lead to a situational attribution; (c) *evaluative extremity*, a more polarized evaluation of the target person and his or her behaviour will lead to a dispositional attribution (assuming evaluative consistency), while relatively neutral behaviours are more likely to be interpreted as being "caused" by the situation.

In summary, it seems necessary to expand attribution theory to include evaluative aspects of the attribution process. A full picture of attributional processes underlying the actor-observer difference must take into account both the attitude towards the person committing a specific behaviour and the evaluation of this behaviour. One way of doing this is to incorporate balance theory notions into the conceptualization of attribution processes.

5

Attribution Theory and the Analysis of Explanations

M. Lalljee

This paper attempts to place current ideas concerning attribution processes within the wider context of a psychology of explanations. Other chapters in this volume concentrate on an exposition of the theory and its major schools (Harris and Harvey, Chapter 3), on the problem of the reflexivity of the concepts involved (Harré, Chapter 6), and on some of the problems in its account of the differences between actors' and observers' explanations of events (van der Pligt Chapter 4). In this chapter, a number of the central assumptions of attribution theory are challenged, and the essentially intra-psychic orientation of attribution theory is located within an analysis of interpersonal and societal processes.

Two notions central to attribution theory

Central to current ideas concerning attribution processes are the notions of (i) explanations in terms of causality, and (ii) the distinction between attributions to internal or external causes. Both these notions figure prominently in Heider's work (Heider, 1958). In his account of the naive analysis of action, Heider seems to regard causal explanation as the paradigm case of lay explanations and distinguishes between personal and impersonal causality. However, the analysis of personal causality soon distinguishes a number of different sorts of factors. The concept of "Power" (whether or not a person has the capacity to perform a particular act) is distinguished from a motivational factor, which includes both the person's effort and his intention. In the same analysis, Heider also distinguished between different sorts of environmental factors. He mentions in this context particularly the concepts of luck and of difficulty, thus recognizing the heterogeneity of explanations in terms of the environment.

Explanations in terms of causality have traditionally been considered central to the scientific enterprise. However, they are not the only sorts of explanation that have been considered. A recent paper by Buss (1978) points out that teleological explanations have often been considered vital especially with regard to the explanation of human action. Explanations in terms of causes must not be confused with explanations in terms of reasons. Buss argues that to explain one's own behaviour in terms of causes, unless it is odd or unintended, is to make a category mistake. Though some philosophers of social science want to maintain that any explanation of human behaviour in terms of causes is inadequate, Buss allows that observers may well make causal explanations of the behaviour of others. He uses this argument with good effect in the analysis of actor-observer differences. But Buss's argument that it is impermissible for a person to explain his own behaviour in causal terms does not seem adequate. He notes that a number of philosophers have tried to analyse intentions as a particular sort of cause, but more importantly, even if it was unanimously agreed that intentions were to be treated differently because they were a conceptually different sort of explanation, it would still not be adequate to justify Buss's view. Even if it is some kind of conceptual error to treat reasons as causes, it may well be that the layman makes that conceptual error in his explanations. The question for psychologists would be to understand how the layman interprets explanations in terms of reasons and how he interprets explanations in terms of causes.

The argument can be clarified by considering the examples presented by Buss. He argues that just because an explanation is couched in causal terms, it should not be accepted at face value as a causal explanation. When a person says "What caused me to walk out of class was the boring lecture", the idea, Buss claims, can be expressed more accurately by the formulation "The reason that I walked out of class was that I found the lecture boring". Consider the following plausible explanations in answer to the question "Why did you go and talk to him?"

   (i) I talked to him because I felt sorry for him.
   (ii) I talked to him because he was all by himself.
   (iii) I talked to him in order to make him feel at home.

Whether the first two are seen primarily as reason explanations or causal ones and, indeed, whether the third is seen as some implicit causal explanation (perhaps being based on the notion of my being impelled by feelings of duty and responsibility), are surely empirical questions which cannot be decided on the basis of conceptual analysis. The general questions are of two sorts. One concerns the layman's interpretation of cause explanations and reason explanations. Are these perceived as being fundamentally similar or different and if the latter in what ways? The second question concerns the presentation of one formulation of the explanation for an event rather than another. This latter question has been a long-standing issue in the study of attribution processes and can be satisfactorily resolved by including an interpersonal dimension in what has so far been intra-psychic theory.

Finally it should be pointed out that explanations in terms of reasons and explanations in terms of causes do not exhaust the types of explanation that have been distinguished by philosophers. Thus Bunge (1959), besides distinguishing four types of causal explanation, also enumerates eight types of non-causal explanation. These include statistical explanations, dialectical explanations and explanations based on claiming that a particular event is an instance of a general class. Such distinctions may be of value to psychologists in so far as they can be related to cognitive or interpersonal processes.

A second major tenet of attribution theory involves drawing a central distinction between causes that are internal to a particular person and those that are external to him. To treat such a distinction as fundamental is to minimize the importance of the heterogeneity of the explanations that fall into each category. Thus "person" explanations include explanations in terms of a person's mood, his physiological state, his personality trait, his past behaviour, his role, goal and social category. These are likely to be very different in terms of their predictive value, in how far they are seen as being under the control of the actor, and in terms of attributions of responsibility and blame. It is these features that have frequently been considered the underlying rationale for constructing explanations in the first place.

Situational explanations too encompass a diversity of possible factors. Thus Heider himself distinguishes between cases where the external cause is the physical environment, and cases where it is another person. Even where the external cause is another person, there are important distinctions to be made. Brown and Lalljee (in press) have suggested that in the case of criminal acts, one such distinction is between cases where the person precipitating the event is also the victim of the offence (as is often cited in cases of rape) or some third party whose actions influenced the perpetrator. Further the criminal law distinguishes those situations that could have been reasonably foreseen and for which a person is held liable even if he did not intend to commit a particular action (Cross and

Jones, 1964). We attribute responsibility for getting into or creating particular situations or allowing them to happen, even when environmental factors are the immediate cause of the behaviour.

The lack of homogeneity of personal and environmental causes needs to be stressed. Even though a number of relevant distinctions were introduced by Heider, these have frequently been lost sight of in other influential work on attribution processes (e.g. Kelley, 1967; Jones and Davis, 1965; Nisbett *et al.*, 1973). Van der Pligt too questions the wisdom of presenting people with pre-determined response modes through which they can offer their explanation of what is going on (Chapter 4). However, Heider does stress that the perceiver achieves predictability over the varied events in his environment by referring phenomena to stable underlying conditions. Foremost amongst these underlying invariances are the motives of others. Perhaps man sees himself as having more control over the motives of others than over other aspects of his environment. Further Heider argues that by and large we only make attributions to personal or environmental factors as opposed to invoking explanations that involve both personal and environmental factors. He claims that this is the case because the latter sorts of explanation have little predictive value.

But Heider's view that the underlying invariances of the world are either environmental or personal dispositions and that people generally explain events in terms of personal or environmental factors, but seldom include both elements in an explanation, must not go unchallenged. The latter is an empirical question, one that cannot readily be answered by experiments that use as their dependent variable rating scale indices of attributions of causality to personal or situational factors. Data collected by the present author (Lalljee, 1979), allowing subjects to explain events in their own words rather than through rating scales, shows that people frequently use explanations that invoke both personal and situational elements and that explanations in terms of personal factors, situational factors, or involving both personal and situational factors are systematically related to the event to be explained. The underlying invariance, ascription to which fulfils only one of the functions of an explanation, may not be in terms of personal or environmental dispositions, but, as will be argued later, may reside in a socially accepted schema or pattern.

Thus two of the central tenets of attribution theory have been shown to be limited. The heterogeneity of person and environmental explanations in terms of their implications for control, predictability and blame makes this questionable as a central distinction. Further, explanations are not simply causal, and the proper study of explanations should incorporate this fact. An appropriate starting-point for the psychology of explanations would be the analysis of explanations offered in everyday life as a stepping stone towards developing a functional taxonomy.

Information gatherer or hypothesis tester?

The notions of explanations in terms of causality and of internal/external attributions are embodied in a theory of attribution processes put forward by Kelley (1967). Kelley explicitly sets out a theory about the way in which the layman assigns causes to events. He suggests that it is fruitful to look at the layman rather like a scientist in the way in which he collects information. Following Heider and John Stuart Mill, the central concept that he invokes is that of co-variation between different events in order to make attributions of causality. Kelley's concept of cause seems to be that of co-variation. Such a view of causality achieved prominence with the work of Hume, but it is by no means the only concept of cause. A number of writers have argued that causality involves more than co-variation and includes some conception of generative mechanism or power in a cause to produce the effect (Wallace, 1972). In fact this latter conception of cause seems much closer to the initial analysis suggested by Heider (1944). Again it is not necessary for psychologists to enter into this conceptual debate, but it does raise the interesting question concerning how causes are looked upon by the layman. Kelley's theory goes on to specify what sort of information a person uses in order to make attributions to internal and external causes. He enumerates three sorts of information:

(a) consistency information — concerning the individual's reaction to the entity over different occasions;

(b) distinctiveness information — about whether the individual's reaction occurs uniquely when the thing is present and does not occur in its absence;

(c) consensus information — information concerning the reactions of others to the same entity.

Thus if an entity is experienced in a particular way by all observers (high consensus), if a particular individual responds to it in the same way on different occasions (high consistency) and if he responds to it differentially from his responses to other entities (high distinctiveness), the cause of the reaction is attributed to the stimulus. Kelley's conception of the scientist is very much that of the inductivist. He approaches nature with no theories, but counts instances of events in particular classes under different conditions and arrives at his conclusions from there.

Kelley's ideas concerning the pervasiveness of these three types of information and their influence on the attribution of causality to forces internal or external to the person have attracted a great deal of attention. A number of studies have been conducted exploring these ideas. Two main categories of study can be distinguished.

The first category includes studies where the information concerning consensus, consistency and distinctiveness are presented and manipulated within a questionnaire. Typically subjects are presented with a brief description of an event as well as consensus, consistency and distinctiveness information, and asked to rate the cause of the event along selected rating scales. For instance McArthur (1972) presented subjects with items concerning the occurrence of an event (e.g. "John laughs at the comedian") and manipulated the other information presented to the subject through statements such as "Almost everyone who hears the comedian laughs at him" (high consensus) or "Hardly anyone who hears the comedian laughs at him" (low consensus). Similar manipulations were made of consistency and distinctiveness information.

The second category of study includes experiments where subjects have typically been asked to make attributions of a target person's behaviour on the basis of information of his behaviour as well as information concerning the behaviour of others in the same situation. For instance, Wells and Harvey (1977) asked their subjects to read the report of the procedure of a psychological experiment (such as Nisbett and Schachter's study on receiving electric shocks) and presented them with information (not always authentic) about how other people had behaved during the experiment. Subjects are then told about how a particular person behaved and asked to make attributions concerning the causes of his behaviour. The results of both sorts of experiments are broadly supportive of Kelley's hypotheses, though just how important consensus information is to the subject is in dispute (see Nisbett and Borgida, 1975; Wells and Harvey, 1977, 1978; Borgida, 1978).

In spite of such apparent support for Kelley's theory, its central notions have a number of difficulties that have been obscured by the experimental formats used. Though information about how a particular person behaves on other occasions and about how other people behave in a particular context is relevant to our explanations of his behaviour, it is unlikely that they operate in terms of the essentially inductive and general information search that Kelley postulates. These notions will now be analysed further and through them an alternative model of the processes involved in explaining events will be presented.

Certainly the behaviour of other people with regard to the entity or of the same person over time may play an important role in the explanation provided for a person's behaviour. In many circumstances it would be adequate as an answer to the question "Why did he do it?" to say that "Everyone does it" or "He usually behaves like that". However, even in such instances, what is offered as an explanation is not just a piece of information that is the result of an inductive information search. To say that "Everyone does it" may not have anything to do with attributing causes for events. It may be essentially a way of denying that this particular individual has any *unique* characteristics that need explaining. Similarly the explanation "He always does it" denies that this particular occurrence of the action needs further explanation, since it can be regarded as a case of one sort of regularity. So while the behaviour of other people and of the same person over time may well be relevant to the explanations provided, they may not operate essentially as bits of information that one uses to sort out questions of causality, but as explanations that may be socially acceptable and adequate in a given context. Kelley (1967) maintains that consensus information refers to the information about the behaviour of all or most other people with regard to that entity but it is most unlikely that this statement can be taken at face value. "All" or "most" could be read literally to refer to counting instances of the human race. Clearly that cannot be what is meant. Could it perhaps refer then to counting the members of a particular group — for instance "most Americans" or "most middle class Americans" or "most white middle class Americans"? Consensus information manipulated within the course of an experiment may perhaps be interpreted by the subjects within the context of such a group rather than in terms of some notion of "all" or "most" people.

The theory in this sort of slightly modified form is also likely to be inadequate. It is most unlikely that information concerning the behaviour of any one group would be considered relevant for a variety of different sorts of events. Thus one might legitimately explain the apparently odd dress of an adolescent by saying that "They all dress like that". Such an explanation may be seen as adequate because we accept that as far as dress and certain other forms of social behaviour are concerned the "adolescent group" may be seen as the appropriate and acceptable source of behaviour. For other activities other groups may be called on for sources of information concerning how people behave. In the case of stealing, for instance, it seems unlikely that the explanation "They all do it" (in the case for instance of an adolescent) is likely to be generally regarded as a satisfactory explanation. The general point here is that though information about how "other people" behave is relevant, the relevant "other people" will vary with different classes of act. Kelley's broad inductivist model where the person simply counts the number of people in the group who behave in a particular way and compares one individual's action with this must be replaced by a much more selective being who looks to a variety of different groups for information he considers relevant for a variety of different sorts of behaviour.

Similar problems can be found with the concept of consistency. Consistency information refers to how the person behaves on other occasions. This has been construed in the experimental paradigms used as to whether the person referred to "almost always" or "hardly ever" behaved in the particular way with reference to the particular object. Again the notion has a generally inductivist flavour. The perceiver counts the instances of the occurrence of a particular reaction before a particular entity and arrives at an attribution of causality from that. Though the person's behaviour on previous occasions is indeed relevant to the explanation provided for his behaviour, does such information operate in the way described by attribution theory? "He always does it" may well count as an adequate explanation for "Why is he going for a walk at 6 p.m.?" but it is hardly likely to be adequate as an explanation for "Why is he going for a walk at midnight?" even though the number of occasions on which he went for a walk at that time might be identical in both cases. What is different is the pre-existence of a social schema of plausible springs of action into which one explanation fits and the other does not. Further, consistency cannot be ascertained by counting instances of the behaviour. If a person divorced four wives in five years, one might well explain his fifth divorce with the remark "He's always doing it", but if he went for a walk at 6 p.m. four times in five years one could hardly think of his "doing it often". The general point is that consistency cannot be sorted out simply by counting instances. What is considered "doing it often" is different for different sorts of events and further there are certain sorts of behaviour for which consistency may be an adequate explanation and other types of behaviour for which it is not. Thus Kelley's empty inductivist who engages in a broad and comprehensive information search along particular dimensions cannot work. His provocative theory does however lead to a new range of questions that can be developed by considering what sort of alternative might function in its place.

Both Kelley and Heider based their hypotheses about how the layman arrives at attributions of causality on John Stuart Mill's ideas concerning scientific method and in particular on Mill's method of difference. The history of science presents a viable alternative model, that of the scientist as a hypothesis-tester rather than information gatherer. An alternative to the Heider/Kelley approach would suggest that the layman already approaches an event with a rich store of hypotheses concerning its explanation. He has in advance a set of hypotheses about why the event happened from the time he has classified the event. Rather than engaging in a general inductivist search along the lines suggested by Kelley, this alternative approach would suggest that he then looks for specific items of information to distinguish between his hypotheses. Take, for example, the instance of stealing mentioned earlier. On learning that a particular child has stolen something, Kelley would imply that the explainer would then search for information concerning consensus, consistency and distinctiveness in order to sort out the causes of the event. The alternative model suggested here would imply a different sort of process. The explainer is likely to approach an event with a store of hypotheses. He may believe that children steal "because they come from poor homes" or "because they aren't given enough pocket-money", or "because of a dare", and then seek information that will enable him to choose between these theories. In the experimental paradigms so far used to test Kelley's ideas, the experiments have looked at information *use* in a very restricted context — what is needed are studies concerned with information *search*. In this context a variant of the sorts of factors that Kelley mentioned may be reintroduced. When do people seek information about the behaviour of others? When do they ask how the person behaved on previous occasions?. Perhaps this sort of information becomes most important when the person has no adequate cultural theory for the event. Thus when the prospective explainer has found out that the child did have enough money, and did not do it for a dare, and has run through his other cultural theories, then perhaps he asks questions such as "Has he ever done it before?". It is plausible to suggest that it is particularly when a person runs out of specific hypotheses will he search along a wide variety of general dimensions.

In brief then the argument presented attempts to show that Kelley's theory concerning how people make attributions is inadequate. Kelley's inductivist who counts instances along dimensions of consensus, consistency and distinctiveness must be replaced by an explainer who comes to an event with a store of hypotheses concerning its explanation, and seeks disambiguating information. Some of these hypotheses will embody culturally shared theories about the event. What our cultural theories are, how they are transmitted and when they are invoked become vital considerations for a psychology of explanations.

Interpersonal considerations

Attribution theory has generally been concerned with intra-psychic processes. The general assumption made in the study of attribution processes is that on encountering an event a person makes an attribution of causality either to personal or to environmental factors. This approach has led to problems when trying to relate language to the attribution of causality to person and situation poles. The central argument of this section is that a speaker has a range of explanations open to him all of which may be true. The interpersonal context of the explanation may be the critical factor in understanding which explanation is presented. Consideration of this interpersonal dimension may lead to the solution of one of the long-standing problems in attribution theory.

Thus in their influential paper on actor-observer differences in the attribution of causality, Nisbett *et al.* (1973) discussed the interpretation of the statement "I chose chemistry because it is a high paying field" as compared with "I chose chemistry because I want to make a lot of money". They suggest that the former should be treated as an attribution of cause to the entity (Chemistry — because it is a high paying field); and the latter as an attribution of cause to the person (I — because I want to make a lot of money). Nisbett *et al.* found that subjects tended to explain their own choices of college major and of girlfriend in terms of the entity, while they explained the choices of their best friends more in terms of the characteristics of their friend. They relate this to their general thesis that actors explain their own behaviour more in terms of situational factors, while observers are more likely to explain the same behaviour in terms of the dispositional characteristics of the actor. Nisbett *et al.* do consider the possibility that the difference between entity oriented and person oriented explanations as given in the example above could be a difference of language use rather than one of attribution of causality. They seek to reduce the weight of this argument by suggesting that similar differences can be found even when subjects do not have to provide the explanations themselves but have to choose between explanations worded in entity and dispositional terms. Ross (1977) returns to the problem with a different example — "Jack bought the house because it was secluded" (entity formulation) as compared with "Jill bought the house because she wanted privacy" (person formulation). He suggests that it is unlikely that these by themselves refer to differences in attribution of causes to personal or situational factors. It does indeed seem unlikely that such a difference refers to fundamentally different ways of perceiving the causes of a particular act. In order that either of the two explanations for the event be true, the other must also be true and is indeed implied by it. It would be nonsense to say that "I chose chemistry because it is a high paying field but of course I don't want to make a lot of money" or "I chose the house because I like privacy but of course the house is not secluded". Van der Pligt gives a very full account in his chapter of the difficulties that Attribution Theorists have had to struggle with in their use of this apparently straightforward pair of concepts. The differences between the two formulations may not be a function of different perceptions of causality but of different interpersonal contexts in which the explanations are presented.

If we are to study explanations as events that take place within particular social contexts, a variety of concepts that have been used in the analysis of discourse become relevant. Rather than take the view that a person is making attributions of causality to personal or environmental factors, an alternative approach, one which has been explored with reference to other issues, would hold that for any event the speaker has a range of alternative explanations all of which may correspond with the facts. Schegloff (1972) in his analysis of how people refer to a particular location points out that any particular place may be referred to in a variety of ways all of which may be equally true. Thus in specifying where my notes are, a variety of formulations from "in front of me", or "on the desk" through to "in Oxford" or "in England" may all be true. Of course the presentation of a particular formulation is not random and Schegloff attempts to analyse some of the concepts that are relevant to the formulation of place on a particular occasion. Similar arguments could apply to the formulation of time. In response to the question "When did it happen?" answers ranging from "At six o'clock" or "In the evening" through to "At Christmas" or "When I was at college" could all be true, and one would expect there to be some systematic principles governing the formulation of time. Adopting such an approach to the study of explanations will involve emphasizing the importance of the context in which the explanation is given.

The importance of context and of understanding the communication system between inter-actors has been emphasized by a number of writers. Thus Rommetveit (1974) stresses that language must be studied in terms of communication between people in a particular context and examines some of the concepts that will be necessary to analyse communication. He argues that communication is based on some shared knowledge and expectations concerning what is relevant. Encoding involves anticipatory decoding, decoding aims at reconstructing what the speaker intends to make known. In his review of discourse processes, Coulthard too stresses the importance of assumed shared knowledge in understanding the realization and interpretive rules of speaker and listener (Coulthard, 1975); and the notion of background expectancies in understanding how an inter-actor orients himself to his context has been stressed by writers concerned with ethnomethodology (see Garfinkel, 1967). Related ideas have been put forward by Grice (1957, 1975) who presents a theory of meaning based on the intentions of the speaker. Of relevance here is his notion that speakers and listeners adhere to the cooperative principle in conversation. Not only does this cooperation concern the mechanics of speech but to certain tacit agreements that the participants will be informative, truthful, relevant and clear.

This leads us to the first principle which may underly the presentation of a particular explanation. (i) *Assumptions concerning the knowledge of the other*. In conversation one undertakes to be informative. Thus if the speaker thinks the listener knows that chemistry is a high paying field or that the person referred to likes privacy he will respond with the formulations "He chose chemistry because he wants to make a lot of money" or "He bought the house because it is secluded". Indeed one could easily envisage the speaker apparently presenting a person attribution to one person and a situational attribution to another depending upon his assumptions about what the listeners already know. The listener is likely to register a chain of interpretations for an utterance (Clark, 1978). Using memory and reaction time experiments, Clark has explored what interpretations are made and the intermediate assumptions a listener has to make in order to interpret an utterance. The interpretation of explanatory utterances and the way in which they are related to judgments of causality and assumptions of the knowledge of the participant is another potentially promising area for the study of explanations.

(ii) *The relationship between the inter-actors*. One aspect of the

relationship between people that has frequently been considered fundamental by social psychology is that of affiliation (see Brown, 1965;
Argyle, 1969). The relationships between this dimension and the related
concept of interpersonal distance to a variety of stylistic, syntactic and
extra-linguistic features has been considered by a number of writers
(e.g. Joos, 1962; Robinson, 1972). However, little attention has been
paid to the content of speech and the way different content areas may be
relevant to different sorts of relationship. Assumptions concerning what
sort of information the other person wants and expects will no doubt be
related to the set of explanations provided. The intimacy of the content
of the explanation provided should be related to the intimacy of the
relationship.

Another central consideration may be that of role. Schegloff (1972)
points out that the formulation of place depends upon the speaker's
assumptions concerning the group membership of the other. One
pervasive aspect of this may be that of role. Thus one would expect that
the explanation for an accident given to a policeman and to a parent
would be very different — even if issues concerning blame, responsibility
and so on were irrelevant — because of the belief that people in such
relationships are interested in different things. The acceptability of a
particular excuse would also be dependent upon the relationship of the
people involved. Thus, as Scott and Lyman (1968) point out, a
depressed husband may obtain sympathy from his wife because his
favourite team has lost an important game, but the same explanation for
his depression will appear odd if offered to his boss. Further, a society
permits certain sorts of people to adopt certain sorts of acceptable
explanations. As Secord and Backman (1974) have noted, a lower-
echelon employee may explain his actions by saying "I was only following
orders", but such an explanation is considered unacceptable for
someone more senior. Thus each participant will approach the interaction with certain assumptions of what the other considers relevant
both in terms of information and in terms of acceptable explanation
within that relationship.

(iii) *Topic and activity implications.* Of central relevance in
Schegloff's analysis for the study of explanations is the notion that a
particular formulation of place is relevant to the topic or activity to be
pursued. Thus the answer to "Where's John?" may well be "In the
library", if the speaker would like to have a word with him straight away
or "still in Oxford" if the speaker was thinking of organizing a party. The
choice of saying "I went to Zermatt" rather than "I went to Switzerland"

would also influence the topic in the unfolding of the interaction. Similarly the explanation for buying that house may be presented in different ways depending upon its topic and activity implications. If it is to another parent who lives in the neighbourhood an explanation may be offered that incorporates the local school. If to a horticulturist, the explanation may be in terms of the garden.

(iv) *Interpersonal consequences.* In his work on the philosophy of language, Austin (1962) points out that language is not simply a means for making statements that are true or false, but that it has consequences. "Saying things will often, or even normally, produce certain consequential effects upon the feelings, thoughts or actions of the audience, of the speaker or of other speakers" (p. 101). Attribution theory has paid some attention to the consequences of an explanation for the speaker himself. There have been a considerable range of studies into what has been called "self-serving biases" in attribution theory (see Zuckerman, 1979 for a review). Whether or not these are properly conceived of as biases is not of concern here. What is important is that explanations may serve to apportion praise or blame, to enhance or lower esteem. This may be achieved by presenting the appropriate sort of explanation for an action in a particular context. These "accounts" through which people attempt to excuse or justify their behaviour has been documented in the now classic paper by Scott and Lyman (1968) and elaborated by Tedeschi and Reiss in Chapter 12 of this volume. Where attribution theory has looked upon the attribution of cause and related questions concerning attribution of blame essentially as intra-personal events, Scott and Lyman see the excuses and justifications presented to other people very much as interpersonal actions.

Further, just as explanations can serve to excuse oneself from blame, so they can be used to focus blame or praise on some other person, or more generally attempt to persuade him to act in particular ways. A relevant example may be that of a child who has been caught stealing. The same person may present a range of different explanations to the variety of participants who may be involved in the episode. The shop-keeper may be told "He did it because you put them in a tempting place" if the intention is to get the shopkeeper to locate them differently; the child's parent may be told "he did it because you didn't give him enough pocket money" (if the objective is to give the child more money) or perhaps "because they were in such a tempting place" (in order to console), and in general conversation at the pub in terms of "because they are poor" or "because of the nature of youth today" or some such. In each of these cases the effects that may be produced by a particular explanation may be vital to their presentation in a particular context.

These are some of the factors that are likely to be related to the presentation of one explanation rather than another. These concepts can also be used to analyse whether or not the explanation will be accepted by the other person. Thus the explainer may make false assumptions concerning the other's knowledge, his criteria of relevance or the nature of their relationship. Further he may wish to embark on some topic or activity other than the one directed by the explanation provided, and finally he may desire particular consequences different from those desired by the explainer.

The approach taken in this section has been that explanations should be treated as events occurring within an interactional framework. Explanations are usually provided in response to questions, and indeed the approach taken here has been that the explainer is responding in terms of his assumptions concerning the intentions of the questioner. Questions too can be formulated in different ways which will have implications for the nature of the relevant answer. Thus, when asking about the same event the questioner may ask "Why did he steal the sweets?" or "Why did he steal?" or "Why did he break the law?" and the answers considered relevant in these cases will also differ. The specific context in which the question is raised is then an important element in the way in which the explanation is formulated. Thus returning to the example given by McArthur (1972) "John laughs at the comedian. Why?" the approach taken here would suggest that the appropriate answer would be given within the context in which the question was asked. Why ask the question in the first place? By doing so the questioner is already singling out the event as being worthy of explanation. The question could be asked in at least two rather different contexts.

(1) The questioner had heard the joke the comedian had just made and did not think it funny;

(2) The questioner, though he has not heard what the comedian has just said, knows that John does not usually laugh at comedians.
Raising the question in either of these differing contexts already implies different previous knowledge and assumptions. In fact they imply a different set of plausible explanations, and are likely to result in different sorts of search for information at the intra-pyschic level rather than search that is similar in nature, as implied by Kelley, as well as different explanations at the interpersonal level.

Thus we have argued against the attribution theory conception of the person as essentially concerned with making attributions to person or environmental causes. The alternative model proposed is that of a person providing an explanation to another in a particular social context. A range of interpersonal factors have been explored which can be seen as relating to the explanations presented and to their acceptance or rejection by the other.

Historical and cultural processes

The importance of the historical and cultural location of a social event has been stressed in an extremely influential paper by Gergen (1973). In Gergen's far-ranging discussion, he makes the point that the general emphasis of attribution theory of seeing people as origins of their own behaviour may be a culturally based phenomenon. Harré (Chapter 6) discusses the ethnocentricity of much of the work on attribution processes. Concern with prediction and control so pervasive in writings about attribution processes may be the function of a particular sort of religious and social orientation and different groups may see their control over the world in different ways. Research on locus of control, which can be seen as investigating systematically different ways of explaining events, shows significant differences as a function of societal factors. In his review of the literature, Phares (1976) suggests that American blacks are more externally oriented than whites, and that people of lower social status are more externally oriented than those of higher social status.

The relevance of historical and cultural location is particularly vital for the study of explanations, since particular cultures not only have different sorts of explanations open to them but also have different systems of categorization, and their cultural theories of the nature of events in the world and their conceptions of man may all be systematically different. It is within the context of these cultural categories and theories that any particular explanation will be invoked. In this section, some of these issues will be touched upon. The objective is to illustrate the issue and to emphasize the importance of the societally given in the analysis of explanations.

Different cultures construe the unity of the world in different ways. In the West, there is a fairly clear distinction between the animate and the inanimate. Further, man has traditionally been seen as fundamentally different from other beings, though the advent and popularization of Darwin's thought now permits explanations of human behaviour in terms of the continuity with other animals in a way which would have been considered outrageous a century ago. Other cultures assert a greater continuity between classes of being and ascribe life and agency in ways very different from that of the West (see for example, Levy-Bruhl, 1928). Ascribing "life" to rocks, and "agency" to trees, as well as ascribing particular powers to dead ancestors over those who are still living obviously make possible a range of explanations that are not open to most Westerners. The conceptions of particular sorts of events have also undergone considerable changes, often as a result of scientific advance. The cultural conception of an event would be related to the sorts of explanations for it that are dominant and readily acceptable in that culture. From the sixteenth century onwards illness has been generally conceived of as something entirely physical and has been characterized by a "body orientation" (Herzlich, 1973). Herzlich suggests that this was closely related to the development of anatomy and physiology. In France today however illness is seen in psycho-social as well as organic terms and the former sorts of explanations receive consideration as well as the latter. In her study of the conceptions of illness in present day France, Herzlich found that central to their notions of the causes of illness was the person's way of life, much of it to do with urbanisation with its noise, pollution and other hazards. Extrapolating from this one might expect that someone living in the city seeking to explain his illness in terms of the environment would find such an explanation readily available, but if a person living in the country attempts to explain lack of health with reference to the country environment (and Herzlich does refer to one such example), he would find it more difficult to make that explanation intelligible because it goes against the prevailing cultural conception of the causes of illness.

Herzlich does refer to the fact that illness is seen in different ways by different cultures. An important instance of this can be found in the work of Ngubane (1977) on Zulu medicine. Apparently the Zulu distinguish between two classes of illness: those that they see as the result of natural causes where the treatment is seen as empirically based and about which the Zulu may readily consult Western trained doctors, and those that are seen as rooted in the conditions of the Zulu social order where the cause is seen as mystical rather than natural and the treatment takes symbolic rather than empirical forms. Indeed the notion of illness as caused by sorcery or witchcraft is not open to a typical Westerner, but plays a vital role in the explanatory system of many other societies. The notion of witchcraft and the systematic way it is used in the explanatory system of the Azande, when it can be invoked and the consequences of its invocation have been discussed by Evans-Pritchard (1937), who emphasizes the coherent and functional role it plays in their explanatory system and their society.

Besides considering the relationship between different aspects of the world and the cultural conceptions of different sorts of events, man's conception of himself would make a fundamental difference to the sorts of questions that are considered explanation-worthy, the sorts of explanations sought, and those that are likely to be considered acceptable. There seems to have been little work done in this area. Thus while reviewing research on socialization, Zigler and Child (1969) point out that the orientation of different researchers in the area can be conceptualized in terms of whether they see the child as primarily active or primarily passive, and whether they see him as fundamentally good or fundamentally evil. But what of the parents' views of the child? Do they see him as active or passive, as good or evil? If he is seen as primarily active, then presumably his activity does not have to be explained, but passivity will, and vice versa. Assumptions concerning the inherent goodness or otherwise of children has played an important part in educational debate (see Tucker, 1977). But our conception of the child has undergone marked changes and Coveney (1967) has documented the changes in the portrayal of the child in English literature. Early representations under the influence of Rousseau and the romantics portrayed the child as innocence; twentieth century treatments, after the publication of Freud's essay on infantile sexuality, are very different. Tucker also quotes Aries who maintains that the whole notion of childhood is something that has been built up in Europe in the last 300 years. Before that apparently the notion of the child as a separate sort of category of person did not exist. This would suggest that certain explanations and acceptable excuses for a child's behaviour in terms of his childish status ("He's only a child") would be unacceptable and attribution of powers to the child to accomplish certain ends would also be different. Again Margaret Mead (1928) has suggested that the conception of adolescence prevalent in the West is not shared by other cultures, and again the particular sorts of explanations for the behaviour of an adolescent would be constrained by the nature of the cultural conceptions of that stage of life.

In the more limited domain Averill (1974) puts into historical perspective the contrast in current psychological thinking, and presumably in lay thinking, between emotions and intellect. Emotions are generally seen in negative terms. They are looked upon as irrational, brutish, "biological", and less than completely within our control. Supporting evidence for such a view of emotions by the layman can be found in the study of McArthur (1972), who showed that emotions are seen as more situationally caused than, for instance, are actions. Such a conception of emotions enables one to offer explanations of emotional behaviour in terms of "being carried away" and serve as a device for reducing blame. Averill argues that the distinction is the result of a tradition in Western thought that goes back to Plato and is based on preconception and simplistic conceptualization rather than evidence. Certainly different cultures see emotions in very different ways (Izard, 1971). It also seems likely that emotions are by no means the only area where different cultures may ascribe different degrees of control to human functioning. Thus Scott and Lyman (1968) report that in first and second generation Italians in America the belief that sex is the inevitable product of biological factors if a male and female are alone together can serve as an excuse for sexual relations, at least for men. But lest this seems an argument entirely in favour of historical and cultural differences, it may be worth referring to the work of Douglas (1970) who has argued that attitudes to the self and to the body are related in systematic, if complex, ways to more general aspects of social structure and cosmological beliefs.

Concluding comments

Attribution theory has been concerned with only a limited subset of issues that should be considered by a psychology of explanations. Its focus has been exclusively on intra-personal processes, and indeed with a limited subset of these. The analysis provided here has attempted to show that interpersonal and societal processes are a vital part of any psychology of explanations. The inter-relationships that have been drawn between these three levels implies that investigation of all these levels is vital to the understanding of explanations in everyday life.

The emphasis on causal explanation, and on the perceiver's making attributions of causality to personal or situational forces may have proved a productive starting point in an unexplored area; these tenets now remain as unnecessary theoretical and empirical blinkers. Broadly, attribution theory ignores a variety of social processes. Its conception of how people make attributions, characterized here as that of an inductivist counting instances along dimensions of consensus, consistency and distinctiveness, ignores the fact that a person already has a variety of plausible explanations for an event. Rather than engage in a general inductive information search he is more likely to look for specific information to help him sort the explanations he already has. The information search for different sorts of events is likely to be different, though systematically guided by his hypotheses. These hypotheses are unlikely to be idiosyncratic, many must be culturally derived. Further, the conception of the person as making attributions to personal or situational forces fails to take into account the fact that explanations are provided to other people in particular contexts. An analysis of interpersonal contexts leads to the view that people would make systematically different sorts of explanation in different sorts of context. Indeed a person may, for one and the same event, make person attributions in one interpersonal context and situational explanations in another. Finally, explanations have to be acceptable, a concept that highlights their social nature. They are embedded not only in interpersonal context but in societal contexts as well.

Thus an analysis of explanations must involve consideration of a range of different sorts of processes. The broad categories into which different cultures classify different sorts of events and the cultural conceptions of these events form the backdrop within which particular sorts of explanations for an event may be developed. In order to relate these explanations to a particular instance, the individual engages in a search for relevant disambiguating information. The explanation is provided to particular other people in a given social context and has both intra-psychic and interpersonal consequences. Widening one's perspective to include the processes discussed clarifies the shortcomings of attribution theory in its own domain of interest and points to a new range of issues that are susceptible to empirical investigation.

6

Expressive Aspects of Descriptions of Others

R. Harré

Introduction

The critical discussion of any project in social psychology must include the consideration that the activities of social psychologists themselves are social psychological events to which the theory, or theories, that are being promoted must be applicable. Nowhere is this more strikingly the case than when what is being promoted is a psychological theory about ordinary theories. Here the psychologist is peculiarly vulnerable: he will be making claims about the activity which he himself could be accused of engaging in (if calling what he does "ordinary theorizing" is indeed an accusation) and he must suffer anything he says to be used in evidence, possibly against himself. The example of a psychological theory about ordinary theories that I want to examine for what this potential reflexivity throws up is a theory which has had a very clear exposition in this volume (Harris and Harvey, Chapter 3) and which is much adverted to elsewhere in the book and has had an influence throughout the social psychological literature. This is, of course, attribution theory (Heider 1958; Jones and Davis 1965; Kelley 1967; Jones *et al.*, 1972), the theory of the way dispositions and other explanatory properties and conditions are attributed to other people by speakers.

Amongst the speakers who make attributions to other people are social psychologists, so attribution theory which has been offered to us as a theory *in* social psychology, must also be examined as a theory *of* social psychology. Some of the work in attribution theory has been particularly naive with respect to this reflexive demand. In particular, I shall single out work of Kelley *et al.* (Kelley, 1967; 1972a, b; see also Harris and Harvey, this volume). The absence of any consideration of the reflexivity requirement can only be due, I believe, to the assumption by many attribution theorists that they can study the causation of action, in particular the causation of the action of making an attribution, without themselves making attributions to others, in much the same way as ordinary people describe and judge their friends. Further, in order for this assumption to be justified, there would have to be some theory that encouraged the treatment of the causes of action as external determinants and indeed that is just what we find in Kelley's studies. What we need to know about Kelley's model of ordinary explanations is that the schema he proposes is one which applies logical rules of causal inference to identified causal candidates (Kelley, 1972a, b). The candidates his scheme allows are any forces which are understandable as being within the person, within the environment, or coming from some combination of the two. There is a stronger form of his argument in which *any* causal candidates are so catergorizable — that is that these three ideas will account for *any* cause one advances for why somebody did something — and it is not always clear in his writing which form of the argument is being endorsed; but the weaker and the stronger versions share the notion that what the explainer is doing is reacting to some combination of such causes and attributing the appropriate one as a matter of logical information processing, the question of differences in causal status between environmental and personal causation entirely shelved. According to this underlying theory Kelley can, for example, talk of the determinants of attribution as "situation and target person" (!) and compound this peculiar way of talking by speaking of an attribution by the subject (the speaker) to the target (the one spoken about) as the "behaviour".

Such terminology is not neutral. Quite apart from the orthodox methodological difficulties it raises, which Lalljee (Chapter 5) and van der Pligt (Chapter 4) deal with, this sort of talk leads us to look upon the attribution not as part of a considered, or even unconsidered, piece of deliberate action in which all kinds of matters germane to the involvement of the subject — so-called — or actor, can be brought into the investigation, but merely asks us to see it as a Humean concomitance between an external treatment and an external response to that treatment.

A first step in freeing ourselves from the naiveté of such forms of investigation as have been practised by Kelley *et hoc genus* is to drop this curious terminology in favour of more accurate forms of description. I will return to detail these below. Now, by paying attention to the implicit metaphysical theory which, via the choice of terminology, is controlling the investigations undertaken by Kelley, we can free ourselves of unacknowledged assumptions. Then the problem of understanding the way people describe others can be approached in a much more empirical fashion. In particular we must raise the question of the reflexivity of attribution theory as an empirical fact about psychologists — such a question can be formulated only when the Humean metaphysics of causality has been cleared away. Kelley knows that *he* is not attributing processes, properties, moral qualities, etc. to a target person on the basis of situational determinants. He knows he is a rational being with his own collectively sanctioned personal projects in the light of which he says things about others, e.g. his subjects. Our problem, as reformers, is to persuade Kelley that the people he has studied are rather like himself. So, a *desideratum* of any treatment of the problem of understanding the systematic character of ordinary explanations must deal with the possibility that those who are studying ordinary explanations are themselves giving an ordinary explanation, or if they are not, they must justify their decision not to do so.

In order to understand what one is being offered in a published report in the social psychological literature as it is currently produced, we must ask "How was the material which is publicly represented in the literature as 'results' generated?" This is particularly pressing when we are assessing material produced in the United States, since the very particular character of the social world that has been created in that culture makes for a heavily ethnocentric influence on any work. The most prominent ethnocentric features for which one must be on the lookout can be brought out by pursuing the question of whether the work was done by asking people to deal with, and produce, documents, or whether it was concerned with actions and speech in the real world. There is a very strong tendency in the United States to create a surrogate world of paper, "documents" which for many practical purposes stand for real things and, in particular, for real people. We must ask, then, whether the studies reported are studies of how people handle personality documents — for example how people make written attributions of explanatory psychological attributes to others, or deal with others' written attributions. A survey of the literature shows quite unequivocably that most of the literature presented as the "results" was generated from documentary work undertaken by the folk. On the rare occasions when the studies presented people with non-documentary data to think about, the people's deliberations were cast willy-nilly into an attributional form that made sense only if the data *had been* documentary in the first place. Orvis *et al.* (1978), for example, asked people to consider the causes of their spouse's behaviour (as they remembered it) but then coded the results as if the behaviours had been presented to the subjects in a form that only allowed certain sorts of explanations to be offered, i.e. as documents reporting the events as some combination of personal and environmental cause, rather than as memories of events with nego-tiated meanings, troublesome definitions, unspoken reproach, implied blame and so on and so forth.

The ethnocentricity of much of the work is also revealed by teasing out the implicit values which are central to the way in which the enterprise has been carried out. In particular, it seems clear that middle class American values are prominent. This is revealed perhaps most vividly in the Jones *et al.* (1961) study of people's attributions about applicants for a job. People were presented with a recording of someone applying for either an astronaut's or a submariner's job and saying things the subject had been forewarned would be either consistent or inconsistent with a successful self-presentation (the submariner/astronaut pair was chosen because subjects could be told that good presentation in one interview was bad presentation in the other, so the experiment could neatly be designed to use only one set of recordings). When the applicant was heard to be saying things consistent with the job he was applying for (e.g. if it was for the submariner's job, being obedient, cooperative and friendly) the subject found nothing particularly informative about his behaviour — on the other hand, if he said the wrong things, subjects concluded that he *really was* demanding rather than obedient, author-itarian rather than cooperative, etc. As Jones and Davis (1965) and Kelley (1972, a) later interpreted it, this was a concrete example of the importance of out-of-role behaviour in generating explanations; it became a cornerstone of attribution theory that the social events to be investigated were special ones, odd ones, where the experimenter could easily manipulate the story to make the behaviour look unusual or peculiar: other, more normal behaviour, in more naturalistic settings, was cold-shouldered out of the reckoning for being, by definition, unin-formative to the lay explainer. It is most striking that in-role behaviour carrying out set routines does not call for special explanations from the folk, whereas out-of-role behaviour does; but it seems that the first thing to say is that this is a feature of social life as it is lived in the United States. It is unlikely to be true of other cultures. It may not even be wholly true of the United States. In their methodological researchers American microsociologists (such as Garfinkel) have tended to show that where the social action is improvised the folk are in possession of explanatory frameworks which, if called for, they can produce. The second thing to say is that this feature, namely that routine behaviour does not call for explanations, reveals further assumptions not only amongst the folk, whose attributions are being studied, but amongst the psychologists studying them. The very idea than an experiment can be used to study folk psychology and its method of theorizing suggests that such theorizing is, as it were, "brought on" by certain conditions. This depends upon the idea that people are automata to be trained rather than actors in a drama of self-presentation to be produced. This reflects a very deep-seated feature of the social order in the United States, namely the routinization of a great many forms of social interaction, a matter to which I shall be returning later.

Now this assumption, which is very deeply involved in the way attribution theory investigations have been carried out has been noticed by some investigators. Jones and Davis, for example, do notice the possibility that there are self-presentational factors at work (ibid., pp. 236−246). I shall be arguing later that the matter should be turned on its head, that is we should be asking whether there is anything but self-presentational matters at work.

The conclusion of all this suggests that there must be two sides to attribution theory — taken as a theory of how people attribute causality in their explanation of social events — if it is to be a viable field of investigation at all.

(a) There must first, of course, be the investigation of how we can explain other people's actions. I shall be arguing that such an investigation must involve a form of theorizing which brings together dispositionalist attributions modulated by the well-attested principle that the sets of dispositions displayed by human beings, are, or tend to be, particular to the kinds of occasions they take themselves to be acting out. And there must be a theory of expressive self-presentation. These elements in any theory of social action are not independent, since the set of dispositions which a person reveals by acting in certain ways on a particular occasion are partly explicable as elements in an expressive self-presentation. Action can be seen as a demonstration for other people providing them with evidence to come to believe that the actor is the way he wants to seem to be. Getting people to assign one's actions to a certain set of dispositions is a move in the game of generating impressions by expressive action. Ultimately, that game is, of course, directed to the more universal human projects of maintaining dignity, seeking for respect, and avoiding the contempt of others.

(b) The moment one introduces some sense of reality into the theorizing, that is begins to pay attention to the dramaturgical conventions of self-presentation involved in the kind of action which one is investigating, one must, if we follow the argument in the first section of this paper, take this point reflexively. In order to understand how psychologists might set about explaining the actions of their fellow-actors, including, of course, their own attributions about other folk, we must pay attention to the self-presentational dramaturgy of social psychologists. Social psychologists are no more immune to the contagion of the cognitions they study than are microbiologists against their viruses; the latter, of course, take stringent precautions against infection, but I can see no evidence of this amongst attribution theorists. Duck (1981) makes the point that social psychologists in general are astonishingly slow to recognize themselves in the people they study, and I want to bring out how attribution theorists, as Americans, scientists and researchers concerned with ordinary attributions, are particularly, and dangerously, slow. On what conventions do they act in order to present themselves on occasions of doing social psychology as they would wish to seem to be? Now one must ask, according to what "self-image of the age", to use Alastair McIntyre's felicitious phrase, are these presentations organized? And the answer is, of course, "As scientist". Now, if we return to the considerations of the first two sections of this paper, that is the ethnocentric features of attribution research as conducted in the United States, these features become immediately explicable as self-presentational conventions in a dramaturgy of what in that culture is taken to be presenting oneself as "scientist". The peculiar terminology that we noted in Kelley's writings, such as "situation and target person" and the use of the word "behaviour" to describe a mode of speaking, and the uncritical use of the word "experiment", are revealed as rhetorical devices in the "social work" done in the expressive order to demonstrate (provide evidence for) the reading by others that psychology is, or aspires to be, a science.

Do we need the rhetoric of scientism over and above the rhetorical devices in use amongst the ordinary folk? I am not clear that any good justification has been produced for a scientistic rhetoric. In general, the dramatization of real life events involves highlighting some aspects, radically simplifying much of the action, subjecting the plot to aesthetic and other criteria which are not normally present, at least in a dominant form, in everyday life. And, indeed, the same goes for a dramatization of what it is to play the role of scientist. The use of a technical terminology and the performance of "experiments" are very superficial features of what it is to be a scientist in, say, a biological or physical field. The underlying interest in the causal mechanisms of nature is obscured by paying attention only to those rather superficial features of the drama. The ethogenic approach insists that every account must be taken seriously as a form of dramatic self-presentation, but examined ironically as a representation of the motivations of those taking part in the event, and folk psychology is shot through with this kind of irony. In that event it must have methodological priority until it is demonstrated to be defective. If for example one discovers that the asymmetry in attribution of traits (depending upon whether one is oneself the actor or one is attributing these traits to others as actors) is a feature of the dramaturgy of self-presentation in everyday life, this must be carried forward reflexively to understand the pseudo-scientific terminology of social psychologists themselves. For example, if a social psychologist such as Kelley attributes to his subjects dispositions or traits to make assymetrical attributions, what role does that play in his own dramaturgy of self-presentation? Would, for example, he attribute that trait to himself, qua psychologist?

The propositional-inferential assumption

I have pointed out the extent to which the work done by most investigators in the field of attribution research is highly ethnocentric. It involves assumptions which are unexamined, largely, I believe, because they are the very stuff of social process in the United States. Now, we have still to show that the ethnocentrism of the investigators generates bad methodology. One feature to which I drew attention was the use of a documentary form in the usual work. Written descriptions of people, situations, etc. feature as the material upon which the folk are asked to work, and rating-scales and similar documents are the devices by which they are asked to make their attributions. In consequence the skills that are drawn upon are those involved in understanding matter which is presented in either written or some other verbal form. Now this is a quite distinctive kind of activity from that which is involved, say, in gossiping. In the gossip I have listened to many enjoyable sessions of character-assasination, the material produced is rich in attributions, in ordinary explanations of the behaviour, from social to motor, of other people. Now, what is involved in using a methodology which concentrates the attention of the folk on documents? Clearly, one unexamined assumption is that attribution is a mode of propositional reasoning, since the folk are asked to consider descriptions of people and situations and then to perform a propositional act, namely marking a rating-scale. Now it may be that the way in which attribution, though it takes the form of a propositional expression, is "done", is as a mode of perceiving. Though I do not wish to be thought defending that particular proposal myself, it must be taken into account as a possibility. It is easy to see, if one looks at Kelley's revealing remarks, (1973, pp. 107–128) that the issue of *how* attribution is done, i.e. by what cognitive processes the attributive sentence is arrived at, is pre-empted by the choice of methodology. At the risk of going over familiar ground let us remind ourselves that the methodology adopted by Kelley, and a very large number of other experimental social psychologists investigating social explanations, involves presenting people with hypothetical stories which they are asked to explain by indicating the degree to which various possible candidates might have caused the reported events. Not only is the *form* of the explanation (attribution of cause) fixed (why not allow people to redescribe the events? or deny they happened?) but the very processes the psychologist advertises himself as being concerned with — the translation of perceptions of the world into cognitions about it — are entirely cut out of the picture: instead of a psychology of how causes (if we limit ordinary explanation to just that) are *seen* — in the ordinary sense of "anyone can see the husband's to blame" or "can't you see he's being driven to it" etc. — one has instead a methodology for the investigation of how causes are *logically arrived at* from the psychologist's own perception and representation of the world.

The position I am defending for interpreting the conditions under which folk explanations are given, and their meaning, is that we should at least begin with dramaturgical assumptions. But by adopting the documentary/laboratory method, Kelley has pre-supposed that the processes of ordinary folk attributions are propositional/inferential rather than, let us say, impression-management/expression-production. He has not even entertained the possibility that the psychological processes are comparable to those by which actors perform in a play. Now just as his choice of method has effectively prevented the raising of the question of whether the features of folk attribution are perspectival, to be understood on a perceptual analogy, so he has effectively prevented a raising of the question of whether they are dramaturgical, to be understood on the analogy of the way actors produce their performances. So some key questions simply cannot be raised by virtue of the ethnocentric assumptions which have been built into the methodology, and as I shall show in a later section, there are more possibilities than those I have raised here.

The danger of slipping into a propositional inferential way of thinking about psychological processes is perennial. Even Secord and Backman (1974) — admittedly quoting Eckmann, though with approval — fall into a similar muddle. "The *face* conveys information about the nature of an emotion", they say (p. 48), missing altogether the distinction between "expressing an emotion" which one might do with one's face and "giving evidence for the inference of the existence of an emotion" which is a wholly other matter, since it presupposes that the emotion is, as it were, hidden, and the facial expression is not part of it. This way of talking pre-empts the question of the emotion theory to adopt. Darwin's view, which now seems to be well-established, is that the actual musculature and its movements is to be considered as a formative part of human emotions.

If I have sounded rather severe in my attitude to Kelley's work, it is not because it is wholly without merit. Kelley notices that members of collectives are possessed of a variety of schemata according to which they identify the sources of the action of others. But this merit, important though it is, is seriously undermined by the assumption that these are inferential schemata. It seems to me clear that such an assumption is a direct consequence of the adoption of the documentary methodology, which is itself a direct consequence of the ethnocentricity of the investigators.

But adopting, for example, and for the moment, a dramaturgical way of treating the process of folk explanation, or attribution of dispositions, praise and blame, etc. to others, allows us to introduce Kantian schemata into our analytical apparatus, and to consider whether, in all of this we are deploying for our own projects' sake, *Weberian ideal types*. So that when we discover empirically what sort of attributions have been made, on what kinds of occasions, we must also ask in order to unravel the underlying processes by which these are done, how, on these occasions, each of us has seen the other; *as* "a villain", *as* "bureacrat", etc. . . .

REINTERPRETATIONS OF THE "DATA"

A very influential piece of work done in attribution theory is Jones and Nisbett's (1972) account of the differences between a performer's and an observer's view of an action. Their proposal is that this difference is due to differences in the information available to the two people and to their different perceptual viewpoints: the actor knows more about the history, etc. of the action, and the actor is more attentive to the things around him that he needs to navigate to carry the action out. The observer does not know the background to the action, the man's intention and so on: and, as a matter of Gestalt principle, his eye is drawn to the performer rather than to the background against which he moves. According to Jones and Nisbett, these two differences account for actors' tendency to attribute the causes of their behaviour to the environment (other people, fate, requests, demands, coercions and so on) and for observers to attribute them to the performer himself (his intentions, longstanding dispositions, traits, beliefs, policy and so on). The question is, will a strictly perceptual/informational account really cover it?

If we look at the matter dramaturgically we have to ask what sort of personal presentations are involved in the events documents describing which have been the major source of published work on attribution theory. It seems clear that what is at stake is the success of a personal impression in the eyes of others as one expresses oneself as self-reliant and *trained* to respond automatically, to produce the routine required so that failure must be put down to some sort of disposition and similarly so must success. It seems clear, then, that the asymmetry that is apparent in the Jones and Davis discussion of the attributions to job candidates, that is that appropriate action does not seem to call for explanation, is just because it fulfills in perfect measure the dramaturgy of self-presentation as "trained". The routinization of life would, of course, be prepresented dramaturgically by the explanation of action as straight determined. Now it is also clear why the actor-spectator paradox appears, since if the culture calls for me to present myself as fully trained, to respond automatically to the demands of the situation, then of course the only thing that can go wrong is some untoward event in the environment with which I have been trained to deal. Now it is easy to see why the actor will tend to explain failures environmentally, but in his self-presentations with inter-actor, will want to represent inter-actor as ill-trained, i.e. not possessed of traits, dispositions etc. which represent the routinization of action from his point of view. What I should stress is that what I am invoking is the idea of the culture's effect on people — not the more personalistic idea of individual desire and disingenuousness. One example of what I do not mean is Bradley's (1978) "self-defensive attribution" which accounts for the assymetry by the personalistic theory that blaming everyone but oneself is a good strategy for a performer when things go wrong, but not when things go right. What I am saying here is that since a theory of self-defence like this cannot do for accounting for *ordinarily* "successful", i.e. run of the mill, actions, we need to look above the personal level of explanation and ask how such an assymetry of attributions could come about as a consequence of the culture, peer-group, etc. being constituted in such-and-such a way, or having this or that rule of conduct. Here I favour the idea that our culture — and the American culture — has amongst its prescriptions the rule that we should be, and be seen to be, competent trained performers of *any* social behaviour, including the most mundane; in other words, the rule that any piece of social behaviour is up for potential critical evaluation before one's peers. Once again it is worth returning the point of the first section, that since the very methodology which has been adopted by social psychologists pursuing these studies is itself an instance of the dramaturgy, i.e. the publication of the results is itself a step in the presentation of oneself as fulfilling one's training in the routinization of an activity, that dramaturgy cannot be brought under scrutiny as a topic of interest. Thus we get a feature of the local ethnography offered as a law of nature. This is exemplified by the idea that an in-role behaviour does not need explanation.

If we turn away from a culture in which the question of training and routinization is paramount and must necessarily dominate attribution theory at its first level or reflexively, we can find enormous variety of other forms of folk-attributions. There are those which involve the grace of God; there are those which involve the machinations of witches, there are those which involve attributions of wickedness, bad faith, and so on, there are those which involve the attributions of party loyalty, or even ideologically self-concealed class-position, and so on. It would be of the greatest interest to systematically investigate the kinds of attributions that are made in a confessional, both by priest to the parishioner and the parishioner to those he has wronged. There is a vast literature of attributions in folk explanations among the Azandi and other Africans, stemming from Evans-Pritchard's seminal works on these matters. This material, which has the virtue of being non-experimental and not involving folk work on documents, lies fallow for the next generation of attribution-theorists.

CONSEQUENTIAL CAUTIONS

In order to transform attribution-theory from a theory in social psychology to a theory *of* social psychology, a theory which includes itself, we must take note of a number of points.

(a) The act of attribution must, as it were, "pass through" impression management. From the point of view of one who wishes to present himself as making scientific attributions I have already pointed out that much of the work of ascribing psychological attributes and moral stances to others involves dramaturgy, but it is important also to see that these attributions, and discussions about their correctness among the folk, are also liable to rely upon personal projects of actor and attributor alike, personal projects which involve efforts to be seen and "have" certain propositions and intentions. Long ago, John Austin pointed out that the best way to pretend to be a window-cleaner is to clean the windows. In the same spirit it may be that we shall discover that the folk believe that the best way to seem to have proper dispositions and intentions is indeed to have them, though providing evidence that one has certain dispositions in what one says and does is a rather complex project.

(b) If this is the case we ought to expect that the accounts that people give, or systematic discussion in speech, are a gloss on the actions of self and others; one ought not to expect these to be in one to one correspondence with actions as true descriptions of causes, interpretations of the actions and intentions of others, i.e. in accordance with the meanings and intentions of those actors. But accounts must be seen as part of the apparatus of expression-management on any particular occasion (see Tedeschi and Reiss's chapter for one view of this). In the ethogenic theory it is only in the long run that there is an expectation of the content of accounts and the meaning and intentions of actors must be coordinated, since in the end the same body of knowledge is deployed in accounting as is deployed in acting. Once again this point illustrates that attribution theory, like any other theory of psychology, must take account of the radical distinctions between a competence-theory which sets out systematically the knowledge necessary to act adequately in a certain milieu, and a performance-theory, the theory of how on particular occasions the appropriate actions are generated. Account analysis, the ethogenic version of attribution theory, whether folk or professional, is only unproblematic when it is considered as the source of a competence-theory. This distinction has not been taken by attribution-theorists who suppose that they themselves as attributing psychological processes to actors, are immune from that distinction.

Kellian performance-theories, whether folk or professional, are epistemically more complex since, as I have pointed out, performances always involve some form of impression management and that involves folk-attributions at the performance level, so as to be attributed to the "right" contingencies and that, of course, is a meta-intention of an actor in a particular situation. Now we have yet to investigate in any systematic way the meta-intention of attribution-theorists to themselves in making folk attributions, i.e. as members of a scientific collective to those that they are pleased to call subjects.

Attribution theory and the work of Jones

The studies that are summed up in Jones and Davis (1965), the *locus classicus* of attribution theory, derive from Heider (1958) and by virtue of that fact alone are more conceptually sophisticated than the simple experimentalist work with which I have been so far concerned. Nevertheless, the studies reported in that important article almost wholly miss the self-presentational aspect of social life, which I have been at pains to emphasize in my criticism of the documentary approach adopted by Kelley. Partly as a consequence of this, and partly as a reason for this neglect, Jones's work seems to assume dispositionalist psychology, i.e. that whether lay or professional, the form of the psychological theory is the attribution of the disposition. Now, of course, this is just the leading and problematic feature of folk-talk about other folk. How does it come about that people do use dispositionalist talk in their discussions with others? The language, as Ryle (1949) and Bromley (1977) have pointed out, is full of dispositionalist terms. How is this accounted for by attribution theory? If it is itself dispositionalist, it will see no particular peculiarity about ordinary people's dispositionalist talk and see no particular reason to have to account for it. Certainly the Jones and Davis (1965) model of explanations was strongly dispositional, assuming that people process information about an action for the sole purpose of arriving, if possible, at a disposition of the actor's that would account for it; quite why dispositions should be assumed to play such an important part in people's explanations of the social world was left unexamined. More recently, qualms among attribution theorists about the coherence of the "dispositional/environmental cause" pair have encouraged some thinking about dispositions, but this has tended, with the exception of Monson and Snyder (1977), to be a matter of rethinking how best to define dispositional versus environmental attribution (e.g. Ross 1977; Buss 1978) rather than any symptom of a doubt about the validity of the dispositionalism that Jones's theory shares with ordinary theorizing; the occasional voices one hears actually offering alternatives to this dispositionalism (e.g. Kruglanski's ends/means, 1975) are cries from the back of the room and do not have much effect on the attribution theory speeches at the front.

The most important contribution of Jones to social psychology has been the famous actor-spectator paradox. The paradox, let us remind ourselves, is that A's action will be explained by A as externally caused, but by his audience B as personally caused; the very same action now carried out by B will be attributed by B to the environment but by A to B. There can be no question of the reality of this phenomenon, it seems to me. But it is by no means unproblematic: Antaki and McCloskey (1978) have demonstrated, in a study summarized in van der Pligt's chapter, that the appearance of the paradox in folk psychological theorizing depends upon the expressive state of the game, i.e. the moral climate, in which the events in question are to be explained. So that if some kind of personal merit, value, prestige, etc. is at issue, somewhere in the background of the event, then one would expect the actor-spectator paradox to appear in an asymmetry of attribution between oneself and another. But the explanation of how it can be that Jones and Nisbett propose this paradox as a universal law must surely be the ethnocentrism of the investigators, which reflects the moment by moment personal competitiveness that is such a characteristic feature of society in the United States. So the first caveat one must enter derives both from Antaki's empirical studies and reflection on the conditions under which the empirical work to reveal the asymmetry between actor-spectator attributions is carried out.

But there is a second feature of this paradox which is worth further contemplation. Why is it that the asymmetry of attribution exists in those *milieux* and under those moral conditions under which it does exist? What is it a reflection of? One view which has become popular is that the actor-spectator assymetry ought to be considered as an illusion either analogous to a perceptual illusion, or reduceable to one. Certainly Nisbett, in an empirical paper demonstrating the theory (Nisbett *et al.*, 1973) lays great stress on the perceptual angle: "the major reason for the divergent perspectives (of actors' and observers' accounts) is probably a simple perceptual one" (ibid., p. 154). Now a perceptual illusion involves non-disposable ways of seeing and hearing, etc. which we systematically discount. It is the non-disposability of perceptual illusions which is a central feature of the concept of illusion as we ordinarily use it and this distinguishes illusions from mistakes and errors. Now it seems clear that there is some element of the Jones and Nisbett asymmetry which can quite properly be assimilated to the idea of an illusion. The question remains, I think, as to whether that illusion should be seen to be reduceable to different ways of perceiving the same event from different standpoints as if it were a simple matter of perspective, or whether this should be considered as a metaphorical use of the notion. Nevertheless, the question of the non-disposability and the discountability both arise. I would argue something like this : provided that the moral climate is stable, i.e. that the interaction between the actor and spectator involves a generally competitive relation, then one would expect that the tendency to explain mistakes and errors in a similar way to that which is found in the Jones-Nisbett asymmetry would continue. But it might well be that the stabilization of long-term personal relationships involves the ritualization of the Jones-Nisbett asymmetry, that is, this simply becomes a way of speaking and its cognitive content is discounted for most cases, unless some expressive purpose is to be served. There ought to be evidence in transcripts of family events such as discussions escalating into quarrels, which would enable one to get at this hypo-thetical feature of talk to see if it could be empirically founded. Attribu-tion theory workers themselves come tantalizingly close to giving us the sort of data we want here: Orvis *et al.* (1978), for example, ask for accounts of couples' misunderstandings, but choose to take snapshots of the data rather than anything more sensitive to the way such accounts are negotiated between partners: each misunderstanding is treated as a *case* (the preoccupation with documents again) and the partners are segregated to give separate accounts. The data are frozen still more by being categorized not according to, say, statements' use in self-defence, exoneration, blame, etc. — obvious categories when the moral climate is a defensive or rationalizing one — but in the ubiquitous causal attribu-tion categories.

But why, in a deeper sense, do Jones and Nisbett get their results, and Antaki gets his? We have to look a little more closely at the dramaturgy of the set-up in the experiment. Provided there is a clear display of the moral climate in which the attributions are to take place, as is achieved in Antaki's study, then we are able to see how far the dramaturgical demands on that moral plane affect the way explaining speech is produced. But where there is no dramaturgy and no clear indication of the moral climate, actors, it seems, fall back on exhibiting the relevant conceptual relations, in this case what they would exhibit would be the conceptual structure of the concept of the person. Now an attribution theory would appear as disguised conceptual analysis. We owe to Glenn Langford (1978) a very subtle investigation of the necessary conditions for a being to have the concept that it is a person among persons. Those necessary conditions have some interesting consequences. Suppose we consider the relationships between concepts held by two persons A and B. Langford has demonstrated that A must suppose that B sees him A as a person of lesser degree of autonomy than A takes himself to be. So A must present himself to B as within an explanatory framework coordinate with that conceptual distinction, i.e. as being in command of himself. But B actually sees A as like himself, hence B presents A to himself B in an explanatory framework coordinate with that conceptual distinction. Now, it seems that whatever A attributes to B will make B seem less autonomous to himself, but whatever A attributes to himself, particularly if he wishes B to continue to see him as an autonomous being, when he is in error or incompetent, as not "himself". The Jones and Nisbett paradox, then, appears quite straightforwardly as a reflection of the conceptual structure of the concept of a person as it is and must be maintained by those who see others as persons too.

Summary

What, then, for the methodology of attribution theory? Before I, as commonsense theorist, can make attributions about your mental state, the courses of your actions, and so on, I must:

(i) have my own dramaturgical project worked out and your role in it defined, as clown, straight man, partner, and so on, since *my attributions to you will subserve my scenario*;

(ii) I must also have some grasp of your dramaturgical project and my role in it, hence I can decode your actions to spot your meta-intentions and projects. Only then do I know how to read the evidence you are feeding me and to find my own evidence if my project runs counter to yours.

What about the attribution theorist considered reflexively? Well, as a social scientist he too has a project of self-presentation and it is to give grounded explanations of whatever it is that he has been able to discern as a non-random pattern of reality. The argument of this paper is intended to suggest that the best move for those who wish to present themselves as social psychologists is to deploy a form of explanation that is already present in the very attribution processes they are trying to understand, since that form of explanation is sanctioned by its similarity to those in the natural sciences and, even more particularly, to those used in linguistics. The social psychologist must begin by deploying an analytical model. The dramaturgical standpoint which I have been using for expository purposes in this paper is only one among many such possibilities. Having revealed the texture of the event he wishes to understand he must come to see it in terms of two cognitive processes, both involving personal intentions and public symbolic actions including speech. There is the disambiguation of the events in question to the degree the occasion demand, and secondly, there is the justification of the actions taken relative to them and the negotiation of those justifications as a public process relative to the given moral climate. In that way the social psychologist will have produced both an attribution and an explanation of the attributions that have been made by those who are taking part in the event.

In their interesting paper which forms Chapter 3 of this volume Harris and Harvey make some thoughtful criticisms of the use of the ethogenic approach in the study of attribution. Essentially their criticisms, or perhaps one ought to say more accurately, their reservations, reduce to two. Are we to explain the mistakes, accidents and incoherences of everyday life in the same sort of terms as we would explain the successful and orderly aspects of it? It is to the latter that the ethogenic approach seems particularly apt. To this I would be inclined to reply that the excesses of ethnomethodology have at least had this upshot, that we must understand the way people cope with accidents and incompetences, misfires and misplays, is itself part of the presentational devices by which they strive to maintain themselves in good standing in the eyes of others and so maintain their moral career. The first question to ask is, "Do people feel demeaned by certain happenings?" and if they do feel so demeaned, how do they cope with that? By what ways are these demeanings remedied? So, a natural extension of the ethogenic way of looking at the process of the genesis of everyday life can, I think, include accident.

A more serious point is their view that there is a role for experimental work to test hypotheses. Now I do not wish to rehearse the standard objections to the experimental way of conducting empirical research as opposed to, say, the observational or role-replication, and so on. Suffice to point out that what is taken to be an experiment in traditional social psychology is that appropriate to the testing of a simple causal relation which is thought to obtain between one sort of *event* and another. Now, it is not at all clear that social life consists of events. Another central doctrine of the ethogenic approach is that much of social life is to be considered as the modulation of structures with the preservation of certain invariances, or, in other cases, the genesis of structures from pre-existing structured templates such as the rules of action which pre-exist the performance of a ceremonial occasion. Now you cannot test structural hypotheses by the old-fashioned, simple-minded experiment. Structural hypotheses in all the natural sciences are tested by the replication of the reality of which one supposes one knows the structure. For example, the test of whether we really understand the structure of an organic molecule is if we can synthesize it. If we really understand the grammar of a language, we can produce for ourselves, from that understanding sentences which are recognized by the folk as grammatical. Similarly, in social psychology, if we really understand the knowledge, beliefs and skills that are required for the production of a piece of social life, and an ordinary explanation of it, then we ought to be able to use that knowledge to reproduce it. There are no Humean causal relations in social life. The genesis of social action — and let us not forget that an explanation is an action — is Aristotelian in character. It involves agents and structured templates and the formation of structural products. It is like anatomy; it is not like kinematics.

7

Telling and Reporting: Prospective and Retrospective Uses of Self-Ascriptions*

J. Shotter

> But if we had to name anything which is the life of the sign, we should, we should have to say that it was its *use*. Wittgenstein: The Blue and Brown Books

In what follows, among other things, I want to mount (with Harré, this volume) an *ethogenic* critique of work in so-called "attribution theory" — that loose assemblage of experimental studies in social psychology claiming their ancestry in the writings of Heider (1958), Jones and Davis (1965), Kelley (1967), and Jones and Nisbett (1972). I want to criticize it for its lack of a proper, overall theory of the actual nature of everyday social life, and for its misleading account both of what in daily life it takes the "naive psychologist's" basic task to be, and of the nature and part played ordinarily by the psychological explanations people give of their own and other people's behaviour. My main concern is to contribute to the attempt to set out what some of us consider to be a much more realistic account of the "naive psychologist's" conduct (Harré and Secord, 1972; Shotter, 1975; Gauld and Shotter, 1977; Harré, 1979) — conduct which, incidentally, we by contrast would say is not naive at all, but displays a high degree of social competence, the nature of which it is our aim to explore.

Before turning to a consideration of attribution, in line with my main concern, I want to discuss a number of issues to do with everyday life in a "moral world" (Shotter, 1980, in press a, in press b). My concern will be with what I shall call "practical explanation".

*Written while a visiting professor in the Department of Psychology at the University of North Carolina at Charlotte. I would like to thank everyone there for the excess of "southern hospitality" extended to me at that time — myth was made reality.

People's use of actions in expressing their states and statuses

Morally, it simply is not open to us to do just what we want when we please. What we have a right to do in one situation, we have no right to do in another; conditions we have no obligations to satisfy here, we must attempt to satisfy there; privileges accorded to us now, we may or may not be accorded tomorrow; and so on. Our moral world is an ever changing sea of opportunities and limitations, enablements and constraints, invitations and rejections, with its character transformed by each action which takes place within it.

I want to discuss what might be called the "political economy" of interpersonal relations in such a world. The currency at stake is made up of the rights and duties, privileges and obligations which, on the one hand, people claim or demand for themselves, and which, on the other, are placed upon them or acceded to by others. The having of such rights and duties, etc. is not something people can just do on their own.

Clearly, while essentially concerned still to retain one's membership of one's society, people act whenever they can to increase their rights in relation to other members of their society and to reduce their obligations to them; there being point to such an aim, of course, only if one does remain a member, one's currency otherwise becomes valueless. Thus at every moment, where one is, how one is placed in terms of what one has a right to do and what one is being required to do, is important knowledge in determining one's momentary action. Those who do not properly grasp where they are, so to speak, do not know how to act in ways appropriate to their situation. But how do we, in such a sea of change, keep a grasp upon our position within it?

Strangely, it is unusual to spend most of our time in bewilderment and confusion. Normally, we know what we are doing and why, we know how we stand, and we grasp what those around us are at also; at least we do so to an extent sufficient to conduct most of our mundane activities with some degree of success. The many difficulties and dilemmas possible in theory in social life — as Wittgenstein (1953) noted in the case of language — hardly ever arise in the normal conduct of daily life. Actual human institutions seem to be structured so that in practice such problems are either minimized (see Shotter, in press b, for a discussion of how in a social order "dilemmas of responsibility attribution" are minimized), or they are carefully avoided, or they are dealt with in some other way — perhaps by being treated as special, and removed from the realm of "real-life" and conducted within circumscribed arenas, such as in "theatres", or on "playing fields" or "campuses" (Huizinga, 1949). Or perhaps again, what raises a difficulty in theory turns out in practice to be a foundation tenet of actual social life, something simply taken for granted.

For instance: the fact that people in daily life are unable to provide distinctive empirical evidence in support of what they tell (or avow) of themselves to others, although it raises many problems in theory — in the causes/reasons debate, say (Buss, 1978; Harvey and Tucker, 1979) — raises few problems in practice. In daily life, the fact is that we assign people a right to make such unsupported self-ascriptions, to make as Abelson (1977) calls them "non-observational self-ascriptions". The normal functioning of social life is founded upon such a convention; it could not operate as it does without it. For, being accorded the right of having most of what they say or do taken seriously and responded to without question is a part of what it is for human beings to be treated as *persons*, for them to be accorded their status as full and competent members of their society. It is only normal to request explanations of people's conduct when it is enigmatic or suspicious in some way (Peters, 1958; Scott and Lyman, 1968), when what the agent has in mind is not immediately perceptible, or if perceptible, not easily acceptable to others; or when, perhaps, their behaviour seems not wholly to be under their own control, not an action of theirs (Taylor, 1964). In conferring upon one another such a right, people give one another the opportunity to use self-ascriptions in asserting their states and statuses in relation to one another; and while people may simply assert things of themselves and have them accepted or rejected by others, they may also be invited by others to make such assertions and they may accept or ignore them as they see fit. The tension in every moral transaction follows from the existence of such options, each party to it is able to act in ways that other parties may neither desire nor expect.

In using a self-ascription in a status-assertion, I may, for example, say to a woman "I love you". In so saying, I may, but I usually do not mean that I have carried out an extensive observational analysis, à la Bem, of my inner states and outer behaviour — my heart rate, breathing, sexual arousal, time spent looking at her, and attempting to be near her, etc. — and have made my statement as a report which sums up the results. There are, as I will discuss below, occasions upon which such reporting is appropriate, but is questionable in a way in which a status-assertion is not. The fact is that here my declaration is not a reporting but a telling; it is a moral statement which once uttered (whatever its causes) commits me to going on in the future with the woman to whom it is uttered in a way different from my relations to her in the past. Now, my status in relation to her is changed; that was my reason for my utterance. I am now, however, vulnerable to her rejection of me, my status is not yet as I desire. Hence the circumspection which is always associated with such declarations. If she accepts me, then the new rights she accords me over her person are tempered with new obligations. Thus when next I am off to a football match with the boys, and have not consulted her beforehand, she will say to me reproachfully, "But I thought you said you loved me?" And I will feel guilty and embarrassed. Realizing the commitments involved, we do not make such declarations lightly.

Above I am using my self-ascriptive utterance in a *prospective* manner, in an attempt to project the whole of myself in a certain way towards the future. And I sense the risk to my self in my project falling to the ground and coming to naught. However, in suggesting that the statement "I love you" is usually used in such a way (by men?) does not rule out the possibility of it also being used *retrospectively*, as a report upon one's state of being, as Bem's (1967) "self-perception theory" would suggest. People do on occasions find themselves puzzled as to why in the presence of a certain person their hearts go "pit-a-pat", and they feel compelled to gaze at them with rapt attention. Then they may report that such events are happening "because, I suppose, I must love you". But then they could go on to say, "But I'm not ready for it yet, let's just go on as we are for a bit longer". Thus clarifying that their statement *was* meant as a reporting and not as a telling. Further, as a report, their statement could be quite wrong: to be fascinated or attracted by a person is not necessarily to be in love with them; rather than your liking them, your inner goings-on may be due, if you are already locked in an unavoidable attachment to them, to your hatred of them, or to some other sentiment that you might have regarding them. In formulating such a report upon the events leading up to and constituting one's current state, one's self is split: an aspect reports while an aspect is reported upon. The uncertainties and risks in relation to myself in such retrospective uses of self-ascriptions, in which only a part of myself is actively involved, are clearly ones of quite a different kind to those in prospective uses, in which I risk the whole of myself. To be wrong in one's report is not to be the wrong person.

The ethogenic perspective

I shall return to make a few more comments about the different logical grammars of telling and reporting in a moment. Here, however, is a convenient point at which to break off in order to say something about the ethogenic perspective, and my relation to it.

For the purposes of this book, my approach here may be considered as essentially an *ethogenic* one (Harré and Secord, 1972), being concerned with how ordinary, everyday social life is actually made to work by the human beings who conduct or perform it. Ethogenists are interested in the devices, techniques, procedures, methods, ways, stratagems, ploys, etc. (most unfortunately, I think, all called "mechanisms" by Harré and Secord, as if such devices could function independently of those who use them) which people actually *use* in "bringing off" their aims in social life, not just anyhow, but in a "rationally accountable" or "socially responsible" manner.

Following Harré and Secord, it might seem that ethogenists should study only what already exists in social life. They state their position as if, on the one hand, there was a pre-established set of devices available in social life, and on the other, users of them, who, if they possess any competency at all, have such devices at their disposal. But such a view would be tantamount to the old idea, scotched by Wittgenstein and his followers (e.g. Winch, 1958), of people as first being given a language, with words having meanings, and so on, which exists independently of its use in social life, and of it then being put to use by people in their social conduct. Such may indeed be the case with large tracts of social life, in which later generations inherit pre-formed "conventional", "ritual", or "rule-governed" structures from their predecessors; and Harré's and Secord's "dramaturgical standpoint" is well suited to their study. But one cannot appeal to such pre-established structures in accounting for the ultimate meaningfulness of behaviour. People are not just rule-users and rule-inheritors, they are also rule-makers; and as the rules governing social life must be made in the course of its actual conduct, and are only intelligible in relation to the context out of which they arise, rules as such cannot be the source of order in social life. There must be a non-rule-governed way in which people can be meaningful to one another, due to the intrinsic intentionality of all human action (Shotter, in press, b). Rules may be necessary if one is to perform in a socially skilful or competent manner, or to discourse upon or account for one's social conduct, without being necessary to meaningful conduct *per se*.

For to perform incompetently is often still to perform in a socially meaningful way, as the parents of every child can attest.

There is thus another side to the ethogenic coin than the concern just with routinely available, preformed devices: there is the concern also with how such devices may be brought into existence in a society in the first place, with how they might be transmitted to new members of it, or with how once in existence they may be developed and changed — a concern with broadly "developmental" issues (Gauld and Shotter, 1977) rather than with "dramaturgical" ones. Here, rather than social competency being taken for granted, its very existence is rendered problematic. This does not, however, prevent our concern from still being an ethogenic one, for now we may be concerned with, among other things, the actual devices available in a society for transforming incompetency into competency (Shotter, 1973, 1974, 1978). Unfortunately, we must add, ways of transforming competency into incompetency will interest us also (see Goffman, 1968, and Garfinkel, 1956, for discussions of "status degradation ceremonies") — such is the danger in "attribution theory", as I shall argue in a moment, if it is taken too seriously as an account of how people actually do do things in everyday life: in ignoring or distorting the actual processes necessary to people making and maintaining the social order in which they live, it may help to render them incompetent in its making and maintenance. Such concerns clearly relate to our interest in the previous section, in status-assertions and status-assignments, as well as to Harré's (this volume), in who or what the expressive order in a society allows people to be.

I shall return to matters of status below; here I want to carry my "developmental" concern with the use of non-preformed devices further: clearly, such apparently routinely available devices as promises, loyalties, agreements, commands, accusations, excuses, endearments, insults, tellings, reportings, etc. are not things which endure in and of themselves as objectively existing entities in the world. Being quite invisible and intangible, and only existing "intersubjectively" within certain patterns of interpersonal relation, they are constructed and reconstructed as and when required, to meet the changing exigencies of daily life. Existing only dynamically, they may exist explicitly at one moment and only implicitly the next. As such, they could just as easily fade from existence as remain in it. And one can easily imagine societies, or particular face-to-face relationships, in which, for instance, the social "skills" of promising, uttering endearments, or being loyal had been all but forgotten (as in Ik society — Turnbull, 1973), or alternately, elevated into high ritual skills (as in traditional Japan); just as "deference" is supposed to be disappearing from English society. The categories in terms of which people account for their relations to one another, and self-consciously think of themselves as having to one another, may change in many ways, from one moment in history to the next (Gergen, 1973).

However, as such categories wax and wane, one's personal actions do not necessarily gain or lose their immediate moral force. The effect of one person's action upon another, with regard to status assignments, status demands, and their satisfaction, does not depend upon that action as first being seen as falling into one or another category of action, and only then its precise moral content appreciated, and acted upon. It may do; but especially in face-to-face exchanges people's actions derive their force very largely from the context in which they are used. Thus the raised eyebrow, for instance, is not usually first interpreted as either an insult, a question, or an expression of surprise, and then reacted to; it is reacted to directly by the recipient stopping speaking, hesitating, attempting to explain, offering apologies, etc. In other words, people usually react to their immediate circumstances, rather than at one remove, to their categorization of them. As Harré (this volume) points out, attribution and kindred processes are not necessarily modes of propositional reasoning; they are, I shall argue, only most unusually so, and are in fact usually "done" as a mode of perceiving (a suggestion of Harré's — this volume — but one which he draws back from supporting himself). As I have suggested elsewhere (Shotter, 1978, in press a, b), people may affect one another directly and immediately in a wholly non-propositional manner, understanding in detail how to use their actions to achieve particular effects in people much as carpenters and other artisans understand how to wield their tools in shaping the materials they work on. In becoming socialized into a society, people clearly first learn its practices before they learn the theory (or the moral rhetoric) of them; they first learn how to act before learning how to account for or to justify their actions. It is only later, when they already have some expertise in actual social manipulations, that as children they learn to discourse upon their conduct — and we all know of children who, even at six or seven years old, are able to argue: "I didn't mean it. I wasn't being rude. That's not rude . . . anyway, she was rude first". Moral practices initially precede the rhetoric of them, although later, of course, they come to include it.

Though my concerns below, then, will largely be with "developmental" issues, and with the ways in which, in everyday life, we cope with the puzzles and difficulties they raise, my consideration of them will still be disciplined by the same considerations disciplining all ethogenic investigations: any accounts offered must attempt to render explicit, in one way or another according to one's purposes, what is *already there* implicitly in the actual nature of daily social life. Or, to put the matter another way: the explicit *uses* and *functions* proposed for people's actions must not distort or render inoperable the implicit uses or functions of those actions in making actual daily life work.

As Harré (this volume) illustrates, the dangers of such distortions are not unreal; the ethogenic concern with *actual* social practices in making and maintaining the social order is of crucial importance; it can serve to highlight particular concerns in, and constraints upon people's actions not always present in laboratory experimentation. For instance, I have already argued that a part of what it is to attribute or ascribe moral autonomy to a person is to ascribe to them the right to make "non-observational self-ascriptions" as "I don't believe you," "I've changed my mind", "I love you", or "I want coffee", and to have them taken seriously even though there are no observational criteria to warrant them. The necessity to ascribe such a right or status to people does not arise out of anything empirically discoverable about people and their behaviour; indeed, empirically, even in daily life, people probably fail to take one another seriously on a large number of occasions. The necessity that they do not always do so is one of a logical kind: without the ascription of such rights to one another, the maintenance of a social order by those who are members of it — for who or what else is there to maintain it? — would be impossible (Shotter, in press, b). Subjects in experimental studies are not always ascribed such a right; for the purposes of science, the normal moral order is often suspended.

It is for these reasons, and others still to be discussed, that although my "developmental" approach may seem to be at odds in some ways with Harré's and Secord's "dramaturgical standpoint", I still consider it to be essentially an ethogenic one, complementary to their standpoint, and far removed from that of attribution theorists.

An hermeneutical model of social perception

Classically, psychologists have tended to think of people's behaviour as something caused, as something which appeared as a final result of, or in "response" to, a sequence of antecedent events; it was not something which people could, as social agents, in and of themselves just "do". Ethogenists do not want to reject this causal story in its entirety, for while they do want to assume that people themselves can be responsible for at least some of the things they can be observed as doing, they do not want to assume they can be responsible for them all. In general though, rather than being interested in the causes of people's actions, ethogenists are interested in the *uses* to which they may be put, as "invitations" or "opportunities" for future action, or as expressions serving to order or determine the nature of future social events. For people may use their actions either instrumentally, as means to an end, or expressively, in claiming a special status and thus a distinct kind of treatment by others.

While one may be puzzled as to what events, exactly, led up to the occurrence of a particular present event, another quite different kind of puzzlement is to do with what, irrespective of the event's cause, the event *means*, what it is the means to, what it indicates, points to, specifies, etc. What is the person doing in doing it? Ethogenists would claim that a goodly number of the puzzles one faces in coping with everyday social behaviour are puzzles of the second kind rather than the first. And the aspect of "ordinary explanation" which interests me is how, when the indications in people's actions are insufficiently clear as to the uses they intend them to serve, those indications are "explained" or made clear. I am interested in what I shall call "primary" or "practical explanation" rather than "secondary" or "rule-regulated explanation"; in what actually "explains" or clarifies a person's social behaviour rather than what "counts as" an explanation of it, i.e. an account. An example will help to make clear what I mean here; consider the following episode:

> They were walking very close now. Her hand brushed more than accidentally it seemed against his. He grasped it. She turned towards him, startled, eyebrows raised, a questioning look. He smiled and squeezed her hand more tightly in his. She turned away, head slightly bowed. He loosened his grip and silently her hand slipped away.

Here, the man "explains" his gripping of her hand, I would claim, by his smile: he makes clear by it that he does not intend to drag her off by force, or to exert greater physical control over her, but just to initiate greater physical intimacy while still respecting her personhood — in response, perhaps, to her "invitation". And in so claiming, I am offering, of course, a secondary or rule-regulated explanation, an account, the accuracy of which may only be properly established in negotiation with those to whom it is applied. Hence the initial uncertainty as to its precise nature. To continue with my account, I claim that she in turn "explains" by her look and by the inactivity of her hand that either her "invitation" was in fact accidental, not actually an invitation, or, "on second thoughts" she is withdrawing it. As a result of this exchange, he realizes that while she is still prepared to undertake an indefinite range of projects with him — her continued presence there indicates that — she is probably not at this stage prepared to investigate further with him the possibility of a more physical relationship between them. His status in relation to her in at least this sphere of activity, is now, at least to a degree, somewhat more clear; and it will be a while before he takes her hand again. But as their relationship progresses, in the course of them explaining *themselves* (not their actions) to one another, what was a vague, global and unformulated mode of relationship, is progressively shaped, specified, or formulated at a practical level by them in their actual conduct of it. But how do actions like "smiles" and "failing to grip another's hand" serve to make more clear the intent in an earlier action; what is involved, practically, in them "explaining" themselves to one another in this rather mindless fashion? For clearly, nothing like categorical perception and propositional reasoning was involved in the above episode.

The primary process involved in such "explanations" is not, I want to claim, anything like the inferential, "information processing" procedures proposed by attribution theorists (e.g. Kelley, 1967; Jones and Nisbett, 1972) — nor, for that matter does it illustrate the kind of "mindlessness" studied by Langer (1978), in her experiments upon people performing highly practiced skills, as if following a "script" — but by a very different kind of process. For, to repeat, one is puzzled not by one's ignorance of what led up to a person's action, but by what their action actually *is*, by what it is that the person is actually trying to do in performing it — by their "smiling", their "turning away", or their "eyebrow raising", and such like.

In modelling the process involved I shall draw, not from the natural sciences, but from "hermeneutics", the discipline to do with the interpretation of (originally biblical) texts (Palmer, 1969; Ricoeur, 1970; Taylor, 1971; Gadamer, 1975; Gauld and Shotter, 1977). There, one's understanding of the precise part played, or function served by a particular expression or piece of text is clarified by constructing (or reconstructing) the larger whole, its context, the wider scheme of things the author had in mind in expressing himself so; the construction being shaped and limited by having to accommodate the item of text in its every aspect. Thus the process does not begin with a pre-established order of things to which puzzling facts must be assimilated, with them being explained as particular instances of the general rules or laws constituting the order, with their uniqueness thus lost. It begins with the puzzling facts in their full individuality — known globally to be of a certain kind (text, facial expressions, or whatever), or course — and then proceeds by degrees in a back and forth process from part to whole, and from whole to part again, to articulate an order adapted to the undistorted accommodation of the initial facts. Or, to put the matter another way, in the process, an initially global, superficial and undiffer-entiated grasp of an action's meaning is transformed into a well articulated grasp of its actual meaning. And rather than an inference from a pre-established order, the process involves the creation of a wholly new order of things within a globally determined whole. The action is understood by its being "framed", one could say.

Interestingly, one of the best sources to turn to for just such a discus-sion of the perceptual process is Heider (1958). Not only does he distin-guish quite clearly between perception and inference, but he also describes perception as a "constructive process" in which a "whole" or "unified structure" is produced within which events may be "embedded", and which results in our "direct experience of them as being the events they appear to be". He distinguishes between percep-tion and inference as follows:

> Perceiving is experienced as a direct contact with the environment; it is a means whereby objective facts enter the the life space . . . Then there is inference through which we arrive at conclusions on the basis of the existing contents of the life space. (Heider, 1958, pp. 15 – 16)

But how can an "objective fact" come into existence in the life space? By the stimulus, the "distal stimulus" as Heider calls it, using Brunswick's (1934) terminology, being "*embedded* in the total situation" (ibid., p. 37). And what precisely he means here he illustrates in his discussion of the results he and Simmel obtained in studying people's perceptions of events in a cartoon film they made. In the film, a large triangle T, a small triangle t, and a circle or disc c move around, while a large outline rectangle with a movable part — typically seen as a one-room house with a door — remains stationary (Heider and Simmel, 1944). In their experi-ments they were able to manipulate a number of things, among them the global schematism within which the movements were perceived. But,

> As long as the pattern of events shown in the film is perceived in terms of movements as such, it presents a chaos of juxtaposed items. When, however, the geometrical figures assume personal characteristics so that their movements are perceived in terms of motives and sentiments, a unified structure appears. (ibid., pp. 31–32).

Seeing the events globally as "personal" rather than "mechanical" seemed to "make sense" in terms of them manifesting invariants more easily in that mode — motives and sentiments — than in the alternative mode. Heider's and Simmel's experiments may be criticized, however, in a way not unrelated to Harré's (this volume) concern with the over-use of "documentary" material in psychological investigations: such experiments are not typical of what happens in real life; they are parasitical upon it. In their experiment, the subject is cast in the role of the 3rd-person observer; in real life, one's usual position is as a 1st-person performer or as a 2nd-person recipient. In both such positions one has a status quite different to that of 3rd-persons: one is able to intervene in and modify the action; one is involved in and required to maintain the action; one must attend to what is intended, and ignore what just happens (what is not intended); and so on. Elaborating on the last point, 3rd-persons may — because they do not face the task of attending to what an actor intends them to attend to — attend to quite different things, in quite different ways than 2nd-persons. As 2nd-persons in everyday life, we do not have that right, unless we are physicians or ophthalmologists, etc. to step out of our "personal involvement" with people, and attend to aspects of their behaviour to which they do not intend us to attend. As 3rd-persons we may notice all kinds of unintended, revealing behaviour, otherwise ignored by 2nd-persons — hence our unease as 1st-persons, when attempting a tricky interpersonal performance, we notice ourselves being observed.

The rights, duties, privileges and obligations of the different "persons" (1st, 2nd, etc.) in everyday social life seem to me to be of crucial importance. The meaning of the episode between the man and the woman, which I referred to at the beginning of the section — written, of course, with "insider's" knowledge — was quite transparent to them; they were making it transparent as they went along. And had the woman failed to make her intent clear in her look and limp hand (or should it be "had the man failed to grasp her intent"?), then she could have done something further, perhaps said, "Please . . . not yet", or whatever expressed her intention best. For they are constructing in miniature, in an hermeneutical back and forth between whole and part, a social order, a common world between them of which neither is the sole creator. What happened — where they stood and where they now stand — while known to them, is somewhat opaque to outsiders. They (outsiders) might *infer*, assimilating the observed events to pre-established schemes, that indeed an offer of physical intimacy was ventured and sadly rejected, but what that rejected offer meant in the context of the man's and woman's whole relationship — that it was the 100th such occasion in a 100 day ritual walk in the woods, and thus the last, decisive rejection — would most certainly escape them. Predicting at least the continuation of the relationship, they would be surprised to observe that at the end of their walk, according to their pact, the man and woman parted, never to meet again. But the ability of outsiders to infer as much as they do comes, I suggest, from their ability to assimilate what they observe to pre-established schemas constructed during their direct involvements in 1st/2nd person exchanges.

Tellings and reportings, avowals and appraisals

Returning now to consider the uses to which self-ascriptions may be put, we can see now how on an hermeneutical model, but not an inferential one, it is possible for people to *progressively* reveal to one another, in their interactions, what they have in mind. The procedure involved is, in fact, a "developmental" one, involving processes of a differentiation and specification *within* a pre-existing, but initially only globally articulated totality. In this context, the "specificatory" nature of thought and action has been discussed by Gauld and Shotter (1977, p. 127) while elsewhere (Shotter, in press, a) I have suggested that in such "specificatory" processes, the "parts" produced within the whole are always open to yet further internal differentiation and specification in relation to one another — but only in terms of their "already specified specifiability", in terms of what they are already. Rommetveit (1976) has also described just such a model. He suggests that whatever is made known in verbal communications may be "conceived of as expansions and/or modifications of a pre-established shared *Lebenswelt*" (op. cit. p. 206). And in discussing the progressive development of a shared social reality — using the example of a question and answer game — he goes on to point out that an "answer at every successive stage is nested onto what at that particular stage has already been established as a shared social reality (or unquestioned, *free information*)" (ibid., p. 207). Having already suggested that a *Lebenswelt* constitutes "*the initially shared, unquestioned, or free information* onto which your very first question is nested or *bound*" (ibid., p. 206). An interpretation of what a person might be doing in their behaviour can be arrived at, Rommetveit would suggest, by a systematic analysis of the way *bound* information is nested in already known *free* information.

I am now in a position to clarify further the distinction between telling and reporting, between explanation by revelation and explanation by description or classification, between the saying of such things as "I want coffee" and statements like "The coffee spilling incident did indeed rather turn me against him" (the type of reports, presumably, figuring in Nisbett's and Bellow's (1977) experimentation, upon which I shall be commenting below). Ryle (1949) calls the two kinds of uses "avowals" and "appraisals" respectively, and I have already discussed their different prospective and retrospective uses. And it is important to emphasize that the distinction between them inheres *in the uses* to which people put their actions or statements, and not in the form of the statements themselves.

While the prototypical form of avowal may be first person, present tense, self-descriptive statements such as "I am thinking", many such statements may also serve equally well as reports, or combine both an appraisal with an avowal function, e.g. in saying "The whisky's burning my mouth", one might be saying "I feel the whisky burning my mouth . . . help", or "I feel something (avowal); it is most likely the whisky which is burning my mouth (appraisal)". Furthermore, many other statements or actions *not cast in anything like that form* may, nonetheless, serve the same function: witness in this respect what the man and woman "tell" one another in their actions.

It is in their "logical grammars" (Ryle, 1949) that telling and reporting may be distinguished (Heaton, 1976); that is, it is in what they imply for one's future action, being in receipt of one or the other of them, that is important. While statements or actions used as reports or appraisals may be checked out for their truth or falsity by reference to observational data, to establish whether the state of affairs depicted in the statement exists in reality, telling or avowals are treated in quite another way. For someone to demand that I make available to them the particular observational data upon which I based my avowal "I want coffee" would be distinctly odd, for in fact, as I mentioned before, there are none (Gauld and Shotter, 1977, p. 45). Such a someone may insist, and go so far as to say "Look here, I've checked out your brain states and the rest of your physiology, and as far as I can see, you're just not in a coffee-wanting state at all". To such a one I could still say, "Nonetheless, I still want a cup of coffee . . . to 'punctuate' my day . . . to get a lift from the caffeine in it . . . to compare it with the last cup of coffee I had here . . . to be sociable as everyone else has one . . . to have something to throw in your face for being so boringly insistent . . ." and so on.

While I may *justify* my wanting coffee by any one of a potentially infinite set of *reasons* appropriate to the context in which they are offered, it makes no sense to ask me to prove my wanting "true", in terms of it having the proper antecedents. Thus in other words, avowals do not have to be warranted like reports, by reference to facts, to any antecedently or currently existing states of mind, body, or anything else, as they simply are not used like reports. They are used by people to reveal to others what they currently have in mind — what their needs, interests and desires are, etc. — in an attempt to order future action; executed now, they function to change the shared social reality within which the next action must occur. And rather than them being evaluated for their truth or falsity, as depicting already existing states of affairs, avowals may be evaluated for, say, the degree of sincerity with which they are uttered: i.e. whether the use claimed for them by the one performing them, is indeed the use they actually intend them to have, for people may have altogether different, more hidden intentions than those they reveal in their performances. For instance, I cannot claim to be sincere in wanting coffee if immediately it is offered me, I either ignore the offer, or, I accept it but put the cup down again instantly, and ignore its existence from that moment on — unless, that is, I wanted the coffee to perform some kind of bizarre insult upon those involved in providing it for me. Thus, while reportings may be evaluated as to whether they are true depictions, and that is their *use* to depict and describe, avowals require evaluating much more broadly as to whether their apparent use is their true usage — something which is only revealed as the actions following from them progressively unfolds.

In criticism of attribution theory: the rights and duties of persons

At the heart of attribution theory is the assumption that "the person-perceiver's fundamental task is to interpret or infer the causal antecedents of action" (Jones and Davis, 1965, p. 200). Given my views expressed above, it is clear that to the extent that such an assumption is considered to be fundamental, I think that it is wrong: in everyday social life the person-perceiver's fundamental task is hardly ever that of inferring the causal antecedents of action, but that of attempting to grasp what in their actions people have in mind — a task of quite a different kind: an hermeneutical task conducted from a 2nd-person standpoint, rather than an inferential task from a 3rd-person stand-point. And on most occasions, person-perceivers are successful in their task; only occasionally do we fail to grasp quite what it is that people are up to in their actions. And it is most unusual for people's actions to be so bizarre that one can perceive no sense in them at all; only then does one resort to a causal analysis, as to what might have produced such a disturbance in normality, in the attempt to restore it (Peters, 1958; Taylor, 1964). Thus normally, I am claiming, people quite literally "explain" their actions in the course of their performances, each action in an exchange serving to clarify the actions preceding it.

It may be worth commenting at this point that the position I am taking here is somewhat to the "left" of Harré (this volume) and other "account analysts", as well as Buss (1978) and Shotter (1975), for I am suggesting that not only is the person-perceiver not primarily interested in knowing the *causes* of people's actions, but that they are not (primarily) interested in knowing their *reasons* either: primarily, they want to know what the person has "done" in his or her action, how by their action they have transformed the shared social reality — changed "the definition of the situation" — in which the person-perceiver must act. The need for people also to know their own and one another's reasons for their actions arises, I would claim, out of the fact that the world of everyday life is a "moral world" (Shotter, 1980a), which works in terms of people's rights and duties as members of a society. And within it people have a right to question the legitimacy of one another's actions, and to ask whether they are appropriately "grounded" in, or are a proper part of, the society's shared social reality; just as by the same token everyone also has a duty to ensure the legitimacy of their actions.

As in many other experimental studies in psychology, the normal moral order implicit in daily life is either suspended, or considerably modified in studies by attribution theorists. Nonetheless, it is clearly enjoying a great vogue at the moment in claiming to meet the demand for a psychology more appropriate to daily life. As one exponent (Ross, 1977) of it claimed recently:

The current ascendency of attribution theory in social psychology culminates a long struggle to upgrade that discipline's conception of man. No longer the stimulus-response (S-R) automaton of radical behaviourism, promoted beyond the rank of information processor and cognitive consistency seeker, psychological man has at last been awarded a status equal to that of the scientist who investigates him.

It is the claim that the struggle is over that I wish to contest, that its culmination in people being awarded the status of scientists is an achievement to be applauded. While such a status carries with it certain rights — the right to question whether things are what they seem, etc. — it also entails certain duties — to act only in relation to logical and explicitly formulated theories, for instance: both such rights and duties are quite different from those in ordinary daily life, in which ordinarily, things are what they seem to be, and people only account for things in unquestioned, taken-for-granted terms. To award ordinary people the status of scientists, from, perhaps, an egalitarian desire to attribute to everyone the ability to conduct the supposedly most highly valued activity in our time, is, I think, misplaced; it is a status which is clearly inimical in many respects to the normal living of everyday life; a quite different moral order is involved. Attribution theorists fail to take such "moral" issues into account. In, for instance, failing to distinguish between tellings and reportings, between the prospective and the retrospective functions of self-descriptions, and in treating them all as reportings, they have failed (while claiming exactly the opposite) to accord the same social status to their subjects as themselves.

As I have already intimated, in everyday life, people in general (let alone scientists in particular) must treat one another as having the ability to make avowals, and must take such empirically unsupportable self-ascriptions seriously; in large part, people are normally treated as meaning what they say they mean (Cavell, 1969), and as being as they present themselves as being (Goffman, 1959). Along with this right, however, goes a duty: to be accounted competent members of their society, people are also expected to act responsibly; that is, even if all alone, they must be ready to answer for what they do, to monitor and evaluate their own actions in terms they share with others in their community. (And such a concern with self-monitoring and accounting is, of course, central to the ethogenic approach — see Harré and Secord, 1972.)

Without such abilities, and without the rights and duties, the enablements and constraints in society carefully structured (it seems) to nurture such abilities and maintain them in existence, social life as we know it would be impossible.

An actual social order does not just allow for the existence of socially autonomous individuals, able to make and justify "nonobservational self-ascriptions", it demands it (Shotter, in press,): if a social order is to endure, then of necessity — for human beings are not born with, as far as we can tell, any particular species-specific way of life — it must be possible for the elements within it, who conduct it, to identify transgressions of it, and for the transgressors to help make restitution. The elements of the order, unlike atoms, have no intrinsic valencies; they must maintain their social order by their own efforts. Without such individually responsible and accountable elements, without in fact *persons*, a social order would fall apart.

Other unities will not do as the basic elements for such a self-maintaining order, a moral order: for the purposes of social psychological theory, we might take certain personal relationships, "transpersonal" unities — e.g. mother/child, husband/wife, boss/worker, teacher/pupil, etc — as the basic elements constituting a social order, for as persons, people exist only in the context of their relations to one another, not in isolation at all. On such a view, *joint acts* (Denzin, 1977, p. 29) or *joint action* (Shotter, 1980a) between people, rather than the acts or actions of individuals becomes one's basic subject matter — a view which I think, in theory, is correct. In the "moral world" of everyday life, though, such transpersonal unities cannot be accorded any moral unity or autonomy, for in practice they are not accountable. Joint acts are produced by people interlacing their actions in with those of others, thus what they each intend and what is actually produced between them, may be widely discrepant. In such genuinely *social* activity, people may remain deeply ignorant as to what it is, really, they are doing (or why), not because the "scripts", etc. supposedly in them somewhere are too vague, or too well practised (Langer, 1978), or too deeply buried in them to bring out into the light of day, but because the formative influences shaping their conduct are not entirely there in them to be brought out: some important influences exist in the situations between people. Other people's actions are often just as much a formative influence in determining what people do as anything from solely within themselves. Joint action thus raises difficulties for the maintenance of a moral order and requires special treatment: its occurence is either minimized, prevented, or groups of people functioning as unities in society at large must, by law, organize themselves such that they *are* accountable, and the group then counts legally as a person.

Crucial to the conduct of daily life, then, are the rights and duties, privileges and obligations of human beings as persons: though a distortion of social psychological reality, the concept of persons able to take responsibility for their actions, is necessary to the existence of a self-maintaining social order, just as a rational, social order is necessary to people conferring such autonomy upon one another — the right to make unsupported self-ascriptions and the duty to be accountable for them. Attribution theorists pay no attention in their studies to these factors, necessary to the normal continuation of everyday life.

THE "FINDINGS" OF ATTRIBUTION THEORISTS: TELLING MORE THAN WE CAN REPORT

Nowhere are the unfortunate consequences of this failure made more apparent than in implications drawn from work by Nisbett and Wilson (1977), and Nisbett and Bellows (1977). They report studies in which people, after having done something within the context of an experimental manipulation, are asked to report upon what seemed to have "caused" what they did. The same general result was obtained time and again: people seemed unable to give any accurate reports on factors which quite clearly influenced their behaviour.

As they report it, such a result seems surprising, especially so, for as Nisbett and Wilson (p. 232) are at pains to point out, it is "obvious to anyone who has ever questioned a subject about the reasons for his behaviour or evaluations, that people readily answer such questions". But, given their results, it would seem that we should put very little trust in what people say; the very title of their paper — "Telling more than we can know" — suggests that the idea that people themselves are the best authority upon what they themselves think, feel, need, etc. is suspect. As Nisbett and Bellows (1977, p. 624) conclude, " . . . it should be clear that the present findings raise serious methodological questions concerning the validity of subject reports as a tool of social science investigation".

But how should we react to these "findings"? Firstly, when the confusing and misleading language in which they are reported is clarified — the confusion between telling and reporting, reasons and causes, knowing and believing, and suchlike — the results are, in one sense, I think, trivial. They merely report once again the already well-known fact that while we do many things in social life, intellingently and intelligibly, in quite skilful ways, *it is quite normal not to be able to report upon how we do them*. Talking is just one such activity. To mimic what Ryle (1949, p. 30) said on this point in discussing people's ability to reason before (and after) Aristotle extracted rules of logic, we could say:

> Explicit rules of grammar were first extracted by Chomsky, yet men knew how to talk before they learned his lessons, just as men since Chomsky, and including Chomsky, ordinarily speak without making any internal reference to his rules.

Practice, in many spheres of social life, normally precedes the theory of it. To assume otherwise is to believe in what Ryle calls the "intellectualist legend", the crucial objection to which is this: if execution of an intelligent act requires the execution of some prior intelligent theorizing to provide the plan for the action, then either such theorizing itself is unplanned, in which case it cannot be intelligent, or it is conducted by reference to a plan fixed in advance, which again is not intelligent. We are not ordinarily able to report on our own inner workings.

Nisbett and his associates only succeed in surprising us by their results by misleading us into thinking that they are talking about tellings as well as reportings, and by making us feel that we have no right to be telling people all over the place about ourselves, as we cannot be trusted to be accurate. If that really were the case, why should we trust them when they say what their results were? The fact is, contrary to what Nisbett and Bellows fear about the validity of subject "reports" as a tool for social scientific research, there is nothing else for the social scientist to use except his subjects' avowals: what they tell us they see, feel, want, believe, dream, etc.

Furthermore, by suggesting that we should sell our right to mean what we say and to have what we say taken seriously, for a mess of causal theorizing, Nisbett and his associates obscure the true character of the phenomenon under study; namely, its intrinsically social nature. Their whole approach leads them to suggest that it is the *individual* who is unaware of the "causal" processes which, going on inside him or her somewhere, influences his or her behaviour; as if with special "awareness training" or suchlike, he or she could become aware of them. Another interpretation of Nisbett *et al.*'s results might be that people's unawareness stems from the fact that the experimental setting is a genuine social situation in which subjects must interlace their actions in with aspects of the situation not under their control, aspects of it due to other people, the experimenters in fact. In such circumstances, the outcome is a product of *joint action*, and as such cannot be linked by the individual to any specific intentions of his or hers, hence the inability of the individual properly to account for it. The individuals involved in joint action are unaware of how its outcome is produced because, to repeat, it is not a process going on wholly *within* them; it is something shared between them and others.

While I can be held responsible for what I avow of myself — for what I write here, for instance, in saying, "I think attribution theorists are wrong" — it is unreasonable to expect me to be able to account for things to which I have only partially contributed; nor should I (or any other individual) be accorded the moral right to do so. The meaning, the usages served by the outcomes of joint action are matters for negotiation (Harré and Secord, 1972; Shotter, 1974).

CONCEPTS AND PEOPLE'S CONTROL OF THEIR OWN BEHAVIOUR

Attribution theorists have, however, turned up some interesting and important results, few more so, I think, than those demonstrating the apparent cognitive control of emotional and other physiological and motivational factors: examples here are the "misattribution studies" of Valins and Ray (1967) and Storms and Nisbett (1970) in which people are misled into attributing their fear, or their insomnia, to other than their seemingly original sources, thus changing the degree of their severity — one is reminded here of Levi-Strauss' (1963, Chapter 10) story of how, in a similar "reattribution" procedure, a shaman helps a woman through a difficult childbirth. Given such remarkable results, what precisely am I complaining about when I say (a) that attribution theorists fall foul of the "intellectualist legend", and (b) that they obscure the real nature of social processes? How can such misguided people produce such effective results? Because, I think, there are other than empirical methods for producing effective results in the social world, there are conceptual methods, too; something which makes a social world quite different from a physical world of matter in blind but lawful motion.

Let me try to clarify what I mean here by approaching my point about the different functions of self-ascriptions in daily life reflexively: people put in possession of a new language — having been socialized into the practices from which it draws its usages — are able to express new things, to put into an ordered and intelligible form what would otherwise remain chaotic and inexpressible. They may make new status-assertions, both to others and *to themselves*; literally, they may understand — in terms of knowing what one must actually do — how to take on new modes of being in the world. While new empirical theories (reports) may extend one's grasp upon what one already knows, the ability to make new status-assertions (tellings) may extend the kind of person one can be.

Let me extend this point by asking which of the two functions, prospective telling or retrospective reporting, attribution theory itself serves. When looked at in this way it becomes clear, I think, that the studies by attribution theorists — and indeed many other studies in experimental social psychology — founder in a deep misunderstanding of the difference between the uses of conceptual analysis and experimentation in science. The task of elucidating the language and the important concepts in terms of which we actually conduct our daily social life is not one in which experimentation need play a primary part, for it is not primarily a task of an empirical kind; it is a conceptual one. And as Heinrich Hertz said in 1894, concerning confusions as to what in physics "force" and "electricity" actually were:

> . . . we have accumulated around the terms "force" and "electricity" more relations than can be completely reconciled amongst themselves. We have an obscure feeling of this and want to have things cleared up. Our confused wish finds expression in the confused question as to the nature of force and electricity. But the answer which we want is not really an answer to this question. It is not by finding out more and fresh relations and connections that it can be answered; but by removing the contradictions existing between those already known, and thus perhaps by reducing their number. (Hertz, 1956, pp. 7-8)

Similarly, Heider (1958, p. 4) remarks:

> . . . we shall not attain a conceptual framework by collecting more experimental results . . . It is our belief that in the field of interpersonal relations, we have a great deal of empirical knowledge already, and that we can arrive at systematic understanding and crucial experiments more rapidly by attempting to clarify theory.

There is a case for non-empirical research in social psychology; but at the moment empirical and non-empirical research is confounded.

To clarify our social concepts we need to remind ourselves of what it is normal to do or say in our society. To do that, we must confront ourselves, either in actuality or imagination, with different particular situations, and simply *ask ourselves*, "What normally should be said or done here?" And, in general, we do not need any reference to evidence in giving a reply, for given our status as competent members of our society, we must, by definition of what it is to be competent, already know it. In other words, we ought usually to be right; the extent of our ability to articulate that knowledge correctly is, however, limited, it being a matter of skill at inventing and organizing the appropriate pattern of questions for ourselves, bearing in mind also the massive richness of the landscape to be mapped. Thus, as Cavell (1969) adds, the claim that in general we do not require evidence does not rest upon a claim that we cannot be wrong about what should be said or done, but only that it would be unusual (i.e. not normal) if we often were. So-called "experiments" often serve exactly this function in social psychological research, as reminders, as "hints" (Tajfel and Fraser, 1978, p. 12), or as "demonstrations" (McGuire, 1973) of what in fact we must already know about how people conduct themselves in daily social life.

Now if studies in attribution theory are studies of this kind, namely conceptual analyses disguised as empirical testing — and I think that there is a good case to be made out that they are (McGuire, 1973) — this need not mean that they have no importance for us: on the contrary. As Gauld and Shotter (1977, Chapter 12) and Smedslund (1978) have suggested, such systematic analyses may bring an explicit order to otherwise unsystematic phenomena. And such "forms of order" are, in their prospective function, of undoubted importance in every sphere of our lives: helping us to make order where none yet exists.

But if that is what the "theories" proposed in "attribution theory" do do, and I think it is, then that is quite another story. The evaluation of their worth needs to be done in terms very different from those used to evaluate a properly empirical theory for its truth: to the extent that conceptual rather than empirical matters are at stake, thought experiments are just as appropriate a tool to use as actual experiments; and the "experiments" should test, not whether such "theories" truly or falsely describe already completed events, but whether in the explicit transformational (Levi-Strauss, 1963; Barthes, 1973) or relational structure (Craik, 1943) they parallel or distort the implicit forms of order already existing in our daily lives. Only if they do parallel them without distortion can they be used, prospectively, to guide us effectively in planning and deliberating upon our way forward (Shotter, 1978); otherwise, quite literally, they will be misleading; they will mislead us into treating one another in ways quite contrary to the currently normal forms of moral order implicit in the ways we treat one another now.

To conclude: attribution theory, as any useful conceptual scheme in psychology should, both gives us new ways in which we might express ourselves in the world, and directs our attention to some extremely important phenomena. But it radically misleads us, I have claimed, regarding the light in which we should see them, and thus misleads us over their implications for our relations to one another in constituting the social order of daily life. It misleads us by ignoring, in its concern only with causal matters, the multifarious uses to which people actually put their actions in social life, and the importance of some of these activities in both making and maintaining a social order. It was Vico who in 1744 showed (Vico, 1975; Shotter, in press,) that as long as people act in "common sense" terms, they may both pursue their own self interests while inevitably contributing to the maintenance of a social order. For although people may try to increase their own autonomy, their own power and powers to act as they please, autonomy is a characteristic only conferred upon one by others. Thus it cannot be increased unless others act towards one in accordance with one's new status-assertions; they may refuse to do so. Clearly, it is common sense to act in ways which others cannot justifiably reject; one must be able *to account for* one's self-assertions; one must know what new status one can justify for oneself — given one's current status, of course.

People cannot remain living as persons simply by using the social order pre-existing in our society; if they do try only to live *off* it and not to an extent *for* it, then the processes concerned with its repair and maintenance will fall into disuse, and all the subtle patterns of inter- personal relations now possible in our society will fail to endure — and perhaps we shall become like mindless particles of matter, clashing up against one another in meaningless but nonetheless orderly ways, that is, if we treat ourselves as such for long enough. This seems to me to be the kind of path we are on in much of modern psychology, and rather than guiding us away from it, and back to "common sense" — as it claims — attribution theory seems to me to take us another step along the way.

Luckily, there is a "crisis" in social psychology currently (Smith, 1972; Gergen, 1973, 1978; McGuire, 1973; Elms, 1975; etc.). That crisis cannot simply be resolved, for it reflects, I think, the intrinsic conflict and uncertainty, the natural "tension of opposites" inherent in all social and organic life; it must be lived with. And it can be lived with if (along with other oppositions) we learn to recognize the differences between *empirical* and *conceptual* modes of investigation, between self-descriptions and ascriptions of a *retrospective* and of a *prospective* kind, between a *causal-explanatory* framework and its associated methodology and an *hermeneutical-understanding* one. At the moment, these two distinct options remain hopelessly confounded; fragments of one are made to serve purposes of the other, evaluated sometimes in their own terms, sometimes others. No wonder the new pathways open to us at the moment are unclear.

8

The Cognitive Psychology of Self-Reports

P. Morris

Introduction

Asking people why they behaved in a particular way is a central part of our social life. However, this does not guarantee that the answers which are given are always, or even often, reliable. When considering human action from a philosophical standpoint Austin (1962) remarked that while ordinary language was not the last word in answering the questions raised, it was the *first* word and a worthwhile starting point. Similarly, it would seem reasonable for psychologists to begin with the ordinary, everyday explanations of their actions which people offer.

Unfortunately, a strong case can be made out for not trusting at least some of the explanations that people offer for their own behaviour. In this chapter I want to consider these arguments. I believe that the criticisms of the reliability of self reports are appropriate to introspections on some cognitive processes, but not to others, including some of the explanations that people offer for their actions. In this chapter I will attempt to identify the types of cognitive processes which are not open to introspection, and those for which introspection may add valuable information. I will outline a model of the cognitive system and discuss the place of consciousness within this system. The criticisms of self reports and the model of the cognitive system will, I hope, help to clarify when introspections are useful in explaining actions, and when they may be misleading.

Limitations on explanations of our own actions

If we are to explain our own behaviour to someone else we must have knowledge of the processes which led to the behaviour. However, one of the earliest observations of psychologists who attempted to introspect upon their mental processes was that much cognitive activity was not available to consciousness. William James (1890) commented upon the flights and perches of thought where only the conclusions of thought processes appeared to be consciously perceived. In the first years of this century the Wursberg group found that not only problem solving, but even the simple comparison of two weights led to no conscious experiences which would explain how the processes took place (see Humphrey, 1951). If one sets oneself the simple task of thinking of a word beginning with C and considers afterwards how one came to think of "cat", or whatever, it is immediately apparent that one is aware of little if anything of what must be a complex cognitive process. The word comes into one's mind. Indeed, if many such processes were open to introspection then cognitive psychology would not be the difficult subject that it is.

That most cognitive processes are not available to introspection has for years been accepted by cognitive psychologists, even though the actual limits of introspection may be disputed (e.g. Pylyshyn, 1973; Neisser, 1976; Hampson and Morris, 1978; Evans, 1980; Morris, 1980). Subjects in experiments are not expected to have privileged access to their cognitive processes. Such knowledge as they do have will come from their observations of their own and other people's behaviour, and since elaborate experimental control is usually necessary for the identification and measurement of these components of cognitive processing, the observations offered by subjects on the nature of their cognitive processes are rarely illuminating.

The fact that many, probably most, of the processes that interest cognitive psychologists are not open to introspection does not specifically undermine confidence in ordinary explanations of actions, but it does raise doubts. Many of the questions that are asked about actions seem to imply that the questioner believes that the person questioned has some special knowledge about why he did what he did. Such knowledge *might* come from nothing more private than self observations of behaviour in the past, but they seem to assume much more than this: they assume the person has knowledge of consciously experienced motives, intentions, plans and expectations.

The issue, then, hangs upon the extent to which people are aware of their intentions and expectations and to what extent the things of which they are aware are really involved in determining the actions they take. Even if we are not aware of many cognitive processes, it may be that those relating to planning and selecting our actions *are* conscious. We certainly feel as if we consciously decide upon our actions. If you asked me "Why did you think of 'cat' when I asked for a word beginning with C?" or "Why did you just put the kettle on?" I would probably reply "I don't know" to the first question and "To make some coffee for my wife" to the second. In other words, I believe that I can answer the second question, and know that I cannot answer the first.

If people consistently reported ignorance of the processes underlying most cognitive processing but gave answers to questions about their reasons for actions, this would be a first step towards subdividing cognitive processing into that which is and is not available to introspection. Unfortunately, in many cases people will answer questions about their behaviour with apparent confidence when we have reason to believe that they are not aware of the causal factors. Sometimes the person may be aware that they are guessing to avoid appearing ignorant, foolish, or not in control of their own behaviour. Sometimes, however, they may really believe that they are giving a causal account, when experimental manipulations will show that they are not.

The problems raised by introspective data have stimulated a series of attacks upon the value of such data to psychology. From Watson (1913) onwards psychologists in the behaviourist tradition have criticized introspection. The 1960s and 70s saw the reacceptance of introspection within mainstream psychology, but the nature of the introspective process and its reliability has remained in dispute. The latest critique of introspection comes from Nisbett and Wilson (1977) who are particularly concerned to attack its use in explaining actions.

Recent objections to subjective reporting

Nisbett and Wilson (1977) claim that when people attempt to report upon higher order cognitive processes they do so not on the basis of true introspections but upon their *a priori* theories about the causes of behaviour. Accurate subject reports will therefore only occur by coincidence when the subjects' beliefs about the causes of behaviour happen to coincide with the real cause. To the extent to which Nisbett and Wilson are correct then explanations of actions offered by subjects will be appropriate only by accident. It is therefore necessary to review Nisbett and Wilson's arguments in some detail so that their interpretations can be evaluated.

Nisbett and Wilson begin by reviewing research on cognitive dissonance and self attribution. As they say, the view of Festinger (1957) and other dissonance theorists is that the cognition "I have done something unpleasant without adequate justification" is unpleasant and leads to a revision of the attitude towards the behaviour to avoid discomfort. The central idea of attribution theory is that people strive to discover the causes of their own responses and those of others, and the attribution of the cause will lead to many attitudinal and behavioural effects. Nisbett and Wilson reviewed all the insufficient justification and attribution studies in which both behavioural (or physiological) measures and verbal reports were obtained. They found that in twenty-two such studies, while the predicted behavioural changes were found, no differences in the verbal reports occurred, and in a further six cases the behavioural effects were more statistically reliable than the verbal reports. In only three studies were differences in verbal reports more statistically reliable than behavioural changes. In the five instances where data was available no significant correlation between verbally reported state and behavioural measures was found. In general, verbal reports of changes in evaluation or motivation were not related to actual changes in observable responses. Nisbett and Wilson go on to argue that subjects in these types of studies must show not only awareness of the existence of an evaluation or motive state, but awareness of a change in the evaluation or state. If a change has taken place but they cannot report it, then they cannot be aware of the nature of the cognitive process which has occurred. They point to studies by Bem and McConnell (1970) and Goethals and Reckman (1973). In these, subjects shifted their evaluations as a result of the experimental manipulations, but claimed at the end that their current attitudes were the same as those preceding the experiment.

Nisbett and Wilson note that a direct approach would be to ask subjects why they behaved as they did in insufficient justification and attribution studies, yet they could find only one report of such a procedure, and this found no subjective awareness of the processes. Nisbett and Wilson report unpublished data on such questioning. The consensus of this evidence was that many explanations were offered by subjects for the changes in their behaviour but very few mentioned the experimental manipulation. If the hypotheses was explained to them, they claimed they had not reasoned that way themselves. As Nisbett and Wilson say, "the explanations which subjects offer . . . are so removed from the processes that investigators presume to have occurred as to give grounds for considerable doubt that there is direct access to these processes" (p. 238).

Nisbett and Wilson go on to point out that there are several other areas in which subjects appear to be unable to report upon the processes leading to their responses. These include the weightings assigned in complex judgment tasks (Slovic and Lichtenstein, 1971), subliminal perception (Dixon, 1971), problem solving (Maier, 1931) and the effect of the presence of other people on helping behaviour (Latané and Darley, 1970). For example, creative workers describe themselves as bystanders, observing only the results of the problem solving process, the factors leading to the solution being hidden from conscious view (Ghiselin, 1952).

Perhaps the most social activity in this review is helping behaviour. Latané and Darley (1970) found that while the sounds of distress coming from another room became less likely to lead to an individual rushing to help as the number of other people in the room at the same time increased, both the subjects themselves, and others asked about the situation, denied that the presence of other people affected the willingness to help.

Nisbett and Wilson then report a series of experiments which they carried out to investigate people's ability to "report accurately on the effects of stimuli on their responses". In the first study subjects initially learned word pairs which were selected to increase the probability of giving related words in a subsequent word association task. Thus, for example, one pair was *ocean-moon,* and subsequently subjects were asked to name a detergent with the probability of saying "Tide" having been increased by the word pair. Although the priming occurred, subjects seemed unaware of the influence of the learned words.

In the next two studies the subjects showed a strong preference for objects at the right hand end of a display, when asked to choose, for example, between four identical stockings. No subject spontaneously mentioned position as influencing their choice and virtually all denied it when asked.

In a later experiment subjects watched an interview on teaching methods with a person who had "a European accent". In one condition the interviewee was autocratic and intolerant, in another he was pleasant and enthusiastic. His appearance, accent and mannerisms did not change, but subjects who saw the autocratic interview rated these as irritating, while those who saw the pleasant interview rated them as attractive. Subsequently, the subjects denied that the interviewee's general behaviour had influenced these ratings.

Nisbett and Wilson's final set of three experiments involved subjects reporting that some variable had influenced their performance when they did not actually differ from a control group. For example, in one study students were asked to predict how much electric shock they could take. One group were "reassured" that the shock would do "no permanent damage". Eighty per cent of these subjects said that the phrase increased their predictions, and the control subjects when questioned said it would have increased theirs, however, there was no difference in the predictions of shock that could be taken.

Nisbett and Wilson conclude that "it may be quite misleading for social scientists to ask their subjects about the influences on their evaluations, choices or behaviour (p. 247)". The reports that subjects give are systematic and match those given by "observer" subjects who simply read verbal descriptions of the experiment. Nisbett and Wilson propose that subjects do not consult their memories to report mediating processes, but simply make judgments about how plausible it is that a particular stimulus would have influenced the response.

CRITICISMS OF NISBETT AND WILSON

Smith and Miller (1978) claimed that Nisbett and Wilson (1977) are in danger of circularity in their argument. Since the latter's position is not falsified if demonstrations of correct verbal self reports are given, their theory is testable only by observing whether self reports are correct when they do or do not match the subjects' judgments of the plausibility of the stimulus causing the response. This criticism is unconvincing. Not only is the alleged circularity not established, since there seems no reason why evidence about subjects' *a priori* causal theories should not be independently gathered, but at least part of Nisbett and Wilson's case is made when they establish that in some situations subjective reports do not match the known causes. It is then up to their opponents to specify those situations in which self-reports can be accepted.

Smith and Miller accuse Nisbett and Wilson of expecting subjects to be aware of what has been effectively hidden by the experimental design. The between subjects design of, for example, the "Tide" study makes it impossible for the subjects to be aware of what is being experimentally manipulated. Here again the criticism seems to miss its mark. The higher frequency of "Tide" responses in the condition in which "moon-ocean" were previously learned indicates that prior exposure to the pair influenced performance. Presumably, the subjects were aware of this prior exposure. Nevertheless they did not report any link between the prior pair and the "Tide" response. All that can be claimed is that since such cueing is only one of the causes of the recall, while it has high priority for the experimenters for obvious reasons, subjects may concentrate on reporting more important causes. Even if some of Nisbett and Wilson's examples may be faulted as Smith and Miller argue (the latter, for example, suggest a possible reinterpretation of the stocking experiment which I will describe later) the general point remains that the subjects in Nisbett and Wilson's experiments were unable to report the causal relationship between the conditions to which they had been exposed and their subsequent response, even when specifically questioned about the manipulated variable.

Smith and Miller re-analysed one of Nisbett and Wilson's experiments, and demonstrated that although, overall, subjects did not agree upon the variable which influenced judgments, positive relationships were found when the analysis compared the subject's own rating with their report on how the information had influenced the rating. While similar weaknesses in the data analysis may mar the other studies in which no difference in performance was found even though subjects claimed that they had been influenced, this brings into question only a small part of Nisbett and Wilson's case.

Towards the end of their paper Smith and Miller comment that "Tasks that are novel and engaging for subjects, such as choosing a college or solving challenging problems often seem to evoke accurate introspective awareness of process (p. 361)". I will return to this point later.

Shotter (this volume) draws a distinction between telling and reporting and criticizes Nisbett and Wilson for misleading us into thinking that their results apply to telling as well as to reporting. In Shotter's terminology instances of telling are used "in an attempt to project the whole of myself in a certain way towards the future (p. 160)". Reports are used retrospectively to refer to already completed actions or events. They may be checked for their truth by observations. Instances of telling, however,

> do not have to be warranted like reports, by reference to facts, to any antecedently or currently existing states of mind, body or anything else . . . They are used by people to reveal to others what they currently have in mind — what their needs, interests and desires are, etc. — in an attempt to order future action (p. 171)

Shotter sees the danger in Nisbett and Wilson's approach of what people say not being taken seriously. Many statements made by people are, according to Shotter, cases of telling, not reporting, and as such are playing an important part in the social interaction.

Shotter is right to point out that comments about one's state may serve different functions and certainly some sense can be returned in this way to what might, following Nisbett and Wilson, be considered senseless, or at least useless, assertions. However, Shotter only defends cases of telling against the Nisbett and Wilson attack and Shotter's account of telling appears to exclude explanations. An explanation is directed towards clarifying something that has already happened; its primary function is not to influence what others do in the future, as is the purpose of telling, but to justify what was done in the past. They refer to, and are warranted by, antecedently existing conditions, as Shotter specifically says telling is not. Statements that refer to already completed actions are reports in Shotter's terminology, and Shotter's definitions of telling and reporting seems to place explanations firmly as cases of reporting. The point then remains that Nisbett and Wilson have made out a *prima facie* case against the reliability of subject's reports concerning the causes of their behaviour, while commonsense suggests that such reports are sometimes appropriate and helpful.

White (1980) develops a criticism initially made by Smith and Miller (1978) that Nisbett and Wilson wish to distinguish between cognitive *processes*, which are not available to introspection, and the *products* of such processing, which may, on occasions, be consciously available. Both White and Smith and Miller (1978) point out the problems in deciding what is a product and what a process. While these arguments seem valid they make little impression upon the Nisbett and Wilson position which does not depend upon the process/product distinction but upon the inaccuracy of subjective reports. Nor does the vagueness of terms like process and product undermine their usefulness as first approximations to a description of what may be available to introspection.

White argues that because the subjective reports discussed by Nisbett and Wilson were often obtained some time after the event, conscious experiences may well pass unnoticed and be forgotten. He also reminds us of the problems raised by any attempt to study consciousness. There is no logical reason for assuming that any behaviour, including reports purporting to be introspections, require consciousness for their occurrence; nor is there any test for the presence or absence of consciousness. Accepting these arguments does not damage the Nisbett and Wilson case so far as this chapter is concerned. Even if White succeeds in showing that they are saying little about consciousness he does not detract from their assertion that people frequently cannot report the causes of their behaviour. That people may fail to attend to or remember their conscious experiences actually strengthens Nisbett and Wilson's case. White goes on to provide evidence of subjects being better than observers at identifying the factors which influenced their decisions and shows that Nisbett and Wilson's method of analysis might have been too insensitive to reveal a difference. This throws doubt upon the Nisbett and Wilson hypothesis that both experimental and observer subjects make their judgments in the same way, based upon their theories of the causes of the behaviour, but it still leaves the frequent inaccuracy of subjects to be explained.

There are other criticisms of Nisbett and Wilson which might be raised. For example, if a difference is found in a behavioural measure, and no difference in a subjective measure, this may reflect the insensitivity of the subjective measure rather than a lack of an underlying effect. Also, since within-subject comparisons tend to be more sensitive than between-subject comparisons, when subjects report that they were influenced by a variable, although their group does not differ significantly from a control group, the problem may result from the insensitivity of the test between experimental and control groups rather than a failure on the subject's part. Do the conditions involving observer subjects differ sufficiently from the experimental conditions for differences to be expected on any theory? One might whittle away at the Nisbett and Wilson data, but the impression remains that there is a core of truth that many processes which social psychologists have assumed to be either taking place at a conscious level, or open to conscious examination are, in fact, opaque to introspection. The question is, which processes, and what implications can be drawn?

What processes are available to introspection?

Nisbett and Wilson (1977) claimed that they were considering "higher-order processes". They begin with the example questions "Why do you like him?" "How did you solve this problem?" "Why did you take that job?" and say that "In our daily lives we answer many such questions about the cognitive processes underlying our choices, evaluations, judgments and behaviour". A great deal seems to be included in Nisbett and Wilson's concept of a higher-order process. They appear to see no need to distinguish between aspects of behaviour which would normally be described as intentional and those for which the concept of intentionality seems inappropriate. Yet it is intentional acts for which people are held responsible and for which explanations will usually be expected. Nisbett and Wilson's example questions gloss over this important distinction. Taking a job is usually an intentional action, but liking someone is not. It seems perfectly reasonable to ask "How or why did you choose that job?", but bizarre to ask "How or why did you choose to like him?" Notice, incidentally, how Nisbett and Wilson's third question on problem solving falls between the other two. In some circumstances, where the person has tried out different strategies, "How did you solve this problem?" can be a question about intentional behaviour, but the actual processes which take place when a problem is solved are not under intentional control. However hard we may will ourselves, to solve a problem, the actual solution will depend not upon our willpower, but upon other cognitive processes.

The distinction between intentional and what I shall call non-intentional cognitive processes seems essential when considering those actions for which explanations are expected. "Non-intentional" is used in preference to "unintentional" because the latter term may carry the implication that intentional processes might be possible in the given situation. Excuses such as external influences (e.g. being pushed), ignorance or absentmindedness are appropriate to unintentional actions, but not to non-intentional processes. The incorporation of the intentional/non-intentional distinction into everyday expectations implies a general recognition of an important difference between chosen, responsible components of behaviour and those for which the concepts of choice and responsibility, at least in their everyday senses, are not appropriate. As I commented at the beginning of the chapter, the processes that have been studied by cognitive psychologists are rarely illuminated by introspections. But these are almost invariably non-intentional processes. Introspections have been very valuable in cognitive psychology where the behaviour has involved intentional components. So, for example, subject's reports of their strategies in trying to memorize word lists often help to explain their performance (e.g. Morris and Reid, 1970; Paivio, 1971).

If it is accepted that it is reasonable to distinguish between intentional and non-intentional aspects of behaviour, and that explanations are normally expected for intentional but not for the non-intentional components, we can ask whether Nisbett and Wilson, as the most recent and influential opponents of introspection, have established a case against the reliability of subject reports about both their intentional and non-intentional behaviour.

When the Nisbett and Wilson evidence is examined it soon becomes apparent that most, if not all, of it concerns non-intentional behaviour. They begin with the poverty of subjective reports in cognitive dissonance and attribution studies. Their evidence can be taken as demonstrating that Festinger and others were either incorrect or writing metaphorically when they attributed the reasons for their findings to cognitions such as "I have done something unpleasant without adequate justification". The processes underlying the results of the dissonance and attribution studies are not conscious ones, but neither is the behaviour involved intentional in the way that choosing a job is intentional. Subliminal perception and problem-solving, in the forms which Nisbett and Wilson discuss, are non-intentional. So are their experiments on associative cueing, personality judgments and estimates of electric shock resistance.

Both the stocking experiment and the helping behaviour research of Latané and Darley (1970) do seem, as described by Nisbett and Wilson, to involve intentional behaviour. However, the stocking experiment is odd in that subjects were asked to choose between identical stockings! Right hand end positions were chosen more frequently than others, but we would not expect position to be adopted by subjects as a basis for a reasoned decision. It is more plausible to accept Smith and Miller's (1978) suggestion that the position effect is a consequence not a cause of the way people make their decisions. If subjects compare each stocking with the earlier ones, and take the one that they are now considering and holding as the best, unless it is poorer than an earlier one, then there should be a strong tendency for the last examined stockings to be chosen. If this is the case, the subjects should be able to report criteria for making comparisons, but not that they chose the right hand stocking because it was at the right hand end because they did not.

Turning to the Latané and Darley (1970) experiments, this again is an unusual situation for the study of intentional behaviour. The assumption is that the point at which subjects rush to help when alone is a base-line representing, as it were, the triggering of the helping response, and that if subjects do not help so readily in other circumstances it is because they choose to inhibit their helping behaviour. It is just as reasonable to assume that the helping behaviour response will be triggered at different thresholds in different conditions. Some of these conditions are studied by Latané and Darley and give interesting information about the helping response. There is no reason, however, to assume that the studies tell us about the intentional inhibiting of a helping response.

To summarize, I have argued that it is important, when considering the reliability of people's explanations of their behaviour, to distinguish between intentional and non-intentional behaviour. While Nisbett and Wilson's studies extend the evidence that many non-intentional processes are unavailable to introspection they do not produce convincing evidence that people make inaccurate reports on their reasons for carrying out intentional actions. It is these actions for which explanations are usually requested, and for these actions that explanations are most confidently offered.

A hierarchical model of the cognitive system

Is it possible to incorporate the evidence upon those cognitive processes which seem open to introspection and those which are opaque into an acceptable model of the cognitive system? If it is, then, the eivdence from introspection may help our understanding of the system, while at the same time we may clarify what will and what will not be available to people asked to explain their actions. First, then, some consideration of the structure of the cognitive system.

Broadbent (1977) restates a principle which he says he was taught by Barlett and took for granted in his youth, namely, that the human processing system operates on many levels, some of which modify or control the operation of others. He comments that: "When therefore investigators of twenty or thirty years ago discussed and experimented upon single channel theories of human performance, they were speaking in a context of accepted multi-level theory and were talking solely of the top level of control (p. 182)". He quotes an example of Kenneth Craik's. Writing in the 1940s, he pointed out that when the Commander-in-Chief of Fighter Command orders a sweep over some area, he does not have to add that Spitfire number so and so must have so many gallons of petrol, have its guns loaded, plugs cleaned, etc. These details are delegated to subordinates. Craik argued:-

In just the same way, for rapidity and certainty in action, it is essential that certain units of activity, such as looking at an object, walking, grasping, using words, or balancing one's body, should be delegated to lower levels . . . (Craik, 1966, p. 38)

I shall assume that Broadbent, Bartlett and Craik are correct in identifying the need for the cognitive system to be hierarchical, (evidence for this view will be found in Broadbent, 1977). For present purposes I want to concentrate upon the top level of control, the equivalent of Craik's Fighter Command C-in-C. I shall refer to the system which is responsible for the top level of control as BOSS, a term which, I hope, carries the right implications of its function. I choose "BOSS" in preference to the term "central processor", which has been current in many views of cognitive psychology, because in some models the central processor does not serve a top-level control function.

Below BOSS are all the cognitive systems involved in perceiving, remembering, performing actions and so on. These systems will themselves be complex, hierarchical, interactive and frequently modified. They are the subject of most cognitive psychological research. Here, however, I will refer to them collectively as the EMPLOYEE systems. The purpose of BOSS is to control the EMPLOYEE systems to ensure that they function for the fulfillment of the general programme, the plans, the intentions of the overall system.

Because there is no general agreement about the structure of the cognitive system it is difficult to give examples of EMPLOYEE systems whose existence would be accepted by everyone. The following should, therefore, be taken as examples of the type of processes involved rather than as a claim that these particular processes actually exist. This said, examples of the EMPLOYEE systems would be iconic memory, feature detectors, logogens, episodic and semantic memory, and motor programmes controlling the actual production of movement and speech. EMPLOYEE systems are those parts of the overall system which either (a) convert the incoming physical energy into the format used by the cognitive system (e.g. words, semantic categories, the objects of visual perception) or (b) use that information to act upon the external world in fairly stereotyped ways which do not require BOSS for their direction or (c) control low level specific activities required to fulfil a BOSS command.

BOSS will be brought into operation when a new general plan must be put into operation, or when novel conditions demand the greatest control and flexibility in the responding of the system. At any particular time, therefore, BOSS may be engaged in running an executive programme which has been pre-determined by internal conditions, such as the overall plan for the day's activities, or by the needs of the organism which require high order control for their satisfaction; at other times BOSS may be directed to controlling the response to external changes, where these changes are novel and the responses various and important. One could, perhaps, push the business analogy further and equate the needs which determine the selection of BOSS programmes to shareholders to whom BOSS is eventually responsible. It is assumed that many activities do not require BOSS to intervene. A new skill, for example, may at first demand BOSS control, but, as it is perfected BOSS is freed to control other activities. In common with most of the research on limited processing capacity in the cognitive system it is assumed that BOSS has some limitation upon what it can process at any given time. It is also assumed that, in order for BOSS to control the functioning of the EMPLOYEE systems, data from these systems is made available to BOSS in a suitable format to allow the control of the overall functioning of the cognitive system.

It is, I hope, obvious that there is a high degree of correspondence between what we would describe as intentional activities and the functioning of BOSS. BOSS controls the overall plan which we are following at any particular time. As such it is responsible for the direction of our actions. In everyday life our talk about intending and choosing is concerned with the flexible control of our actions and deals with actions at a high level. That is, we choose or intend to, e.g. meet a friend, but we do not talk of choosing to make the specific bodily movements involved. In other words, we talk about plans, choices and intentions just as would be expected if they were part of the functioning of a BOSS system which controlled the main strategy of our actions but which was not responsible for more than initiating the specific behaviour required.

CONSCIOUSNESS AND BOSS

I wish to argue that conscious experience is part of the functioning of BOSS. This claim is far from novel. As long ago as 1890 William James wrote in the "Principles of Psychology" that: "The distribution of consciousness shows it to be exactly such as we might expect in an organ added for the sake of steering a nervous system grown too complex to regulate itself" (p. 144). More recently, Shallice (1972) has suggested that the cognitive system is controlled by a large set of "action systems", only one of which can be activated at any given time. He equated consciousness of X with the currently dominant action system receiving input from a selector mechanism which represents X. The selector mechanism has the dual function of providing the activation which leads to a particular action system being dominant and of setting the goal of the action system. In this system percepts correspond to selector inputs from the perceptual system, intentions to selector inputs from a previously dominant action system. The dominant action system controls the functioning of lower level components in the system.

In so far as the present discussion is concerned there is little difference between Shallice's model and the BOSS-EMPLOYEE system outlined earlier. In the BOSS system, Shallice's action-systems are programmes which are entered into BOSS. Shallice concentrates upon the programmes that control behaviour and avoids the implication of a separate part of the system responsible for overall control. Such parsimony is desirable if it can be maintained. Problems begin to arise when other than developed action systems are considered. I believe that a richer model than Shallice's is required to contain the conscious activities involved when developing a new skill, considering possible alternative future actions (see, e.g. Mandler, 1975, p. 53), planning one's day, etc. as well as to include other aspects of consciousness such as emotions. Also, one is conscious of more than an X, the specific information relevant to the dominant action system; one is conscious, for example, of a whole visual array some of which is relevant to current actions, some of which is not. I share with Shallice the belief that one is conscious of the inputs from lower level processing systems. It is this feature of consciousness which has led Miller (1962), Neisser (1967), Nisbett and Wilson (1977) and others to argue that we are conscious of the products of mental processing not the processes themselves. I suggest that a whole range of information is made available continuously to BOSS in a format suitable for the activation of BOSS programmes, if the situation so requires. Some of the information will be acted upon, and that will produce the phenomena of attention and the subjective experience of apperception (Wundt, 1912).

Consider the properties of your own consciousness. In perceiving and in imaging what is experienced is certainly highly processed and elaborated and many of the phenomena of perception, for example, size and shape constancies, seem designed to make the content of consciousness both stable and rich in potentially useful semantic information. This is, I suggest, because this is the nature of information appropriate to BOSS functioning. We are conscious of input which may require flexible actions by BOSS. This includes inputs of all kinds, visual, acoustic, but also emotional, as well as such things as pains. We are not conscious of information from bodily systems, such as those maintaining homeostasis until flexible actions (e.g. taking off clothing) are required. Some systems may never have developed information routes to BOSS and we are always unconscious of them. We are conscious of the relevant information when carrying out a difficult task, such as driving round a crowded roundabout. When learning a new skill we are often conscious of what we want to do, but cannot carry it out slickly. Gradually, with practice, we cease to be conscious of many learned skills, unless the situation becomes one needing novel, flexible control. When not dealing with a complex task, the apparently unitary stream of consciousness continues, occupied now with planning future actions or reviewing what has happened in the past. All this suggests that consciousness is related to the operations of BOSS, involving the input to BOSS, and, probably, some of the processes which go on within BOSS.

I believe that the equating of consciousness with the information supplied to and being processed in the BOSS system gives an account which is not only compatible with our experience of consciousness, but also assumes the philosophical position on the relationship between mental experience and the physical world which has fewest problems. I am claiming that consciousness is what it is like to be, as it were, inside the BOSS system. The advantages of this are that there then seems some sense in the very existence of consciousness. Otherwise, the evolution of consciousness would be bizarre, even if, as Wassermann (1979) has argued against Popper and Eccles (1977) it is logically possible that the evolution of human behaviour has been associated with the develop-ment of mental epiphenomena which, just by chance, have the integrated, consistent properties that they do. If the products of mental processing of which we are conscious are produced for a purpose, then the oddity of the very reason for their production is removed. Nor does one have to face the interactionists' problem of how mental events cause physical changes. White (1980) complained that in a model such as Shallice's one can take away consciousness and the model continues to function as before. But this is a inevitable property of any account of consciousness other than an interactionist one where mental events intervene causally in the physical world. It does not seem desirable to turn to the interactionist account, with all its attendant problems con-cerning the suspension of the physical laws if a less problematic account exists. On the present account consciousness is not dismissed as irrelevant, as an epiphenomenon, but, from the individual's own aspect, it is crucial, since it is part of the working of his highest level of functioning. Further discussion of the model and its philosophical position is not appropriate here.

Does this account of the link between BOSS and consciousness have testable implications, or is the argument circular? The accusation of circularity is certainly tempting since with the vagueness of our current knowledge of the cognitive system it is not always obvious which processes should be designated EMPLOYEE, and which part of BOSS. The danger of beginning to define processes on the basis of their conscious or unconscious functioning therefore exists, and if allowed would make the model circular. However, neither BOSS nor the EMPLOYEE systems are, in fact, defined in terms of consciousness, but according to their functions in the cognitive system. Further study of the processes in overall control of our behaviour will, I presume, be carried on, as in the past, without reference to consciousness, and as more is known about the BOSS system so the plausibility of the identification of consciousness with BOSS processing can be examined. Also, there are many cognitive processes which are obviously not BOSS processes. If examples of such processes can be found where we are conscious of the process, rather than its result, then the present account will be shown to be invalid. One such possibility would be iconic memory, which must precede most perceptual processing and is obviously not a BOSS process. Several attempts to estimate the duration of the icon have used the duration of the conscious experience of the briefly presented stimulus assuming the conscious experience to be equivalent to the icon (e.g. Haber and Standing, 1969). Such an assumption is clearly inconsistent with the present model. However, Coltheart (1980) has recently argued convincingly that the icon is not equivalent to the conscious experience in these experiments. The point, for present purposes, is that it is possible using empirical evidence to refute the BOSS-consciousness model.

IMPLICATIONS OF THE BOSS MODEL FOR EXPLANATIONS OF ACTIONS

I have claimed that we are conscious of at least some of the processes that occur in BOSS, but not of the processing in the EMPLOYEE systems. I have argued that we are conscious of the information made available for the flexible control of our overall behavioural strategy, and of some of the processes making use of this information, but not of the processes which make the information available. Earlier, I argued that we feel as if we can introspect about our plans and intentions, but not about processes such as probing memory. Neither Nisbett and Wilson

(1977) nor other critics of introspection have presented arguments which imply that we cannot report reliably upon our intentions. I have also argued that intentional behaviour is behaviour controlled by BOSS. Talk about intentions should eventually be translatable into talk about BOSS, when more is known about the BOSS processes.

When all these arguments are put together we have reasonable grounds for admitting people's explanations of their own actions as at least one respectable source of information on the causes of their behaviour. Not only do we feel that we can sometimes give explanations in terms of our plans and intentions, there is no good evidence that such explanations are less reliable than other reports which people make, and the BOSS-consciousness hypothesis provides an account of why these introspections may be more reliable than introspections about lower cognitive processes. If the BOSS-consciousness hypothesis is correct then intentions, plans and choices are part of the processing of the highest level of the cognitive system, with which consciousness is associated. When questions are asked concerning the functioning of this part of the system, then some useful subjective reports may be anticipated.

There will, however, remain many questions which cannot reasonably be answered with introspective reports. It is pointless to ask for introspections on processes which take place in the EMPLOYEE systems. They are not consciously experienced and will not be open to introspection. I agree with Nibsett and Wilson (1977) and those who preceded them in believing that it is risking misleading reports to ask for introspections on such processes. The BOSS-consciousness account suggests a test question which can be asked prior to any request for introspections. If the account is correct, then we can ask "are the processes about which I will request introspections, ones which involve either the directing of the person's behaviour in a flexible way in a fairly unpredictable situation, or a report of the information currently available to the person which will be used for this directing?" If the answer is "yes", then BOSS processes will probably be involved with conscious experiences which may be introspected. If the answer is "no" then introspections may be worse than useless, they may mislead. Questions such as "Why did you take that job?" may produce illuminating self-reports; questions such as "Why do you like him?" "Why did you forget my name?" will not. The danger is that subjects may feel that they should answer the latter types of questions. They may feel that an account is required of them, or that they can, indeed give useful information. However, their reports are likely to be couched in terms appropriate to BOSS but irrelevant to the processing by the relevant EMPLOYEE system. An analogy might be that of a managing director of a business who has never observed his employees at work being ask how some skilled member of his staff carries out his task. His reply, if he had to give one, would be a mixture of guesswork, prejudice and personal experience often wrongly applied. He might, however, be able to make useful comments about his own job, just as introspections about BOSS processes may be valuable.

Other cognitive limitations on explanations of actions

Not all questions about the reasons for actions are questions demanding introspections, and the reliability of subjects' answers is then another problem which cannot be discussed here. Even when introspections might be of value there is no guarantee that they will be given. Subjects may base their answers upon observation of their own behaviour, their own inferences about why they did what they did, or they may use, as Nisbett and Wilson suggest, commonly accepted plausible accounts of why an action is being performed. The difficulty of knowing when a subject is giving an honest introspective report and when, through incompetence at introspection or social pressure to say the right thing, he is making up a report has dogged the use of introspection since its first use in psychology, and will always make such data less reliable than that which can be observed and repeated publicly.

Even when a subject is cooperating fully, he is limited by the problem of describing the content of his consciousness. We can only learn to name those subjective experiences which occur sufficiently regularly in similar external conditions for a person who already knows the language to judge that the individual he is teaching is, in these particular circumstances, having a particular type of experience. He can teach about tickles, itches, pains, etc. in this way, but when an experience is not regularly linked with some known observable situation, or has not been regarded as important enough by language users in the society for a word to have been adopted to name it, then an introspecting subject will be unable to describe his experiences. Also, because of the way in which the names for subjective experiences are learned, there is no way of confirming that the experience which you, for example, call a tickle is the same as that which I call a tickle. All that we know is that we talk about the experiences consistently, when there is evidence that can be used. If I stroked the palm of your hand with a feather, and you giggled with laughter, and then reported that you felt a searing pain in your hand I would suspect that you did not know the meaning of the words "pain" or "tickle". Normally, these oddities do not arise, and this can be taken as some evidence for the consistency of the understanding of those words in common use which refer to mental experiences and for the similarity between individuals of the mental states to whcih they refer. Nevertheless, the limitations upon any unusual explanation relating to a mental state, remains.

Even if subjective reports upon the reasons for their actions are taken as evidence for the processes which led up to the actions, the reports will be no more reliable than any others involving memory for past events. Studies of eyewitnesses' memories, where objective checking is possible, reveal frequent recall errors, which are made worse by the asking of questions about the events (see Bull and Clifford, 1979 for a recent review). The accuracy of memory depends upon the type and amount of processing at the time when learning takes place, and the availability at the recall stage of cues appropriate to the memory trace initially laid down (see e.g. Morris, 1978). Some of the factors which led up to a particular action may play only a fleeting part in the ongoing cognitive processing and may be poorly encoded, or uncued at the time that an explanation is required.

Finally, even if my BOSS/EMPLOYEES model is correct, only some questions about intentional actions can lead to useful replies. A point will soon be reached when the questions leave the province of BOSS and move to the EMPLOYEE systems. Take, for example, my reply to the question "Why did you just put the kettle on?" which was "To make some coffee for my wife". If I am then asked "But why did you put it on just *now*?" I will soon be drawn away from reporting upon processes to which I have any introspective knowledge. I do not know how I decide when to put on the kettle; I may not know why I thought of doing so. The reasons for these lie outside BOSS processing. They are no longer the result of activity in the system in overall control of our actions, but of the lower level systems which supply information to BOSS, or of past circum-stances which have determined the nature of the programmes run in BOSS. So, if we looked for the reason for my putting on the kettle just now we would have to consider EMPLOYEE systems such as internal clocks, or past events which led to the development of the programme which I follow during a normal morning, and so on. The limits of intro-spective awareness of our reasons for acting are rapidly reached. Of course, we may still be able to offer useful information when taken beyond them, and forced to consider our memories of what we do and why.

In this chapter I have reviewed some of the arguments that have recently been advanced against the reliability of subject reports. If these arguments were valid they would lead to serious doubts about the reliability of people's explanations of their actions. However, I hope that I have shown that intentional actions are not covered by this evidence, and that an examination of the nature of the cognitive system and consciousness suggests that valuable information on the reasons for intentional actions may, in some circumstances, be accurately reported by subjects.

9

Personal Constructs and Private Explanations*

S. Wilkinson

This chapter is about the role that ordinary explanations can play in research on one particular topic within social psychology: impression formation in dyads. I will be trying to show how according a central importance to individuals' own explanations has had a crucial influence on my own research, leading me away from traditional experimental methods to an ordinary language, case study approach. Furthermore, I will be arguing that this kind of approach not only affords proper respect to its "subjects", but is a prerequisite for an adequate investigation of impression formation — because traditionally oriented studies just cannot encompass the essential nature of the process. The chapter will thus be a specific demonstration of how working with ordinary explanations can enrich the psychologist's understanding of personal and social life. In presenting this, I will be concentrating on the conceptual and methodological issues that most clearly develop the overall theme of this volume, rather than examining particular individuals' explanations of impression formation in detail (although some examples of these will be given).

More specifically, I have three particular objectives. Firstly, I hope to demonstrate that while impression formation within relationships can be considered as a competent social performance (in that it is smoothly incorporated into continuing social interaction), and as such amenable to "public" explanation, it is also essential to view it as a highly individual and very personal activity, necessitating the exploration of "private" explanations. While other contributors to this volume — for example, Canter and Brown (Chapter 10) — have stressed public

*This is based on research conducted at the Dept. of Psychology, University of Surrey, for which the support of a Social Science Research Council studentship is gratefully acknowledged. I would also like to thank Peter Stringer for helpful discussion.

explanations, my principal concern here will be with private meanings. My second objective is to indicate how two particular theoretical perspectives have contributed to this line of study. These are ethogenics (Harré and Secord, 1972; Harré, 1979) and personal construct theory (Kelly, 1955, 1969). I will focus more especially on the latter, which is particularly suited to my emphasis on private explanations, and will follow up some of the implications of taking it seriously; for fuller discussions of the ethogenic perspective, see Harré (Chapter 6), and Shotter (Chapter 7) (both this volume). My final — and more general — objective is to convey a "user's eye view" of ordinary language, case study research — its joys and problems. I hope to emphasize the unique advantages of working with people's own explanations of impression formation, yet also indicate the considerable conceptual and methodological problems associated with obtaining, evaluating and interpreting such explanations. I will also present a few short excerpts from my data transcripts: this is only partly in illustration of my arguments; it seems to me essential that in an account of research on ordinary explanations some ordinary explanations should appear — and they make fascinating reading.

Background to the research

Firstly, to put the research into context, it is necessary to explain some of the rationale for undertaking it. The initial impetus was a dissatisfaction with most of the existing research in the area. This shows only too clearly the consequences of reliance on the traditional view of psychology as akin to a natural science — for example, Hull (1952) — and the associated model of man as essentially passive and reactive, operating according to natural laws and principles. The adequacy of this conceptual stance has been widely debated in recent years: see for example, Arnold (1976), and many social psychologists, in particular, now acknowledge its limitations — for example, Armistead (1974).

The ramifications of this view seem particularly pervasive when surveying the literature relating to impression formation in dyads. First, one encounters massive conceptual oversimplification. This appears principally in the fact that the topic itself spans two areas of mainstream social psychology which are traditionally separated and distinct: person perception and friendship formation. It is supposed that the impressions we form of other people can be studied independently of our relationships with them; however, I would want to argue that the two are inseparably interlinked, and should be studied as such.

Secondly, each of these areas has had its own research paradigm, which has evolved little since its inception and has dominated most of the studies in the field: in person perception, Asch's (1946) studies of trait centrality; in friendship formation, Byrne's (1961) studies of attitude similarity (sometimes referred to as "the attraction to a stranger paradigm"). Both, however, are firmly laboratory-based, involving individual "subjects" in simple and artificial judgment tasks on the basis of a limited amount of highly-controlled stimulus material. I would want to argue that studies of this type show little respect for their "subjects" as people and as individuals, and are focussing on something which bears very little relation to what goes on in everyday life. By imposing a predetermined framework (checklist, rating scale, question-naire, etc.) on an individual's impressions, all the richness and subtlety of her/his personal viewpoint and its meaning to her/him is lost — and a very impoverished view of the impression formation process is consequently obtained. Furthermore, in their isolation of variables to be studied on a single occasion, with (usually) a single "subject" in the laboratory, these studies lose sight of the fact that impression formation is a complex, dynamic, and above all, inherently *social* process. It normally takes place as a component of two-way interactions, which are themselves part of the larger purpose of getting to know someone. For an adequate study of the process, then, I would stress as a minimum requirement the need to consider individuals' *own* accounts of their impression formation, within the social context of a developing relation-ship.

A handful of recent studies have moved outside the old restrictive paradigms, shifting their emphasis, in Antaki and Fielding's terms (this volume, p.28), from an information-processing to a representational mode. However, it seems to me that they have not gone far enough. For example, within person perception, Bromley (1977) and Rosenberg (1977) are working with open-ended descriptions of actual acquaint-ances — but both consider static, "one-off" impressions, devoid of social context, and employ reductionistic forms of data analysis. In his work on friendship, Duck (for example, 1973) has attempted to integrate the fields of person perception and friendship formation — but only by subsuming impression formation as an early stage of friendship, which fails to consider the *interplay* between impressions, and a developing relationship. Individuals' own impressions are obtained (but restricted by a Reptest format) and change over time is considered, but the studies are very limited in scope and do not really enter into the meanings or the social dynamics of the process at all. It seems abundantly clear that in these fields, at least, workers have been constrained by the traditional model of man and associated methods of study.

Elaborating an alternative perspective

Beginning from an altogether different conceptual stance — that of psychology as a distinctively human science and man as an active, self-determining agent (see, for example, Shotter, 1975, and this volume) — it seemed that it might be possible to gain a much deeper understanding of impression formation. The perspectives of Kelly (1955) and Harré and Secord (1972) seemed to have several essential similarities, but perhaps most crucial was their focus on the individual as active constructor of and reporter on her/his own social life — in line with my own priorities for study. I was particularly drawn to personal construct theory because, taken as a meta-view, and interpreted in its broadest and fullest sense (most users of it never get beyond the repertory grid technique), it seemed to have wide implications for the kind of research I was interested in; this is also true of ethogenics, but construct theory has a more specific concern with private explanations. Beyond this, Kelly's view seemed to have particularly interesting — and relatively unexplored — further implications for the re-shaping of social psychology in a more humanistic direction, while Harré's view has been explicitly developed along these lines. (I will defer a discussion of Kelly's far-reaching suggestions until a later section.)

The important emphases of personal construct theory seem to me to be as follows. First, in stressing that each person deals with the world (including other people) by placing her/his own interpretative framework over it, personal construct theory establishes a *necessity* for studying individuals' *own* viewpoints in order to understand them at all. Furthermore, Kelly makes it abundantly clear that people *are* able to describe their own realities: as Salmon (1979, p. 222), comments, "If Kelly is associated with any single remark, it is probably his suggestion that if you want to know something about someone, you should ask him" (this is, sometimes, referred to as Kelly's "first principle") — indicating that people's own words are to be the primary data source. It may be noted that this is very much in line with Harré's contention that man not only controls his own behaviour, but can *account* for it.

Secondly, Kelly's emphasis on each individual's viewpoint as personal and unique (individuality corollary) provides a firm rationale for idiographic investigation, each individual being of interest as a subject of study in her/his own right. This led me to case studies: there is no reason why these should not be viewed as scientific — see, for example, Dukes (1965); Shapiro (1966) — but to regard them as the basis for a whole social psychology may well entail a much wider conception of the scientific enterprise than that traditionally held by psychologists. I will return to this issue later.

Thirdly, Kelly suggests that the basis of social behaviour is one's attempt to understand the other's viewpoint (sociality corollary). This directs one's attention both to *why* the social context of impression formation (that is, its location within two-way interactions, themselves part of a developing relationship), is important, and to *how* it operates to shape the process: your view of X will be influenced by your view of her/his view of you; similarly, X's view of you will be influenced by her/his view of your view of her/him. The corollary thus emphasizes the need to study the reciprocal perspectives of individuals in relation.

This applies to the psychologist as much as to those she/he studies: she/he can only enter a role relationship with her/his "subjects" by endeavouring to construe their construction processes. Kelly stresses the essential continuity between psychologist and lay-person (after all, they both have the same objective of trying to understand the world), and following on from this the need to account for the behaviour of both in the same terms. (This is part of his argument on the necessity for reflexivity, an issue central to psychology, but rarely given consideration — as Harré, p.139, this volume notes.) I would regard this as having important implications for "subject" and "experimenter" roles within social psychology, and, particularly, as indicating the need to break down this distinction and move towards regarding both as participants or collaborators in the same enterprise. (As a first step in this direction I refer to my "subjects" as "participants".) The extensive literature on experimenter effects and demand characteristics (for example, Orne, 1962; Rosenthal, 1966) testifies to the fact that the traditional role of the social psychologist has been somewhat ambivalent: she/he has been viewed as exerting a pervasive influence in her/his research, but this has nevertheless been seen as "confounding". Kelly's position implies a new role for the social psychologist: embedded in the research, rather than directing or observing it; actively utilizing her/his presence rather than attempting to remain detached and "objective". This seems far more appropriate for a *social* psychologist than detachment. Taking these arguments seriously and applying them to my own research, I must be prepared to study the dynamics of impression formation in relationships by being in relation myself: I therefore participate in the research as a dyad member. The acceptability of the idea that one can *only* investigate social relationships by being in relation oneself is a further issue whose implications I shall pursue later.

The research methodology

The methodology used has been developed and refined over several sets of studies, to reflect, as far as seems practicable, the concerns amplified above. Essentially, it involves case studies of individuals in relation. Participants are simply individuals who are interested in finding out more about themselves and their relationships; those involved in pilot studies were mainly university students but these in turn recruited a wide circle of friends and acquaintances. I am included amongst them, and considered to have the same status as any other participant. In the later stages of the study participants were strategically selected* from those who participated in the pilot studies, which also served a training purpose. The criteria for selection were a high degree of introspective interest in one's own impression formation and an ability to articulate this to others — characteristics suggested by preliminary work as desirable for maximizing quality and quantity of information obtained. I would not want to suggest that the methodology used is only suitable for this type of individual, but rather to argue for flexibility of design: modifying the techniques used or considering alternatives ones when working with other types of people.

Each participant is given a very full briefing on the rationale behind and objectives of the research, and is encouraged to comment on it at any time. She/he is then assigned, simply on the basis of a mutually convenient initial meeting time, to a same-sex dyad, and is introduced to her/his partner. In general terms, the members of a dyad are simply requested to monitor their impression formation while getting to know each other, interacting freely on a number of occasions over four to six weeks. They set the parameters of their own meetings: time, location (a

*Strategic selection involves utilizing the individual cases that best fit one's criteria for study. It is rarely used in a psychology which has pre-occupied itself with issues such as representativeness and generalizability, but is common in other branches of science. A detailed rationale for it may be found in Glaser and Strauss (1967), while a further example of its use in social psychology is provided by Rapoport and Rapoport (1976).

reasonably "homely" room is available for coffee and conversation if requested), length, etc. and decide when to actually terminate the research period (some continue to meet beyond it!). More specifically, they are asked to record the following information, by means of an unstructured account, as soon as possible after the first meeting: impression of partner, and its basis; partner's likely impression of self, and its basis; details of the relationship being formed. After subsequent meetings they note changes in both sets of impressions and the relationship, and how these interact. I should perhaps note that this procedure is not intended to be a real-life analogue in any way — simply a particular research context designed to aid the participants in examining their own impressions.

Once the sequence of meetings is over, the dyad members are asked to summarize the proceedings and evaluate the research and its methodology. They also provide a range of additional information, again via unstructured accounts, to put the meetings into context — the data from the actual interactions is viewed only as the "core" of each case study. This further information consists of biographical data; an outline life history; details of past and present social networks and significant relationships; and material relating to the self-concept.

The analysis, which considers each dyad as a separate single case and examines the perspectives of both participants and their interaction within the relationship, is also within the framework of personal construct theory. In selecting a framework, I had two guiding concerns. The first of these was to keep a sense of the relationship as a whole while looking at the finer detail of it. The second was to consider dyadic impression formation both in its wider sense as a competent social performance and in its narrower sense as essentially very individual and private. (As will probably be apparent, these led me to reject an ethogenic analysis, for while this may have illuminated the social dynamics of the relationship, there seems to be very little place in it for what is essentially very personal.)

A construct theory framework seems to fulfil both my criteria in the following way. I can retain a sense of the whole relationship in terms of purposes and patterns of construing: the objectives of action (understanding/prediction of the world, including self and other, as laid down by Kelly's fundamental postulate) and the means by which these are achieved (general principles of use of a construct system). However, on this I can superimpose finer detail of the individual's own particular purposes (including, particularly, the importance of core role construing), and the content, organization and use of her/his own particular construct system. With respect to my second criterion, the sociality corollary provides for an understanding of the social dynamics of the relationship in highly personal terms: by considering how each individual's view of her/his partner's impressions influences her/his own impressions and how these in turn influence the developing relationship: this can also be related back to and understood in terms of the individual's own purposes and specific constructions. A further important feature of the research is that all my interpretations are taken back to the individuals involved — both to provide feedback for them and to elicit comment and critique. It seems particularly important to negotiate and intermesh my outsider's perspective with the insiders' views in the dyads where I am not a participant member.

I would now like to turn to a consideration of what working with ordinary explanations is actually like: the kind of data that are obtained, the particular advantages of them, and at least some of the problems and issues that arise in attempting to interpret them. I will also return to some of the wider implications of the approach I have taken.

Advantages of an ordinary language approach

The most immediately apparent advantage of obtaining individuals' own explanations of their impression formation is the tremendous richness and complexity of the accounts they give. This may seem an obvious point, but when confronted with this type of data, the degree of attention to detail and the extent of individuals' insights is truly impressive. Two very brief examples — chosen more or less at random from typical transcripts — will serve to illustrate this assertion:

I also like looking at her, she has a lovely face and looks at me a lot while she talks, which is important. I had a fleeting impression at one point that there was something in her face which betrayed a slight weakness. She has a strong face, full of determination, yet kind, but somewhere there was a suggestion of weakness, maybe the way she uses her mouth sometimes. I made a mental note to look for that again.

. . . the edges of the initial impression have softened as the framework has been built on. For example, I think I perceived A's directness/mettle as "tougher" on the first encounter than I do now. It's very difficult to assess exactly why — partly, one suspects, because she admits to being sensitive to say, being lonely (on leaving home (meeting 2)), needing to lose a few pounds in weight, etc. At the base of it all is the fact that one can identify with these commonplace problems/worries.

It seems to me that these data alone amply confirm the view that traditional studies of impression formation are impoverished.

As soon as one begins to analyse these accounts, it becomes apparent that this kind of approach and methodology generates insights into the impression formation process which a more traditional investigation could not even begin to achieve. To illustrate this I will give examples of two processes which appear in several transcripts, and which seem to be central to the way in which individuals explain and account for their impression formation.

First, the extent to which individuals refer their impressions of their partners back to their own self-impressions is remarkable: virtually all participants indicated extensive self-other comparisons. Additionally, it appears that an important feeling behind this process is an uncertainty about the self:

> I was impressed both by her academic subject background and by the careful, articulate way she expanded on her field of interest (problem-solving, lateral thinking, concept formation, etc.). Somewhere around this point I began to feel over-awed by B's obvious ability and very conscious of the gaps in my own knowledge/ability. My own self-image embodies the idea that I am below average where rational, analytic thought is concerned. Consequently, I am impressed by this ability in others.

Similarly, in this example:

> Difficult to admit, but I think that someone as collected as C appeared to be on the 1st meeting (and the fact that she's pretty, intelligent) makes it more difficult to empathise. If one feels self-conscious (which I did on the 1st occasion) there is a greater tendency to hold oneself up as some kind of a mirror to the other person. If one is feeling very together then, even with strangers, the self-image matters less (ideally, not at all, *but!*) . . . .

Secondly, it is evident just how important it is for individuals both to define this relationship and to fit it into the context of others they have or have had. Again, the aspect of this that seems crucial is what their relationships reveal about themselves. For example:

> We talk about all sorts of things, from the emotional to the scientific, concrete to abstract and back. I'm not conscious of holding anything

back. But I feel somehow that something is missing. Thinking about the close friendships I have, first of all they're mostly with men. Secondly the women I have as close friends are very aggressive and pride themselves on their intellect. Neither of these statements are true of D. But what is the implication of that for the closeness of the relationship? Another point is that all the men I have as close friends have both male and female qualities. They too are aggressive, but they are also emotional, interested in the human condition and all of that. So obviously I feel drawn towards people who span a wide range of responses, interests, characteristics etc. Where D doesn't quite fit this is in the fact that she is very female. She's not aggressive — all her extroversion is manifested in her friendliness, caring, interest in others, relaxed manner. She is outgoing, but in no way seeks to conquer. I am attracted by that, I like it. I think I would like to have a mother like her. But in a friend I want the masculine dimension as well.

These kinds of insights seem to suggest that we should be working towards a much wider understanding of impression formation — and, indeed, that a reconceptualization of the process based on its place in and interplay with a developing relationship and its relation to past relationships and other events in the individual's life, is long overdue. I would propose, for example, on the basis of the examples I have given, that one vital element is a complex process of self-exploration and definition.

A second major joy (or series of joys) of this type of research lies in the participants' reactions to it. They seem to find it both interesting and enjoyable (the level of enthusiasm is often surprising), but more importantly, they find it of value to them. It is worth noting that many of the benefits which emerge are of immediate use to the participants themselves: they appear either during the course of the meetings or as a direct result of them, and do not depend on applying "knowledge" gained from this research in some distant future context. The process of participating in the research constitutes a learning experience in itself, and often generates insights which individuals feel will be valuable in future interactions. Here is an extract from one participant's evaluation:

First of all it was very enjoyable!!! Second, I really do think that it "got at" some processes of impression formation in that I was able to analyse the "instinctive" . . . I found it quite rewarding in that I was surprised how much of the impression formation process is based on hard concrete fact, although they emerge fleetingly packaged together into one global positive or negative packet. I gained in that I *could* (but maybe not *will*) be more consciously and actively searching for clues with future newcomers. I could also apply this to people whom I tend to fight shy of meeting, i.e. people who are strange in any way — outside the norm. Consciously searching for clues could take one's mind off the strange part, i.e. a handicap. This could apply to anyone with whom one feels ill at ease.

Participants also seem to value the research for itself: to approve of its aims and methods and (particularly) to appreciate the contrast with more traditional research. Typical comments were:

It's more "real" than anything I have come across in text books and treats people as subjects rather than objects — therefore more likely to tap true real relationships.;

Valuable research. I feel it "got at" something — even I was surprised at myself! Difficult to see how questionnaires etc. would have tapped the nuances and the flux embodied in the impression-formation process.

This sort of positive evaluation in turn feeds back into the research. With this type of approach one experiences a remarkable working relationship: rapport is easily established, the level of cooperation is high, and the volume and standard of data is thereby maximized. Finally, it is notable that one obtains "personal" as well as "professional" benefits from adopting a participant role. Just like the other participants I found I both enjoyed the meetings and learnt more about myself and my impression formation.

Thus far I have presented a very positive picture of this type of research; I will now redress the balance by discussing some of the problems I have encountered, particularly those associated with the evaluation and interpretation of accounts — although these in turn have been a valuable aspect of the research, leading me on to consider its wider implications.

Issues and implications

First of all, in ordinary everyday life, we do not normally turn our attention to the dynamics of impression formation, but simply get on with the business of living out our relationships. However, this does not mean that individuals have no insight into the precesses taking place: if you ask them they can explain them, as Kelly's "first principle" and Harré and Secord's "open souls doctrine" would indicate, and as I hope the examples I have given illustrate. The problem becomes one of assisting people to articulate this knowledge, or in Antaki and Fielding's terms (this volume, p.27), of helping them translate "unconscious or unrealized" information into definite "private explanations", which can then be communicated directly via accounts. It is because this is such an unfamiliar activity that people need assistance with it. My methodology, construed as a "guided exploration" of impression formation — in that individuals are asked to monitor the process during several pre-arranged meetings over a limited period of time and to provide certain kinds of information as they do so — is an attempt to provide this kind of assistance with minimum interference, although in itself it is only one kind of answer. Other workers within the field of personal construct theory are grappling with this problem: see, for example, Mair's (1970) "Conversational Model", and Bonarius' "Reptest Interaction Technique", Eland et al. (1979). A similar concern can also be seen in the ethnomethodologists' procedures for assisting people in examining "background assumptions", and in Harré and Secord's rule-breaking (here the rationale is that even if people cannot articulate the rules that order their social conduct, they may be aware of violations of them).

Researchers of a more traditional persuasion often level the old objections to introspective techniques at the use of individuals' own accounts: reliability, accuracy of reports, reactivity, etc. I want to argue that these criticisms are just not appropriate in this context. If we are attempting to study a person who actively interprets reality in her/his own terms, then her/his own account of those terms is the only acceptable primary source of data. It does not matter whether this account is "accurate" or "reliable" (whether or not we accept that there is a "correct" view): she/he acts on each situation as she/he sees it, and it is this — or what she/he chooses to tell us of this — that is significant. The argument of reactivity (here, that in focussing an individual's attention on her/his own impression formation thereby changes it in some way) can also be stood on its head: the researcher who adopts the kind of perspective I have suggested is not trying to minimize her/his influence in the investigation, but to actively utilize it as part of the study. Along with this goes an increased awareness of the new role and a commitment to monitoring its effects. I will say more about this in a while; see also Canter and Brown's chapter (this volume) for a different perspective on "the explainer's role". In some ways, of course, this new social psychology can be seen as less reactive than the old: it interferes with its "subjects" less, studies them in natural social situations, and gives maximum credence to their own phenomenal accounts.

A much more significant line of criticism relates to the possible limitations of accounts. It seems important to consider the adequacy of individuals' own accounts as explanations of a complex social phenomenon such as a social relationship — and there are indications that there may be problems here. In one sense, as Shotter (1977; Chapter 7, this volume) argues, an individual does not possess "in her/his head" all the necessary information to explain his impression formation. She/he cannot explain her/his actions with reference to her/his inner processes because these are only one element of action: in a complex social situation action is joint or shared — between the inner processes of each actor and the outer processes of the situation. Each individual thus has only partial knowledge of it. Similarly, Radley (1978) emphasizes that relationships are not based on the coming-together of two isolated, private worlds, but on what happens "between people": on experience which is shared and lived through together. Shared experience would appear to be central to an understanding of relationships — but to what extent does this method tap into it? It seems clear that any one individual's account cannot constitute an adequate representation of the situation and all its intersubjective elements; can this be attained by the integration of accounts from both participants, including their views of the relationship (viewed as a product of the shared experience of their interactions)? I think the answer is "only partially", but that this is not necessarily a limitation of the methodology — but rather a question of whether shared experience *can* be subjected to meaningful empirical investigation.

This brings me to the associated problem of the interpretation of accounts. While it appears that the individual can only partly explain her/his own action, the psychologist is doubly distanced in trying to explain someone else's. As Shotter (this volume, p.159) comments, there is quite a gulf between the insider's "informed" perspective and that of someone attempting to interpret the action from the outside. (Interestingly, this is in line with the attribution theorists' interest in actor-observer differences — see, for example, Jones and Nisbett (1972).) The first step in trying to interpret someone else's explanations — as personal construct theory points out — must be to achieve an understanding of how she/he sees the situation (that is, to construe her/his construction processes). Personal construct theory also points to the way of doing this: by becoming an insider oneself. The psychologist who really wants to achieve an understanding of social relationships must be prepared to do so by being in relation herself/himself and by subjecting his own experience to rigorous analysis. This must, of course, be tempered by both a heightened awareness and a clear analysis of one's influence in this role; and one must also consider the wider issues involved. Central amongst these would appear to be the extent to which any one individual's relationships are particularly characteristic of her/him, and whether the psychologist in relation is any different from the layperson in relation.

However, while I am included in the research as a dyad member (and thereby achieve greater understanding of this particular social relationship), the problem is not solved with regard to the other dyads in which I am not a participant and to which, it is clear, I have no privileged access. Does this mean that in following up the widest implications of a personal construct theory approach one can *only* investigate one's own relationships? Furthermore, if this is so, what kind of social psychology would we then have? (N.B. Stringer (1979) hints at an answer to this question.)

I believe it *is* the case that the fullest insights will only be achieved by studying one's own relationships — but that this only appears unacceptably restrictive if one sees the psychologist as the centre of the action. A shift in perspective reveals a varied team of researchers, collaborating on an investigation, and within which each member (regardless of "professional" status) is considered as an expert in her/his own relationships. One important implication of this would be to dissolve the distinction between "ordinary" and "scientific" explanations — although this need not mean (at least initially) that there would be no distinction between psychologist and layperson. The psychologist may still be regarded as possessing a battery of "professional" skills, but instead of using them to investigate "subjects" she/he would turn them to an investigation of her/his own relationships and pass them on to others to enable them to do likewise.

This type of social psychology would therefore be characterized by in-depth investigations, conducted by individuals who would be participating principally to explore their own relationships, and who would thus be the primary beneficiaries of the knowledge gained (which would consist of intensely personal and largely qualitative data). But is this science — and could anything be communicated beyond the investigators themselves? I believe the answer to both these questions is "yes" — for the following reasons.

First of all, patterns found in one case may be found in others: hence it is possible to look for similarities in processes between people. At the very least, comparisons and contrasts between individual cases may lead to the establishment of a body of "case law" (Bromley, 1977). In addition, Herbst (1970) argues that by examining a single case for data on behavioural variables, and then "adding on" more similar cases, one obtains a set from which behaviour principles characterizing the type can be derived — his ultimate quest is for a general theory. Also, Harré (1978) suggests that we may be able to identify universals (if we want to) from comparisons of individual cases — but by looking for underlying *structural* homologies (as in linguistics) rather than laws at the level of action. These, however, are answers from within a traditional view of science. I believe that the implications of this type of research are much more exciting if one takes a much wider view of the scientific enterprise than that habitually entertained by psychologists.

The view I am suggesting is based on a paper by Sloman (1976).* Sloman regards the central aim of science as extending man's knowledge and understanding of the universe. In working towards this he emphasizes the importance of our knowledge of possibilities: indicating that it is crucial to establish what sorts of things are possible and impossible — and how and why they are. However, beyond the deline-ation and exploration of possibilities, Sloman is concerned with ways of increasing the range and types of possibility that are open to us. He shares this emphasis on the expansion of possibilities with Kelly (see also Wilkinson, 1980), who says, for example:

> The humanistic researcher looks for what man can do that he has never done before, rather than conclusive explanations of what man has been doing all the time. (1969, p. 104)

It is Mair (1970) who indicates *how* personal data may be communicated and constitute part of the scientific endeavour, viewed in these terms. Individual insight may be viewed as contributing to a body of actualities and possibilities, in that what is revealed as an actuality for one person thereby becomes a possibility for another — and thus broadens the range of options for future action and explanation. In this way both our personal possibilities and our view of man and what he can do are continually extended. It is to this end that a fully elaborated personal construct study of private explanations may lead.

*I am grateful to Jonathan Potter for bringing this to my attention.

10

Explanatory Roles

D. Canter and J. Brown

An outline of the chapter

The purpose of the present chapter is to "situate" explanations, to put them into context. Ordinary explanations are given for a variety of reasons and take on a wide range of forms. As a consequence, any explorations of explanations in daily use requires an examination of the role of the *explainer* vis-a-vis that which is being explained, as well as the role of the *explanation*. In other words, this chapter moves towards a typology of explanatory roles based upon the relationship between the explained event and the person doing the explaining.

The discussion of explanatory roles embraces many of the issues dealt with separately by other contributors to the present volume. For example, van der Pligt focusses on people with different perspectives on events (as actor or observer), Harris and Harvey examine how people deal with causal attribution and Shotter emphasizes the different kinds of explanation which exist. Other contributors discuss the problems of the reliability and validity of whatever explanations are collected for study. All these issues are different aspects of how explanations may differ from each other. The present chapter contributes to that debate by drawing attention to the role of the person providing the explanation.

Our categorization of explanatory roles also has a purpose beyond the integration of the diverse issues raised by the students of explanatory behaviour. This is to enable social scientists to move beyond the study of explanations *per se* and to provide a framework which will facilitate their *use* of explanations as part of a broader research enterprise. Put simply, we believe that ordinary explanations are of great value to the day-to-day functioning of society and that they therefore ought to be of assistance to the development of a psychological understanding of that society. Indeed, as we shall argue in more detail later, we see any explanation provided by a psychologist to be an inevitable member of the family of explanations provided by people with other, different roles in society. This raises the question of how psychologists' explanations differ from those provided by mere mortals. We anticipate that the answer to this question will prove of more value to the clarification of the social contribution of psychology than did the earlier debate on the difference between psychology and common sense (cf. Joynson 1974).

The explanation of the roles which explanations play in the explanatory activity of those who explain, especially if we are attempting to explain the role of explanations in the activities of those who are providing explanations of explanatory roles, can become rather abstract and tortuous! Let us, therefore, set the reader on a simple track by summarizing the points to be discussed in the remainder of this chapter.

(1) Ordinary explanations are of direct value and relevance to systematic, scientific psychology. By ignoring them psychologists miss an important gateway to much of human experience.

(2) The study of ordinary explanations requires research *in situ*. They must be examined in their natural habitat. This has consequent implications for the appropriate research methods and modes of validation.

(3) Those who generate explanations as part of their daily lives do so on the basis of varying degrees of (a) expertise and (b) involvement in the events or experiences they are explaining. It is therefore possible to categorize the givers of explanations in a way which has implications for the kind of explanation given.

(4) The psychologist, like all others who explain, has a place in any category scheme of explanatory roles. By making more flexible use of the roles available psychologists can increase the power and range of their explanations.

One final point of introduction. The arguments in this chapter are the outcome of a number of years of applied field research. Examples are therefore, drawn from studies of house purchasing; behaviour in fires; nurses' conceptualizations of ward design; Salvation Army hostels and studies of prisons.*

It has been our recurrent discovery that people in all these situations can and do give articulate accounts of their experiences — even "old lags" in Salvation Army hostels. Accounts, moreover, which have constituted a rich yet useable data base for analysis and theory construction.

*Acknowledgement: We are grateful to all our colleagues for the insights and data they have shared with us, much of which has been drawn on for this chapter. In particular we owe a debt to Ivor Ambrose, John Breaux, Cheryl Kenny, Ray Oakley, Kathy Rees and Jonathan Sime.

THE MAN IN THE SALOON BAR

It has often been suggested that psychologists, if they know anything of human behaviour and experience, know it of people in unusual situations. Hospitals, universities and other institutions have provided the cannon fodder for psychological trench warfare. It is only recently that there has been a welcome resurgence of interest in ordinary folk in everyday settings; an interest in their hopes, desires, explanations and beliefs. The person sitting down for a drink of an evening in the saloon bar at last has emerged as someone whose views can be treated scientifically. It is too much to hope, of course, that such psychological interest would be unfettered by two or more generations of laboratory based social research. The ordinary explanations which form the basis for this book are still too often elicited in the clinical confines of the experimental laboratory or at best in the informal discussion of students with their tutors.

That even such a disembodied, laboratory approach can be fruitful is shown by how much can be learned at the empirical level as demonstrated by Harris and Harvey, or of the philosophical structure of ordinary explanations, as shown by Pettit. However, it is our contention that even those students of explanations who have given their respondents most benefit of the doubt, such as Harré, have nonetheless omitted to consider two important aspects of the significance of the explanations they are studying.

The first major significance of everyday explanations is that they play a primary role in social discourse. The explanation which a politician gives for a course of action may have far reaching consequences, and even though the explanation which the same person gives for why he is drinking whisky instead of beer may be less newsworthy, it is still a potentially noteable ingredient of the experience of the saloon bar. If we are to understand political decisions, drinking habits, or any of the other aspects of human action which are of psychological concern, then the accounts which actors themselves give of why they perform as they do must surely be incorporated into our theories and models.

The second significance of explanations follows from the first. The people who provide the explanations will have different roles in relation to the phenomena which they are explaining. In other words, explanations occur within a context. This context needs to be explored if we are to understand fully any explanation and its significance.

It is important to emphasize that the identification of the significance of the context of an explanation derives from looking at explanatory behaviour as it occurs. In essence, then it is the very "ordinariness" of the explanations we are studying which provides a pointer both to their importance and their differentiation.

EXPLANATIONS IN CONTEXT

Our interest in the role of explanations and of those who explain derives not from a direct psychological interest in ordinary explanations, *per se*, but in the requirements of studying situations which exist. The questions which have lead us to esteem ordinary explanations and the work on which we wish to draw in order to illustrate our argument, has its root in what might be called the "Environmental Perspective". As has been discussed on a number of occasions (Canter *et al.*, 1975; Canter, 1976) there are many aspects of the human experience of physical settings, of practical and theoretical significance, which cannot be studied within the laboratory. Thus from its early recognition as a field of inquiry, environmental psychologists have gone out into the environment with which they are concerned. The essence of a prison, for example, or of how people buy houses cannot be dissected and studied in even the most benign laboratory. It is necessary to approach the people in the settings themselves. Furthermore, unlike the tradition of ergonomics, or industrial psychology, the criterion against which to consider these different settings cannot be established independently of any exploration of the experience of the setting. It is essential to understand what the users of the setting wish to achieve from them and within them. It is therefore necessary to explore with the people responsible for creating, managing, or using any particular place their aspirations and conceptualizations. In other words, it became a natural part of our research to talk to people and to listen to their explanations of the events and processes we were exploring. As indicated in earlier publications (Canter *et al.*, 1972; Brown and Sime, in press), these are fundamental requirements of our research and led us to utilize account gathering procedures which bear a distinct relationship to the approach advocated by Harré and Secord (1972). However, we became aware that we were drawing upon these accounts and explanations for many different purposes and that our respondents had, inevitably, a variety of roles in relation to the topics of our concern. It is important to realize that the context of the study and the nature of the problems we were studying were always taken to exist independently of our research inquiries. What

happens to people in a building on fire is a matter about which manu-
facturers, officials, firemen, journalists and the public at large want to
know. The appropriate role for a Salvation Army Hostel within the
community is a matter of direct concern to many authorities, public and
private. Thus what we are studying plays an organic role in the world at
large. This is very different from the identification of any given explanation as an examplar of an academic concern. If a respondent in a
research interview is provided with an account of an event, and asked to
provide explanations of it, a process which is remarkably similar in both
the attribution studies discussed by Harris and Harvey and the ethogenic
approach as discussed by Harré, then many of the naturally occuring
concomitants of any explanation provided are severed from the situation
under study.

As researchers we require explanations for a variety of reasons. We
therefore epitomize a range of possible conditions under which explanations may be given. We are thus not acting any differently, at one level,
from the wide range of people, lawyers, doctors, car mechanics, shop
assistants, junior executives, ships captains, or firemen, who require
accounts and explanations as part of their day to day activities. Similarly
material we collect as psychologists must be regarded as having many
similarities to a wide range of other accounts and explanations which are
collected by people in the course of their duties. The example of reports
given by journalists, or statements taken by police from witnesses, comes
to mind here. These systematic attempts at recording, in an unbiased
way, events which have occurred, and the reason for them, must overlap
in methods and usage with many of the accounts which we ourselves
gather. The fundamental difference, of course, is that as social scientists
we are attempting to collect the information in order to build up
generalizable models, not just to understand the particular events in
question.

The problem of the reliability and validity of explanations is also
addressed by all those who collect them. As discussed by Brown and Sime
(in press) the stringency with which checks are applied depends upon the
use to which the data are being put. Thus the checks of the investigative
journalists Woodward and Bernstein in their uncloaking of the Watergate conspiracy were less demanding than, say, inquiries by the police
leading to prosecution of the conspirators.

For the moment, our purpose is to demonstrate that the variety of uses
we make of explanations inevitably overlap with the uses which other,
ordinary folk, may make of them. Consequently, by considering the

context of ordinary explanations we are throwing light upon the broader issues of the role of explanations in everyday life.

The uses of explanations

BACKGROUND FROM THE EXPERTS

One of the inevitable starting points for a piece of field research, if the researcher can muster enough humility, is that the information available about the setting being explored is going to be available mainly to those who use or manage that setting. In other words, the researcher is in the role of novice. The expert is the respondent whom he approaches. So, for example, the account which an estate agent gives of the housing market, or which a prison governor gives of the issues involved in running a prison are both important sources of expertise. It is not really possible to carry out an intelligent study of the psychology of house buying, or an evaluation of a prison design unless the views of estate agents or prison governors are taken into account. For example consider one estate agent's exploration of his role in the house buying process:

> . . . . . We are the only participants in the whole business of property transfer that has the incentive to see the whole thing through; our fees are only paid if we succeed, having said that obviously one is absolutely straight in what one does . . . . .

Whatever credence is placed upon this statement it is important to bear it in mind when developing any further aspects of a study of home buying. It certainly lead us to examine more closely the role of estate agent in the whole process and to question others on their activities.

ESTABLISHING RAPPORT

Obtaining this information requires establishing a type of rapport with respondents which is not usually considered necessary if the researcher is dealing with, for instance, undergraduate psychology students. Giving a senior manager, or somebody who has been running a large organization for many years, a semantic differential to complete is to display a form of insult and social distancing. In order to obtain "expert" testimony it is necessary to demonstrate to those who are being approached that they do indeed have a significant role in the research enterprise. One of the most direct ways of doing this is to give them a good opportunity to provide detailed accounts and explanations of their experiences. It is precisely because the researcher is prepared to listen to the interpretations of the respondent that the respondent is prepared to explore the ways in which his expertise can be fully utilized.

Consider a further example from interviews with estate agents:

> . . . . . Our image is maligned. In the media we are often portrayed as shady, garrulous men, carrying brief cases, wearing spectacles and a trilby hat, ready to rip off some poor unsuspecting applicant . . . .

Whilst the image described may not add much to the study of house buying, the fact that the researcher is prepared to listen attentively to it is an important stage in the developing of a working relationship with the expert whose views are needed.

Of course useful background information for the processes being studied is frequently also provided by these rapport-establishing explanations. For example, when it is learned that many prison governors will fully accept the conflict inherent in their role, between attempting to create a rehabilitative establishment yet maintaining security, then it is clear that no simple taking of sides, or focusing on one aspect of prisons, will reach the level of complexity or sophistication which is already accommodated within the management structure. Thus the explanatory accounts which are provided by respondents who are part of the system being studied are a prerequisite for structuring, directing and elaborating research objectives.

OBTAINING DIFFERING PERSPECTIVES

Besides the use of ordinary explanations for establishing contact and gaining background information, there is a third reason for using ordinary explanations. This can be related more directly to perspectives derived from personal construct theory (Kelly, 1955) and the elaboration of the notion of environmental role (Canter and Walker, 1978; Canter, 1976). The organizational literature has frequently pointed to the significance of understanding the patterns of role and role/rule relationships which make up any organization. What derives from this literature is the awareness that the functioning of a role creates and is facilitated by a role related perspective. Thus in looking at any existing system it is necessary to understand the perspective of the different individuals involved in making the system function. This of course frequently becomes a major research enterprise in its own right (as reviewed for Environmental Research by Canter, 1976). The main point here, though, is that in order to understand fully the perspective associated with a role it is necessary to have the role incumbent provide an explanation of the system as he sees it.

A comparison of agents' and house buyers' view of the house detail circulars distributed by estate agents provides an instructive example here. A typical comment from an estate agent was:

> If we attempt to provide details strictly within the limits set by the applicant we may miss out on a sale because another agency, sending in another range happened to include something which "appealed" to the buyer.

On the other hand, buyers frequently expressed views such as the following:

> Most of the things they sent us were in the top quarter of the price range and a lot were above it. Not a bad move on their part as we ended up paying more than we originally intended.

Clearly their differences in perspective are a useful and interesting basis for further exploration of the experiences involved in home buying.

Once again, then, generating an ordinary set of explanations in the form of an account by a role incumbent of his own context provides crucial information for the understanding of any situation under study. The researcher is in a position to gain information from a range of role figures and so build up a composite picture. Often such a pooling of viewpoints is beyond the scope of any one participant in the situation being studied.

ACCESS TO INFORMATION NOT OTHERWISE AVAILABLE

When we are making use of explanations given by a role incumbent we are trying to gain access to information which is not available in any other form. However, the assumption is that the representatives of the various role groups with whom we deal will not vary too greatly in the explanations they give. This is an assumption which will have more or less validity depending on the particular circumstances. The problem is discussed by Harris and Harvey in relation to the concept of social desirability. However, it can be contrasted with the use of ordinary explanation precisely because there is no other information available on the matter concerned. The most clear example of this can be drawn from our research into human behaviour in fires (Canter, 1980).

It is in the very nature of buildings on fire that observation of actual events or simulations of possible events are unlikely to be valid. It is therefore only possible to explore what actually occurred, and why, through discussions with people who have been involved in a fire. In such a case we are using the fire victims as a unique source of information; as witnesses in their own drama. As with many explanations we wish to ensure that the information we get is as trustworthy as possible. We constantly need to corroborate the information against whatever other sources are available. A fire in a building is one example of a situation in which the account being given cannot be replaced by any other source of data. However, there are many other cases which have similar properties. Take another example with which we have been concerned; why people use Salvation Army hostels. It seems to be in the nature of the users of these hostels that there is little knowledge of them other than descriptive statistics. It is also the case that their lifestyle and experience of the world may be expected to be very different from those who live within permanent homes. Yet if accommodation is to be provided of a suitable form for these people it is essential to understand their view of the hostels, their experiences and their explanations as to how they come to be in them. Once again, as with the victims of fire, the estate agent or prison governor, a structured questionnaire or set of behavioural observations is likely only to reveal the paucity of the researchers' understanding of the actors' world and to obscure the possibility of any understanding of their experiences.

Collecting explanations *in situ*

There are many ways of collecting explanations of significance to psychological understanding. Yet if the explanatory role is to be revealed through the collection procedure that procedure needs to have certain properties. Many of these properties have been elaborated by Harré (1979) in his advocacy of "account gathering". A more detailed description of the actual processes used by the present authors has been given by Brown and Sime (in press). Various reports also provide examples of the results achieved with these interview techniques (e.g. Canter, 1980; Brown, 1979; Ambrose and Canter, 1979).

For the present chapter, however, three general aspects of the techniques used in the examples discussed are worth mentioning.

The first point is that the researcher's explanation of his purposes in talking to the participants is a crucial aspect of the interviewing process. It is essential that the researcher shares with the participant some common understanding of the reasons why they should talk to each other. This usually involves the interviewers in explaining their own roles and purposes in the research process as well as the role which they perceive their informant is having. It is instructive that this reciprocation of explanations can reveal information and processes which the most ardent questioning leaves hidden. It is by this "sharing" that a relationship of negotiation may be established in line with the model of clinical psychology and discussed by Harré and Secord (1972).

The second important aspect of an explanation harvest is that it is fruitless to pretend that the researcher does not have a set of issues in which he is interested. These issues form an implicit agenda to the discussion. At the end of the meeting the topics covered may well be checked against the agenda to ensure that no matters of interest have been avoided. Thus, although it is the informants' perspectives and conceptualization which are the focus of the discussion it is understood by all parties what the purpose is for the discussion.

A further point which emerges from these considerations is that it is essential for the informants to understand the framework of the discussion in which they are to take part. Typically, this involves establishing, through pilot work, the most comprehensible "instruction" which will allow the respondents to provide their own account. Thus after an introduction to the purposes of the research, the role of the interviewer and the nature of the discussion, the interviewer will say, for example in the study of fires: "Please tell me everything that happened from the moment you were aware that something was wrong".

Or in the study of people in Salvation Army hostels the "instruction" was: "Please tell me how you came to be in this hostel and what happened before that".

One important point about these opening questions is that whilst they are completely open ended they have an implicit structure to which the informant can relate. In essence they imply an account of a series of fire episodes with middles, beginnings and endings.

The statements made are usually tape-recorded and then verbatim transcripts are made for later content analysis. The procedure is time-consuming and requires skills at each stage which are not normally learnt on undergraduate courses; this is especially true of interviewing techniques. We believe the effort is worthwhile because of the access it provides to otherwise unknown processes and experiences.

Consequently, interview training procedures are adopted for those engaging in research using accounts data; e.g. the Salvation Army study referred to earlier used volunteers comprising Salvation Army Officers and hostel wardens. They came to Surrey University in order to receive training in accounts interviewing techniques.

The purposive use of explanations

It has been argued that society runs on ordinary explanations. They are the lubricant which enable the pattern of social contracts to operate from one day to the next. It is therefore not surprising to discover that many groups, who are not professional social scientists, utilize and indeed systematically collect ordinary explanation in order to facilitate their daily activities. All professional groups require accounts from their clients, couched in ordinary language, as the starting point for their professional services. Indeed, it may be pointed out, *en passant*, that one of the most likely long term benefits to accrue from the study of ordinary explanations is the development by professional groups, or the sophisticated computers which will eventually replace them, of more effective working relationships with their clients.

Professional groups require explanations for precisely the same reasons that we do as researchers. They need to establish *contacts*, to obtain *background* information and to gain an understanding of the *perspective* of those whom they would serve. The client also has *unique information* upon the events and their causes which it is necessary for the professional to use as the starting point in his investigations. The doctor starts by identifying from the patients the cause of their coming to see him; the architect requires an explanation of why a building is considered to be necessary for the organization. Even a lawyer, who may be seeking in the account given by his client to identify which reasons for action may be legally acceptable and which are not justifiable in law, nonetheless must begin by exploring his client's own explanation of what happened. Such dialogues with clients are a far cry from the attribution theorists explanations of the social perceptions of untrained observers highlighted by Harris and Harvey. Yet there are important parallels.

Many groups, professionals, social scientists and others, are in effect, collectors of explanations which they are required to digest and present. Consider the journalist, especially the investigative journalist, or even the policeman obtaining witness statements. Where these people carry out their job conscientiously and in as unbiased a way as possible their material may often be of direct value to social research. We have certainly found that the statements collected by the police from the witnesses to a fire can be fruitfully content analysed and generalities derived from them (Canter 1980). Of course, the accounts, which are gathered by journalists or the police have different purposes. A journalist may wish to make an interesting story which in the end will help to sell his newspaper, whilst the policeman is attempting to identify the prime cause of a crime and to establish who was responsible and so can be accused of it.

What is highlighted when the everyday occurrence of ordinary explanations is examined is that, just as the researcher will have special reasons for collecting his explanations, so will the person providing the explanations have a variety of purposes for giving them. It seems likely that the account which an individual might give of what happened in a fire, and why, may be quite different if it is given to a doctor, a journalist, a lawyer or a policeman. This is not to say that the individual is going, necessarily, to bias or distort his account for the different recorders. It is rather to point out that it is precisely because explanations are part of the fabric of society, precisely because they are an aspect of interaction between individuals, that they will be expected to take on different content and structure for different purposes. In Harré's paper, he discusses the importance of the elicitor of the account understanding the scenario or context of the account given. Expressing this crucial idea another way, if explanation is seen as only being fully comprehensible when considered in context, the nature of explanations is likely to vary from one context to another, even if ostensibly it is an explanation of the same event. Giles (1979) has shown that many aspects of language change from one situation to another. It is therefore not surprising to realize that the content of what is said may well change also. It follows that the student of ordinary explanations must explore the relationships those explanations have to the different contexts in which they may be presented.

What then of the validity or acceptability of any particular explanation? If as researchers we wish to make use of explanations as a central aspect of our research then we need to establish the trustworthiness of the explanations we are given. The conventional approach to reliability and validity in the psychometric literature does not seem especially appropriate for considering this issue. Certainly if it is fundamental to our argument that we would expect variations in the same account under different conditions, then the conventional notion of reliability is inappropriate. If we also accept that different ways of obtaining information may be expected to have consistent variations, we cannot accept conventional notions of validity either. In their advocacy of account gathering Harré and Secord (1972), or even more recently, (1979) are surprisingly vague on this methodological issue. Bromley (1977) is one of the few psychologists who has addressed this matter directly, drawing upon the analysis of argument proposed by Toulmin (1958) and the approach to evidence which exists in the legal context. He has demonstrated that the structure of ordinary language can be systematically studied and utilized without reliance on psychometric notions. We have taken this argument a little further (Brown and Sime, in press) and demonstrated that there are a whole series of checks and counter-checks, of corroboration and search for disconfirmation, which are possible in a thorough authentication of accounts.

What emerges, however, from this consideration of the validity and reliability of explanations, is that it must be dependent on the context in which the explanation is given. In other words, the role which the person who is explaining has in relation to the events he is describing. Thus any exploration of explanations must utilize an understanding of the explanatory roles which may exist. Students of attribution theory, as described by Harris and Harvey, have long suspected that whether the person is giving an explanation of behaviour relating to themselves or to another will influence the type of explanations which is drawn upon. In the experimental context of much attribution theory, this is the major role differentiation which can be established. However, it is clear when ordinary explanations are dealt with, that a much greater variety of roles are possible. An understanding of the structure of these roles, of the way in which people differ in relation to the phenomena they are explaining, is fundamental both to the evaluation and understanding of the explanations which are given as well as being an important topic for study by the student of ordinary explanations.

Facets of explanatory roles

In order to take the discussion of the context and purpose of explanations further we would like to propose some ways in which informants may differ in their relationships to what they are explaining. These are proposals which it is hoped will generate a more thoughtful approach to the consideration of the different conditions under which explanations may be given.

LEVEL OF EXPLANATORY ANALYSIS

The differences we put forward for consideration are, in effect, ways in which an explanatory role may generate varying levels of explanatory analysis. The concept of "level" in this context is an admittedly clumsy one, but it is intended to capture variations in both the intensity and richness of the explanations being given. It is clear from daily discourse that some explanations may be dismissed as trivial or superficial whilst others are regarded as profound. We suspect that this variation underlies much of the discussion of the value or otherwise of "ordinary" explanations. We are therefore suggesting that there are at least two aspects of the context of explanations which, although qualitatively different, do combine to produce differences in explanatory level. These two aspects of explanatory context are most easily thought of as two different ways of categorizing people who give explanation. One may be characterized as the degree of *involvement* in the situation which the person is explaining, the other is the extent of their *expertise* with regard to that situation. Both these categorizations (or "facets" to use a more formal term, cf. Shye, 1979) imply differences in degree of intensity or level of explanatory analysis which can be provided. In other words we are suggesting that the variety of explanatory roles which are available may be built up from a scheme which combines both the amount of involvement, and the degree of expertise which the person giving the explanation has, in relation to the entity they are explaining. Each role is seen as having two constituents. Together these two facets coalesce to provide a description of any particular type of explanation. Let us examine these facets in more detail.

Facet (A): involvement. Consider three different degrees of involvement with a situation which are possible: (i) incidental, (ii) social and (iii) personal. A situation which a person happens upon and in which they play no special role is one for which their involvement may be regarded as extrinsic to the situation or "incidental". The informant has no function within the events he is explaining. A passer-by, who notices a fire in progress and an arson investigator who examines the resulting debris are both similar in that the event they describe has an existence independently of them. So long as they are merely observers of it their actions and explanations are incidental to the phenomena they describe.

A second level of involvement occurs when the reporter has a social relationship with others in the events being explained. The person who explains and who experiences the situation share some common notions. A neighbour who sees a fire and gives an account of it, or a hostel warden who explains why people use his hostel, both draw upon a relationship to their subject matter which is socially significant.

The third level of involvement occurs when a respondent gives an account of phenomena of which they are an integral part, phenomena which would not exist without their involvement. In this case they are providing an insight into a situation which is very much part of their unique personal experience. The person who describes what happened when he woke to find his home ablaze or the prison governor describing his prison, both have a personal involvement which it is essential to understand if the explanatory role is to be appreciated.

Facet (B): expertise. Quite distinct from the degree of involvement is the degree of information or expertise which the individual draws upon, or has available to him to draw upon, when giving an explanation. By degrees of expertise is implied the amount of special information or special knowledge, which may result from training, or may be a product of prior experience. Three levels of expertise are proposed: (i) publicly available, (ii) special to the situation and (iii) special to the role.

Much of the expertise which somebody giving an explanation uses is publicly available. Knowledge of how commonly used, simple equipment works, e.g. a box of matches, or the routines through which people go in public, e.g. looking in an estate agents window, are of this kind. This may be all the expertise required of an individual in order to provide an explanation. That such expertise is in the public domain implies that the explanations built upon it will take a form which is distinct from those requiring more special knowledge.

In some cases the expertise drawn upon to provide an explanation is only available to people who have access to a particular situation. It is not available except to those who also experience that situation or similar ones. Knowledge of the dialogue which takes place between an estate agent and his client, or of the gradings in trustworthiness used to categorize prisoners is available to all those who have used the services of an estate agent or visited a prison. This situational experience provides a basis for a level of explanation beyond that publicly available.

A further degree of expertise can be recognized as being unique to the role which a person has in the event being explained. Of particular note is the difference in role between somebody who initiates actions and

somebody who is a passive victim of them. A person providing an explanation of their own behaviour, in a fire for example, would usually draw
upon knowledge of the circumstances which is unique to their own
reasons for being in that situation. Or consider our estate agent again.
When giving his view of the housing market he is drawing upon expertise
derived from his role within that market. When discussing the
experiences of first-time buyers he is drawing upon his special knowledge
of the situation. On the other hand, when commenting upon govern-
ment policy he is only likely to have access to publicly available understanding of those mysteries.

The example of the estate agent shows that levels of expertise can vary
within one person in relation to different issues. As a consequence the
type of explanatory role which a person can take may vary in relation to
the event he is explaining.

TYPES OF EXPLANATORY ROLE

Any one of the levels of involvement can be combined with any one of
the degrees of expertise to provide a type of explanatory role. It is
assumed, and is certainly amenable to future research, that the nature
of the constituents of any role, so defined, would provide an understanding of the types of explanation which would be provided by people
within the role. In other words, the hypothesis is being put forward, for
future validation, that the nature of any explanation given will be a
function of both the involvement and expertise of the person providing
the explanation. Involvement and expertise, it should be emphasized,
are with regard to the event or experience being explained.

Other contributors to this volume have focussed on variations in types
of explanation. Some detailed cross-reference between our proposals
and theirs awaits future discussion and empirical evidence. However, it
is suggested for example that the distinction between dispositional and
situational explanations (reviewed for example by van der Pligt) is likely
to require greater refinement in order to map onto the variations in
explanatory role defined. We would nonetheless anticipate that the
range from external sources of explanation (such as situations) to
internal sources (such as dispositions) would be likely to parallel both the
increase in involvement and expertise.

A further prediction, for further test, which derives from considering
the two aspects, or facets, of explanatory roles is that the more similar
the constituents which go to make up a role the more likely are the types

of explanations associated with them to be similar to each other. This is in essence the principle of contiguity (Foa 1958). By proposing a two-facet framework for describing roles, then, we are also putting forward a category scheme which will generate more specific empirical explanations.

The way in which combinations of involvement and expertise can give rise to a definition of roles can be readily illustrated by taking two extreme examples. A person who has only incidental involvement with a situation and draws upon expertise which is publicly available may be given the title of a "neutral observer". We would usually feel uncomfortable about the personal motivations which such an observer would ascribe to the situations he is explaining. We would tend to use the more directly overt aspect of the situation they perceived and attempt to corroborate those with other people's accounts of the same overt actions. By comparison, consider an informant who is personally involved in a situation and is giving information which is based upon his unique and special experience of his role in that situation. We might, for want of a better term, label such a role as that of a "client". We would expect the motivational components and those causal forms of explanation which rely upon the individual's view of himself in that situation as being an important component in the explanation which he gives. A factual account of events would be taken far less seriously if given by someone in this role. Such an account would be questioned very directly for its personal significance.

Between these two extremes there are a variety of possible combinations. Table I summarizes these various combinations and assigns labels to the role position. It will be noted that at the right hand side of the diagramme the person is seen as having some degree of involvement in the situation. Thus we have a person who may be an *occupant of*, a *victim of*, or a *consultant to*, the circumstances he describes. In contrast to this, on the left hand side of the diagramme, are listed a *witness*, an *expert* and a *specialist*. The principle of contiguity around which the diagramme is built leads to labels with the most similar facet profiles being next to each other. This helps to summarize a great variety of ways in which the roles can differ. It is a partial order scalogram (see Shye, 1979; or Shye and Elizur 1976). The level of explanatory analysis is held constant at each point down through the diagramme. However, at each level across it is possible to have qualitatively different types of role although they may be associated with equal levels of overall "degree" of explanation. Thus the *expert* who is brought in to look at a fire, drawing

TABLE I. *A PARTIAL ORDER FOR EXPLANATORY ROLES*

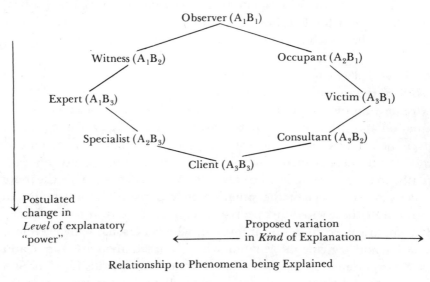

Relationship to Phenomena being Explained

(A) *Degree of Involvement*
1. Incidental
2. Social
3. Personal

(B) *Amount of Expertise*
1. Publicly available
2. Special to situation
3. Special to role

upon his particular training and commenting on that one event with which he has no particular interaction, may be contrasted with a *victim* of that event who, whilst personally involved in the fire, only draws upon an understanding of the human activities within it which is publicly available. There is a sense in which these two individuals only have the same amount of power of explanation to draw upon, although their circumstances are so different. Another example can be provided by contrasting the *specialist* with the *consultant*. According to our definition the *specialist*, whilst having a role within the situation and not being socially involved within it, is drawing upon information which is unique to his contact with such similar situations. The *consultant*, on the other hand is actually changing or influencing the situation. He may even have direct personal profit to gain from changing it. However, much of what he can utilize is only available to him because of his being part of the situation, not because of any particular aspects of his role.

This model is referred to as a "partial" order because there are two distinct routes through it. There are thus two compatible orders in which the various roles can be placed. What this demonstrates is that many of the properties which need to be taken into account when considering explanatory role, may well be a function of qualitative differences between the basis of those roles rather than quantitative differences in terms of the amount of information or the power of the explanations which they may give. It can thus be argued that as one moves across to the right of the diagramme verification, in terms of internal consistency and corroboration, would need to be explored. On the other hand, as one moves across to the left of the diagramme a more open, publicly attestable, form of verification against external criteria can be brought to bear. The power of a model such as that in Table I lies in the way in which it can summarize exisiting discussions within the literature and the way in which it points to new insights. It is therefore interesting to examine the types of explanation which Antaki presents and those which Pettit elaborates and to see whether or not they are likely to map at all on to our model of explanatory roles. This in effect becomes an empirical prediction, that if a person falls into a particular role vis-a-vis a situation which he is explaining, then he will draw on particular classes of explanation. Such predictions await elaboration in particular research contexts.

A role for the psychologist

One of the difficulties which is raised when we elaborate the roles which are available is to link these roles to the psychologist's use of and study of ordinary explanations. Does the psychologist move through all these different roles and make use of them? Or is there some unique role which he must try to take when presenting explanations and behaviour or making use of it? It is hoped that our model will generate debate on this important aspect of the use of ordinary explanations. However, our model does lead to some intriguing suggestions. If we take the notion of involvement, i.e. the degree to which the investigator plays an increasingly active role in the phenomena being studied, we have three levels equivalent to the incidental, social and personal, i.e. neutral observer, engaged spectator, participant observer. These roles involve minimal to maximum contact with the subjects/respondents. The setting of studies also tends to be ordered on a public-private continuum similar to availability of expertise. Thus laboratory based study is conducted in the private world of the experimental psychologist, whilst field studies are set in the world of the participant. An intermediate situation can be exemplified by the elicitation of information about a real world phenomenon from participants, but removed from settings where the events take place, e.g. interviewing house buyers about their purchasing experiences in their own home. Thus we can describe three types of role for psychologists which we can impose on the model, as illustrated in Table II.

(1) a casual or neutral laboratory based role, exemplified by the notation 1,3, equivalent to the label *expert*.

(2) an engaged spectator in an "intermediate" setting, exemplified by 2,2, equivalent to a label such as *investigator*.

(3) a participant observer in a field setting, exemplified by 3,1, or the label *victim*.

What is interesting is that these exhibit qualitative differences, i.e. they are all on the same level of explanatory analysis.

TABLE II: *A PROPOSED ROLE FOR SOCIAL SCIENCE EXPLANATIONS*

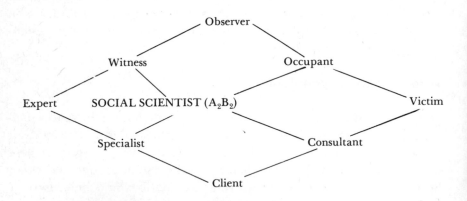

It will be noted that the role of the investigator occupies the central position. It describes social involvement and expertise which is special to the situation. In other words a role which derives from an interaction between individuals and in which information drawn upon is special to that particular interaction. This seems to us the most comfortable role for the psychologist in studying the applied issues of real world environments. If his involvement is more personal then doubts will be cast upon the validity of comment. If it is too detached the studied behaviour becomes removed from reality. There is a worthy literature elaborated on the artefacts of laboratory based studies (Rosenthal 1966, 1969; Orne 1962, Adair 1973). What is interesting about the role in the configuration is in terms of the contiguity principle alluded to earlier. Putting it another way, if we were to establish correlations between all the different roles, then the role in the middle would have the highest average correlation with all the other roles. It is interesting to explore whether this is what the psychologist should search for or what he should try to break away from. Nonetheless, it does suggest that the specification of a model for explanatory roles provides new ways of thinking about the nature of psychology in general.

Concluding comments

It has been argued that a real-world oriented psychology inevitably draws upon a range of explanations. It has been shown that these are the range of explanations which are available to many other people in society. It has been further demonstrated that the meaning and significance of these explanations derive from the context in which they occur and the purposes for which they are given or elicited. It follows from this that the validity of any such explanation could only be understood in relation to the role which the person giving the explanation had in relation to the situation or phenomenon he was explaining.

This argument opens up the necessity of establishing the variety of roles for explanation which might exist. This is necessary both in order to understand the structure of explanation and in order to identify the relevant forms and variety of verification which might be necessary for any particular explanation.

It was argued that the degree of involvement which a person had in a situation and the specialness of the expertise upon which they drew, combine together to give what we called a partial order of explanatory roles. This partial order indicated the existence of at least eight distinct roles which could be ordered in terms of the power of the explanatory analysis which might be expected to be associated with each. It was also illustrated that qualitative differences between these roles in terms of the personal or social involvement which they represented also helped to distinguish between them.

Finally a suggestion was made that central to this whole structure of explanation could be identified a role which may well characterize that of the research psychologist. This helps to define further what the psychologist's task is in studying ordinary explanations.

In conclusion then, by studying the nature of the ordinary explanations which are available to psychologists, we have identified the possibility that the types of explanations which the psychologist obtains are unique to his role, but may throw light on explanations achieved in other circumstances because of the special properties of that role. We can also see that slight changes in the balance of this role would lead him to take on different explanatory perspectives. In terms of the labels we have assigned, more personal involvement leads him in the direction of being a consultant and more incidental involvement pulls him in the direction of being a witness. A different emphasis drawing upon knowledge unique to a role leads him in the direction of the type of explanation provided by a "specialist", whereas drawing upon experience more publicly available puts him in the role of the occupant of the situation. Intriguingly, this model suggests that there are other explanations which are distant from those available to psychologists. These derive from both the role of the client and the role of neutral observer. Once a psychologist takes on either of these relationships to a situation he is likely to provide types of explanation which are wholly different from those which are uniquely available to him as a psychologist.

11

Negation, Synthesis and Abomination in Rhetoric*

D. Gowler and K. Legge

Since the giving and grasping of meanings is the mechanism of much of the patterns of social interaction, greater *precision* of the delineation of *meanings* is what corresponds in the social sciences to the development of greater *accuracy* of the *measurement* of parameters in the physical sciences. Harré and Secord (1972, p. 132) "The Explanation of Social Behaviour".

Introduction

Following Harré, we understand the psychology of ordinary explanations to be principally concerned with the exploration of the "giving and grasping of meanings", as this process, and the meanings themselves, occur variously in different social contexts. The origins of our interest in this branch of psychology lie in our work on the evaluation of planned organizational change (Gowler and Legge, 1978). Briefly, our experience not only convinced us that such applied research questions the validity of the very positivist paradigm that promotes these activities, but also, given our special concern with the impact of organizational change upon individual perceptions and performance, that we were dealing with the vexed question of meanings (Menzel, 1978). But, as Harré (1978) argues, the "old methodology", i.e. the utilization of methods used by physical scientists, is likely to result in the elimination or displacement of meaning.

*This work was supported by the Medical Research Council and by the Social Science Research Council. We are also pleased to acknowledge our epistemological debts to Rom Herré, Tom Lupton and roy Payne and the generous assistance received from many colleagues. Additionally, we are greatly indebted to our co-fieldworker, Neil Millward, who not only contributed one of the accounts, but also recorded the songs. And, finally we are particularly grateful to John Cook and Ben Fletcher, who with unfailing courtesy questioned our own contributions to "calculated vagueness" and "ambiguous presentation".

ORDINARY EXPLANATIONS OF SOCIAL BEHAVIOUR

Given this dilemma, we not only turned to the "qualitative methodologies" (Filstead, 1970) but also began to collect "wild" or "natural"
data, e.g. documents, stories and songs that "exist" independently of the
research methods concerned, in comparison to the "cultivated" data
which are literally created by the stimulus of "instruments" or "treatments". Inevitably, then, we have been drawn to the work of those social
scientists who record and analyse accounts of individual and interpersonal behaviour (Lyman and Scott, 1970). In the light of our special
interests, we found the literature on the occupational and organizational bases of deviant behaviour (Bryant, 1974; Ditton, 1977;
Klockars, 1974; Mars et al., 1979; Miller, 1978; Sagarin, 1977) to be of
particular relevance.

In the course of these methodological wanderings, we became
interested in the application of the work of cognitive consistency
theorists (Gowler and Legge, 1975) and, more recently, in the development of attribution theory (Heider, 1958; Jones et al., 1972). When
pursuing this particular methodological trail, we eventually came upon
Harré and Secord's view that:

If we follow the paradigm of non-positivist science, explaining
behavioural phenomena involves identifying the generative "mechanisms" that give rise to the behaviour. The discovery and identification
of these "mechanisms" we call *ethogeny*. We believe that the main
process involved in them is self-direction according to the meaning
ascribed to the situation. At the heart of the explanation of social
behaviour is the identification of the meanings that underlie it. Part of
the approach to discovering them involves the obtaining of *accounts* —
the actor's own statements about why he performed the acts in question,
what social meaning he gave to the actions of himself and others. (1972,
p. 9; added emphasis)

As illustrated in sections below, these ideas (plus Harré's (1978) outline
of the principles of ethogenic approach) provide our theoretical
rationale for linking the method of the "identification of the meanings"
of actual accounts to their contexts.

Turning now to the question of accounts, we focus this chapter upon
those that may be described as rhetorics. The focus is thus on meaning
rather than motivation and, given this emphasis, we have "backgrounded" the Burkean definition of rhetoric (that is, the verbalizations
of motives — for a recent comment on this see Taylor, 1979).

We define rhetoric narrowly as the use of language to
(a) justify and legitimize actual or potential power and exchange relationships;
(b) eliminate actual or potential challenges to existing power and exchange relationships,
and, at a deeper level,
(c) express those contradictions in power and exchange relationships that cannot be openly admitted or, in many cases, resolved.

Obviously, when defined this way, rhetoric is placed squarely in that class of behaviours labelled "political", so frequently ignored by psychologists, but which colour and direct many everyday activities, especially in occupational settings (Gowler and Legge, 1980).

Consequently, it is argued here that the rhetorician uses accounts to manipulate what we have termed the process of categorization, and that, in doing so, he has access to four textures of meaning, i.e. contrast, negation, synthesis and abomination (see sections on digital textures of meaning and analog textures of meaning below). The use of these rhetorical accounts does not depend solely upon the clarity of meaning produced by the sharp definition and contrast of differentiated sociolinguistic categories, i.e. what we have termed digital communication, but also involves the use of ambiguous and implicit meanings generated by undifferentiated sociolinguistic categories, i.e. analog communication (Wilden, 1972). As suggested by the title of this chapter, it is these ambiguous and implicit meanings that are our central concern.

The chapter is then composed of two main parts. In the first, mainly conceptual, part, i.e. the sections on categorization and meaning, we begin by constructing a typology of textures of meaning (see Fig. 1), which is then related to digital and analog forms of communication. Here we found it necessary to draw upon concepts of sociologists and sociolinguists (Berstein, 1971; Cicourel, 1973; Giglioli, 1972) from outside the conventional limits of psychology, making the point, perhaps, that "everyday life" may not conform to the boundaries set by the academic disciplines. Additionally, we have incorporated the work of those anthropologists who have studied the relationships between meaning, communication and culture (Douglas, 1975; Leach, 1976) and the symbolic order of social life (Babcock, 1978; Douglas, 1966; Sahlins, 1976; Turner, 1974).

In the second, mainly empirical part of this chapter, i.e. the sections on ethogenic analysis and on the structure and function of rhetoric, we

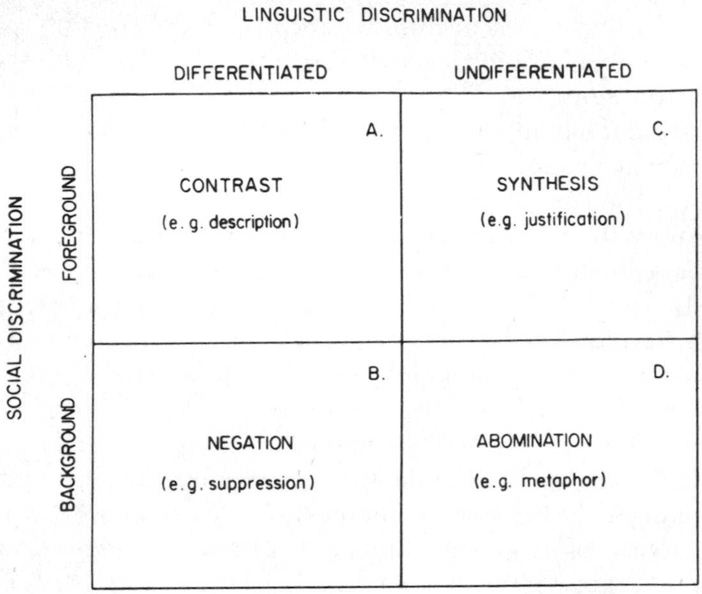

LINGUISTIC DISCRIMINATION

Fig. 1. The process of categorization and the double discrimination of meaning.

introduce and relate Harré's principles of ethogenic analysis to our empirical material and we present two accounts collected during our early fieldwork of the impact of organizational and environmental changes on employee perceptions and behaviour (Brown, 1971; Gowler, 1969, 1970; Legge, 1970). We use these accounts to show that, as rhetorics, they combine the functions of attributions, cautionary tales and myths. Moreover, in Fig. 2, these distinctions are analysed in terms of the four textures of meaning identified above.

This approach, we believe, illustrates the fact that, in natural settings, accounts are semantic "black holes", where meanings are so impacted that positivist, scientific methods, which ultimately rely upon the manipulation of discrete "chunks" of date, are clearly inappropriate. Nevertheless, in the section on the structure and function of rhetoric, an alternative, reflexive approach to the analysis of such date is presented, using a version of Levi-Strauss' (1963) structural method of determining the meaning of myth (see Fig. 3).

Finally, in our conclusions, we suggest that a psychology of ordinary explanations might fruitfully emulate those "field" sciences, e.g. archaeology, where the reconstruction of date in context replaces the disaggregation of date out of context.

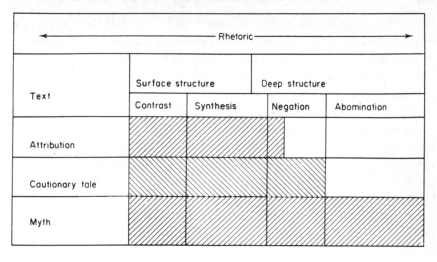

Fig. 2. The structure and function of rhetoric.

TEXT	COLUMN 1	COLUMN 2	COLUMN 3	COLUMN 4
A.	Girl assembler crippled mentally (an epileptic – head?)	Spoilt by mother	Receives help from group	Leaves firm, result of workers action
B.	Girl assembler crippled physically (leg)	Very close relationship with friend (lesbians)	Gives help to friend	Leaves firm result of supervisor action, but returns

Fig. 3. The structural analysis of myth.

Categorization and meaning

The point of departure for this chapter is signposted by Fig. 1 below, which is a formal representation of the proposition that the process of categorization provides a flexible and multiform framework of meaning. More specifically, it illustrates reciprocal relationships between two analytically distinct determinants of the process of categorization. In Fig. 1,

    (i) the horizontal axis represents a modification of the "Whorfian hypothesis", which asserts that our categorization of the world is patterned by the *structure* of language (Bernstein, 1971; Whorf, 1941) and

(ii) the vertical axis represents a modification of the sociolinguistic perspective, which asserts that our categorization of the world is a function of language embedded in the experience, performance and anticipation of *social interaction* (Cicourel, 1973; Giglioli, 1972).

Our approach not only combines the lexical and grammatical "characteristics" of language (horizontal axis), but also relates this combination to the selective effect of culture, represented here by Douglas' (1975) concept of submerged or "backgrounded" categories (vertical axis). The result is a fourfold typology of textures of meaning (frames of cognitive significance), permutations of which are available to the would-be rhetorician. Indeed, we would argue that these textures of meaning, i.e. contrast, negation, synthesis and abomination, provide the necessary cognitive-linguistic sieves for the shaping and manipulation of interpersonal communication and influence. In other words, they are assumed to be functionally requisite for all forms of oral, written and situational rhetoric.

The form and function of these textures of meaning are discussed in detail below, but suffice to say that our choice of the term "texture" was influenced by its relatively wide range of perceptual connotations, for example, its evocation of three-dimensional patterns of structures that appear to vary in shape, density and feel when perceived in different contexts (Fox 1969). Furthermore, the visual and tactile connotations of the term are intended to suggest a correspondence between these textures of meaning and objective conditions in the physical world.

LINGUISTIC PERFORMANCE AND COGNITIVE CONSISTENCY

To consider the horizontal axis of Fig. 1 first, it is suggested here that interaction between the lexical and grammatical characteristics of language create differentiated and undifferentiated textures of meaning (Fillenbaum and Rapoport, 1971). Other things being equal, words and sentences shape and convey either precise (differentiated) or blurred (undifferentiated) meanings. However, the introduction of the *ceteris paribus* clause in the foregoing sentence raises the difficult issue of assumptions. Whilst these are modified as this analysis progresses, it is necessary to discuss them in some detail at the outset.

First, our definition of the differentiated/undifferentiated dichotomy effectively assumes that language and meaning are identical. Although this is often taken for granted in everyday life, it is now criticized from many academic quarters. For example, sociolinguists argue hat it over-states the influence of purely linguistic characteristics of language upon meaning. As Cicourel states,

> Linguistic features of speech bound the meanings exchanged only in a formal sense; thus there are obvious articulations between syntactic structures and semantic ones, but the syntax is also misleading because it conveys the impression that the formal appearances of bounded sentences are in close correspondence with interactional meaning structures. Linguistic theory does not address the larger horizons of meaning (codes, repertoires, code switching, choices available within repertoires) indexed by the syntax and intonational variations of talk invented or imagined by the participants for making speech socially relevant. (1973, p. 78)

It is also important to note that our assumption of a close corrspond-ence between language and meaning is likely to result in the situation where the written or oral expressions of undifferentiated (unclear) meanings are labelled as inadequate cognitive-linguistic performances. Thus, the individual believed to generate and/or convey such "blurred" meanings may be charged with "low intelligence", "having a poor vocabulary", "not having a proper command of the language", "using jargon", "given to waffle", "muddled thinking" or even "mentally ill". (Of course, this is not to deny that such interpretations might be well-founded.)

The second major assumption underlying the horizontal axis of Fig. 1 involves a facet of human cognitive development, i.e. the articulation of perception, which implies that individuals acquire and maintain stable and unequivocal (differentiated) textures of meaning. This assertion, however, is subject to the general criticism levelled at cognitive consist-ency theory. Under this assumption, of course, undifferentiated textures of meaning are believed to be unstable and to result in the arousal of cognitive dissonance. Nevertheless, the undifferentiated elements in the matrix provide possible counter assumptions, e.g. that individuals do at times create and utilize cognitive inconsistency.

These assumptions are stated here, in part, because in some of their forms, they apply to attribution theory. For example, the first assump-tion outlined above, i.e. that there is a close correspondence between language and meaning, is built into those laboratory attribution research designs using the manipulation of predetermined verbal and written statements. The second type of assumption commented upon here, i.e. that individuals acquire and maintain "unequivocal" textures of meaning, is made by those who state or imply that it is the drive for cognitive consistency that promotes the attribution of naive, causal statements about everyday life. For example, Aydin and Markova recently commented that

> Attribution theory assumes that *in order to bring structure and meaning to his world a man ascribes transient and variable actions and events to their relatively invariant underlying causes and reasons.* When information about causes of and reasons for actions is not readily available or is ambiguous, we may assume that *the perceiver's general assumptions and expectations* about people and their actions play an important role with regard to the way causal attributions and inferences about intentions are made. (1979, p. 291; added emphasis)

We have also stressed the assumption of cognitive consistency because as Jones *et al.* point out

> While there are clear differences between attribution theory and the theories of cognitive consistency their intellectual roots have much in common. Many basic ideas of the former derive from the two major cognitive consistency theorists, Leon Festinger and Fritz Heider. (1972, p. xi)

However, these and other assumptions come into high relief in the following sections of the paper, where, among other things, it is suggested that "rhetorical man" operates at a high level of "attributional complexity" (Jones *et al.*, 1972, p. xii), by combining and manipulating both digital and analog forms of communication and meaning.

BACKGROUNDED INFORMATION AND IMPLICIT MEANINGS

Before discussing the dichotomy comprising the vertical axis, it is necessary to consider the fundamental assumption upon which this whole analysis rests. This is that language not only provides a classification of "things", but also moulds our environment and locates us at the centre of a logical and relatively reassuring social space (Leach, 1972 (1964), p. 48). As Leach also observes,

> . . . . . . I would emphasise that this whole process of carving up the external world into named categories and then arranging the categories to suit our social convenience depends upon the fact that although our

ability to alter the external environment is very limited, we have virtually
unrestricted capacity for playing games with the internalised version of
the environment which we carry in our heads. (1976, p. 36)

As argued above, this linguistic aspect of the process of categorization
results, *ceteris paribus*, in what we have termed differentiated and
undifferentiated textures of meaning. But, as Leach points out, the
socio-cultural aspect of this process also arranges these categories and
meanings "to suit our social convenience". In order to represent this
idea, we turn to Douglas' (1975) distinction between foregrounded and
backgrounded information.

Thus, the vertical axis of Fig. 1 represents a form of social discrimination, where people in everyday interaction select the linguistic discriminations appropriate to their circumstances. Consequently, this double
discrimination (i.e. social and linguistic discrimination) results in some
categories/meanings being neglected. However, the disuse of
categories/meanings is not only an outcome of "natural selection", but
also a consequence of direct and indirect social prohibitions. In other
words, categories/meanings may be either neglected or rejected. On this
point Douglas takes a firm stand, and contends that

It seems hardly worth noting that some matters are deemed more worthy
of scholarship than others. If there is any one idea on which the present
currents of thought are agreed it is that at any given moment of time the
state of received knowledge is backgrounded by a clutter of suppressed
information. It is also agreed that the information is not suppressed by
reason of its inherent worthlessness, nor by any passive process of
forgetting: it is actively thrust out of the way because of difficulties in
making it fit whatever happens to be in hand. (1975, p. 3)

Further, she continues to press home the argument, concluding that

*When the background of assumptions upholds what is verbally explicit,
meanings come across loud and clear*. Through these implicit channels of
meaning, human society itself is achieved, clarity and speed of clue-
reading ensured. In the elusive exchange between explicit and implicit
meanings a perceived-to-be-regular universe establishes itself pre-
cariously, shifts, topples and sets itself up again. (1975, p. 4; added
emphasis)

We have emphasized Douglas' reference to the relationship between
culturally determined backgrounds and verbally explicit meanings in
order to relax the *ceteris paribus* assumption about the purely linguistic

(lexical and grammatical) determinants of meaning assumed by the horizontal axis of Fig. 1. Put another way, both well-defined and ill-defined semantic domains are a product of the process of linguistic and social discrimination.

Finally, it is necessary to realize that a *ceteris paribus* clause may also be applied to the dichotomy comprising the vertical axis of Fig. 1. Briefly, this representation of socio-cultural context is used here to provide a conceptual foothold from which the analysis of more complex situations may be attempted. For example, on some occasions, e.g. during certain rituals, backgrounded information and implicit meanings may be foregrounded and made explicit under conditions of tight social and symbolic control. These questions, however, come into sharper focus in the following two sections, where we consider each of the textures of meaning in turn.

DIGITAL TEXTURES OF MEANING

In this and the following section, so that we may later develop the theme that "rhetorical man" manipulates highly complex attributions that encompass and go beyond the attribution of cause and effect in everyday life, we consider the textures of meaning in terms of a distinction drawn from communication theory. Thus, we contend that "contrast"/"negation" and "synthesis"/"abomination" are characteristic of digital and analog communication respectively. We define "digital" and "analog" communication in the same terms as Wilden, who, in reference to computers asserts that

> The digital computer (e.g. an adding machine) computes by discrete steps, whereas the analog computer (e.g. a slide rule, a clock) employs continuous functions, which are then digitalized by the observer. In the on/off processes of the digital computer, "no", "not", "zero", and "minus" are all possible, whereas in the analog computer, one cannot say "not". The digital computer operates by means of "either/or" identities, which, along with a way of saying "not", are the sole prerequisites of any kind of analytic logic. But the analog computer communicates on the basis of "more or less". Consequently, identity is an impossible operation in analog communications. (1972, p. 24)

In the light of this definition the correspondence between the differentiated/undifferentiated and digital/analog dichotomies needs little by way of further comment. Nevertheless, this question of digitalization leads directly to the discussion of the differentiated textures of meaning identified by cells A (contrast) and B (negation) in Fig. 1.

First, cell A in the matrix represents the differentiated and fore-grounded texture of contrast and includes the sharp distinctions used to construct the semantic scaffolding of any description. But, whilst the texture of contrast provides the discriminations necessary for the deline-ation and transmission of meaning, it is by no means sufficient for this purpose. Those who assume that it is may be compared to those who would "positively" define a fishing net as a regular pattern of knots and line. But research models and methods must also cope with the "negative" definition of a fishing net as a collection of holes.

Turning to cell B of Fig. 1, this represents the differentiated though backgrounded texture of negation, which is perhaps more readily understood as a form of suppression, or act of denial. And, as illus-trated below, examples of denial are manifested in forms of "etiquette". But here Babcock's comments are most significant, since she states that

There are certain dangers inherent in celebrating the negative, and in focusing on the negative we run counter to some of the strongest psycho-logical habits of our culture and to the still tenacious positivist emphasis of social science. (1978, p. 14)

Babcock goes on to suggest that symbolic inversions are a form of "cultural negation", and comments that

All symbolic inversions define a culture's lineaments at the same time as they question the usefulness and the absoluteness of this ordering. . . . they remind us of the arbitrary condition of imposing an order on our environment and experience, even while they enable us to see certain features of that order more clearly simply because they have turned insight out. (1978, p. 29)

And, in so far as "imposing an order on our environment" includes the foregrounding and backgrounding of meaning, the concept of symbolic inversion may be said to apply. But here we restrict the definition of "negation" to its simple dictionary sense to mean any act of denial, examples of which abound in the ethnographic literature, especially in studies concerned with kinship terminologies, where they frequently take the form of categorical prohibitions. For instance, Humphrey recently reports that, amongst the Mongols,

> In general, the names of seniors of either sex, reckoned by relative gener-
> ation and age, are not used in address by juniors, although they may be
> used in reference. In the latter case such names are usually slightly
> disguised. . . . (1978, p. 91)

And, significantly, she continues to make the point that,

> This prohibition on the use of the names of seniors does not, however,
> amount to a taboo; it is more a matter of respect and decorum, a custom
> which is followed without the notion of very serious consequences if it were
> to be broken. Seniors, on the other hand, can use the personal names of
> juniors freely. *This differentiation between seniors and juniors should be
> seen in context of the general use of honorific words and expressions in
> dialogue between people of different status.* (1978, p. 9; added emphasis)

The idea of backgrounding information is nevertheless a controversial
matter in Western cultures, where such ideas run counter to "rational,
scientific norms". Indeed, the whole notion of suppressed information
and implicit meanings is often regarded as evidence of primitive
behaviour, social deviance and/or individual neurosis, or at best, the
province of *double entendre*. Certainly, as far as positivist research
methods are concerned, these assertions raise problems about verification, measurement, etc. which are so psychologically and sociologically
disturbing that, like the categorical prohibitions of the so-called
"irrational" and "superstitious", they are quite firmly backgrounded.
Indeed, to rank a problem as worthy of scientific investigation, it is
necessary to assume that the phenomenon concerned permits the
establishment of firm boundaries, and to deny those messy manifestations of undifferentiated textures of meaning, e.g. anomalous
categories, ambiguous symbols, analog communication, so often denied
their place in human thought and action.

ANALOG TEXTURES OF MEANING

The undifferentiated elements in Fig. 1 are defined here as those
forms of analog communication which (a) suppress the boundaries
created by digital communication (synthesis) and (b) fill in the "gaps"
created by digital communication (abomination). Thus, in cell C, Fig.
1, we contend that, in the continuous flow of everyday life, the distinctions drawn by the textures of contrast are blurred through the
deliberate use of words, phrases, symbols and behaviours that have

multiple meanings. And, as such, they are used to synthesize both differentiated and undifferentiated textures of meaning, and to lubricate communication. It is also suggested that such ill-defined though foregrounded devices provide excellent raw material for what elsewhere we have termed the "rhetorics of justification" (Gowler and Legge, 1980). For example, in our own work on occupational rationales and ideologies, we found that "professional" workers deal with the many pressures stemming from environmental change by having recourse to a dialectical defence, i.e. justification, of their authority and access to scarce resources.

Central to the typical content of these justifications are direct and indirect appeals to "altruism" and "expertise", as they often juxtapose and conflate expertise (skills, knowledge, competence) and altruism (selflessness, humanitarianism, impartial commitment). For the naive attribution theorist, of course, such accounts may be seen as oblique ways of presenting acceptable causes and effects as the very juxtaposition of these meanings implies that, seen causally, it is through expertise one exercises altruism. Interestingly enough, the rationalism of our culture "backgrounds" the alternative causal sequence, i.e. through altruism to expertise, since this smacks of "miracles" and "quackery". However, the protestant work ethic neatly deals with this possibility by converting "altruism" into "hard work", "application" and/or "proper motivation".

An example of this expertise/altruism dichotomy is provided by Bender, who, in a recent article on the future of community psychology, comments that

> If the psychology profession has a valid claim to having *usable skills* then it surely has an ethical commitment to *provide these skills to all who might benefit from them.* Thus, psychologists have a moral obligation to provide services for clients in places other than hospitals and in areas other than the traditional ones of mental illness and mental handicap. The elderly, the physically handicapped, children of one-parent families, and the "at risk" in general are equally deserving of psychologists' attention. Such *services* cannot possibly be provided by psychologists institutionalized in hospitals. (1979, p. 9; added emphasis)

The emphasis on the term "service" here is inserted to illustrate how analog textures of meaning suppress the boundaries created by digital textures of meaning and, whilst the term "service" offers a useful shorthand expression for, say, "the altruistic provision of appropriate expertise", it also serves to reduce the dissonance and interpersonal conflict created by the fundamental semantic differences (different-iation) between altruism and expertise. These differences are high-lighted, for example, in Gowler and Parry's discussion on the role of the clinical psychologist:

> . . . . . altruism, which is by definition, *unbounded*, self-denying, valid in its own terms, and concerned with the whole person, stands in opposition to expertise (forms of specialization) which is *bounded*, self-affirming, validated by external criteria (e.g. utility), and concerned only with particular aspects of a person. (1979, p. 54)

Given this semantic difference, the term "service", via analog communication, achieves a synthesis of altruism (thesis) and expertise (antithesis).

At this point, it is necessary to emphasize two important issues. First, it is useful to clarify the distinction between negation and synthesis. Thus, in negation, through the suppression of certain socio-linguistic choices, a number of meanings and other behaviours are not realized. For example, in Great Britain, certain royal persons cannot be addressed by their first names even by close acquaintances. Among other things, such etiquette symbolizes the fact that even the possibility of any reduction of the social distance between certain royalty and their potential subjects is not to be entertained. In synthesis, however, ambiguity is deliberately introduced in order to maintain and/or conflate meanings whilst at the same time suppressing their contradictions (whether or not such a synthesis is achieved).

Second, as suggested above, there are circumstances when such ambiguities are utilized. For example, not only are they a feature of professionals' rhetorics of justification and legitimation, but also of the "calculated vagueness" of the fortune teller (Miller, 1978; Tatro, 1974), the "ambiguous presentation" of the amateur trader in stolen goods (Henry, 1978) and the bland evasions of "official spokesmen". Further-more, ambiguous meanings, whether created by language, behaviour, objects or events, are taken for granted in much of everyday life and, as such, do not necessarily arouse dissonance or promote confusion and conflict.

There are, nevertheless, certain ambiguities, as represented by cell D in Fig. 1, that comprise the texture of abomination. As Bailey comments

People or objects or events which will not fit into a known category are likely to be regarded with fear, with contempt, or even with loathing: they are not likely to be overlooked. This quality of catching attention makes the unexpected action strategically advantageous: but it can also be perilous. Furthermore, the quality of being unexpected shades into another quality, that of being abominable. Thus, it is not marginality alone which renders the half-breed or the transvestite or the calf with two heads monstrous: rather it is the fact that each culture picks out certain categories of the unexpected, and marks them as *intrinsically* beyond comprehension: they are "unnatural". Anyone who attempts to understand or explain these unexpected combinations, let alone anyone who displays them, is likely to arouse immediate and unreasoning hostility. (1977, p. 184–185)

And, as certain anthropologists (e.g. Douglas, 1966; Leach, 1964; Lévi-Strauss, 1963; Norbeck, 1977; Sahlins, 1976; Tambiah, 1969) have discussed at great length, such abominations appear as prohibitions or taboos, especially about such everyday human activities as eating, speaking and physical contact. There are, however, arenas e.g. theatres, circuses and some committees (Bailey, 1977) where licensed comics, clowns and chairpersons transform abominations into absurdities, thus reinforcing their essential ambiguity.

Given this argument, i.e. that textures of abomination carry a heavy affective charge, they may be seen to function as metaphors, which, as Turner points out

. . . . . bring into relation a number of ideas, images, sentiments, values and stereotypes. Components of one system enter into dynamic relations with components of the other. (1974, p. 29)

As such, they both mediate and obviate other textures of meaning. Further, it is the associated implications of such metaphors that provide their analog functions, (although, obviously, we are not suggesting that all metaphors are abominations).

We wish to emphasize that these abominable meanings not only *relocate* other meanings but also that this function is frequently achieved without any change occurring in themselves. In other words, they are, like myths, a form of semantic catalyst that confutes the conventional (Wagner, 1978), and, as such, they also convey a unique type of ambiguity. It is this quality that distinguishes the textures of abomination from those of negation. Whereas the texture of negation becomes ambiguous through suppression, the texture of abomination is suppressed because it is ambiguous. Second, at the level of action, failure to observe negation, e.g. not to conform to the rules of etiquette, is to run the risk of social and, in some cases, supernatural sanctions. Conversely, breaches of the rules of abomination, e.g. taboos, always involve a supernatural sanction and, in some cases, social sanctions (Norbeck, 1977).

Following this discussion of the ideas represented by Fig. 1, it may be evident why we now suggest that the attribution theorist's model of man as a "naive social scientist" (see Harris and Harvey's chapter in this volume) might be reviewed in the light of the notion that the attribution theorist (as scientist) is a naive rhetorician. Put another way, in so far as attribution theorists also manipulate ambiguous meanings (by say "backgrounding" them in their models and research methods) they themselves engage in a rhetoric that attempts to recreate their "subjects" as flawed images of themselves ("sophisticated" scientists), who are unfortunately given to cognitive lapses resulting from either an inadequate intellectual endowment, poor linguistic performance and/or faulty logic.

In the following section, however, we move towards Harré's ethogenic model where he argues that

Account analysis reveals the knowledge of social meanings, situations, standards of propriety and so on required by a competent social actor in the continuous meta-activity of interpreting and justifying what has been done in this or that episode. (1978, p. 63)

Ethogenic analysis

Our interpretation of Harré's (1978) position is that ethogenic analysis involves the analysis of individual accounts, supplemented by an intensive research design that distinguishes between the synchronic and diachronic aspects of the context. Given this, we now apply this conceptual frame, along with our own model of the process of categorization, to data collected during intensive fieldwork conducted in two Northwestern factory workshops in the first six months of 1967 (Gowler, 1970; Millward, 1968).

To summarize this fieldwork situation, the firm's wage payment system was subject to structural and cultural "pressures" not envisaged in its design. For instance, labour and product markets influenced the operation of the organization's control systems, especially the forms of payment and allocation of work. The consequences of this were that a number of managerial aspirations, e.g. low unit costs and a stable, satisfied labour force, were not realized.

Viewing this situation in terms of Harré's injunctions, Gowler (1970) identifies a number of structural imperatives, amongst which he includes certain rules, procedures and conventions, the investigation of which appears to equate with what Harré terms synchronic analysis, i.e. ". . . . . the analysis of social practices and institutions as they exist at any one time. . . . (1978, p. 46)". Gowler also employs what Harré terms *diachronic analysis* (i.e. "the investigation of the stages and process by which these practices are created and abandoned, changed and unchanged") to explore how the "tensions" existing within and between the factors identified above created a number of self-reinforcing processes that introduced "unplanned" structural, behavioural and attitudinal changes. This interest in the emergence of "pathological" organizational forms is the hallmark of the Manchester Business School group of organizational theorists (Gowler and Legge, 1973, 1975, 1978; Legge 1978a, 1978b; Warmington *et al.*, 1977).

Central to this case study is Gowler's description of how "typical" members (Harré, 1978) of the work organization, e.g. supervisors and assemblers (i.e. workers assembling components for electronic equipment) were influenced by these synchronically and diachronically defined factors. The outcome of this was said to be (i) pressure on the supervisors to increase and maintain productivity in the face of growing uncertainty, and (ii) pressure on the operators to reduce productivity in order to reduce uncertainty. As Gowler reports, another result of this conflictual state of affairs was anxiety and labour turnover on the part of the assemblers, accompanied by frustration and low morale on the part of the supervisors.

When seen in the light of Harré's ethogenic principles, this case study may be reinterpreted in such a way as to include "accounts" omitted from Gowler's original analysis. This revised version not only suggests that pressures stemming from structural differentiation, e.g. the division of labour, control systems and markets, increased the psychological and social distance between supervisors and assemblers, but that this "gap" was expressed and contained by culturally determined devices, e.g. accounts, jokes and songs. It is the analysis of these accounts, jokes and songs that, we suggest, conforms to the centrepiece of Harré's argument, i.e. through ethogenic analysis, it is possible to comprehend the "semantic structure" of "lived episodes", and thereby to construct a picture of how people mutually construct their interpretations and performances of everyday life. Consequently, in the following section, two accounts are analysed in terms of the textures of meaning outlined in Fig. 1, whilst being related to the contextual (synchronic and diachronic data) discussed above.

Before we commence, however, it seems important to enter a caveat about Harré's injunction that one should draw a sharp distinction between synchronic and diachronic analysis. We find this dichotomy to be theoretically suspect and, certainly, methodologically difficult. Whilst there is not space to develop an adequate critique here, we believe that this dichotomy (i) tends to "background" the emergent (Goldner, 1967) and covert (Ditton, 1977; Mars *et al.*, 1979) nature of social interaction, and (ii) as such, also encourages the very positivistic espistemology and methodology that Harré has been at pains to criticize. Furthermore, it is the emergent properties of all institutions and individuals (Claxton 1979) that not only embarrasses our research methods, but also, *inter alia*, such practical, everyday intentions as the design, implementation and evaluation of planned organizational change. Indeed, such emergent processes are frequently backgrounded by being categorized as "messy data" and/or "political factors". What is more, the type of data presented and analysed in the following section, i.e. accounts, is often perceived and rejected as manifestations of these political processes, i.e. not reliable or significant information. But, more frequently, it is just simply ignored.

THE CONTEXT AND FUNCTION OF TWO ACCOUNTS

At the outset, it should be emphasized that these accounts (each one collected from a different supervisor in separate workshops) not only reflect managerial values and beliefs about productivity, morality and rewards, but also, whilst appearing to represent real events, have the structure of myths. We return to discuss this mythic quality in the next section. In the meantime, as recounted by supervisors during casual conversation, these accounts or texts are as follows.

A. A girl subject to fits, an epileptic, who was said to have been "spoilt by her mother", took advantage of her condition and received an unusual amount of help from her workmates. This help consisted of the gift of completed assemblies and enabled her to meet her production targets. A supervisor noticed that the operator concerned began to fall short of her quota but, before he could take action, the girl had left the firm. The supervisor was subsequently informed that other workers in this girl's group had refused to continue their support. The reason given for this withdrawal of help was that the girl gave nothing in return.

B. A girl with a crippled leg became very friendly with the worker sitting next to her. Their relationship was so close that they were known as "a couple of lesbians". Their superior believed that the crippled girl was helping her friend, who made little or no attempt to improve her performance or to repay this assistance. Eventually, the supervisor confronted the girls with this and threatened to separate them. This resulted in both girls giving notice and each actually left the factory. However, the crippled girl returned to the firm, having found difficulty in finding suitable employment elsewhere.

At first glance, these stories seem unexceptional and, indeed, one might ask what all the fuss is about. However, it must be emphasized here that the wage payment system, or more precisely changes in the wage payment system, created both operational and moral dilemmas for supervisors and assemblers. For example, the supervisors were responsible for the output of components of a given quality whilst at the same time maintaining fixed production targets. These responsibilities were linked with the assemblers' wage payment system, where the management had set closely monitored standards of performance related to various levels of pay. Under this system, each worker "contracted" to maintain a certain standard of performance in return for a guaranteed wage, i.e. a form of "measured daywork", which, at that time, was popularly supposed to require supervisors of high calibre, possessing above average technical, administrative and "human relations" skills. Nevertheless, it is clearly evident, in the circumstances reported by Gowler, that the supervisors concerned did not possess or exercise such qualities and skills.

These issues apart, two rules appeared to produce a constellation of difficulties for these supervisors. The first was that, once having contracted to maintain a given quality and quantity of output, an assembler was not then allowed to fall back to lower levels of performance. This rule was upheld even though an assembler might be transferred to another unit where she (all these workers were women, though the supervisors were men) would have to perform similar operations on slightly different components. If, for whatever reason, an assembler fell regularly below the agreed level of output, she was required to undergo a period of retraining, and if, after this, she did not meet her original contractual obligations, she might be dismissed.

The management's justification for these rather rigid regulations was that:

(i) since standards were scientifically set by their work study experts, a 100 performance on task A was no different from a 100 performance on task B. Consequently, a transfer from task A to task B should create no difficulties for the operator, and

(ii) if they allowed assemblers to vary their performance at will, the whole system would be undermined and, effectively, would revert to the conventional piecework scheme which they had recently abandoned in favour of the measured daywork system.

But since the assemblers challenged these managerial views, and given the other factors described by Gowler, it is not surprising that they tended to contract for levels of performance well below their ability to achieve them. An obvious outcome of this was that many operators had either a considerable amount of spare time (having completed their contractual obligations) or continued to produce extra components for which they would not be paid.

These classic difficulties gave rise to the second rule (which is referred to in both accounts) that any operator discovered giving completed components to another would be dismissed. Again the management's rationale for this rule was that this practice not only undermined the "individual contract" basis of the wage payment system, but also it created other managerial difficulties, e.g. in workflow administration and quality control.

The supervisors were then caught in a web of conflicting demands. If they pressed the assemblers to contract for levels of performance which the latter could not maintain, they might have then to dismiss them. If, on the other hand, they left assemblers to contract low levels of performance, they had either to tolerate the latter "wasting time" or producing components that might be "illegitimately distributed" to those who, for one reason or another, could not fulfil their contractual obligations.

Against this background, and viewed functionally, accounts A and B may then be said to be either:

(i) *attributions* made by "leaders" in conditions of extreme uncertainty (Green and Mitchell, 1979);

(ii) *cautionary tales* used to socialize new personnel (and researchers);

(iii) *myths* that permit the statement of what "would be difficult to admit openly and yet what is patently clear to all and sundry that the ideal is not attainable" (Douglas, 1967, p. 52), or

(iv) *rhetorics* that combine the three functions identified above.

We suggest that organizational change (or any other type of change in everyday life) will be reflected in the form and function of rhetoric.

Indeed, the increasing quantity of rhetoric is itself an indicator of social and organizational change.

In the following section, this typology of functions is mapped onto that of the textures of meaning to provide a conceptual framework for an analysis of the two accounts (hereafter referred to as "texts") quoted above. This conceptual framework is represented in diagrammatic form in Fig. 2 below.

The structure and function of rhetoric

In Fig. 2, attributions are treated mainly as observable surface structures composed of a set of contrasts organized into a causal sequence. But, as illustrated in the diagramme, "wild" (as opposed to "cultivated", researcher contrived) attributions, also involved some synthesis and, by definition, certain negations. This is the inevitable consequence of the fact that wild texts are "messy" or "dirty" data, contaminated by ambiguous presentation, calculated vagueness, and other "toxic" elements.

These wild texts, however, are composed of much more than a net of sharp contrasts organized into a dissonance reducing, causal sequence. For instance, such texts, e.g. everyday accounts, jokes, fairy stories, myths and songs, are not merely exotic forms of attribution, but also "fragments" (Harré, 1978, p. 45) of a mutually constructed web of shared meanings (culture) and, as such, parts of a broader more encompassing script. Furthermore, given this is the case, the would-be psychologist of everyday life might well emulate the field archaeologist by unearthing all fragments (shards) on site and then envisaging how they combine into more comprehensive and comprehensible wholes (pots).

We emphasize this injunction because, as illustrated in Fig. 3 below, this "archaeological" exercise might be attempted through the methods suggested by structuralists (in this instance, Lévi-Strauss), which exercise, as Piaget (1971 (1968), p.136) comments, calls for a special effort of reflective abstraction. Moreover, this approach is not only consistent with the "process of categorization" and "double discrimination" discussed above, but is also suggested by the data themselves, since, fortuitously, one text is the mirror image of the other.

The construction of Fig. 3 is discussed in detail below when these texts are treated as myths. But, meanwhile, column 4 offers a neat example of how different meanings emerge when contrasts within texts are complemented by contrasts (as oppositions) between texts. Thus, text A indicates that, whilst the "problem" was removed, i.e. the "delinquent" operative left the firm, this was the result of the assemblers taking independent action and, effectively, usurping the supervisor's powers. Text B, on the other hand, actually reverses this state of affairs, since in this story, the supervisor exercises his powers, but only to find that the "problem" (in the shape of the crippled girl) returns. Consequently, if these are treated as a single text, these two "causal" statements are transformed into a single "correlation". This, in these circumstances, is that supervisory power is inversely related to supervisory problem-solving, which thereby changes diachronic cause and effect into a synchronic correlation.

If this seems speculative and far-fetched, it should be noted that Gowler, in his original report, writes

. . . . . . the workers did not regard the supervisors as competent in either a technical or social sense, and certainly they did not regard their power as legitimate. These attitudes stemmed from the relative lack of technical expertise on the part of these supervisors and also from certain cultural values held by the workers. What is meant by a "relative lack of technical expertise" is not that the supervisors were deficient in knowledge about the component being manufactured but they were unlikely to be able to make one. At the least not at the speed and precision achieved by the assemblers. (1970, p. 107–108)

Moreover, since authority, i.e. legitimate power, is a necessary resource in hierarchically organized interpersonal relationships (Cohen, 1975; Legge, 1978b) and, given that, in such circumstances, technical competence is a major source of this managerial asset, these supervisors found themselves in the unenviable position of having to accept responsibility whilst being denied legitimacy. Moreover, this stress-inducing vulnerability tended to surface on those relatively frequent occasions when the supervisors had to exercise their disciplinary powers to enforce the assemblers' contractual obligations.

This technical incompetence and related lack of authority was neatly encapsulated in one of the assemblers' publicly chanted work songs:

They say that at *Widget's* it's a wonderful place,
But the organization's a shocking disgrace.
The chargehand and foreman, and manager too,
Stand with their hands in their pockets,
With nothing to do.

They stand on the floor and they bawl and they shout;
They shout about things they know nothing about:
For all that they're doing they might as well be
Shovelling coal on the Isle of Capri.
(Sung to the traditional tune of the "Mountains of Mourne", and recorded at the firm's annual dance. *Widget's* is a fictitious name and the emphasis is added)

Turning now to these texts as *cautionary tales*, it is suggested by Fig. 3 that the latter involve a fair degree of negation. First, the dramatic nature of these stories is heightened by the use of contrasts, e.g. persons and events, that are stigmatized and threatening. Thus contrasts carrying a heavy affective load are used to deflect attention away from more pragmatic questions such as "Is dismissal the inevitable consequence of being detected at the illegitimate disposal of completed components?" In other words, we suggest that the sensational nature of these details (plus significant omissions) serves not only to demonstrate that retribution eventually overtakes the wicked, but also to "blot out" or "background" meanings that, either for etiquette or social convenience, could not be overtly expressed.

On the interesting question of retribution, Heider (1958) argues that this familiar theme may relate to the individual's desire to maintain harmony or balance within and between sentiments and cognitions. For instance, cognitive consistency combines with moral fervour to produce such epigrammatic cautionary statements as "people get their just deserts" and "crime does not pay". However, in these texts, retribution is also conveniently pressed into service on behalf of the dominant group, providing a clear example of how rhetoric not only utilizes, but goes beyond, mere causal attribution. Furthermore, it is this rhetorical aspect of cautionary tales that reveals how thin is the moral veneer on pragmatic intent. And, since it is intention that links attribution with context and action with meaning, the analysis of cautionary tales should prove especially fruitful.

As commented above, however, rhetoric goes beyond the meanings and functions of cautionary tales. Thus, the deep structures of these texts not only involve negative forms of etiquette and selected omissions, but also make covert recognition of ambiguous categories (Gowler 1972) and unspeakable meanings, i.e. abominations. Put simply, rhetoric also incorporates myth. To demonstrate this "covert recognition" of abominations, we now turn to the controversial methods of analysis of structural anthropology (Lévi-Strauss, 1963), which, *inter alia*, assume the "existence of an unconscious meaning of cultural phenomena" (Rossi, 1974, p. 7).

Figure 3 adapts Lévi-Strauss' approach to the decoding of myths (Larrain, 1979). Before discussing this matter more fully, it seems useful to outline the characteristics of this method by reference to Lévi-Strauss' influential analysis of the Oedipus myth (see Wilden, 1972) for an example of the influence this style of work upon that of Lacan). Lévi-Strauss suggests that through trial and error, it is necessary to break down such data into their "gross constituent units or mythemes" (1963, p. 211), then to treat these mythemes as counters to be arranged in such a way as to produce columns of items that exhibit common features. Thus, as illustrated by Fig. 3, Lévi-Strauss goes on to issue the instruction that

> Were we to *tell* the myth, we would disregard the columns and read the rows from left to right and from top to bottom. But if we want to *understand* the myth, then we will have to disregard one half of the diachronic dimension (top to bottom) and read from left to right, column after column, each one being considered as a unit. All the relations belonging to the same column exhibit one common feature which it is our task to discover. (1963, p. 214–15)

Next, he suggests that one should then consider the relationships between the relations, i.e. the bundles of "common features". This method, he argues, not only reveals meanings of myth which "get thought in man unbeknownst to him" (Lévi-Strauss, 1978, p. 3) but also that it

> . . . . . . eliminates a problem which has, so far, been one of the main obstacles to the progress of mythological studies, namely, the quest for the *true* version, or the *earlier* one. On the contrary, we define the myth as consisting of all its versions . . . . . . (1963, p. 216–217)

Returning to our example of such analysis, Fig. 3, column 1 may be said to represent the common feature of extreme forms of physical disability and column 2 extreme forms of interpersonal behaviour. Column 3 represents extreme (asymmetrical) forms of reciprocity (see Gowler, 1970, p. 112–120) and column 4 extreme social sanctions. Then, to reduce this further by compressing columns 1 and 2 into extreme behaviour (physical handicaps are socially defined and managed, Goffman, 1964), and columns 3 and 4 into extreme retributions, we have the proposition that excessive behaviour is related to excessive sanctions.

There are, however, deeper levels of meaning revealed when each column is viewed in terms of its internal contrasts, and again the themes of extremes and excesses emerge. For example, column 1 internally contrasts extreme forms of physical disability, i.e. one "end" of the body against the other (head/leg), which, incidentally, is an example of the common theme of "polarity" found in much symbolic classification (Needham, 1963). Column 2, on the other hand, internally contrasts extreme forms of "affection", between kin and non-kin, and in column 3 there emerges the opposition between individual and group reciprocity. Finally, column 4 contrasts workers-and-leaving with supervisors-and-returning.

This material, of course, may be subjected to even deeper, contextually related analysis and, whilst space does not permit further excursions into "reflexive abstraction", one last point seems worth extra comment. This is that the dominant theme of "excess" may be viewed in terms of a deep concern, on the part of the élite involved, to maintain and manipulate the "proper" balance both within and between status, effort and reward. Alternatively, if the idea of *excess* is converted into the idea of *surplus*, then returning to our analysis of the context, this is the core concern of the supervisors. Thus, to recapitulate, the assemblers created a surplus (either in spare time or in completed components) in an attempt to resolve conflicting pressures in their situation (Gowler, 1970, p. 122). But the very creation and disposal of this surplus resulted (at least from the management's point of view) in reprehensible forms of social behaviour and (from the workers' point of view) the exercise of severe negative sanctions. This situation was equally unsatisfactory for the supervisors, since the existence of the surplus in either of its forms was certainly unacceptable. Furthermore, given their vulnerability, e.g. their relatively low level of technical competence, they were disadvantaged when confronting the assemblers about questions of effort, quality and productivity. Yet, paradoxically, attempts to reduce the size of the surplus might result in lower performance and labour wastage.

Finally, when viewed in the broader context of our interest in the evaluation of organizational change, it could reasonably be argued that the introduction of the "measured daywork" method of payment (the firm had previously operated a conventional bonus system) created new problems of managerial control, especially in the regulation of the surplus, which management were unable to perceive, let alone solve. When viewed in the even broader socio-political context, a Marxist might argue that this situation constitutes a manifestation of a major "contradiction of capitalism", whereby the surplus value of labour is not available to either workers or employers. We add this radical perspective to remind the would-be psychologist of everyday life that, outside the laboratory, behaviour has political meaning and interpretation, which, apart from the political persuasions of those involved, makes it difficult to sustain the belief that science is separate from politics. This perspective inevitably returns us to the vexed question of research method.

Conclusion: meaning and methods

In the analysis of the texts as myths, it will have been noted that we have made no reference to the question of "synthesis" (see Fig. 2). This is because this texture of meaning rests mainly in the words used in an account. And, given that the texts reported above were recorded after they had been recounted in casual conversation, the precise form of words used have obviously been distorted by the act of recollection and transformation into written form. This difficulty does not affect the validity of the structural analysis of these texts as myths, for reasons made evident above, in particular because this method is more concerned with form than content. However, to give an example of the use of verbal synthetic ambiguity used in this situation, the following assemblers' song (recorded at the same time as the one reproduced above) is presented:

> We are the *Widget* girls, some of the *Widget* girls,
> We are awful-mannered, *sell our fags for tanners*,
> We are respected where'er we go.
> As we go marching along the street, doors and windows open wide.
> All the lads and lasses say,
> "*Widget* girls are passing by". (Emphasis added)

The line emphasized in this song is an example of the ambiguity created by a word that has two or more meanings (cf. the way the word "development" is used in rhetorics of justification and legitimation, Strauss, 1977). Here we contend that the word "fags" is used not only to represent the ambiguous nature of their exchange relationships with their employers, but also the "now-you-have-it-now-you-don't" characteristics of the "surplus", i.e. extra components and spare time. Like cigarettes (and food) they are simultaneously both consumed and saved.

Furthermore, readers are invited to speculate on the range of semantic possibilities offered by the word "fags".

Methodologically speaking, we suggest that this material would seem to have little meaning unless "contextually" interpreted. To reiterate Harré:

> When we are studying the interactions of social life we are dealing with an entity which has unitary social meaning as a whole and which we cannot partition into purely formal meaningless elements, take them separately and expect them to generate the elements of the same socially meaningful effect that was produced by the unpartitioned ensemble. One might say that the ensemble has a unitary semantic quality. The semantic quality of the presence of that entity to a knowledgeable perceiver is lost the moment it is partitioned into purely formal elements (1977, p. 35–36).

To some extent, the formality of our "double discrimination" of the determinants of meaning model, Fig. 1, contradicts this injunction. However, we contend that Fig. 1 provides the researcher with four questions to ask of certain types of data, each of which is related to a cell in this matrix and, especially in the case of "negation" and "abomination", demands contextual, holistic interpretation. Without necessarily accepting our theoretical justifications, the four textures of meaning could also be used to generate a range of questions to ask of the *content* of any verbal or written account. For example, this schema may have something to offer the clinical psychologist when interpreting material collected from clients.

These contextual and holistic interpretations require that we turn to the "field" sciences, e.g. geology, archaeology, and ethology, for our methodological exemplars, since these not only suggest that we find meaning *in* context, but also that meaning *is* context. We might then, perhaps, achieve a social psychology that replaces validation with evaluation, and prediction with sensitization (Gergen, 1973).

As far as cognition is concerned, this analysis might be seen to suggest that adult individuals are not only capable of three distinct modes of thought, i.e. causal, dialectical and mythic, but also of switching between them by using rhetoric. We stress adult individuals because these cognitive abilities appear to require both emotional maturity and an experience of a wide range of social situations.

Finally, we suggest that this analysis requires a theoretical/methodological pluralism (Bell and Newby, 1977) that is yet to be accepted by many social scientists, but which is crucial for the investigation of what we understand by a psychology of ordinary explanations.

12

Verbal Strategies in Impression Management

J. T. Tedeschi and M. Reiss

Introduction

William James (1890) noted that individuals have multiple selves; rather than possessing a single self, each of us is composed of various identities. In their dramaturgic analyses of human social behaviour, Burke (1952) and Goffman (1959) claimed that in each social situation people adopt one or another of their various identities in order to influence the interaction. The specific social identity that a person adopts in a social interaction can have a marked impact on how others react to him or her. For example, a person who is perceived as having high status or prestige will usually have more influence over others than someone who adopts a social identity that does not entail these attributes. Thus, it is not surprising that persons actively create, promote, and maintain specific social identities by engaging in tactics that convey desired impressions to interactants. One common occurrence of this impression management occurs when individuals account for their actions, or, as the phrase explicitly has it, "explain themselves" to others. Thus, people offer ordinary-language explanations of their behaviour and such explanations often serve a self-presentational function. These and other impression management or self-presentation tactics may convey identities that correspond to an individual's self-image, or they may misrepresent the individual's conception of himself.

The present paper is concerned with those impression management tactics used by individuals who face social predicaments. Schlenker (1980) defines a predicament as "any event that casts undesired aspersions on the lineage, character, conduct, skills, or motives of an actor" (p.125). In order to ascertain whether he faces a predicament, the actor (i.e. the person upon whose actions we are focusing) must make some judgment concerning the attributions and perceptions that others are forming of him. So, the impression-management process involves two sorts of explanations. The first is the actor's personal explanation, interpretation, or diagnosis as to whether the situation entails a predicament or potential predicament. If the cognitive explanation or definition of the situation as a predicament is reached the actor should become aware that some sort of impression management is required. He will then probably offer a public account for the predicament-provoking actions in order to avoid or escape their undesired implications. This second form of explanation is the major focus of our chapter.

Central to the realization that one faces a predicament is the belief that others attribute to oneself causality and responsibility for the event in question. In general, an actor faces a predicament whenever he engages in a behaviour that he believes others consider morally blameworthy or failing to meet some standards of achievement. Under these circumstances the actor projects an identity as an immoral or incompetent person. The undesirable implications of these identities are typically at variance with the image the actor would like to convey. So, in a sense the actor is a naive attribution theorist, drawing conclusions about the inferences others make about his behaviour. In addition to influencing the actor's decision concerning whether he faces a predicament, these inferences will affect the explanations that he will use to deal with it. Thus, our analysis of impression management must also consider how individuals make attributions.

In the first section of this paper we lay the groundwork for our analysis of reactions to predicaments by explicating concepts, terms and issues relevant to attribution and impression management. This is necessary to understand the circumstances in which individuals will conclude that they face a predicament and the kinds of explanations they will offer. In the second section we will catalogue and describe the ordinary-language explanations that individuals engage in when they find themselves faced with a predicament. In the last section we will point out one application of our analysis by claiming that several social psychological research paradigms can be interpreted as situations in which the experimenter creates a predicament for subjects and observes how they attempt to explain themselves in order to maintain their public image.

Explication of concepts and issues

Social psychologists are in the midst of trying to develop a theory of naive psychology. In a large sense attribution theory and research are concerned with the man (or woman) on the street as a naive, common sense psychologist. According to Heider (1958) and Jones and Davis (1965), each person has developed his own common sense psychology which he uses as a basis for explaining, analysing, and predicting the behaviour of others. This is related to our analysis of predicaments because impression management theory proposes that the self-presentational tactics that an actor uses are based on the attributions that the actor perceives the audience has made concerning him.

The surge of interest in attribution processes among social psychologists has focused primarily on the writings of Heider (1958), Jones and Davis (1965), and Kelley (1967, 1973). Recently, a number of conceptual problems with these seminal works have been raised, some of which are addressed in other chapters in the present volume. Attribution theorists and researchers have often used terms loosely and inconsistently. This has led to ambiguity and vagueness in important concepts and might serve to impede progress in the area (cf. Buss, 1978; Kruglanski, 1975). Because an impression management interpretation of reactions to predicaments requires some analysis of attribution processes, we will start with a critique and clarification of relevant concepts and issues from the attribution literature.

ATTRIBUTIONS AND DESCRIPTIONS

Attribution theorists have failed to recognize a distinction between action descriptions and attributions. Descriptions of behaviour may be divided into those concerned with actions and those concerned with activities (Langford, 1971). Descriptions of actions include the actor's purposes and the connection of the action with social rules. Thus, actions cannot be adequately described by enumerating movements of the body. Activities, unlike actions, are performed for intrinsic reasons and are not directed towards ends or goals. For example, a person may jog or sail a boat frequently not in order to get anywhere, but for the sheer joy that running or sailing provide. Descriptions of actions and activities are carried in the language of a given culture. A person learns in what context which descriptions of behaviour are most appropriate.

Many different descriptions of an actor's particular behaviour can usually be given. For example, one may say that a man is exercising his arm by pushing a pump handle up and down, or that he is pumping water into a bucket, or that he is stealing water from his neighbour's well. Of course, the way that the actor describes his behaviour may be

quite different from the way an observer would describe it. What should
be noted, however, is that the three descriptions differ primarily in terms
of the purpose or aim of the behaviour (cf. Peltit, p.11).

An actor can offer one or another description in order to explain his
behaviour and resolve predicaments that might result from it. Purposes,
goals, intentions and motives are not perceived directly from actions,
but they are typically included in the descriptions of actions. These
descriptions are most probably learned with a particular language. It is
therefore plausible to suggest that the process proposed by current attribution theories is not the typical way that attributions are made.
Observers may not use only the responses in question and their effects in
order to directly make inferences about the actor. Instead, the observers
may use these and other cues in the situation — including props, objects,
social histories, social norms, identification of the parties to the interaction and verbalizations and movements of the actors — as a basis for
deciding which of the relevant and cognitively available action descriptions should be applied in the particular case. The particular action
description chosen will dictate the attributions about the actor which
can be made. Thus, the person faced with a predicament would attempt
to convince observers to choose the action description which leads them
to make the most favourable attributions about him.

The lack of recognition of action descriptions by prominent attribution theorists is illustrated by an example from the theory of correspondent inferences proposed by Jones and Davis (1965). An observer
watches two people, labelled A and B, working together on a task. A
gives orders to B, monitors his performance, and indicates that the
quality and quantity of B's work are inferior. According to the theory,
presuming that no environmental causes for A's behaviour appear to
exist, the observer will tend to regard A's dominating behaviour as
indicative of his personal qualities or dispositions to be domineering. As
Jones and Davis (1965) stated, the "most correspondent inference is that
which assumes with high confidence that domineering behaviour is a
direct reflection of the person's intention to dominate, which in turn
reflects a disposition to be dominant" (p. 223). Our point is that describing the behaviour as domineering already includes the notion of intent
and does not require any further inference. Once the observer chooses
the action description which describes the behaviour as dominating
(rather than one which describes the behaviour as part of a play, for
example), the inference that A intended to be domineering has already
been made. It is true that from a description of a particular behaviour

an observer might draw the inference that the actor is prone to engage in a class of actions which have some common characteristics, such as a disposition to control and evaluate the behaviour of others, but this prediction based on inference is different from the initial dispositional inference itself.

CAUSALITY AND RESPONSIBILITY

Another conceptual problem in the attribution literature concerns the distinction between attributions of causality and attributions of responsibility. There tends to be confusion and ambiguity in much of the attribution work regarding whether the investigators are interested in how people make attributions about the causes of some actions or how people decide whether an individual should be held responsible for the alleged effects (or consequences) of these actions. Cause and responsibility are often used as if they were synomymous concepts.

Perusal of the attribution literature suggests that many authors are interested in a notion of cause consistent with Hume's definition as covariation or regularity in the temporal and spatial contiguity of events. Heider (1958) claimed that the cause of a person's behaviour may be attributed in varying degrees to external (i.e. environmental) factors in the situation, or to internal (i.e. dispositional) factors in the person. Much research and theory concerns itself with variables that affect the extent to which external and/or internal causal attributions are made.

Yet, some investigators focus on variables that affect the degree to which a person will be held answerable or accountable for a particular event and will be called on to explain the action. This is where the notion of responsibility attributions enters the picture. Making an attribution of responsibility requires implications of obligation and duty. Only when a person is capable of making such decisions might he be held responsible for his actions and receive credit or be called on to explain them. If the action or its consequences are in some sense negative (e.g. socially unacceptable), the responsible actor is typically blamed and a debit is created in a moral record kept, unless he can successfully account for the actions. Such debits are often associated with punishments and disapproval. If the action or its consequences are positive, a credit is established on the actor's moral record. According to Strawson (1959) the concept of person was originated as a locus for keeping these moral debits and credits.

A predicament can arise only when a person is held responsible for his or her negative behaviour. A consideration of predicaments therefore requires that cause and responsibility not be confused with each other, although it is tempting to shade cause into because. It should be clear that an actor may cause some negative event but not be held responsible for it. In this case a predicament would not arise and the actor would not have to answer for his behaviour in order to avoid a debit on his moral record. For example, although one professional boxer may physically harm another in the ring, he will not be charged with assault and battery. Although he caused the physical damage, he is not held legally responsible for it. On the other hand, a person whose automobile is cursed with a manufacturer's defect in the parking brake (of which he is unaware) is nonetheless faced with a predicament when the brake fails to hold the parked car on a hill and it rolls into a neighbour's house.

INTENTIONS AND MOTIVES

The concept of intention is particularly important in attribution theory and research. For example, in their theory of correspondent inference, Jones and Davis (1965) hypothesized that if environmental determinants of some behaviour can be discounted, observers will attribute intent to the actor for the effects produced unless there is evidence that the actor (a) did not have knowledge of or could not have foreseen the effects, or (b) did not have the skill or ability to perform the responses. Once the observer attributes intent to the actor, he then makes an internal inference for the actor's behaviour. Further, the disposition, intention or motive attributed to the actor will correspond closely to the description given of the behaviour in question. Heider (1958) also focused on intent, which he defined in terms of the observer's inference that it (i.e. the intent) referred to a plan which served as a basis for the actor's conduct. Attribution of intention to the actor will affect the extent to which dispositional or situational inferences will be made and whether the actor will be held personally responsible for the actions. Other investigators have focused on the attribution of intent *per se*, and are less concerned with its effect on other inferences (cf. Maselli and Altrocchi, 1969).

Let us begin our consideration of intentions and motives by clarifying what we do *not* mean by the terms. Intentions and motives are not factors which exist inside the actor and propel him into the behaviour. In other words, intentions do not serve as the cause of behaviour. As Anscomb (1957) has convincingly argued in her brilliant conceptual analysis, there are serious logical problems with viewing intention as some kind of interior movement that serves to propel or cause behaviour. If intention was this type of interior movement, then it would have to be intentionally brought about by the individual, and the intention to bring it about would also have to be intentional. This kind of reasoning obviously leads to an infinite regress.

According to our view, an intention is essentially a description of what the actor was trying to accomplish by engaging in some behaviour. Assigning intention to an actor assumes that the actor knew what his goal was, believed in the connection between the means used and the goal pursued, and believed he was trying to obtain the goal by the means used. A statement of the actor's intention serves to answer the question, "why did the actor do what he did?", and may also serve to answer the question, "what is it that the actor did?" (Anscomb, 1957). Statements of intention may therefore serve as explanations, reasons or accounts for behaviour.

A motive, according to C. W. Mills (1940), is a set of words that serves as an explanation of actions that are viewed as untoward, unexpected, illegitimate or rule breaking. Peters (1958) further elucidated the concept by characterizing a motive as having three components:

> (a) it is used in contexts where conduct is being assessed and not simply explained, where there is a breakdown in conventional expectations; (b) it is used to refer to a reason of a directed sort and implies a direct disposition in the individual whose conduct is being assessed; (c) it must state *the* reason why a person acts, a reason that is operative in the situation to be explained. The motive may coincide with *his* (the actor's) reason, but is must be *the* reason why he acts. (pp. 35–36)

It is of course possible for an action to have more than one motive.

To clarify the distinction between intentions and motives it should be realized that an intention refers to a reason involving a specific goal of a particular behaviour, whereas a motive refers to an explanation involving dispositions or values of the actor that may lead him to engage in a wide range of related behaviours across a number of situations. Kenny's (1963) differentiation between forward and backward reasons is useful here. An intention refers to the forward goal toward which the behaviour may lead, while a motive refers to why the actor wanted the goal. Schutz's (1967) distinction between "in order to" and "because of" answers is also related. In response to the question, "why did you engage in that behaviour?" an actor may respond, *"in order to* reach a particular goal". An observer might not be satisfied with this kind of answer (which states the actor's intention) and may ask why the actor wanted to pursue that goal. The answer involving "because of. . ." is the kind of explanation that we refer to as a motive.

Intentions and motives are used by observers to evaluate the ethical, moral and social character of an actor, and are important determinants of observers' attributions of responsibility and assignment of blame. Thus, they are intimately involved in predicaments. Observers' perceptions of an actor's intentions and motives will influence whether he faces a predicament. Depending upon the particular motive or intention inferred by observers, the same behaviour may or may not result in a predicament. Consider the case where a doctor breaks a patient's arm. If we infer that the doctor's intention was to ensure that the arm set correctly, no predicament would arise. However, if we infer that the doctor's motive was to cause pain to a patient he would prefer not to treat, then he would face a predicament. Further, when faced with a predicament the actor may try to alter the observers' perceptions of his motives or intentions. In the second part of our example the doctor would try to convince us that we are mistaken, his true intention was to ensure the well being of the patient.

Since a motive refers to a general disposition of a person it has predictive value for other actions of the person. Intentions, however, refer only to specific actions, but not to dispositional factors. Therefore, intentions by themselves have no predictive value for future actions. They help to classify an action into a category as a description, but, as Beck (1966) noted, "it does not classify the man" (p. 156). Similarly, reasons are provided to show how a person explains a particular action, whereas the attribution of motives to the actor suggests the kinds of reasons he might have for performing a number of different actions.

An intention can never be unconscious, but we can have unconscious motives. By definition, an intention refers to the awareness of the actor concerning what he is doing. According to the definitions offered here, all *actions* are intended and all intentions are conscious. A person may deny that he performed an action of the type described by others or may assert that the effects produced by some behaviour he performed were unintentional. However, the actor could never properly say that his *action* was unconscious. Ignorance, unforeseeability of effects and lack of awareness are at the root of unintentionality and serve as the basis for some reactions to predicaments. On the other hand, a person may not be aware that he has certain dispositions and, hence, it may be said that he has unconscious motives. Observers (as well as actors themselves) often search for or infer an unconscious motive for an action when the actor cannot easily offer one, or when the motive offered to explain the behaviour is implausible.

Intentions are not synonymous with goals. It is possible for a person to have goals that he hopes will be achieved by other means than through his own behaviour. Baier (1970) has noted that one may have impossible or Utopian goals, but it is not possible to have impossible or Utopian intentions. We cannot intend what we cannot do. If a person cannot play the piano, then he cannot intend to play it, although he can intend to learn to play it. Also, we cannot intend behaviour that we cannot prevent, such as breathing, although we can of course intend to breath deeply.

EXPLANATIONS, REASONS, MOTIVES AND ACCOUNTS

Explanations of behaviour are usually offered or requested when the rule or goal that is relevant to a behaviour is in question. An explanation is typically a means-goal or a rule-relevant argument to clarify why the behaviour was performed. A reason is an explanation that defends the actor's choice or decision to act as he did. As we have already seen, a motive is an explanation that provides a dispositional answer to the question why. Accounts are explanations for untoward actions whose function is to exculpate the actor from responsibility and blame, or at least to mitigate negative moral judgments made of him. Once intention is stated (or implied in an action description), the number and kind of explanations, responses, motives, and accounts that can be plausibly made for the action are limited.

Sutherland (1959) noted that there are certain types of action for which there can be no explanation in terms of intentions, motives, values or normative rules. There are five different classes of such behaviour: reflex acts, habits, outcomes produced by accident or by mistake, activities and direct expressions of moods and emotions.

It does not make much sense to ask a person why he blinks when you blow air on his eyelids. Such reflexes are strongly affected by immediate environmental factors and are normally elicited without a conscious decision or deliberation by the actor. A causal answer based on physiology could be given for the reflex act, but such reference to neurological processes normally has no social significance.

As William James (1890) stated the matter, habit is the flywheel of society. Because we learn to do some things without having to think about them or even without being aware of doing them, we are freed from the more repetitive and mundane requirements of everyday life. This provides time and energy to think about and learn other things. A person may lock the door of his house (out of a motive for safety or security) in order to prevent burglars from entering. Over time, however, this action may become merely habitual. That is, the person no longer locks the door with the motive of security, and would lock the door even if he knew there was another outer door that was already locked. Door locking has simply become part of the ritual of going to bed at night, along with putting out the cat. Habits are motiveless behaviours.

A third class of behaviour that has no explanation in terms of a motive is that of unintentional responses. These are behaviours performed by accident or by mistake. If a cashier at a check-out counter gives too much change by mistake, he cannot be said to have done it for financial gain. If there is a motive for making the wrong change, then the behaviour cannot be classified as a mistake. Persons are also prone to accidents, particularly when the effects they try to produce in the environment are mediated by complicated machines. An accident occurs when an unforeseen circumstance or event happens by chance and disrupts the line of action taken by the person. To lose one's balance, footing or control over an automobile because of an unseen obstacle or mechanical failure may lead to effects that the individual can no longer control.

Activities constitute a fourth class of motiveless behaviours. A person performs some activities merely for the sake of performing them. A person may suddenly begin singing, and, when asked the motive for singing, may sincerely reply "I don't have any motive; I just wanted to sing". In the same way hunger may not be a motive for the activity of eating. The person may be eating simply because he likes to eat.

Impulsive reactions to emotions or mood states constitute a fifth class of motiveless behaviour, according to Sutherland. Yawning from boredom or throwing things in anger may of course be consciously and deliberately performed, but they may also occur without forethought, decision making, intent or motive.

Accounts are the ordinary-language explanations actors offer when the course of interaction is disrupted and they are faced with predicaments. Accounts are remedial explanations meant to restore the identity that the actor puts forth or to mitigate a negative or unwanted identity fostered by some behaviour. Accounts consist of excuses and justifications (Austin, 1961). Excuses are explanations in which one admits that the disruptive act is bad, wrong, or inappropriate but dissociates himself from it. Justifications are explanations in which the actor takes responsibility for the action but denies that it has the negative quality that others might attribute to it. Both excuses and justifications are intended to serve the impression-management purpose of restoring a more positive identity in front of relevant and important audiences when actors face predicaments. If these accounts are accepted by observers, the actor's predicament may be resolved. He may no longer be considered responsible and blameworthy for the negative consequences that occurred.

Reactions to predicaments

Now that important terms have been defined, we will discuss the kinds of behaviours individuals engage in when faced with predicaments. We will consider (a) excuses, (b) justifications, (c) meta-accounts, (d) disclaimers, (e) apologies and (f) blame.

A TYPOLOGY OF EXCUSES

As can be seen in Table I, excuses can be classified under three general categories. In a predicament an actor may challenge the audience's description of an action by denying any intention to bring about negative effects; the actor may argue that he did not have control over his bodily motions; or he may deny that the behaviour in question was ever performed.

Lack of Intention

One form that denial of intention takes is the claim that the effects resulted from an *accident* rather than through planned actions. Thus, the actor may claim that he accidentally tripped over a tree stump, this caused his rifle to fire, resulting in the death of his hunting buddy. Since accidents are unintentional and therefore motiveless, explaining that some behaviour was an accident reduces the predicament.

On the grounds that one cannot intend what one does not foresee, a *plea of ignorance* also amounts to a denial of intention. There are many reasons why a person might not foresee the consequences of his actions. Any one of these could be used as an excuse. (1) It might be argued that

TABLE I.   A typology of excuses.

Lack of intention or assertion that effects were not planned

Accident
Failure to foresee consequences (plea of ignorance)
    effects unforeseeable
    lack of information
    poor judgment
    distraction by other events
    misrepresentation of events by others
    mistake
    lack of time for deliberation (e.g. crisis)
    inadvertency
Mistook identity of target person
Lack of capacity (e.g. infancy, mental retardation, etc.)

Lack of volition or assertion of lack of bodily control

Physical causes
    drugs
    alcohol
    physical illness (e.g. fainting spell, temporary paralysis, etc.)
    exhaustion
Psychological causes
    insanity or mental illness
    overpowering or uncontrollable emotions (e.g. fear, anger, jealousy)
    coercion by others
    hypnotized
    brainwashed
    somnambulism
Lack of authority

Denial of agency

Mistaken identity (I didn't do it)
Amnesia and/or fugue state

---

no one in similar circumstances could have foreseen the effects that occurred. (2) The actor might not have sufficient information about a state of affairs to foresee certain consequences of his action. For example, an engineer might set off dynamite after taking proper precautions but not be aware that a stray hiker has wandered into the danger area. (3) Poor judgment occurs when the actor fails to foresee the effects of his behaviour but the average person would have foreseen these effects. The excuse of poor judgment may not alleviate the actor of all responsibility for an action, since she may be considered negligent, but it may mitigate the degree of negative reaction to him. (4) Distraction by other events may lead a person to react in unintentional ways. For example, rubbernecking among motorists is a cause of errors that produce collisions. (5) A reliance on the mistaken representation of events by others may also lead to unintentional effects, as when our blasting engineer is informed by others that the danger area has been cleared of all living beings even though, unbeknownst to them, a wandering hiker is in the area. (6) A mistake refers to perceiving or interpreting something wrongly and may involve an action that has negative but unintentional effects (like pushing the wrong button). (7) Under conditions of extreme danger where quick decisions must be taken, the individual may claim he had inadequate time to foresee all the effects of his behaviour. Thus, claiming to experience a crisis may serve as grounds for offering the excuse of failing to foresee the consequences at issue. (8) Inadvertency may also serve as the basis of a claim that the effects were not foreseen. According to Austin (1961a) an act is done inadvertently when in the course of performing some other act, the person failed to proceed with enough care and attention as would have ensured the non-occurrence of the unfortunate event in question. Thus, thinking that it is caused by a deer, a hunter may shoot at the rustle of a bush without waiting to see that another hunter actually caused the bush to move.

An actor may state that the negative effects which befell a target person involved a case of mistaken identity and in that sense the action was unintentional. This excuse is different from that involving a mistake since the latter involves a wrong response while mistaken identity involves a wrong target. A witness may charge that he saw a person carry out a criminal action and this testimony may serve to do harm to the defendant. But it might be a case of mistaken identity. Witnesses are notoriously fallible and hence often unintentionally do harm to innocent people.

Certain classes of people are believed incapable of intending certain actions and thereby have a ready-made excuse. Children seven years of age are not considered as sufficiently developed intellectually or morally to be responsible for their actions. Mentally defective people cannot foresee the effects of their behaviour and hence are typically not held responsible for what they do. Predicaments are often easily resolved by these classes of people.

Lack of Volition or Bodily Control

While a person's body might be involved causally in bringing about certain negative effects, the person might assert that he did not have

control over his body at the time. This lack of control might be attributed to various physiological or psychological factors or to lack of
authority. (It is parenthetically interesting that attribution theorists
tend to ignore the issue of bodily control.) Physiologists refer to involuntary acts, such as a knee jerk reflex, but they do not employ
"involuntary" in a way that would excuse someone for an action he
should not have done. When considering volition we inquire into the
actor's abilities, opportunities, capacity or authority at the time the
action took place (Gustafson, 1963–64). Excuses claiming lack of volition typically involve factors that diminish the person's abilities or
capacities to act otherwise than he did.

Among the physical causes impairing volition are drugs and alcohol.
These pharmacological agents have deleterious effects on behaviour.
They disinhibit antinormative behaviour for several reasons. For one
thing, the person who is "high" has a shortened time perspective and no
longer is inhibited by the consequences of his actions. The person is
engulfed by the emotions of the present to the exclusion of any
consideration of the future. In this sense the usual social controls over
behaviour are removed and the person engages in conduct that is
atypical for him when not under the influence of pharmacological
agents. Physical illness or exhaustion may refer to physiological reasons
why a person could not perform an action expected of him. Thus, a
failure to save another person's life may be attributed to a fainting spell,
temporary paralysis or total exhaustion.

Psychological causes for a lack of control over bodily movements
involve those excuses where the person suffers from some inner compul-
sions or defects or is controlled through culturally recognized means by
some other person. The actor (or his spokesperson — e.g. lawyer) may
assert as an excuse for untoward or antinormative behaviour that he did
not know right from wrong at the time of his action or that an aberrant
interpretation of events led to his action. For example, he can be
declared legally insane or can provide evidence that he is mentally ill. In
either case, it is not considered useful to hold the individual responsible
for his action since negative reactions and retribution would presumably
not be effective in deterring or inhibiting such behaviour, given the
person's state of mental health.

Another excuse claiming inability to control bodily actions is the over-
powering or uncontrollable compulsion produced by such emotions as
fear, anger and jealousy. These are intense, powerful emotions and are
associated with strong reactions. A man who has been threatened by

another may become so fearful that the only way he can function is to do something to remove the fear. This may lead him to take an action that he never otherwise would carry out, and the action may be carried out as if in a dream, or compulsively without planning it. Thus, a policemen at a demonstration may shoot an innocent and unarmed teenager because he interpreted the latter's movement to pull up his pants as reaching for a weapon. The shooting may represent a non-thinking semi-reflex reaction by the policeman who fears for his own life.

Social psychological factors involved in excuses of lack of volition include coercion by others, brainwashing, hypnosis and somnambulism. The issue in each of these cases is the means used by another person to sap the individual's will or freedom to make decisions for herself. In the case of coercion the actor is free to make a decision to comply to or resist the threatener's demands, but it is often not reasonable to expect a normal person to resist the threat of great punishments. The general rule is that it is reasonable to expect a person to comply to threats even by engaging in an untoward or antinormative action as long as the magnitude of the threat exceeds the amount of harm done by the compliant action (i.e. a least-of-evils criterion). The actor may also offer as an excuse for his conduct that he had been hypnotized, brainwashed, or that he acted while asleep and was unable to control himself. Patty Hearst tried to excuse her bank robbery and firing of an automatic weapon to help the Harrises escape from the site of a robbery by claiming that she had been brainwashed by a revolutionary organization and was no longer acting as a free agent. The killers associated with Charles Manson offered the excuse that they had been mesmerized by their leader. His charisma and Christ-like magnetism caused them to lose their capacity to make moral decisions on their own.

A person may deny responsibility for an action by offering the excuse that he lacked authority for acting. There are times when a person is blamed for *not* carrying out an action. In such cases the person may offer the excuse that because he lacked authority he could not have legitimately carried out the particular action. It may be unreasonable to expect a person to engage in unauthorized action even if it is for a good cause.

Denial of Agency

The actor may offer a defence of innocence based on the argument that the event at issue never occurred or that he was not involved in the event. To the charge that he broke a promise and the implication that he is unreliable, noncredible, untrustworthy and a bad person, the actor may claim that he never made such a promise and that the accuser is mistaken in the belief that he did. To the charge that she was seen at a discotheque with someone not her husband, the person may offer the defence that it could not have been her because she in fact was at home with her husband; it must have been someone else.

An actor faced with a predicament could also offer the denial-of-agency type of excuse by claiming that he has amnesia. If he has absolutely no recollections of the actions in question and is not even aware that he performed them, how can he be held responsible for these actions? The cause of the amnesia or fugue state may align this excuse with one of the others discussed previously. For example, the amnesia could have been produced by drugs, alcohol, temporary insanity or hypnotic suggestion.

In all types of excuses, the actor (or his spokesperson) denies that he is responsible for the reprehensible events in question. If it can be shown that the actor is not responsible for the negative behaviours, then he cannot be held accountable for them. The actor can resolve the predicament by admitting that the actions themselves are blameworthy but then dissociate himself from the actions. In justifications, the next kind of response to predicaments we will consider, the actor admits responsibility for the behaviour in question but denies that it or its consequences are blameworthy. The predicament is resolved by demonstrating that the actor's behaviour does not have the negative qualities that other suspect it possesses or implies.

A TYPOLOGY OF JUSTIFICATIONS

A predicament can be resolved if it can be shown that the unexpected, untoward or antinormative action in question does not reveal some defect of the actor's character. Another way of stating this idea is that a defect in character is revealed, and a predicament exists, whenever a blameworthy action has been performed and has not been explained away in an acceptable manner. When a judgment involving a defect in character is relevant, it is usually subject to revision. That is, the identity attributed to the actor is defeasible (Hart, 1949). If a person does harm through mistake of fact, through the effects of drugs or alcohol or fatigue, and so on, his behaviour is attributable to transient factors and not to the more enduring and stable traits, motives and values that typify him as an individual. By blaming a person for a negative action one implies that he possesses some defect in character — for example, negative dispositions or values, or lack of ability.

Justifications are verbal accounts used by actors in an attempt to reverse or neutralize an unwanted identity arising from negative actions. Scott and Lyman (1968) stated that "to justify an act is to assert its positive value in the face of a claim to the contrary" (p. 411). Sykes and Matza (1957) referred to these explanations as techniques of neutralization and Jellison (1977) labelled them social justifications, but whatever they are called, they constitute impression management strategies. The actor is engaged retrospectively in repairing a damaged identity.

There are an unending number of justifications that an actor may offer for his conduct. However, the variety of justifications can be classified into ten major categories (see Table II). In each case the actor or his spokesperson implicitly or explicitly agrees that the actor is responsible for the consequences in question but denies that the act was wrong or bad or faulty. Most of the categories relate the action in question to some norm or rule of society or the particular social group. The norm or rule prescribes or allows the behaviour or defines it as morally neutral (or good). Thus, through the justification the actor offers a socially acceptable description of an action that might have been perceived as strange, unsuccessful, meaningless, bad, immoral, unethical or unexpected by others. Stokes and Hewitt (1976) view accounts in general as attempts to re-align the actor with the norms or rules that govern conduct in the group, despite the fact that the person's behaviour has the appearance of not living up to cultural definitions and requirements. Thus, justifications attempt to make seemingly unacceptable behaviour appear socially acceptable. We will consider the ten types of justifications in turn and mention several justifications that can be classified in each type.

Appeals to higher authority shift accountability for the actions from the actor to some respected person or group. They thereby tend to render the conduct legitimate. Thus, while it is normally considered reprehensible and morally wrong to kill another human being, a hangman does his job (for rather high pay) at the behest of legal authorities and is normally not asked to account for his behaviours. A person may assert that God, Satan, corporation or organizational rules, persons in power, or "voices" commanded him to do as he did. In a study of presidential assassins in the United States it was reported that in no

TABLE II. A typology of justifications.

Appeal to higher authority
    God, Satan, or spirits commanded
    government official commanded
    high status or high prestige person commanded
    organizational rules stipulated
Appeal to ideology
    nationalism or patriotism
    for the revolution
    to protect society or mankind
    to promote the religion or sect
    against oppression
Appeal to norms of self-defence
    self-defence
    reciprocity
    revenge on associate of provoker
            clan and gang wars
            guilt by association
Reputation building
    protection from coercion
    credibility maintenance
    machismo
Appeal to loyalties
    friends
    long-standing understanding or relationship
    gang or group
    peer group, sex, race, etc.
Appeal to norms of justice
    derogation of victim
    equity, equality and social welfare norms
    law and order
Effect misrepresented
    no harm done (no victim)
    benefits outweigh harm
Social comparisons
    condemn the condemners
    scapegoating
Appeal to humanistic values
    love
    peace
    truth
    beauty
Self-fulfillment
    psychological health
    catharsis of pent-up emotions
    personal growth
    exerting individuality
    mind expansion and self-actualization
    conscience or ego-ideal

instance did the assassin feel remorse; they all felt their acts were justified by some transcendent principle of law, divine guidance, or the like (Kirkham, *et al.*, 1970). John N. Schrank, who shot Theodore Roosevelt in the chest from a range of about six feet, reported that McKinley's ghost appeared to him in dreams, a fact that reinforced his view that he was operating under divine guidance.

Appeals to ideology as a system of ideas or symbols often serve to justify otherwise problematic behaviour. If we are to believe their accounts, almost every reprehensible action ever performed by a political figure has been carried out as an act of patriotism. Extreme acts of terrorism are carried out for revolutionary goals. Torture and executions have been justified as necessary to punish heretics and to cleanse their souls and the soul of the nation. According to nearly all the president's men, Watergate-related actions were justified by the imperative to save the nation by keeping President Nixon in office. Whether deceit, subterfuge, "dirty tricks," terror, assassination and warfare are justifiable often depends on the ideological commitments of a particular observer.

Appeals to norms of self-defence essentially state that a grievance has been created by the unprovoked harmful actions of another person or group and that counter-action is justified. According to the norm of self-defence a person has the right to use coercion or force (or the threat thereof) to protect himself, his property, family group, or nation from the unprovoked use of coercion by others. A reciprocity norm justifies harming another person in proportion to the amount of harm he perpetrated first (Gouldner, 1960). In some cultures and subcultures it is justifiable to seek revenge not only against a provoker, but also against his kin or associates. Thus, if one member of a gang attacks a member of a second gang, any member of the second gang might seek revenge against any member of the first gang. In these cases the attacking individual is considered to be acting in behalf of the larger entity and, hence, any harm done to the entity is considered as quid pro quo. As is the case with most justifications, appeals to self-defence may be acceptable to one cultural group but not to another. Thus, Quakers might not accept a self-defence justification even though the person clearly acted to save his own life.

Acts of self-defence may also be justified as reputation building. If one is attacked, he may justify his acts of defence or counterattack by claiming that they are necessary to maintain a positive public image or to save face. If no resistance is offered this time the perpertrator's use of coercion may be repeated. This justification, as well as many others, obviously occurs on both the micro-social (i.e. personal) and macro-social (i.e. group) level.

Credibility maintenance is a related form of reputation building. A source of influence must be believed if he is to be successful in gaining compliance from target persons. Hence, most people are concerned with maintaining at least the appearance of high credibility. Persons (or groups) may indicate that their predicament-arousing behaviour (e.g. the use of force) was necessary because it established the credibility of their threats, and should that credibility be questioned, much worse could happen.

A combination of the credibility maintenance and protection from coercion justifications was used by the United States in the 1960's to explain its presence in the Vietnam war. If America didn't fulfil her commitment to fight for democracy in Vietnam, no one would believe her promises and treaties in other parts of the world, and acts of aggression against allies would probably increase. Henry Kissinger has claimed that later events in Angola, Cuba and Afghanistan support the validity of this justification. By failing to act decisively in the Angolan and Cuban incidents, the Carter administration damaged the United States' reputation and paved the way for the Soviet invasion of Afghanistan.

Finally, reputation building may involve acts characterized as macho. Males sometimes feel it is necessary to show that they are tough, courageous, and able to effectively engage in violent actions. Oscar Lewis (1961) has stated that machismo is an important identity in cultures of poverty. In such cultures many behaviours (e.g. robbery, physical aggression, sexual promiscuity) are justified as demonstrating machismo and thereby serving to build one's reputation.

Sykes and Matza (1957) found that juvenile delinquents often justified their antinormative actions in terms of loyalties to friends or to the gang. Appeals to loyalties may extend to peer groups or to identifications with members of the same sex, race, religion or nationality. Thus, many American Jews who did not experience the Holocaust themselves, nevertheless boycott German products such as cars and cameras. Similarly, many nonreligious women actively support and might even demonstrate for women's admission to the priesthood.

Actors facing predicaments may appeal to norms of justice to explain their behaviour and thereby neutralize the negative identity they have projected to others. For example, the actor may derogate the victim to show that the latter deserved the treatment received. Scott and Lyman (1968) identified four subcategories of accounts that derogate the victim or deny that there even was a victim. In these accounts the victims are identified as either (a) proximate foes who acted in an unfair manner toward the actor, such as an overpunitive teacher or parent; their actions elicited the actor's counter-behaviour; (b) incumbents of normatively discrepant roles, such as homosexuals, pimps and whores, who do not count for much anyway and deserve whatever happens to them; (c) stigmatized groups that are the subjects of stereotypes, such as blacks, Chicanos or Jews; the content of the stereotype tends to justify the actor's conduct; or (d) distant foes, such as Communists, Nazis or capitalists, whose conduct justifies almost anything that is done to harm their interests.

Specific allocation norms of distributive justice may also serve as explanations for problematic behaviour. The failure to work as contracted, the failure to pay someone for work done, or the infliction of penalties or harm on another may all be carried out in behalf of some principle of equity or equality. Thus, workers who feel that they deserve a wage increase may go on strike or stage a work slowdown. Similarly, adherence to existing standards of law and order may serve as justifications for vigilante behaviour or other forms of conduct that otherwise might be considered as representing some negative personal character-istic of the actor rather than some external standards.

In another type of justification actors facing predicaments argue that the effects at issue have been misrepresented. There is a denial that any injury in fact occurred or is likely to occur. The person may admit that he performed the act but assert that the amount of harm done was trifling or negligible or that the victim was so rich or possessed so many resources that he would not experience any decrement as a result of the act. Sykes and Matza found that juvenile delinquents would sometimes deny that they stole a car but instead would represent the act as "borrowing". The actor might also claim that the effects of his action are misrepresented in that only the negative features are noticed. He may argue that the benefits outweighed the amount of harm done and justified the conduct. Thus, Robin Hood justified his behaviour by claiming that he robbed only the rich and used his booty to help the poor. Robin further claimed that the Sheriff of Nottingham misrepre-sented his actions by ignoring their benefits.

Actors may discount the negativity of their behaviour by making comparisons with the behaviour of others. Sykes and Matza refer to condemnation of the condemners as a justification given by juvenile delinquents for their antinormative actions. This type of account states that many other people do the same or worse things and they are not caught and punished; in fact, the behaviour of these others may go unnoticed or may even be praised. This kind of account attempts to undermine the validity of the norms that the actor's behaviour violates and attempts to remove the basis for viewing the behaviour as negative or wrong. It might be wrong to live out of matrimony with someone of the opposite sex if you are one of only a few who do so, but it can hardly be considered wrong if millions of other people are also doing it. Another form of social comparison is with stigmatized groups. The basic idea behind an account of this kind is that no matter how bad the observers might think the actor is, there are entire groups of people who are much worse. Stereotyped characteristics of other ethnic groups are typically used for this kind of invidious comparison.

Questionable actions may be justified by appeals to such universal humanistic values as love, peace, truth and beauty. Thus, Woodrow Wilson viewed World War I as the war to end all wars, and the Defence Department's expenditures of trillions of dollars for weapons and preparations for war are justified as essential to preserve the peace. Nazi medical researchers justified conducting grotesque experiments on human physiology with concentration camp prisoners as subjects on the grounds that this research would contribute substantially to human knowledge. Several famous nineteenth century generals believed the greatest human values were manifested in time of warfare (e.g. brotherhood, self-sacrifice, loyalty, courage) and considered war the most beautiful of all human activities.

With the advent and incorporation into lay culture of Freudian and phenomonological psychologies and the personal growth movements, the focus on the individual and his self-fulfilment introduced important new values into Western civilization. Today, a person may express hostility and negative impressions of another, although such behaviour is normally thought to be in bad taste, and justify the behaviour on the ground that it is harmful to one's psychological health to hold in one's feelings.

Frantz Fanon (1963) argued that individuals in former colonized nations in Africa need to engage in violent overthrow of those who represent foreign cultures. Such venting and catharsis of pent-up hostility is presumed to free the individual from psychological bondage and to promote self-fulfillment and a positive self-image. Similarly, in this age of honesty and openness individuals may be more frank in their self-disclosures, even to the point of dwelling on their own personal growth as well as the personal growth of the others. Nonconforming behaviour such as homosexuality and sexual promiscuity may be justified by claiming that by exerting one's individuality one fosters self-growth and fulfillment.

Self-fulfillment is also used by some individuals to justify antinormative actions such as taking narcotics or hallucinogens on grounds that these drugs expand the mind and promote self-actualization. Finally, persons may justify their conduct in terms of personal conscience or ego-ideal. A personal sense of justice or of right and wrong may lead the individual to engage in actions that appear senseless or excessive to others. Individuals have justified turning in their children or friends for breaking the law by claiming that no one is above justice. Similarly, individuals with strong super-egos may punish themselves excessively for not living up to the high expectations they set for themselves, and some people who place an extremely high value on obedience may beat their child or dog for disobeying an order.

A new vocabulary of justifications has emerged among the me-generation. "I'm getting my head together", "let it all hang out", "feed your head", "if it feels good, do it", "I'm only doing what is right", and other similar expressions have all been successfully used to resolve predicaments within the past decade and a half. Before that time these justifications probably would not have been effective and might even have made the situation worse.

META-ACCOUNTS

Rather than or in addition to providing excuses or justifications for their questionable behaviour, individuals can resolve predicaments arising from such behaviour through the use of meta-accounts. Meta-accounts (Scott and Lyman, 1968) are essentially attempts to avoid explaining or justifying behaviour. Among the evasive meta-accounts are mystification, deferral, referral, identity switching, restatement of intentions and empty explanations.

The technique of mystification involves a statement by the actor that there are reasons for what he did, but it is complicated and would take more time to explain now than is available. Or it might be claimed that the reasons are confidential or secret and hence the very integrity of the actor (which might be in question) prevents disclosure of the reasons for the behaviour. Therefore, observers are asked to defer judgment on the seemingly questionable actions and it is implied that a negative evaluation would be in error. This particular meta-account was employed by Richard Nixon on several occasions during the unravelling of the Watergate cover-up.

Referral involves telling the accuser to seek an account for the behaviour from someone else. An actor might claim to be sick and suggest that the doctor or a family member would be better able at this time to provide a justification of the behaviour in question. The actor might point out that he is a subordinate and that it would be more proper to obtain an account from the person in authority. The subordinate might even claim not to know the purpose of an action ordered by a superordinate.

Identity switching involves the questioning of credentials. What right does the questioner have to ask for an account? The actor might claim that because of his identity or status he is not obliged to explain his actions to the observer. Instead of offering an account the actor might respond with "Don't you know who I am?" or "Who do you think you are?". For example, a teacher may not have the right to ask about an incident in another teacher's room, but the principal may be considered as having a legitimate right to an explanation of the behaviour.

A restatement of intentions might be verbalized by the actor in hopes that the listener will accept it as a justification of the behaviour. Thus, the restatement of intentions takes the place of an account. As Schutz (1967) has pointed out, this "in order to" reason is superficial and simply states that the actor knew the effects that would occur at the time he performed the behaviour. But such an "in order to" reason may be provided by an actor who either does not have or does not wish to reveal a "because of" explanation. That is, an actor who has no acceptable excuse or justification for a behaviour may hedge against an accounting by giving the appearance of answering the questions of observers. Most politicians are quite adept at this form of meta-accounting.

Empty explanations involve a statement that the actor engaged in the problematic action because he wanted to. This explanation suggests that the behaviour in question was volitional and intentional and satisfied some need of the actor's. However, "because I wanted to" is not specific about why the actor wanted to do as he did, nor does such an explanation provide a justification for the behaviour. As is the case with all meta-accounts the "because I wanted to" empty explanation serves to prevent the actor from having to provide a more meaningful accounting of the problematic behaviour.

DISCLAIMERS

Up until this point we have considered reactions of individuals who already find themselves faced with a predicament. They have been called on to explain and account for some behaviour previously performed. It is also the case that individuals engage in a class of behaviours, called disclaimers, when they anticipate that something they are about to do is likely to place them in a predicament in the future.

Disclaimers are prospective excuses or justifications intended to forestall or avoid a predicament. An actor tells an audience what he is going to do and why, so that they will be no mistaking his motives when he performs the action. Hewitt and Stokes (1975) stated that "a disclaimer is a verbal device employed to ward off and defeat in advance doubts and negative typifications which may result from intended conduct" (p. 3). Among the types of disclaimers are hedging, credentialing, sin licenses, cognitive disclaimers and appeals for the deferral or suspension of judgment.

Hedging involves verbal expressions that the actor is uncertain about how others will respond to an action and that he has a minimal commitment to the action. The tentative nature of the whole enterprise suggests that the actor is open to suggestions and would be willing to change his mind if given good reasons to do so. This kind of exploratory probe tests the social waters before the actor takes the plunge. In this way he can avoid negative typifications should he find that such attributions would be the likely reaction to the proposed action. Expressions of intentions may serve as probes regarding causal relationships, social norms or rules, possible descriptions of the action, possible incidental effects, and so on.

Credentialing consists of expressions that establish for the actor qualifications permitting him to engage in an action with the implication that the typical way of labelling a person who behaved in that fashion would be inappropriate in his case. The actor acknowledges that the consequences of his action may be discrediting, but he affirms his commitment to perform it even if others misunderstand his motives. The statement of strong purpose suggests that the actor has a good reason to justify his action, although of course no justification is provided. The quick flash of a police badge by plainclothes officers before a raid is a type of credentialing.

Sin licenses are statements which acknowledge that the actor is about to break a rule and that such behaviour is likely to bring rebuke. The statement has the function of reminding the audience that there are occasions on which any rule may be legitimately violated without considering such behaviour as an indicator of a defect in the actor's character.

Cognitive disclaimers acknowledge that the observer might question the actor's cognitive capacity when the behaviour occurs. However, by anticipating that the observer might think the behaviour is crazy, wierd or strange and acknowledging this possibility, the actor is ensuring that his behaviour will be perceived as purposeful and under cognitive control. The implication is that there is sufficient justification for the behaviour.

The actor may prospectively use the techniques of mystification or deferral (meta-accounts) to disclaim an action he is about to perform. The actor essentially says, "I have good reasons for what I'm about to do, but I can't reveal them right now. So trust me". Similarly, appeals for the suspension of judgment might be made when the actor fears that his future action may be offensive or produce other strong emotional reactions in the observer. Thus, the actor might ask the observer not "to jump all over me before giving me a chance to explain".

It should be noted that many other of the excuses, justifications and meta-accounts already discussed may be offered before the potentially negative actions are performed. In this way they are used as disclaimers to avoid or alleviate a potential predicament. For example, before starting a fight in a bar, an actor might claim that he is quite drunk (disclaiming excuse) or that the target of his attack previously provoked him (disclaiming justification).

APOLOGIES

While excuses, justifications, meta-accounts and disclaimers are attempts by the actor (or someone for the actor) to either deny responsibility for an untoward behaviour or to deny that the total effects of the behaviour are negative, apologies acknowledge blameworthiness. Apologies consist of attempts to obtain a pardon and to mitigate negative evaluations and retribution. Thus, apologies may be used as an impression management tactic to deal with a predicament. According to Schlenker (1980) an apology asserts that the

> undesirable event is not a fair representation of what the actor is really like as a person. The current good self is split off from the past bad self, the part that is guilty is split off from the part that dissociates itself from

the offense and affirms a belief in the offended rule. The bad self is left behind, discredited and vilified by the actor. Thus, the actor evidences rehabilitation. (p.154)

Goffman (cited in Schlenker, 1980) has listed essential elements of apologies. The actor: (a) accepts responsibility and blame for what he did by expressing guilt, remorse or embarrassment; (b) indicates that he knows what the appropriate conduct should have been and believes that violations of the rule should be punished; (c) rejects the problematic behaviour and derogates the bad self that misbehaved; (d) promises to behave appropriately in the future; and (e) performs an act of penance or offers restitution. Apologies may be explicit with regard to some of these elments while the remainder are left implicit. The first element — expression of guilt, remorse or embarrassment — is the most important, however, and is usually explicit. Hence, we will consider these three reactions in more detail.

Psychologists have often discussed guilt as if it consists of at least three components: (a) an acceptance of responsibility for performing a negative action; (b) self-blame; and (c) psychological pain resulting from feelings of lowered self-worth and the need for some form of punishment to alleviate the pain. We would subscribe to the first two elements only. While self-blame may lead to lowered self-esteem and self-punishment, many kinds of responses other than psychological pain may also occur, such as an increased probability of engaging in positive and altruistic actions and of helping others or an increased tendency for an entire reorganization of personality and values (as in religious conversions).

The basic German equivalent of guilt is *Schuld*, which has its origin in the term *schulden*, meaning to be indebted. To express guilt is to admit a kind of moral indebtedness, which the person acknowledges should be paid. This debt may be paid in the form of restitution or punishment or in a number of other ways. The expression of guilt reveals that the offender believes in the cultural or societal rules that were broken by his behaviour. It is therefore clear that as compared to someone who accepts no blame for such an action, the guilty person requires less punishment for purposes of deterring similar future behaviour. Confession is another way of dealing with guilt. The person humbles himself. In all of these reactions to guilt the person tries to manipulate the responses of others and to reinstate himself in the social order.

Remorse indicates that the person is sorry that harm was done and wishes he could undo it. There is more of a focus on the victim than on the self, whereas guilt is more focused on the self than on the victim. Guilt is more oriented toward the rule that was violated, while remorse is more concerned with the harm done to the victim. Remorse suggests that the problematic behaviour was not typical of the actor, whose values normally would preclude performing such behaviour. Thus, remorse, like guilt, tends to mitigate the degree of negative reaction of others to the offender. It is well known, for example, that judges will hand out stiffer sentences to convicted felons who do not show remorse than to those who are remorseful. Remorse involves not only repentance for what has been done but also a resolution to avoid such actions in the future. The remorseful person might indicate that he is going through a process of re-examination in order to understand why he did not live up to his own internal standards of behaviour and is doing so in order not to stray from acceptable moral standards again.

Kelman (1974) has distinguished between actions that deviate from standards of morality and actions that violate standards of propriety. These two kinds of predicament-causing actions spawn different post-transgression reactions from actors. Violations of standards of morality typically involve actions that harm others, society in general, or even the actor himself. Kelman notes that the social controls that are typically imposed for transgressing against moral standards include punishment or the threat of punishment, exclusion from certain roles or groups, and other forms of disapproval. Guilt and remorse are responses that are appropriate following moral transgressions.

Actions that violate standards of propriety are ones that are deemed inappropriate for a person of a particular position, role, age or identity. That is, the actor has failed to behave in a manner consistent with the identity he has put forth as relevant for the interaction taking place. In order to maintain smooth and predictable interaction between persons, there are social sanctions to support and uphold standards of propriety. These sanctions include ridicule, ostracism and contempt. Embarrassment and shame are typical responses of persons who have violated standards of propriety.

Embarrassment typically occurs when an individual has behaved publicly in a way that is discrepant with the identity he wishes to present to others. Unlike guilt, where the person is concerned about his own morality, what is at issue in embarrassment is the information about himself that the individual has communicated to others. Such a discontinuity or incongruity of self-presentation may lead the individual to take any of a number of remedial actions. The actor may try to demonstrate the ability or trait put into question by the discrepency, may pretend that the discrepant behaviour was only a joke, or may allege that he was somehow testing the credulity of the other person. These and other strategems restore the continuity of line in self-presentation and allow the interaction to continue smoothly. Thus, embarrassment communicates to others that the identity disrupted by the predicament is an authentic one, since if the actor did not sincerely believe his own presentations he might not be so concerned about the discrepant behaviour. Embarrassment itself as an emotional reaction thus plays a role in restoring the identity in question.

An impropriety may lead the individual to become concerned about his ability to live up to the expectations of others and whether the identity he has assumed is authentic. It thus raises questions about his position in various social groups or society in general. These concerns are referred to as shame. Unlike embarrassment, where the chief problem is restoring one's identity in the eyes of another, a person who is shamed is concerned about his definition of himself. A typical reaction of a person who has been shamed is an attempt to compensate for the impropriety. If this kind of correction is not possible because the person's aspirations are set too high, the reaction to shame may take the form of self-contempt, depression, self-punishment and in extreme cases, mental illness and suicide.

Most discussions of guilt, remorse, embarrassment and shame imply that these reactions are real; in other words, that the actor is actually experiencing them. While this is probably the case much of the time, it is likely that actors sometimes merely feign these reactions in order to manage the impressions that observers form of them. If an actor can convince others that he is feeling guilt, remorse, embarrassment or shame, when he in fact feels none of these, their reactions to him will be the same as if he really experienced the emotion. The remorseless convicted felon who can successfully act as if he feels remorse will be treated by judges, juries and prison personnel like the truly remorseful felon, and will be one up on his comrades who make no attempt to show remorse.

BLAME

The function of blaming a person is not merely to condemn his action, but also to evaluate his moral worth by comparing moral demerits with merits. Violations of moral rules are debited against the actor's informal record, while praiseworthy and acceptable actions are credited to the individual's record. If this moral bookkeeping shows that the actor's positive qualities and behaviours outweigh his negative ones, then the actor's overall moral character is maintained despite the predicament.

For purposes of assessing responsibility and blame it is necessary to examine a person's intentions and his reasons for acting, rather than his abilities or opportunities (Glover, 1970). The person is identified with his intentions while other factors influencing his conduct are treated as external. Occasionally, however, an actor may not be held responsible for an intentional act if he is not open to persuasion designed to alter his intention. That is, a person whose actions are not guided by deliberation and reasons may be judged as lacking sufficient self-control to be responsible for what he does. Thus, drug addicts may not be able to alter their intentions because they are driven by their physiological dependency. However, such people may not totally escape blame for their actions because they can be blamed for lacking sufficient character to avoid becoming addicts in the first place.

Associating intentions with blame provides incentive for actors to stop and consider the consequences of their actions before engaging in them. This consideration of consequences increases the chances that people will consider moral rules before acting and has the result of making actions more rational. The anticipation that one may be blamed for an action tends to have a deterrent effect that inhibits immoral actions. In this way order is maintained and regulated in human groups.

Since blame is directly associated with intentions, factors that enhance the likelihood that intent will be attributed to an actor will also affect the degree of blame assigned to him. That is, factors that lead observers to make internal rather than external attributions are directly associated with how blameworthy the actor is judged. There are of course a large number of such factors, including the status of the actor, the number of choice alternatives open to him at the time of the action, the state of the actor (his health, anxiety, fear, pain, self-control, etc.), the state of the target, affective or kinship relationships between actor and victim, resources controlled by the actor, the social norms that govern expectations in specific situations, and so on.

Blame does not always lead to punishment, although it does detract from a person's reputation and contributes to a lessening effectiveness in relations with other people. If punishment is to follow blame, it must be justified when there is some reason to believe that it will have a deterrent or rehabilitative effect on the blameworthy person. Utilitarians would add that punishment should be used for these purposes only when it causes less harm than any other equally effective method (Hart, 1949).

While it may appear to an observer that a person is responsible and blameworthy for a negative action, it is sometimes the case that the observer lacks critical information in forming his or her moral judgment. Thus, additional information may cause the observer to change his mind and remove the debit against the actor's moral account. Excuses and justifications serve to provide information about intentions, volition, motives, reasons or explanations that are intended to remove or mitigate the degree of blame assigned to the actor.

Many factors must be considered in ascertaining the extent of a person's blameworthiness. Among these factors are the amount of harm done or intended, the actor's awareness of these consequences to the victim, the victim's character and identity, the actor's conduct in the past, and most importantly, the reason for performing the action. Further, moral accounting may become more complicated when more than one person is involved in planning and carrying out an action. Stover (1972) has suggested that the agent whose action comes first in a causal series which includes the action of a second person is the more blameworthy individual. It might also be argued that the person whose action made the greatest contribution to the harmful effects is the most responsible for these effects.

Just as actors are sometimes not held responsible for intentional acts, they are sometimes held responsible and blamed for unintended effects. Under some conditions these acts might have been excusable, but not in the particular case. Two such general cases are negligence and recklessness. When a person unknowingly or knowingly creates a risk for others he may be considered negligent and blamed for indirectly bringing about the negative effects. Negligence may occur when a person fails to perform an action (or performs it inadequately) and it is reasonable to expect that responsible people would have adequately performed the action under similar circumstances. For example, failing to get one's automobile inspected periodically may be considered negligent when the brakes fail and an accident occurs. Negligence may also be involved when a person misassesses a risk due to haste or insufficient deliberation or when he fails to give her full attention to the execution of her action.

A reckless action is one where the major intended effects are justifiable and morally neutral or acceptable but where the actor is aware that there is some probability of also producing undesired and harmful effects. A reckless person persists in a course of action even though he realizes there is a risk of undesired negative consequences. According to Hart (1949) recklessness is "wittingly flying in the face of a substantial, unjustified risk, or the conscious creation of such a risk". Oberdiek (1972) has suggested that risks are tolerated (a) in direct relation to the supposed benefits of the overall action, and (b) provided that there is informed consent to run the risk by those who are placed at risk by the action. Of course the determination of the degree of benefit, amount of risk, and what constitutes informed consent is no simple matter. Feinberg has commented that "consent is a form of privilege which allows one to have sexual intercourse without committing rape, or to utter false and damaging remarks without committing slander, or to walk on another's land without committing trespass" (1973, p. 57).

SUMMARY

These, then, are the kinds of reactions individuals engage in when faced with a current or potential predicament. We acknowledge that our categorization might not be complete; the reader might have thought of one or another response to predicaments that does not fit into one of our categories or subcategories. For example, while blame is relevant in predicaments where morality is questioned, not all predicaments involve actions that are problematical in a moral sense. Some improprieties may lead observers to make amoral judgments of the actor's behaviour. In these cases fault rather than blame is at issue. Perhaps impression management strategies other than those considered here can be used to deal with these types of predicaments. Thus, additional categories and subcategories may be needed.

In addition, we want to make it clear that the categories and subcategories are not mutually exclusive. For example, some reactions to predicaments may both excuse and justify the actions in question, while others may have elements of both the lack-of-intention and lack-of-volition types of excuses, or elements of both mystification and referral types of meta-accounts.

We will now briefly illustrate one application of our categorization system. Several research paradigms used by experimental social psychologists can be viewed as situations in which the experimenter creates a predicament for participants and studies their reactions to it. While these reactions are rarely interpreted as impression management

strategies used by subjects to explain themselves out of a predicament, we feel that it is plausible and advantageous to do so. Such an interpretation offers a common-sense, social (i.e. interpersonal) interpretation of behaviours that are often considered irrational, problematic, and as due to intrapersonal factors. Rather than considering all these research paradigms as actually studying different processes, and offering different theoretical analyses for each, a consistent and thorough analysis in terms of predicaments and ordinary-language explanations in the service of impression management provides a more general theory and serves the interests of parsimony.

Interpretation of experiments as predicaments demanding impression-managing explanations

Most social psychological research is carried out in the context of laboratories situated in universities and use college students as subjects (Adair, 1973). The students usually know that they are participating in experiments and are aware that they are under the close surveillance of a psychologist or an assistant of the scientist. The psychologist-experimenter controls the setting, stages most of the action, states the rules that will apply to the situation, and limits the range of responses the subjects can make. It would not be surprising if the subjects in these situations are primarily concerned with displaying an identity as a normal, average (or better), healthy, intelligent, cooperative and moral person (Rosenberg, 1965), and engage in self-presentational strategies to do so.

We have suggested that many research paradigms in social psychology can be interpreted as producing predicaments for subjects. Correspondingly, the responses of subjects may be viewed as impression-managing explanations designed to resolve a predicament. It would take another entire chapter for an extensive and detailed treatment of all such experimental paradigms, and the authors are writing such a chapter to complement this one (Tedeschi and Riess, 1981). Here we will illustrate this type of analysis by reinterpreting subjects' responses in one paradigm as explanations offered to resolve a predicament.

ATTRIBUTIONS FOR SUCCESSFUL AND UNSUCCESSFUL PERFORMANCE

Starting with Heider (1958), social psychologists have become increasingly concerned with individuals' attributions for their positive (e.g.

successful) and negative (e.g. unsuccessful) behaviours and outcomes. In the typical methodological paradigms used in this research, subjects first perform some task involving either interpersonal influence or skill-oriented performance (cf. Bradley, 1978 and Zuckerman, 1979, for reviews). For example, subjects act as quasi-teachers or therapists and try to influence another person, or they perform some achievement related task such as anagrams or tests of social perceptiveness. They then receive feedback (usually bogus and randomly assigned) indicating that they were quite successful or had done rather poorly. Finally, they are asked to make attributions for their performance outcomes. It has typically been found that subjects make external, environmental attributions for their failures and make internal, dispositional attributions for their successes. These effects have been referred to as defensive attributions, self-serving biases, attributional egotism, and other similar terms (cf. Bradley, 1978; Miller and Ross, 1975; Riess, Rosenfeld *et al.*, 1980; Snyder *et al.*, 1978; Zuckerman, 1979). However, so-called counterdefensive attributions have also been found; that is, subjects sometimes take personal responsibility for their failures or deny personal responsibility for their successes (cf. Bradley, 1978; Zuckerman, 1979). We will first consider attributions following failure and show how both defensive and counterdefensive attributions can be viewed as impression-managing explanations of performance outcomes that subjects offer to mitigate a present predicament or prevent one in the future. Then we will also interpret subjects' attribution statements for their successful outcomes as impression management strategies designed to engender the most favourable presentation of self that circumstances will permit.

Attributions Following Failure

Receiving feedback from the experimenter indicating that they had performed poorly on the experimental task most probably creates a predicament for subjects. This information casts undesired aspersions on their conduct or skills. It appears that the subject is incompetent, lacks the ability required, or did not put out the effort necessary for success. According to the impression management interpretation, subjects use their attribution statements to explain their behaviour in order to resolve this predicament. In nearly all the experiments conducted, subjects' attributions are public in the sense that they are observed by the experimenter, and perhaps by others (Bradley, 1978;

Miller, 1978; Riess *et al.*, 1980). Thus, these attribution statements can be used by subjects to offer explanations of their behaviour for public consumption. Subjects can resolve the predicament by explaining through their attribution statements that environmental factors external to them, such as bad luck and the difficulty of the task, led to their poor performance, and that factors internal to them, such as their possible lack of ability, skills and effort, had little to do with it. Thus, they imply that they did not cause the failure and therefore should not be held personally responsible for it. The predicament is resolved by deflecting attributions away from factors relevant to character and ability so that the failure is excused in a manner that does not reflect negatively on the subjects themselves. This type of impression-managing explanation is also commonly heard in non-laboratory settings. For example, tennis players are notorious for attributing their losses to such factors as the wind, the sun, the poor playing surface, dead balls, blind judges and bad luck; in other words, anything but their lack of ability. Similarly, students are quite adept at offering a multitude of excuses which externalize responsibility for poor performance on examinations and papers.

In their reviews of the literature, Bradley (1978), Miller and Ross (1975), and Zuckerman (1979) reported some experiments in which subjects made counterdefensive rather than self-serving attributions following failure; in other words, they attributed causality for the failure to themselves. At first glance these results do not seem to be interpretable in terms of impression-managing reactions to predicaments. However, we believe that these counterdefensive attributions can be incorporated into our explanations-for-predicaments framework. Sometimes the best way to deal with the predicament aroused by negative performance feedback is to accept rather than deny personal responsibility. Denial of responsibility for failure may be socially inappropriate at times and can make the person appear overdefensive, egocentric or irresponsible. Defensive attributions therefore fail to resolve the predicament. In these situations offering counterdefensive attributions is often the socially appropriate and acceptable thing to do, as when a coach takes personal responsibility for his team's failures, and when a commanding officer, president, or other type of leader takes responsibility for the failures or improprieties of his subordinates. Ex-president Nixon, for example, took responsibility for his subordinates' actions regarding the Watergate cover-up, although he denied any knowledge of their actions. This probably would have been the best way to deal with the predicament had no subsequent information refuted his claims.

Two recent investigations of reactions to attributions offered by others support the notion that counterdefensive explanations are sometimes the best way to deal with the social predicament resulting from poor performance feedback. In a study by Tetlock (1979) observer-subjects rated individuals who supposedly gave counterdefensive explanations for their performance more positively than those who gave defensive attributions. Mitchell *et al.* (1979) found similar results in a group setting. Group members who made egocentric attributions (e.g. took less than their fair share of blame for failure) were viewed more negatively by other group members than were those who did not.

Bradley (1978) has suggested a further reason why counterdefensive attributions might occur. A person would not want to overly deny responsibility and blame for his failures if there is a reasonable chance that his attribution statements might be invalidated by his own subsequent behaviour or by others' assessment of his performance. This invalidation of the individual's explanation would probably serve to exacerbate rather than reduce the predicament. The person might be seen as a fake, a liar, or as someone out of touch with the reality of the situation. With this idea in mind, Bradley (1978) has begun to clearly specify the conditions under which counterdefensive rather than defensive attributions would be likely to occur. The likelihood of counterdefensive attributions should increase with the possibility that an inconsistency will be revealed between one's own attributions for one's behaviour (i.e. his explanations for failure) and either (a) one's subsequent performance or (b) another person's explanation for one's own performance outcomes. Hence, both defensive and counter-defensive attributions following failure may be viewed as impression-management strategies designed to deal with predicaments and the conditions under which each is likely to occur have begun to be specified.

Attributions Following Success

Thus far we have focused on how individuals use attribution statements to resolve predicaments by explaining away their failures. As mentioned earlier, however, attributions following success have also been widely investigated and it is typically found that individuals make internal explanations for these outcomes. An impression-management interpretation has also been offered for these self-serving attributions (Bradley, 1978; Riess *et al.*, 1980; Tedeschi and Lindskold, 1976, Chapter 4). Individuals attribute their positive outcomes to internal factors, such as their ability and effort expenditure, and play down the role of external, environmental factors, such as luck, in order to explain that they are personally responsible for these outcomes. They are attempting to maintain or promote a positive presentation of self by convincing others that their competence and determination explain their success. Thus, they should receive the social approval, credit, and rewards associated with production of positive outcomes.

Following success actors are faced with a different kind of predicament than we have been considering thus far. Rather than trying to protect or save their public images from the negative implications of failure by disassociating themselves from it, they are attempting to garner the favourable self-presentation that comes with personal responsibility for positive behaviour and outcomes. The "predicament" is aroused because they might not be associated with and get credit for actions that could reflect positively on them. Here they attempt to *entitle* themselves to personal responsibility for their praiseworthy actions by making internal attributions for these actions. In addition, if the actor feels that he already has or can easily obtain personal responsibility, he may attempt to *enhance* others' perceptions of the favourability of his actions, and thereby bask in increased glory.

As mentioned earlier, however, individuals sometimes make external, environmental attributions for their successes. Some of these attributions, which on first glance may seem to be non-self-serving, may actually reflect individuals' attempts to enhance the favourability of actions for which they are already responsible. Data recently collected by the second author indicate that collegiate skiers' perceptions of their success in races are positively correlated with their attributions to task difficulty. In other words, they made environmental attributions for their successful performance, a result which seems inconsistent with the typical notion of self-serving (i.e. ego-enhancing) biases. However, by claiming that the race course was difficult, their success, which has already been established, looks all the better. The greater the difficulty of the course, the more positively one's success reflects on one's skiing prowess. Consequently, these external attributions for success might actually serve to enhance the ski racers' public image. Other elements of these data are consistent with self-serving biases. The racers' perceptions of their success were also positively correlated with attributions to ability and effort (internal factors) and negatively correlated with attributions to luck (an external factor).

Bradley's (1978) and Zuckerman's (1979) reviews also indicate that subjects sometimes do not take personal responsibility for their successes (i.e. they do not make internal attributions). According to our interpretation, here subjects might be acting in a manner that will avoid a future predicament. They may be reluctant to claim personal responsibility for their successes because this might make them appear to be boastful, pretentious, arrogant and selfish. The studies by Tetlock (1979) and Mitchell *et al.* (1979) indicated that individuals who made ego-enhancing attributions for successes were viewed less favourably by subjects than were those who did not offer self-serving explanations. Moreover, if individuals fear that their self-enhancing explanations of their successes might be invalidated by their subsequent actions or by others' assessments of their performance, they may be quite modest in their attributions (Bradley, 1978; Schlenker, 1975). They are avoiding the potential predicament that would probably arise if their positive presentation of self is subsequently invalidated. If subsequent information suggests that one's self-serving explanations for one's performance outcomes might be exaggerated, the person then faces a predicament because he has not lived up to his presentation of self (Goffman, 1959). From an impression management standpoint it is worse to have one's claims of self-worth refuted than to have not made them in the first place. Finally, subjects' failure to take responsibility for their successes may reflect their desire to appear modest (Schlenker, 1975; Schneider, 1969). If others already attribute responsibility for successes to you then there is no need to entitle yourself to responsibility. In this case modest self-presentations might engender the most favourable public image. You will be seen not only as competent, but also as modest about that competence. These modest self-presentations are not effective if others do not already give you credit for the beneficient actions. As Jones and Wortman (1973) have pointed out, "Modesty is becoming to those who are great; what is difficult is to be modest when one is nobody" (p. 1).

SUMMARY

In summary, we hypothesize that individuals will make the attributions for their successful or unsuccessful outcomes which (a) present themselves in the most favourable (or least unfavourable) light, and (b) which they believe they can get away with (i.e. that will not be invalidated in the future). We have begun to specify what the most favourable and least unfavourable self-presentations are in various situations and the factors which affect whether a person thinks his explanation for his behaviour and outcomes might be refuted.

Our goal here was only to illustrate one application of the "impression-managing explanations for predicaments" approach by reinterpreting one topic of interest to social psychologists in terms of it. In another paper (Tedeschi and Riess, 1981) we interpret many domains of social psychological research in terms of predicaments, explanations and impression management. These include (a) induced compliance, (b) post-decision dissonance and effort justification, (c) transgression-compliance, (d) psychological reactance, (e) norms of allocation and reactions to inequity, (f) risky shift, (g) deindividuation and (h) diffusion of responsibility and helping behaviour. It is our belief that this type of theoretical intergration of seemingly diverse areas of research provides an ordinary language perspective for interpreting much of the data generated by laboratory-oriented social psychologists.

References

Abelson, R.P. (1976). A script theory of understanding, attitude, and behaviour. *In* "Cognition and Social Behaviour" (J.S. Carroll and J.W. Payne, Ed). Erlbaum Associates, Hillsdale, N.J.

Abelson, R. (1977). "Persons: A Study in Philosophical Psychology." Macmillan, Basingstoke.

Abramson, L.Y., Seligman, M.E.P. and Teasdale, J.D. (1978). Learned helplessness in humans: Critique and reformulation. *J. Abnorm. Psychol.* **87,** 49–74.

Adair, J. (1973). "Human Subject: Social Psychology of the Psychological Experiment." Little and Brown, New York.

Ambrose, I. and Canter, D. (1979). The Design of Total Institutions, Organizational Objectives as Evaluation Criteria. Paper presented to ICEP, Guildford, 16–20th July.

Anderson, N.H. (1973). Cognitive Algebra. *In* "Advances in Experimental Social Psychology", (L. Berkowitz, Ed.), Vol 7. Academic Press, New York.

Anscombe, G.E.M. (1957, 1963). "Intention." Blackwell, Oxford.

Antaki, C. and McCloskey, J. (1978). Attribution theory and everyday explanations of bad behaviour. MRC Social and Applied Psychology Unit Memo. No. 240, University of Sheffield.

Argyle, M. (1969). "Social Interaction". Methuen, London.

Argyle, M. (1977). Discussion chapter: an appraisal of the new approach to the study of social behaviour. *In* "The Social Context of Method" (M. Brenner, P. Marsh and M. Brenner, Eds). St. Martin's, New York.

Arkin, R.M., Gleason, J.M. and Johnston, S. (1976). Effects of perceived choice, expected outcome, and observed outcome of an actor on the causal attribution of actors. *J. Exp. Soc. Psychol.* **12,** 151–158.

Armistead, N. (1974). "Reconstructing Social Psychology." Penguin, Harmondsworth.

Arnold, W.J. (Ed.) (1976). "1975 Nebraska Symposium on Motivation." University of Nebraska Press, Lincoln.

Asch, S. (1946). Forming impressions of personality. *J. Abnorm. Soc. Psychol.*, **41,** 258–290.

Austin, J.L. (1961a). A plea for excuses. *In* "Philosophical Papers", (J.L. Austin, Ed.). Oxford: Clarendon.

Austin, J.L. (1961b). "Philosophical Papers." Clarendon Press, Oxford.

Austin, J.L. (1962). "How to do things with words." Oxford University Press, Oxford.

Averill, T.R. (1974). An analysis of psychophysical symbolism and its influence on theories of emotion. *J. Theory Soc. Behav.* **4,** 147–190.

Aydin, O. and Markova, I. (1979). Attribution tendencies of popular and unpopular children. *Brit. J. Soc. Clin. Psychol.* 18, 291–298.

Babcock, B.A. (1978). "The Reversible World: Symbolic Inversion in Art and Society." Cornell University Press, Ithaca.

Backman, C.W. (1979). Epilogue: a new paradigm? *In* "Emerging Strategies in Social Psychological Research" (G.P. Ginsburg, Ed.). Wiley, Chichester.

Baier, A.C. (1970). Act and Intent. *J. Phil.* **67,** 648–658.

Bailey, F.G. (1977). "Morality and Expediency: The Folklore of Academic Politics." Blackwell, Oxford.

Bannister D. and Fransella, F. (1971). "Inquiring Man: The Theory of Personal Constructs." Penguin, Harmondsworth.

Barker, R.G. and Wright, H.F. (1963). "One Boy's Day." Harper Row, New York.

Barthes, R. (1973). "Mythologies." Paladin, St. Albans.

Beck, L.W. (1966). Conscious and unconscious motives. *Mind* **75,** 155–179.

Bell, C. and Newby, H. (1977). Introduction : the rise of methodological pluralism. *In* "Doing Sociological Research" (C. Bell and J. Newby, Eds), pp. 9–29. G. Allen and Unwin, London.

Bem, D.J. (1967). Self-perception: an alternative interpretation of cognitive dissonance phenomena. *Psychol. Rev.* **74,** 183–200.

Bem, D.J. (1972). Self-perception theory. *In* "Advances in Experimental Social Psychology" (L. Berkowitz, Ed.), Vol 6. Academic Press, New York.

Bem, D.J. and McConnell, H.K. (1970). Testing the self-perception explanation of dissonance phenomena: on the salience of premanipulation attitudes. *J. Person. Soc. Psychol.* **14,** 23–31.

Bender, M.P. (1979). Community psychology: when? *Bull. Brit. Psychol. Soc.* **32,** 6–9.

Berger, P.L. and Luckmann, T. (1971). "The Social Construction of Reality." Penguin, Harmondsworth.

Berkowitz, L. (1965). The concept of aggressive drive: some additional considerations. *In* "Advances in Experimental Social Psychology" (L. Berkowitz, Ed.), Vol 2. Academic Press, New York.

Bernstein, B. (1971). "Class, Codes and Control (Vol 1): Theoretical Studies Towards a Sociology of Language." Routledge and Kegan Paul, London.

Borgida, E. (1978). Scientific deduction: evidence is not necessarily informative: a reply to Wells and Harvey. *J. Person. Soc. Psychol.* **36,** 477–482.

Bowey, A.M. (1976). "The Sociology of Organisations." Hodder and Stoughton, London.

Bradley, G.W. (1978). Self-serving biases in the attribution process: a re-examination of the fact or fiction question. *J. Person. Soc. Psychol.* **36,** 56–71.

Brand, M. (Ed.) (1976). "The Nature of Causation." University of Illinois Press, London.

Brehm, J.W. (1966). "A Theory of Psychological Reactance." Academic Press, New York.

Broadbent, D. (1977). Levels, hierarchies and the locus of control. *Quart. J. Exp. Psychol.* **29,** 181–201.

Bromley, D.B. (1977). "Personality Description in Ordinary Language." Wiley, London.

Brown, A.J. (1971). Further analysis of the supply of labour to the firm. *J. Man. Studies* **8,** 280–291.

Brown, J. (1979). Motives and moving house. Paper presented to ICEP, Guildford, 16–20th July.

Brown, J. and Sime, J. (in press). *In* "Social Method and Social Life" Brenner, M., (ed.). Academic Press, London.

Brown, L. and Lalljee, M. (1979). Young persons' conceptions of criminal events. (Unpublished manuscript).

Brown, R. (1965). "Social Psychology." The Free Press, New York.

Brunswick, E. (1934). "Wahrnehmung und Gegenstandswelt." Denticke, Leipzig and Wien.

Bryant, C.D. (1974). "Deviant Behavior: Occupational and Organizational Bases." Rand McNally, Chicago.

Bull, R. and Clifford, B. (1979). Eyewitness memory. *In* "Applied Problems in Memory" (M.M. Gruneberg and P.E. Morris, Eds.). Academic Press, London.

Bunge, M. (1959). "Causality: the Place of the Causal Principle in Modern Science". Harvard University Press, Cambridge, Mass.

Burke, K. (1952). "A Grammar of Motives." Prentice-Hall, New York.

Buss, A. (1978). Causes and reasons in attribution theory: a conceptual critique. *J. Person. Soc. Psychol.* **36,** 1311–1321.

Byrne, D. (1961). Interpersonal attraction and attitude similarity. *J. Abnorm. Soc. Psychol.* 62, 713–715.

Byrne, D. (1971). "The Attraction Paradigm." Academic Press, New York.

Cairns, R.B. (1979). "The Analysis of Social Interactions." LEA, New Jersey.

Canter, D. *et al.* (1972). Royal hospital for sick children: a psychological analysis. *Architects' Journal*, 6th September, pp. 525–564.

Canter, D. *et al.* (1975). "Environmental Interaction : Psychological Approaches to our Physical Surroundings." Surrey University Press, London.

Canter, D. (1976). "The Psychology of Place." Academic Press, London.

Canter, D. (Ed.) (1980). "Fires and Human Behaviour." Wiley, London.

Canter, D. and Walker, E. (1978). Role and Housing Assessment. Paper presented to IAAP, Munich, July.

Cassirer, E. (1944). "An Essay on Man." Yale University Press, New Haven.

Cavell, S. (1969). "Must We Mean What We Say?" Cambridge University Press, London.

Charniak, E. (1972). "Towards a Model of Children's Story Comprehension." MIT Press, Cambridge, Mass.

Cialdini, R.B., Levy, A., Herman, C.R. and Evenbeck, C. (1973). Attitudinal politics: the strategy of moderation. *J. Person. Soc. Psychol.* 25, 100–108.

Cicourel, A.V. (1973). "Cognitive Sociology: Language and Meaning in Social Interaction." Penguin, Harmondsworth.

Clark, H.H. (1978). Inferring what is meant. *In* "Studies in the Perception of Language" (W.J.M. Levett and G.B. Flures d'Arcais, Eds), Wiley, London.

Claxton, G. (1979). Individual relativity: the model of man in modern physics. *Bull. Brit. Psychol. Soc.* 32, 415–418.

Cohen, A.P. (1975). "The Management of Myths: The Politics of Legitimation in a Newfoundland Community." Manchester University Press, Manchester.

Coltheart, M. (1980). Iconic memory and visible persistence. *Percept. Psychophys.* 27, 18–228.

Coulthard, M. (1975). Discourse analysis in English — a short review of the literature. *Lang. Ling. Abstr.* 8, 73–89.

Coveney, P. (1967). "The Image of Childhood." Harmondsworth, Penguin.

Craik, K.J.W. (1943). "The Nature of Explanation." Cambridge University Press, Cambridge.

Craik, K.J.W. (1966). "The Nature of Psychology." Cambridge University Press, Cambridge.

Cross, R. and Jones, P.A. (1964). "An Introduction to Criminal Law." Butterworth, London.

Cunningham, J.D. and Kelley, H.H. (1975). Causal attributions for interpersonal events of varying magnitude. *J. Person.* 43, 74–93.

Danto, A. (1973). "Analytical Philosophy of Action." Cambridge University Press, Cambridge.

Davidson, D. (1963). Actions, reasons and causes. *J. Phil.* 60, 000–000.

Davidson, D. (1967). The logical form of action sentences, *In* "The Logic of Decision and Action" (N. Rescher, Ed.). University of Pittsburgh Press, Pittsburgh.

Davidson, D. (1971). Agency. *In* "Agent, Action and Reason" (R. Binkley, R. Bronaugh and A. Marrass, Eds). Blackwell, Oxford.

Davidson, D. (1973). Freedom to act. *In* "Essays on Freedom and Action" (T. Honderich, Ed). Routledge and Kagan Paul, London.

Davidson, D. (1978). Intending. *In* "Philosophy of History and Action" (Y. Yovel, Ed.). Reidel, Dordrech.

Davis, L.H. (1979). "Theory of Action." Prentice Hall, Englewood Cliffs, N.J.

Denzin, N.K. (1977). "Childhood Socialization: Studies in the Development of Language, Social Behaviour, and Identity." Jossey-Bass, San Francisco.

Ditton, J. (1977). "Part-Time Crime: An Ethnography of Fiddling and Pilferage." Macmillan, London.

Dixon, N.F. (1971). "Subliminal Perception: The Nature of a Controversy." McGraw-Hill, London.

Douglas, M. (1966). "Purity and Danger: An Analysis of Concepts of Pollution and Taboo." Routledge and Kegan Paul, London.

Douglas, M. (1967). The meaning of myth, with special reference to "La Geste d'Asdiwal". In "The Structural Study of Myth and Totemism" (E. Leach, Ed.), pp. 49–69. Tavistock, London.

Douglas, M. (1970). "Natural Symbols." Barrie and Rockliffe, London.

Douglas, M. (1975). "Implicit Meanings: Essays in Anthropology." Routledge and Kegan Paul, London.

Duck, S.W. (1973). "Personal Relationships and Personal Constructs: A Study of Friendship Formation." Wiley, London.

Duck, S.W. (1979). The personal and the interpersonal in construct theory: social and individual aspects of relationships. In "Constructs of Sociality and Individuality" (P. Stringer and D. Bannister, Eds). Academic Press, London.

Duck, S.W. (1980). Taking the past to heart: one of the futures of social psychology? In "The Development of Social Psychology" (R. Gilmour and S. Duck, Eds). Academic Press, London.

Dukes, W.F. (1965). N = 1. Psychol. Bull. 64, 74–79.

Duval, S. and Wicklund, R.A. (1972). "A Theory of Objective Self Awareness." Academic Press, New York.

Duval, S. and Wicklund, R.A. (1973). Effects of objective self awareness on attribution of causality. J. Exp. Soc. Psychol. 9, 17–31.

Eisen, S.V. (1979). Actor-observer differences in information inference and causal attribution. J. Person. Soc. Psychol. 37, 261–272.

Eland, F.A., Epting, F.R. and Bonarius, H. (1979). In "Constructs of Sociality and Individuality" (P. Stringer and D. Bannister, Eds.). Academic Press, London.

Elig, T.W. and Frieze, I.H. (1975). A multi-dimensional scheme for coding and interpreting perceived causality for success and failure events. JSAS Catalog of Selected Documents in Psychology 5, 313 (Ms.No.1069).

Elig, T.W. and Frieze, I.H. (1979). Measuring causal attributions for success and failure. J. Person. Soc. Psychol. 37, 621–634.

Elms, A.C. (1975). The crisis of confidence in social psychology. Am. Psychol. 30, 967–976.

Evans, J.St.B.T. (1980) Introspective reports of cognitive processes: a critique. Bull. Brit. Psychol. Soc. 33, 32–33.

Evans-Pritchard, E.E. (1937). "Witchcraft, Oracles, and Magic Among the Azande." Oxford University Press, Oxford.

Fanon, F. (1963). "The Wretched of the Earth." Grove, New York.

Feinberg, J. (1965). Action and responsibility. In "Philosophy in America" (M. Black, Ed.). Cornell University Press, Ithaca, New York.

Feinberg, J. (1973). "Social Philosophy." Prentice-Hall, New York.

Felipe, A.I. (1970). Evaluative versus descriptive consistency in trait inferences. J. Person. Soc. Psychol. 16, 627–638.

Festinger, L. (1957). "Cognitive Dissonance." Stanford University Press, Stanford.

Fillenbaum, S. and Rapoport, A. (1971). "Structures in the Subjective Lexicon." Academic Press, New York.

Filstead, W.J. (1970) "Qualitative Methodology." Markham, Chicago.

Fincham, F. and Jaspars, J. (1979). Attribution of responsibility to the self and other in children and adults. *J. Person. Soc. Psychol.* **37**, 1589–1602.

Fischhoff, B. (1976). Attribution theory and judgment under uncertainty. *In* "New Directions in Attribution Research (Vol 1)" (J.H. Harvey, W.J. Ickes and R.F. Kidd, Eds), pp. 421–452. Erlbaum, Hillsdale, N.J.

Fishbein, M. and Ajzen, I. (1973). Attribution of responsibility: a theoretical note. *J. Exp. Soc. Psychol.* **9**, 148–153.

Fiske, D.W. (1957). The constraints on intra-individual variability in test responses. *Educ. Psychol. Measure.* **17**, 317–337.

Fiske, S.T. (1979). Interpersonal Cognition and Affect: A case for Separate Systems. Paper presented at the annual APA Convention, New York, September 1979.

Fiske, S.T. and Cox, M.G. (1979). Person concepts: the effect of target familiarity and descriptive purpose on the process of describing others. *J. Person.* **47**, 136–161.

Foa, U. (1958). The contiguity principle in the structure of interpersonal relations. *Human Relations* **11**, 229–238.

Fox, J. (1969). Texture discrimination and the analysis of proximity. *Perception* **8**, 75–91.

Gadamer, H.G. (1975). "Truth and Method." Sheed and Ward, London.

Garfinkel, H. (1956). Conditions of successful degradation ceremonies. *Am. J. Sociol.*, **61**, 420–424.

Garfinkel, H. (1967). "Studies in Ethnomethodology." Prentice Hall, New Jersey.

Gauld, A. and Shotter, J. (1977). "Human Action and its Psychological Investigation." Routledge and Kegan Paul, London.

Gergen, K. (1973). Social psychology as history. *J. Person. Soc. Psychol.* **26**, 309–320.

Gergen, K.J. (1978). Toward generative theory. *J. Person. Soc. Psychol.* **36**, 1344–1360.

Ghiselin, B. (1952). "The Creative Process." Mentor, New York.

Gibson, J.J. (1966). "The Senses Considered as Perceptual Systems." Houghton Mifflin, Boston.

Giglioli, P.P. (Ed.) (1972). "Language and Social Context." Penguin, Harmondsworth.

Giles, H. and St. Clair, R. (Eds.) (1979). "Language and Social Psychology." Blackwell, Oxford.

Ginsburg, G.P. (1979). "Emerging Strategies in Social Psychological Research." Wiley, Chichester.

Glaser, B.G. and Strauss, A.L. (1967). "The Discovery of Grounded Theory: Strategies for Qualitative Research." Aldine, Chicago.

Glover, J. (1970). "Responsibility." Humanities Press, New York.

Goethals, G.R. and Reckman, R.F. (1973). The perception of consistency in attitudes. *J. Exp. Soc. Psychol.* **9**, 491–501.

Goffman, E. (1959). "The Presentation of Self in Everyday Life." Doubleday, Garden City, New York.

Goffman, E. (1964). "Stigma: Notes on the Management of Spoiled Identity." Prentice-Hall, Englewood Cliffs, New Jersey.

Goffman, E. (1968). "Asylums." Penguin, Harmondsworth. (First pub. 1961).

Goffman, E. (1975). "Frame Analysis." Penguin, Harmondsworth.

Goldberg, L.R. (1968). The inter-relationships among item characteristics in an adjective checklist: the convergence of different indices of item ambiguity. *Educ. Psychol. Measure.* **28**, 273–296.

Goldberg, L.R. (1978). Differential attribution of trait-descriptive terms to oneself as compared to well-liked, neutral, and disliked others: a psychometric analysis. *J. Person. Soc. Psychol.*

Goldman, A.I. (1970). "A Theory of Human Action." Princeton University Press, Princeton.

Goldner, F.H. (1967). Role emergence and the ethics of ambiguity. *In* "Ethics, Politics and Social Research" (S. Sjoberg, Ed.), pp. 245–266. Routledge and Kegan Paul, London.

Goodman, N. (1965). "Fact, Fiction and Forecast." 2nd edn. Bobbs-Merrill, Indianapolis.

Gouldner, A.W. (1960). The norm of reciprocity: a preliminary statement. *Am. Soc. Rev.* **25,** 161–178.

Gowler, D. (1969). Determinants of the supply of labour to the firm. *J. Man. Studies* **6,** 73–95.

Gowler, D. (1970). Socio-cultural influences on the operation of a wage payment system. *In* "Local Labour Markets and Wage Structures" (D. Robinson, Ed.), pp. 100–126. An abridged version appears in "Industrial Relations and the Wider Society" (E. Rhodes and J. Beishon, Eds.), pp. 287–297). Open University Press, London.

Gowler, D. (1972). On the concept of a person: a biosocial view. *In* "Six Approaches to the Person" (R. Ruddock, Ed.), pp. 37–69. Routledge and Kegan Paul, London.

Gowler, D. and Legge, K. (1973). Perceptions, "the principle of cumulation" and the supply of labour. *In* "The Sociology of the Workplace" (M. Warner, Ed.), pp. 116–148. G. Allen and Unwin, London.

Gowler, D. and Legge, K. (1975). Occupational role integration and the retention of labour. *In* "Labour Turnover and Retention" (B.O. Pettman, Ed.), pp. 99–137. Gower Press, Epping.

Gowler, D. and Legge, K. (1978). The evaluation of planned organizational change: the necessary art of the possible? *J. Enterpr. Man.* **1,** 201–212.

Gowler, D. and Legge, K. (1980). Evaluative practices as stressors in occupational settings. *In* "Current Concerns in Occupational Stress" (C.L. Cooper and R.L. Payne, Eds), pp. 213–242. Wiley, London.

Gowler, D. and Parry, G. (1979). Professionalism and its discontents, *New Forum* **5,** 54–56.

Graham, M. and Pettit, P. "Semantics and Social Science." (forthcoming) Routledge and Kegan Paul, London.

Green, S.F. and Mitchell, T.R. (1979). Attributional processes of leaders in leader-member interaction. *Organ. Behav. Hum. Perform.* **23,** 429–458.

Grice, H.P. (1957). Meaning. *Phil. Rev.* **66,** 377–388.

Grice, H.P. (1975). Logic and conversation. *In* "Syntax and Semantics", Vol 3 (P. Cole and J.L. Morgan, Eds). Academic Press, New York.

Gustafson, D. (1963–64). Voluntary and involuntary. *Phil. Phenomenol. Res.* XXIV, 493–501.

Haber, R.N. and Standing, L.G. (1969). Direct measures of short-term visual storage. *Quart. J. Expe. Psychol.* **21,** 43–54.

Hampson, P.J. and Morris, P.E. (1978). Unfulfilled expectations: a criticism of Neisser's theory of imagery. *Cognition* **6,** 79–95.

Harré, R. (Ed.) (1976). "Life Sentences." Wiley, London.

Harré, R. (1977a). Rules in the explanation of social behaviour. *In* "Social Rules and Social Behaviour" (P. Collett, Ed.), pp. 28–41. Blackwell, Oxford.

Harré, R. (1977b). The ethogenic approach: theory and practice. *In* "Advances in Experimental Social Psychology" (L. Berkowitz, Ed.) Vol 10. Academic Press, New York.

Harré, R. (1978). Accounts, actions and meanings — the practice of participative psychology. *In* "The Social Contexts of Method" (M. Brenner, P. Marshall and M. Brenner, Eds), pp. 44–65. Croom Helm, London.

Harré, R. (1979). "Social Being: A Theory for Social Psychology." Blackwell, Oxford.

Harré, R. and Secord, P.F. (1972). "The Explanation of Social Behavior." Blackwell, Oxford.

Harris, B. (1977). Developmental differences in the attribution of responsibility. *Devel. Psychol.* **13,** 257−265.

Hart, H.L.A. (1949). The ascription of responsibility and rights. *Proc. Aristotelian Soc.* XLIV, 171−194.

Harvey, J.H. (Ed.) (in press). "Cognition, Social Behavior, and the Environment." Erlbaum, Hillsdale, New Jersey.

Harvey, J.H. and Tucker, J.A. (1979). On problems with the Cause-reason distinction in attribution theory. *J. Person. Soc. Psychol.* **37,** 1441−1446.

Harvey, J.H., Arkin, R.M., Gleason, J.M. and Johnston, S. (1974). Effect of expected and observed outcome of an action on the differential causal attributions of actor and observer. *J. Person.* **42,** 62−77.

Harvey, J.H., Harris, B. and Barnes, R.D. (1975). Actor-observer differences in the perceptions of responsibility and freedom. *J. Person. Soc. Psychol.* **32,** 22−28.

Harvey, J.H., Ickes, W.J. and Kidd, R.F. (1976). A conversation with Fritz Heider. *In* "New Directions in Attribution Research (Vol 1)" (J.H. Harvey, W.J. Ickes and R.F. Kidd, (Eds). Arlbaum. Hillsdale, New Jersey.

Harvey, J.H., Ickes, W.J. and Kidd, R.F. (Eds) (1978). "New Directions in Attribution Research" (Vol 2). Erlbaum, Hillsdale, New Jersey.

Harvey, J.H., Ickes, W.J. and Kidd, R.F. (1978). A conversation with Edward E. Jones and Harold H. Kelley. *In* "New Directions in Attribution Research", (Vol 2). (J.H. Harvey, W.J. Ickes and R.F. Kidd, Eds). Erlbaum, Hillsdale, New Jersey.

Harvey, J.H., Ickes, W.J. and Kidd, R.F. (Eds) (in preparation). "New Directions in Attribution Research" (Vol. 3). Erlbaum, Hillsdale, N.J.

Harvey, J.H., Yarkin, K.L. Lightner, J.M. and Town, J.P. (in press). Unsolicited interpretation and recall of interpersonal events. *J. Person. Soc. Psychol.*: Attitudes and Social Cognition.

Heaton, J. (1976). Theoretical practice: the place of theory in psychotherapy. *J. Brit. Soc. Phenomenol.* **7,** 73−85.

Heider, F. (1944). Social perception and phenomenal causality. *Psychol. Rev.* **51,** 358−374.

Heider, F. (1958). "The Psychology of Interpersonal Relations." Wiley, New York.

Heider, F. (1959a). The function of the perceptual system. *Psychol. Issues* 1, (3), 35−60 (originally published, 1930).

Heider, F. (1959b). Thing and medium. *Psychol. Issues* 1, (3), 1−34 (originally published, 1927).

Heider, F. (1960). On Lewin's methods and theory. *J. Soc. Issues*, Supplement 13.

Heider, F. and Simmel, M. (1944). An experimental study of apparent behavior. *Am. J. Psychol.* **57,** 243−259.

Hempel, C.G. (1965). "Aspects of Scientific Explanation." Free Press, New York.

Henry, S. (1978). "The Hidden Economy." M. Robertson, London.

Herbst, P.G. (1970). "Behavioural Worlds: The Study of Single Cases." Tavistock, London.

Hertz, H.H. (1956). "The Principles of Mechanics." Dover, New York.

Herzberger, S.D. and Clore, G.L. (in press). Actor and observer attributions in a multitrait-multimethod matrix. *J. Res. Person.*

Herzlich, C. (1973). "Health and Illness: A Social Psychological Analysis." Academic Press, London.

Hewitt, J.P. and Stokes, R. (1975). Disclaimers. *Am. Soc. Rev.* **40,** 1−11.

Hewstone, M. and Jaspers, J. (in press). Intergroup relations and attributional processes.

To appear in H. Tajfel (Ed.), "Social Identity and Intergroup Behaviour." Academic Press, London.

Himmelfarb, S. (1972). Integration and attribution theories in personality impression formation. *J. Person. Soc. Psychol.* **23,** 309–313.

Hovland, C.I., Janis, I.L. and Kelley, H.H. (1953). "Communication and Persuasion." Yale University Press, New Haven, Connecticut.

Huizinga, J. (1949). "Homo Ludens." Routledge and Kegan Paul, London.

Hull, C.L. (1952). "A Behaviour System." Yale University Press, New Haven.

Humphrey, C. (1978). Women, taboo and the suppression of attention. *In* "Defining Females" (S. Ardener, Ed.), pp. 89–108. Croom Helm, London.

Humphrey, G. (1951). "Thinking: An Introduction to its Experimental Psychology." Methuen, London.

Izard, C.E. (1971). "The Face of Emotion." Appleton Century Croft, New York.

James, W. (1980, 1950). "Principles of Psychology." Dover, New York.

Jellison, J.M. (1977). "I'm Sorry I didn't Mean to and Other Lies we Love to Tell." Chatham Square Press, New York.

Jones, E.E. (1976). How do people perceive the causes of behaviour? *Am. Sci.* **64,** 300–305.

Jones, E.E. and Davis, K.E. (1965). From acts to dispositions: the attribution process in person perception. *In* "Advances in Experimental Social Psychology", Vol 2 (L. Berkowitz, Ed.), Academic Press, New York.

Jones, E.E. and McGillis, D. (1976). Correspondent inferences and the attribution cube: a comparative reappraisal. *In* "New Directions in Attribution Research" (J.H. Harvey, W.J. Ickes and R.F. Kidd, Eds.), Vol. 1 pp. 389–420. Erlbaum Associates, Hillsdale N.J.

Jones, E.E. and Nisbett, R.E. (1972). The actor and the observer: divergent perceptions of the causes of behavior. *In* "Attribution: Perceiving the Causes of Behavior." (E.E. Jones, D.E. Kanouse, H.H. Kelley, R.E. Nisbett, S. Valins and B. Weiner, Eds). General Learning Press, Morristown, N.J.

Jones, E.E. and Wortman, C. (1973). "Ingratiation: An Attributional Approach." General Learning Press, Morristown, New Jersey.

Jones, E.E., Davis, K.E. and Gergen, K.J. (1961). Role playing variations and their informational value for person perception. *J. Abnorm. Soc. Psychol.* **63,** 302–310.

Jones, E.E., Kanouse, D.E., Kelley, H.H., Nisbett, R.E., Valins, S. and Weiner, B. (1972). "Attribution: Perceiving the Causes of Behaviour." General Learning Press, New Jersey.

Joos, M. (1962). The five clocks. *Int. J. Am. Ling.* **28,** Part 5.

Jordan, N. (1966). The cognitive psychology of Fritz Heider. Unpublished manuscript.

Joynson, R.B. (1974). "Psychology and Common Sense." Routledge and Kegan Paul, London.

Kahneman, D. and Tversky, A. (1973). On the psychology of prediction. *Psychol. Rev.* **80,** 237–251.

Kelley, H.H. (1967). Attribution theory in social psychology. *In* "Nebraska Symposium on Motivation", Vol 15 (D. Levine, Ed.). University of Nebraska Press, Lincoln.

Kelley, H.H. (1972a). Attribution in social interaction. *In* "Attribution: Perceiving the Causes of Behavior" (E.E. Jones, D.E. Kanouse, H.H. Kelley, R.E. Nisbett, S. Valins and B. Weiner, Eds). General Learning Press, Morristown, N.J.

Kelley, H.H. (1972b). Causal schemata and the attribution process. *In* "Attribution: Perceiving the Causes of Behavior" (E.E. Jones, D.E. Kanouse, H.H. Kelley, R.E. Nisbett, S. Valins and B. Weiner, Eds.). General Learning Press, Morristown, N.J.

Kelley, H.H. (1973). The processes of causal attribution. *Am. Psychol.* 107−128.

Kelley, H.H. (1977). An application of attribution theory to research methodology for close relationships. *In* "Close Relationships" (G. Levinger and H.L. Raush, Eds). University of Massachusetts Press, Amherst, Mass.

Kelley, H.H., Thibaut, J.W., Radloff, R. and Mundy, D. (1962). The development of cooperation in the "minimal social situation". *Psychol. Monogr.* **76,** (No. 19, Whole No. 538).

Kelly, G.A. (1955). "The Psychology of Personal Constructs." Norton, New York.

Kelly, G.A. (1969). *In* "Clinical Psychology and Personality: The Selected Papers of George Kelly" (B. Maher, Ed.). Wiley, New York.

Kelman, H. (1974). Compliance, identification and internalization revisited. *In* "Perspectives on Social Power" (J.T. Tedeschi, Ed.). Aldine, Chicago.

Kenny, A. (1963). "Action, Emotion and Will." Routledge and Kegan Paul, London.

Kidd, R.F. and Amabile, T.M. (1981). Causal explanations in social interaction: some dialogues on dialogue. *In* "New Directions in Attribution Research, Vol III" (J. Harvey, W. Ickes and R.F. Kidd, Eds). LEA, Hillsdale.

Kirkham, J.S., Levy, S. and Crotty, W.J. (Eds) (1970). "Assassination and Political Violence." Praeger, New York.

Klockars, C.B. (1974). "The Professional Fence." The Free Press, New York.

Kruglanski, A. (1975). The endogenous-exogenous partition in attribution theory. *Psychol. Rev.* **82,** 387−406.

Kruglanski, A., Hamel, I.Z. Maides, S.A., and Schwartz, J.M. (1978). Attribution theory as a special case of lay epistemology. *In* "New Directions in Attribution Research, Vol 2" (J.H. Harvey, W.J. Ickes and R.F. Kidd, Eds). Erlbaum Associates, Hillsdale, N.J.

Kuipers, N.A. and Rogers, T.B. (1979). Encoding of personal information: self-other differences. *J. Person. Soc. Psychol.* **37,** 499−514.

Lalljee, M. (1979). Report to the Social Science Research Council on Research Grant HR 5092 "The explanations provided by young children and adults for actions and emotions".

Langer, E.J. (1978). Rethinking the role of thought in social interaction. *In* "New Directions in Attribution Research (Vol 2)" (J.H. Harvey, W.J. Ickes and R.F. Kidd, Eds). Erlbaum Associates, Hillsdale, N.J.

Langer, E.J., Blank, A. and Chanowitz, B. (1978). The mindlessness of ostensibly thoughtful action: the role of "placebic" information in interpersonal interaction. *J. Person. Soc. Psychol.* **36,** 635−642.

Langford, G. (1971). "Human Action." Doubleday, New York.

Langford, G. (1978). Persons as necessarily social. *J. Theory Soc. Behav.* **8,** 263−283.

Larrain, J. (1979). "The Concept of Ideology." Hutchinson, London.

Latané, B. and Darley, J.M. (1970). "The Unresponsive Bystander: Why Doesn't He Help?" Appleton-Century Crofts, New York.

Leach, E. (1972). Anthropological aspects of language: animal categories and verbal abuse. *In* "Mythology" (P. Maranda, Ed.), pp. 39−67. Penguin, Harmondsworth. First published *In* "New Directions in the Study of Language" (E.H. Lenneberg, Ed.), pp. 23−63. M.I.T. Press, Cambridge, Mass. (1964).

Leach, E. (1976). "Culture and Communication: The Logic by Which Symbols are Connected." Cambridge University Press, Cambridge.

Legge, K. (1970). The operation of the "regressive spiral" in the labour market. *J. of Man. Studies* **7,** 1−22.

Legge, K. (1978a). Work in prison: the process of inversion. *Brit. J. Criminol.* **18,** 6−22.

Legge, K. (1978b). "Power, Innovation and Problem-Solving in Personnel Management." McGraw-Hill, London.

Lepper, M.R., Greene, D.T. and Nisbett, R.E. (1973). Undermining children's intrinsic interest with extrinsic reward: a test of the "overjustification" hypothesis. *J. Person. Soc. Psychol.* **28**, 129–137.

Lerner, M.J. (1970). The desire for justice and reactions to victims In "Altruism and Helping Behaviour" (J. Macauley and L. Berkowitz, Eds.). Academic Press, New York.

Lerner, M.J., Miller, D.T. and Holmes, J.G. (1976). Deserving and the emergence of forms of justice. *In* (L. Berkowitz, Ed.), *Adv. Expe. Soc. Psychol.* **9**, 133–162.

Levi-Strauss, C. (1963). "Structural Anthropology." Basic Books, New York.

Levi-Strauss, C. (1978). "Myth and Meaning." Routledge and Kegan Paul and University of Toronto Press, London and Toronto.

Levy-Bruhl, L. (1928). "The Soul of the Primitive." Allen and Unwin, London.

Lewis, O. (1961). "The Children of Sanchez: Autobiography of Mexican Family." Random House, New York.

Lyman, S. and Scott, M.B. (1970). "A Sociology of the Absurd." Appleton-Century-Crofts, New York.

McArthur, L.A. (1972). The how and what of why: some determinants and consequences of causal attribution. *J. Person. Soc. Psychol.* **22**, 171–193.

Macdonald, G. and Pettit, P. "Semantics and Social Science." Routledge (forthcoming), London.

McGee, M.G. and Snyder, M. (1975). Attribution and behavior. Two field studies. *J. Person. Soc. Psychol.* **32**, 185–190.

McGuire, W.J. (1973). The yin and yang of progress in social psychology. *J. Person. Soc. Psychol.* **26**, 446–456.

Maier, N.R.F. (1931). Reasoning in humans: II. The solution of a problem and its appearance in consciousness. *J. Comp. Psychol.* **12**, 181–194.

Mair, J.M.M. (1970). Psychologists are human too. *In* "Perspectives in Personal Construct Theory" (D. Bannister, Ed.). Academic Press, London.

Mandler, G. (1975). "Mind and Emotion." Wiley, New York.

Mars, G., Bryant, D. and Mitchell, P. (1979). "Manpower Problems in the Hotel and Catering Industry." Saxon House, Farnborough.

Maselli, M.D. and Altrocchi, J. (1969). Attribution of intent. *Psychol. Bull.* **71**, 445–454.

Mead, G.H. (1934). "Mind, Self and Society." University of Chicago Press, Chicago.

Mead, M. (1943). "Coming of Age in Samoa." Penguin, Harmondsworth (first published in 1928).

Mellor, D.H. (1976). Probable explanation. *Australasian J. Phil. Vol 54.*

Menzel, H. (1978). Meaning — who needs it? *In* "The Social Context of Method" (P. Marsh and M. Brenner, Eds), pp. 140–171. Croom-Helm, London.

Milgram, S. (1963). Behavioural studies of obedience. *J. Abnorm. Soc. Psychol.* **67**, 371–378.

Milgram, S. (1965). Some conditions of obedience and disobedience to authority. *Human Relations* **18**, 57–76.

Miller, A.G. (1975). Actor and observer perceptions of the learning of a task. *J. Expe. Soc. Psychol.* **11**, 95–111.

Miller, A.G., Gillen, B., Schenker, C. and Radlove, S. (1973). Perception of obedience to authority. *Proc. 81st Ann. Conv. Am. Psychol. Associ.* **8**, 128–128.

Miller, D.T. (1978). What constitutes a self-serving attributional bias? A reply to Bradley. *J. Person. Soc. Psychol.* **36**, 1221–1223.

Miller, D.T. and Ross, M. (1975). Self-serving biases in the attribution of causality: fact or fiction? *Psychol. Bull.* **82**, 213–225.

Miller, G. (1978). "Odd Jobs: The World of Deviant Work." Prentice-Hall Englewood, Cliffs, N.J.

Miller, G.A. (1962). "Psychology: The Science of Mental Life." Harper and Row, New York.

Miller, I.W. and Norman, W.H. (1979). Learned helplessness in humans: a review and attribution-theory model. *Psychol. Bull.* **86**, 93–118.

Mills, C.W. (1940). Situated actions and vocabularies of motive. *Am. Sociol. Rev.* **5**, 904–913.

Millward, N. (1968). Family status and behaviour at work. *Sociol. Rev.* XVI, 149–164.

Minsky, M. (1975). A framework for representing knowledge. *In* "The Psychology of Computer Vision" (P. Winston, Ed.). McGraw Hill, New York.

Mischel, W. (1973). Towards a cognitive social learning reconceptualization of personality. *Psychol. Rev.* **80**, 252–283.

Mischel, W. (1979). On the interface of cognition and personality. *Am. Psychol.* **34**, 740–754.

Mitchell, T., Berger, R. and Forsyth, D.R. (1979). Reactions to others' egocentric claims of responsibility. Paper presented at the annual meeting of the American Psychological Association, New York City.

Monson, T.C. and Snyder, M. (1977). Actors, observers, and the attribution process: toward a reconceptualization. *J. Exp. Soc. Psychol.* **13**, 89–111.

Morris, P.E. (1978) Encoding and retrieval. *In* "Aspects of Memory" M.M. Gruneberg, and P.E. Morris, Eds). Methuen, London.

Morris, P.E. (1980). Introspective reports of cognitive processes: a defence. *Bull. Brit. Psychol. Soc.* **33**, 33.

Morris, P.E. and Reid, R.L. (1970). Repeated use of mnemonic imagery. *Psychonomic Sci.* **20**, 337–338.

Myles, B. (Ed.) (1976). "The Nature of Causation." University Illinois Press, London.

Needham, R. (1963). (Ed), "Right and Left: Essays on Dual Symbolic Classification." University of Chicago Press, Chicago.

Neisser, U. (1967). "Cognitive Psychology." Appleton Century-Crofts, New York.

Neisser, U. (1976). "Cognition and Reality." Freeman, San Francisco.

Newtson, D. (1973). Attribution and the unit of perception of ongoing behaviour. *J. Person. Soc. Psychol.* **28**, 28–38.

Newtson, D. (1976). Foundations of attribution: the perception of ongoing behaviour. *In* "New Directions in Attribution Research" (J. Harvey, W. Ickes and R. Kidd, Eds.). Erlbaum, Hillsdale N.J.

Ngubane, H. (1977). "Body and Mind in Zulu Medicine." Academic Press, London.

Nisbett, R.E. and Bellows, N. (1977). Verbal reports about causal influences on social judgments: private access versus public theories. *J. Person. Soc. Psychol.* **35**, 613–624.

Nisbett, R.E. and Borgida, E. (1975). Attribution and the psychology of prediction. *J. Person. Soc. Psychol.* **32**, 932–943.

Nisbett, R.E. and Schachter, S. (1966). Cognitive manipulation of pain. *J. Expe. Soc. Psychol.* **2**, 227–236.

Nisbett, R.E. and Valins, S. (1972). Perceiving the causes of one's own behavior. *In* "Attribution: Perceiving the Causes of Behavior" (E.E. Jones, D.E. Kanouse, H.H. Kelley, R.E. Nisbett, S. Valins and B. Weiner, Eds). Morristown, N.J.: General Learning Press.

Nisbett, R.E. and Wilson, T.D. (1977). Telling more than we can know: verbal reports on mental processes. *Psychol. Rev.* **84**, 231–259.

Nisbett, R.E., Caputo, C., Legant, P. and Maracek, J. (1973). Behavior as seen by the actor and as seen by the observer. *J. Person. Soc. Psychol.* **27**, 154–164.

Nisbett, R.E., Borgida, E., Crandall, R. and Reed, H. (1976). Popular induction: information is not always informative. *In* "Cognition and Social Behavior" (J.S.

Carroll and J.W. Payne, Eds). Erlbaum Associates, Hillsdale, N.J.

Norbeck, E. (1977). A sanction for authority: etiquette. *In* "The Anthropology of Power: Ethnographic Studies from Asia, Oceania, and the New World" (R.D. Fogelson and R.N. Adams, Eds), pp. 67–76. Academic Press, New York.

Norman, W.T. and Goldberg, L.R. (1966). Raters, ratees, and randomness in personality structure. *J. Person. Soc. Psychol.* **4**, 681–691.

Oberdiek, H. (1972). Intention and foresight in criminal law. *Mind* **81**, 389–400.

Orne, M.T. (1962). On the social psychology of the psychological experiment: with particular reference to demand characteristics and their implications. *Am. Psychol.* **17**, 776–783.

Orvis, B.R., Kelley, H.H. and Butler, D. (1978). Attributional conflict in young couples. *In* "New Directions in Attribution Research (Vol 1.) (J.H. Harvey, W.J. Ickes and R.F. Kidd, Eds). Erlbaum Associates, Hillsdale, N.J.

Paivio, A. (1971). "Imagery and Verbal Processes." Holt, Rinehart and Winston, New York.

Palmer, R.E. (1969). "Hermeneutics." Northwestern University Press. Evanston.

Peabody, D. (1967). Trait inferences: evaluative and descriptive aspects. *J. Person. Soc. Psychol. Monogr.* **7**, (4, whole No. 644).

Peabody, D. (1970). Evaluative and descriptive aspects in personality perception: a reappraisal. *J. Person. Soc. Psychol.* **16**, 639–646.

Peters, R.S. (1958). "The Concept of Motivation." Routledge and Kegan Paul, London.

Pettit, P. (1975). The life-world and role-theory. *In* "Phenomenology and Philosophical Understanding" (E. Pivcevic, Ed.). Cambridge University Press, Cambridge.

Pettit, P. (1976). Making actions intelligible. *In* "Life Sentences" (R. Harre, Ed.). J. Wiley, London.

Pettit, P. (1978). Rational man theory. *In* "Action and Interpretation" (C. Hookway and P. Pettit, Eds). Cambridge University Press, Cambridge.

Pettit, P. (1979). Rationalisation and the art of explaining action. *In* "Philosophical Problems in Psychology" (N. Bolton, Ed.). Methuen, London.

Phares, E.J. (1976). "Locus of Control in Personality." General Learning Press, New Jersey.

Piaget, J. (1971). "Structuralism." Routledge and Kegan Paul, London. First published as "La Structuralisme", Presses Universitares de France, Paris. (1968).

Popper, K.R. and Eccles, J.C. (1977). "The Self and its Brain." Springer, Berlin.

Prus, R.C. (1975). Resisting designations: an extension of attribution theory into a negotiated context. *Sociol. Inquiry* **45**, 3–14.

Pylyshyn, Z.W. (1973). What the mind's eye tells the mind's brain: a critique of mental imagery. *Psychol. Bull.* **80**, 1–24.

Quine, W.V. and Ullian, J. (1978). "The Ways of Belief" (2nd edn.). Random House, New York.

Radley, A. (1978). Intersubjectivity as a unity of intention. Paper presented to the Annual Conference of the Social Psychology of the B.P.S., Cardiff, September, 1978.

Rapoport, R. and Rapoport, R.N. (1976). "Dual-Career Families Re-Examined." M. Robertson, London.

Reeder, G.D. and Brewer, M.B. (1979). A schematic model of dispositional attribution in interpersonal perception. *Psychol. Rev.* **86**, 61–79.

Regan, D.T. and Totten, J. (1975). Empathy and attribution: turning observers into actors. *J. Person. Soc. Psychol.* **32**, 850–856.

Regan, D.T., Straus, E. and Fazio, R. (1974). Liking and the attribution process. *J. Expe. Soc. Psychol.* **10**, 385–397.

Ricoeur, P. (1970). "Freud and Philosophy: an Essay on Interpretation." Yale University Press, New Haven.

Riess, M., Rosenfield, P., Melburg, V. and Tedeschi, J.T. (1980). The self-serving bias: distortions of perception or description? Unpublished manuscript: Middlebury College, Vermont, U.S.A.

Robinson, W.P. (1972). "Language and Social Behaviour." Penguin, Harmondsworth.

Rogers, T.B., Kuipers, N.A., and Kirker, W.S. (1977). Self-reference and the encoding of personal information. *J. Person. Soc. Psychol.* 35, 677−688.

Rommetveit, R. (1974). "On Message Structure." Wiley, London.

Rommetveit, R. (1976). The architecture of intersubjectivity. *In* "Social Psychology in Transition" (L. Strickland, F. Aboud and K.J. Gergen, Eds). Plenum Press, New York.

Rosenberg, S. (1977). New approaches to the analysis of personal constructs in person perception. *In* "1976 Nebraska Symposium on Motivation" (A.W. Landfield, Ed.). University of Nebraska, Lincoln.

Rosenthal, R. (1966). "Experimenter Effects in Behavioural Research." Appleton-Century-Crofts, New York.

Rosenthal, R. and Rosnow, R. (1969). "Artifact in Behavioural Research." Academic Press, New York.

Ross, L. (1977). The intuitive psychologist and his shortcomings: distortions in the attribution process. *In* "Advances in Experimental Social Psychology, Vol 10" (L. Berkowitz, Ed.). Academic Press, New York.

Ross, L., Green, D. and House, P. (1977). The "false consensus effect": an egocentric bias in social perception and attribution processes. *J. Exp. Soc. Psychol.* 13, 279−301.

Ross, M. and Sicoly, F. (1979). Egocentric biases in availability and attribution. *J. Person. Soc. Psychol.* 37, 322−336.

Rossi, I. (1974). Intellectual antecedents of Levi-Strauss' analysis of the unconscious. *In* "The Unconscious in Culture" (I. Rossi, Ed.), pp. 7130. Dutton, New York.

Ryle, G. (1949). "The Concept of Mind." Hutchinson, London.

Sagarin, E. (1977). "Deviance and Social Change." Sage, Beverly Hills.

Sahlins, M. (1976). "Culture and Practical Reason." University of Chicago Press, Chicago.

Salmon, P. (1979). Children as social beings: a Kellyan view. *In* "Constructs of Sociality and Individuality" (P. Stringer and D. Bannister, Eds). Academic Press, London.

Salmon, W. (1971). "Statistical Explanation and Statistical Relevance." University of Pittsburgh Press, Pittsburgh.

Salmon, W. (1975). Theoretical explanation. *In* "Explanation" (S. Korner, Ed.). Blackwell, Oxford.

Schachter, S. (1964). The interaction of cognitive and physiological determinants of emotional state. *In* "Advances in Experimental Social Psychology", Vol 1 (L. Berkowitz, Ed.). Academic Press, New York.

Schank, R. and Abelson, R. (1977). "Scripts, Plans, Goals and Understanding." LEA, Hillsdale.

Schank, R.C. and Colby, K. (1973). "Computer Models of Thought and Language." Freeman, San Francisco.

Schegloff, E. (1972). Notes on a conversational practice: formulating place. *In* "Studies in Social Interactions" (D. Sudnow, Ed.). Free Press, Glencoe.

Schlenker, B.R. (1975). Self-presentation: managing the impression of consistency when reality interferes with self-enhancement. *J. Person. Soc. Psychol.* 32, 1030−1037.

Schlenker, B.R. (1980). "Impression Management." Brooks/Cole, New York.

Schneider, D.J. (1969). Tactical self-presentation after success and failure. *J. Person. Soc. Psychol.* 13, 262−268.

Schutz, A. (1967). "The Phenomenology of the Social World." Northwestern University Press, Evanston.

Scott, M.B. and Lyman, S.M. (1968). Accounts. *Am. Sociol. Rev.*, Vol 33.

Secord, P.F. and Backman, C.W. (1974). "Social Psychology," 2nd Edn. McGraw Hill, New York.

Selby, J.W. III. (1976). Inferential sets and descriptive versus evaluative aspects of behavioural inference. *J. Person. Soc. Psychol.* 33, 13−24.

Seligman, M.P. (1975). "Helplessness: On Depression, Development and Death." Freeman, San Francisco.

Semin, G.R. (in press). A gloss on attribution theory. *Brit. J. Soc. Clin. Psychol.*

Shallice, T. (1972). Dual functions of consciousness. *Psychol. Rev.* 79, 383−393.

Shapiro, M.B. (1966). The single case in clinical psychological research. *J. Gen. Psychol.* 74, 3−23.

Shaver, K.G. (1970). Defensive attribution: effects of severity and relevance on the responsibility assigned for an accident. *J. Person. Soc. Psychol.* 14, 101−113.

Shaver, K.G. (1975). "An Introduction to Attribution Processes." Winthrop Publishers, Inc, Cambridge, Mass.

Shotter, J. (1973). Acquired powers: the transformation of natural into personal powers. *J. Theory Soc. Behav.* 3, 141−156.

Shotter, J. (1974). The development of personal powers. *In* "The Integration of the Child into a Social World" (M.P.M. Richards, Ed.). Cambridge University Press, Cambridge.

Shotter, J. (1975). "Images of Man in Psychological Research." Methuen, London.

Shotter, J. (1977). Agency and 'accounting': in criticism of Harré and Secord's 'open souls' doctrine. Paper presented to The Annual Conference of the Social Psychology Section of the B.P.S., Durham, September.

Shotter, J. (1978). The cultural context of communication studies: theoretical and methodological issues. *In* "Action, Gesture and Symbol" (A. Lock, Ed.). Academic Press, New York and London.

Shotter, J. (1980a). Men the magicians: the duality of social being and the structure of moral worlds. *In* "Models of Man" (A. Chapman and D. Jones, Eds), British Psychological Society, London.

Shotter, J. (1980b). Action, joint action, and intentionality. *In* "The Structure of Action" (M. Brenner, Ed.). Blackwell, Oxford.

Shotter, J. (in press). Vico, moral worlds, accountability, and personhood. *In* "Indigenous Psychologies The Anthropology of the Self" (P. Heelas and A. Lock, Eds). Academic Press, London.

Shye, S. (Ed.), (1979). "Theory Construction and Data Analysis in the Behavioral Sciences." Jossey-Bass, San Francisco.

Shye, S. and Elizur, D. (1976). Worries about deprivation of job rewards following computerisation. *Human Relations* 29, 63−71.

Sicoly, F. and Ross, M. (1977). The facilitation of ego-biased attributions by means of self-serving observer feedback. *J. Person. Soc. Psychol.* 35, 734−741.

Skinner, B.F. (1957). "Verbal Behaviour." Appleton-Century Crofts, New York.

Sloman, A. (1976). What are the aims of science? *Radical Philosophy.* Spring, 7−17.

Slovic, P. and Lichtenstein, S. (1971). Comparison of Bayesian and regression approaches to the study of information processing in judgment. *Organ. Behav. Hum. Perform.* 6, 649−744.

Smedslund, J. (1978). Bandura's theory of self efficacy: a set of common sense theorems. *Scand. J. Psychol.* 19, 1−14.

Smith, E.R. and Miller, F.D. (1978). Limits on perception of cognitive processes: a reply to Nisbett and Wilson. *Psychol. Rev.* 85, 355−362.

Smith, M.B. (1972). Is experimental social psychology advancing? *J. Exp. Soc. Psychol.* **8**, 86−96.

Snyder, M.L., Stephan, W.G. and Rosenfield, D. (1978). Attributional egotism. *In* "New Directions in Attribution Research, vol. II" (J. Harvey, W. Ickes and R. Kidd, Eds). Erlbaum, Hillsdale, N.J.

Sosa, E. (ed.), (1975). "Causation and Conditionals." Oxford University Press, Oxford.

Stephan, W. (1977). Stereotyping: role of ingroup-outgroup differences in causal attribution of behaviour. *J. Soc. Psychol.* **101**, 255−266.

Stevens, L. and Jones, E.E. (1976). Defensive attribution and the Kelley cube. *J. Person. Soc. Psychol.* **34**, 809−820.

Stokes, R. and Hewitt, J.P. (1976). Aligning actions. *Am. Sociol. Rev.* **46**.

Storms, M.D. (1973). Videotape and the attribution process: reversing actors' and observers' point of view. *J. Person. Soc. Psychol.* **27**, 165−175.

Storms, M.D. and Nisbett, R.E. (1970). Insomnia and the attribution process. *J. Person. Soc. Psychol.* **16**, 319−328.

Stover, R. (1972). Responsibility for the cold war − a case study of historical responsibility. History and Theory **11**, 145−178.

Strauss, A.L. (1977). "Mirrors and Masks: the Search for Identity." M. Robertson, London.

Strawson, P.F. (1959). "Individuals." Methuen, London.

Stringer, P. (1979). Individuals, roles and persons. *In* "Constructs of Sociality and Individuality" (P. Stringer and D. Bannister, Eds). Academic Press, London.

Stryker, S. (1977). Developments in "two social psychologies": toward an appreciation of mutual relevance. *Sociometry* **40**, 145−160.

Stryker, S. and Gottlieb, A. (in press). Attribution theory and symbolic interactionism: a comparison. *In* "New Directions in Attribution Research, Vol 3" (J.H. Harvey, W. Ickes, and R.F. Kidd, Eds). Lawrence Erlbaum Associates, Hillsdale, N.J.

Sutherland, N.S. (1959). Motives as explanations. *Mind* LXVIII, 145−159.

Sykes, G. and Matza, D. (1957). Techniques of neutralization: a theory of delinquency. *Am. J. Sociol.* **22**, 664−670.

Tajfel, H. and Fraser, C. (1978). "Introducing Social Psychology." Penguin, Harmondsworth.

Tambiah, S.J. (1969). Animals are good to think and good to prohibit. *Ethnology* **7**, 423−459.

Tatro, C.H. (1974). Cross my palm with silver: fortune telling as an occupational way of life. *In* "Deviant Behavior" (C.D. Bryant, Ed.), pp. 286−299. Rand McNally, Chicago.

Taylor, C. (1971). Interpretation and the sciences of man. *Rev. Metaphys.* **25**, 3−51.

Taylor, L. (1979). Vocabularies, rhetorics and grammar: problems in the sociology of motivation. *In* "Deviant Interpretations" (D. Downes and P. Rock, Eds), pp. 145−161. M. Robertson, Oxford.

Taylor, R. (1974). "Metaphysics," 2nd edn. Prentice Hall, Englewood Cliffs, N.J.

Taylor, S.E. and Koivumaki, J.H. (1976). The perception of self and others: acquaintanceship, affect and actor-observer differences. *J. Person. Soc. Psychol.* **33**, 403−408.

Tedeschi, J.T. and Lindskold, S. (1976). "Social Psychology: Interdependence, Interaction and Influence." Wiley, New York.

Tedeschi, J.T. and Riess, M. (1981). Social psychological experiments as predicaments requiring impression management. *In* "Impression Management and Social Psychological Research" (J.T. Tedeschi, Ed.). Academic Press, New York.

Tedeschi, J.T., Schlenker, B.R. and Bonoma, T.V. (1971). Cognitive dissonance: private ratiocination or public spectacle? *Am. Psychol.* **26**, 684−695.

Tetlock, P.E. (1979). The social consequences of defensive and counterdefensive attributions. Paper presented at the annual meeting of the American Psychological Association, New York City.

Thibaut, J.W. and Riecken, H.W. (1955). Some determinants and consequences of the perception of social causality. *J. Person.* **24**, 113–133.

Toulmin, S. (1958). "Uses of Argument." Cambridge University Press, Cambridge.

Triandis, H.C. (1977). "Interpersonal Behaviour." Brooks, Cole, Montery, California.

Tucker, N. (1977). "What Is a Child?" Fontana, London.

Turnbull, C.M. (1973). "The Mountain People." Cape, London.

Turner, V. (1974). "Dramas, Fields and Metaphors: Symbolic Action in Human Society." Cornell University Press, Ithaca.

Valins, S. and Ray, A.A. (1967). Effects of cognitive desensitization on avoidance behaviour. *J. Person. Soc. Psychol.* **7**, 345–350.

Van der Pligt, J. and Van Dijk, J.A. (1979). Polarization of judgment and preference for judgmental labels. *Europ. J. Soc. Psychol.* **9**, 233–241.

Van der Pligt, J. and Eiser, J.R. (a) Preferences for the situational option and response uncertainty (in preparation).

Van der Pligt, J. and Eiser, J.R. (b) Attribution and evaluation of the target person (in preparation).

Van der Pligt, J. and Eiser, J.R. (c) Self-other differences in the attribution of trait-descriptive terms: evaluative Vs. descriptive consistency. Manuscript submitted for publication.

Vico, G. (1975). (T.G. Bergin and M.H. Fisch, Eds and trans.). "Principles of the New Science of Giambattista Vico." Cornell University Press Ithaca, New York (3rd edn. orig. published 1744).

Wagner, R. (1978). "Lethal Speech: Daribi Myth as Symbolic Obviation." Cornell University Press, Ithaca.

Wallace, W.A. (1972). "Causality and Scientific Explanation." University of Michigan Press, Michigan.

Walster, E. (1966). Assignment of responsibility for an accident. *J. Person. Soc. Psychol.* **3**, 73–79.

Walster, E. (1971). Passionate love. *In* "Theories of Attraction and Love" (B.J. Murstein, Ed.). Springer Publishing Corp, New York.

Warmington, A., Lupton, T. and Gribbin, C. (1977). "Organisational Behaviour and Performance: An open Systems Approach to Change." Macmillan, London.

Wassermann, G.D. (1979). Reply to Popper's attack on epiphenomenation. *Mind* **88**, 572–575.

Watson, J.B. (1913). Psychology as the behaviourist views it. *Psychol. Rev.* **20**, 158–177.

Weary, G., Rich, M.C., Harvey, J.H. and Ickes, W. (in press). Heider's formulation of social perception and attributional processes: toward further clarification. *Person. Soc. Psychol. Bull.*

Wegner, D.M. and Vallacher, R.R. (1977). "Implicit Psychology: An Introduction to Social Cognition." Oxford University Press, New York.

Weiner, B. (1974). "Achievement Motivation and Attribution Theory." General Learning Press, Morristown, N.J.

Weiner, B., Frieze, I., Kukla, A., Reed, L., Rest, D. and Rosenbaum, R.M. (1972). Perceiving the causes of success and failure. *In* "Attribution: Perceiving the Causes of Behavior" (E.E. Jones, D.E. Kanouse, H.H. Kelley, R.E. Nisbett, S. Valins and B. Weiner's Eds). General Learning Press, Morristown, N.J.

Wells, G.L. and J.H. Harvey, (1977). Do people use consensus information in making causal attributions? *J. Person. Soc. Psychol.* **35**, 279–293.

Wells, G.L. and Harvey, J.H. (1978). Naive attributors' attributions and predictions:

what is informative and when is an effect an effect. *J. Person. Soc. Psychol.* **36**, 483–490.

White, P. (1980). Limitations on verbal reports of internal events: a refutation of Nisbett and Wilson and of Bem. *Psychol. Rev.* **87**, 105–112.

Whitehead, G.I. and Smith, S.M. (1976). The effect of expectancy of the assignment of responsibility for a misfortune. *J. Person.* **44**, 69–83.

Whorf, B.L. (1941). The relation of habitual thought and behavior to language. *In* "Language, Culture and Personality: Essays in Memory of Edward Sapir." Sapir Memorial Publication Fund, Menasha, Wisconsin.

Wiggins, D. (1975). Deliberation and practical reason. *In* "Proceedings of the Aristotalian Society," 1975–76.

Wilden, A. (1972). "System and Structure: Essays in Communication and Exchange." Tavistock, London.

Wilkinson, S.J. (1980). Constructs, counterfactuals and fictions: elaborating the concept of 'possibility' for science. *In* "Recent Advances in the Theory and Practice of Personal Construct Psychology" (H. Bonarius, R. Holland and S. Rosenberg, Eds). Macmillan, London.

Winch, P. (1958). "The Idea of a Social Science and its Relations to Philosophy." Routledge and Kegan Paul, London.

Wittgenstein, L. (1953). "Philosophical Investigations." Blackwell, Oxford.

Whyte, W.H. (1956). "The Organization Man." Simon and Schuster, New York.

Wortman, C.B. and Brehm, J.W. (1975). Responses to uncontrollable outcomes: an integration of reactance theory and the learned helplessness model. *In* "Advances in Experimental Social Psychology", (Vol.8) (L. Berkowitz, Ed.). Academic Press, New York.

Wortman, C.G. and L. Dinzer. (1978). Is an attributional analysis of the learned helplessness phenomenon viable? A critique of the Abramson-Seligman-Teasale reformulation. *J. Abnorm. Psychol.* **87**, 75–90.

Wundt, W. (1911). "Einfuhrung in der Psychologie." tr. R. Pintner "An Introduction to Psychology (1912)." Allen, London.

Zanna, M.P. and Cooper, J. (1976). Dissonance and the attribution process. *In* "New Directions in Attribution Research" (J.H. Harvey, W.J. Ickes, and R.F. Kidd, Eds). Lawrence Erlbaum Associates, Hillsdale, N.J.

Zigler, E. and Child, I.L. (1969). Socialization. *In* "The Handbook of Social Psychology, Vol 3" (G. Lindzey and E. Aronson, Eds). Adison-Wesley, Massachusetts.

Zuckerman, M. (1979). Attribution of success and failure revisited, or: the motivational bias is alive and well in attribution theory. *J. Person.* **47**, 245–287.

Author Index

Page numbers in italic indicate where names are mentioned in the reference lists

Subject Index

European Monographs in Social Psychology

Series Editor: HENRI TAJFEL

E.A. CARSWELL and R. ROMMETVEIT
Social Contexts of Messages, 1971

J. ISRAEL and H. TAJFEL
The Context of Social Psychology: A Critical Assessment, 1972

J.R. EISER and W. STROEBE
Categorization and Social Judgement, 1972

M. VON CRANACH and I. VINE
Social Communication and Movement, 1973

CLAUDINE HERZLICH
Health and Illness: A Social Psychological Analysis, 1973

J.M. NUTTIN, JR (and Annie Beckers)
The Illusion of Attitude Change: Towards a Response Contagion Theory of Persuasion, 1975

H. GILES and P.F. POWESLAND
Speech Style and Social Evaluation, 1975

J. CHADWICK-JONES
Social Exchange Theory: Its Structure and Influence in Social Psychology, 1976

M. BILLIG
Social Psychology and Intergroup Relations, 1976

S. MOSCOVICI
Social Influence and Social Change, 1976

R. SANDELL
Linguistic Style and Persuasion, 1977

H. GILES
Language, Ethnicity and Intergroup Relations, 1977

A. HEEN WOLD
Decoding Oral Language, 1978

H. TAJFEL
Differentiation between Social Groups: Studies in the Social Psychology of Intergroup
   Relations, 1978

M. BILLIG
Fascists: A Social Psychological View of the National Front, 1978

C.P. WILSON
Jokes: Form, Content, Use and Function, 1979

J.P. FORGAS
Social Episodes: The Study of Interaction Routines, 1979

R.A. HINDE
Towards Understanding Relationships, 1979

A-N. PERRET-CLERMONT
Social Interaction and Cognitive Development in Children, 1980

B.A. GEBER and S.P. NEWMAN
Soweto's Children: The Development of Attitudes, 1980

P. SCHÖNBACH
Education and Intergroup Attitudes, 1981

In preparation

W.P. ROBINSON
Communication in Child Development